contents

Preface 7

Prepare for take-off!

1. **Tips for travellers** 11
   - Defining a gap- 12
   - What do you want to do? 14
   - Where do you want to go? 15
   - How long have you got? How much do you want to spend? 17
   - Sort the paperwork 18
   - What to take; Handy items 20
   - Less is best; Packing tips 23
   - Maps, directions and vital information 24
   - Where to buy your kit 25
   - First aid kit 27
   - Looking after yourself; health and safety 28
   - In-country advice 43
   - Belief systems 44
   - Keeping in touch 52
   - And finally...back to Earth after a gap- 55
   - Directory 61

2. **Finance** 69
   - How much will you need? What do you need to pay for? 70
   - Money savers 72
   - Money security 74
   - Sticking to a budget 75
   - Insurance 77
   - Directory 85

3. **Career breaks and older gappers** 79
   - The benefits of being an older gapper 94
   - Arranging a sabbatical 96
   - Finance 100
   - What about the house? 104
   - Directory 114

contents... continued

4. Travelling and accommodation 119
   - Sustainable travel 122
   - Planes 125
   - Trains and Inter-railing 127
   - Buses/Coaches 132
   - Overlanding 135
   - Car 137
   - Ships 139
   - Accommodation: hostels 135
   - Camping 142
   - Hotels 144
   - Directory 148

Your gap-year abroad

5. Working abroad 181
   - Choosing your destination 183
   - Finding a job 184
   - Au pairing 185
   - Internships 189
   - TEFL 191
   - Seasonal work 194
   - Directory 199

6. Volunteering abroad 213
   - Why volunteer? 214
   - Ethical concerns 216
   - What would you like to do? 220
   - What is the cost? 221
   - What to expect 222
   - Safety first 225
   - Directory 226

7. Learning abroad 271
   - Arts & Culture; Design & Fashion; Film, Theatre and Drama 273
   - Music 275
   - Media and journalism; Photography; Languages 276
   - TEFL 282
   - Directory 283

the gap-year guidebook 2011

Editor: Alex Sharratt

John Catt Educational Ltd

Published in 2010 by John Catt Educational Ltd,
12 Deben Mill Business Centre, Old Maltings Approach,
Melton, Woodbridge, Suffolk IP12 1BL

Tel: +44 (0) 1394 389850   Fax: +44 (0) 1394 386893
Email: info@gap-year.com   Website: www.gap-year.com

First published by Peridot Press in 1992; Nineteenth edition 2010
© 2010 John Catt Educational Ltd

All rights reserved. No part of this publication may be reproduced, stored in a retrieval system, transmitted in any form or by any means, electronic, mechanical, photocopying, recording, or otherwise, without the prior permission of the publishers.

Opinions expressed in this publication are those of the contributors, and are not necessarily those of the publishers or the sponsors. We cannot accept responsibility for any errors or omissions.

The Sex Discrimination Act 1975.
The publishers have taken all reasonable steps to avoid a contravention of Section 38 of the Sex Discrimination Act 1975. However, it should be noted that (save where there is an express provision to the contrary) where words have been used which denote the masculine gender only, they shall, pursuant and subject to the said Act, for the purpose of this publication, be deemed to include the feminine gender and vice versa.

British Library Cataloguing in Publication Data.

ISBN: 978 1 904724 926
eISBN: 978 1 908095 008

Designed and typeset by John Catt Educational Limited, 12 Deben Mill Business Centre, Old Maltings Approach, Melton, Woodbridge, Suffolk IP12 1BL.

Printed and bound in Great Britain by Wyndham Grange, Butts Road, Southwick, West Sussex BN42 4EJ.

Contacts

Editor
Alex Sharratt
Email: editor@gap-year.com

Production - Neil Rogers
Design - Scott James

Distribution/Booksales
Tel: +44 (0) 1394 389863
Email: booksales@johncatt.com

Advertising
Tel: +44 (0) 1394 389853
Email: info@gap-year.com

visit: www.gap-year.com

contents... continued

8. Sport ... 313
- Becoming an instructor ... 314
- Getting a job ... 317
- Coaching as a volunteer ... 319
- Playing sport on your gap- ... 320
- Directory ... 323

Your gap-year in the UK

9. Working in the UK ... 347
- Why work on a year out? ... 348
- Writing a CV ... 349
- Getting the job ... 350
- Job surfing; On spec ... 352
- Interviews ... 354
- Gap-year specialists ... 355
- Festivals; Seasonal and temporary work ... 356
- Pay, tax and National Insurance ... 356
- Directory ... 359

10. Volunteering in the UK ... 369
- Benefits of UK volunteering ... 370
- What can you do? ... 372
- Where to start? What qualities does a good volunteer need? ... 373
- Conservation; Animals ... 375
- Volunteering - with pay ... 376
- Directory ... 377

11. Learning in the UK ... 389
- Archaeology ... 390
- Art; Cookery ... 390
- Drama; Driving ... 392
- Languages ... 394
- Music ... 396
- Photography; Sports; TEFL; X-rated ... 397
- Directory ... 399

contents... continued

Appendices

Appendix 1
1a Retakes 427
1b Applying to university 433
1c Universities in the UK 441

Appendix 2
Country info 453

Appendix 3
Business colleges 507

Index 531

Preface

Any time you take time out from the normal pattern of your life to do something completely different –
that's a gap-

Preface

In the days before A level results are released there is always a flurry of media interest but in 2010 there was more than usual. There were two main issues. First the number of students applying for university exceeded the places available by more than 200,000; and second, fourteen percent of graduates had been unable to find a job in the first year since graduation. Competition for university places and graduate jobs is fierce and school-leavers and undergraduates need to consider how to steal a march on their peers. For the 2010 entry to university at least 170,000 applicants failed to secure a place and find themselves on an unexpected **gap**-year. Many will have excellent A levels and be keen to re-apply. All the indications are that the competition for places will be equally intense in 2011. Experience has shown that a well-structured **gap**-year programme can make a difference.

Mary Curnock Cook, the chief executive of the Universities and Colleges Admission Service (UCAS) said, "I believe the golden age of the **gap**-year is over. Candidates who want to achieve a good offer next year need to use their (**gap**-) year strategically to enhance their attractiveness to institutions. People have to be more realistic. They need to go out and use their 'bridging year' to enhance their application. Conceptually a **gap**-year has been when young people take a nice break and go out and see the world. By calling it a bridging year you stress that it should be a focused way to support an application to the course or university you are targeting."

These are wise words but the concept is not new. The first **gap**-year organisations were set up in the UK over 40 years ago with the specific aims of providing school-leavers with the opportunity to develop their personal skills, to utilise their initiative and resourcefulness and to learn about other countries and in doing so to return home with a better understanding of their role in the world and what they wanted to achieve in the future. In recent years the popularity of the **gap**-year has increased with an ever increasing variety of activities available both in the UK and overseas.

The term 'bridging year' emanates from the United States where the concept of the structured **gap**-year has only recently begun to catch on. Eleven year ago in the UK the leading **gap**-year organisations set up Year Out Group primarily to promote the concept and benefits of a structured **gap**-year programme that the CEO of UCAS advocates. The Group's founder members chose the term 'year out' to differentiate from the notion that the **gap**-year should be a 'year off', *ie* a jolly. It is encouraging to see concept of the 'year out' being acknowledged in the US and publically endorsed by UCAS. The message for all those planning a **gap**-year is clear, namely to make sure that you use the time to your best advantage and in a way that will be acknowledged by your chosen university and any future employer.

In general terms university admission tutors look favourably on applicants who can demonstrate that they have a considered plan for their year out programme. Universities know that students who have taken a well structured **gap**-year arrive refreshed and focused and have a very high probability of completing their chosen course. These students are more mature, more globally aware and have acquired skills and experiences that enable them to make a fuller contribution to their course and university life in general. Some universities have capped the percentage of applicants they will allow to defer in order to take a **gap**-year. This suggests they have seen through the recent trend for **gap**-year participants to sign up for very short placements just to get a tick in the box.

The same applies to employers. Employers actively seek graduates who can demonstrate that they have gained valuable skills and experiences during their gap year. Employers are looking for signs of commitment, team work, project and risk management and negotiating skills, global awareness and ideally language skills as well. Recent research by Year Out Group has shown that 60 percent of those taking **gap**-year placements with a Year Out Group member are female. In the UK only 11 percent of female graduates were unemployed one year after graduating compared with 17 percent of their male counterparts. One message from these figures is that young males could benefit more than they realise by committing to a structured **gap**-year programme.

The secret to a successful **gap**-year/year out/bridging year programme (call it what you will; it is what you do with your time that matters) is to research and plan in as much detail as possible. Start by working out why you want to take this time out and what you seek to achieve in the time available. You can then identify the organisations that appear to meet your unique requirements. You can then use this book to obtain advice on how to finance your trip, obtain proper insurance cover and stay healthy and much more besides. When it comes to making the final decision on which project is best for you, there is no better way than to talk to the organisations and people with recent experience of those placements. This will enable you to make an informed decision so that you develop a **gap**-year/year out programme that you will enjoy and will genuinely increase your chances of securing your preferred university place or future job.

Richard Oliver
Chief Executive, Year Out Group
August 2010

Many thanks to all those who have given their time, advice and expertise to help us keep this book as up-to-date as possible.

They are:
Ally Crichton (Gap Aid)
Becci Coombes (GirlsTravelClub.co.uk)
Fair Trade Volunteering
Francesca Toma (CSV)
Gary Hughes (Career Sage)
Hope for Harambee
Jacqui Smith (Tourism Concern)
James Phillips (Medic Alert)
Kim Ireland (Cancer Research)
Kimberley Rowley (Volunteer England)
Linda Whittern (Careers Partnership (UK))
Lisa McGauley (Tick Alert)
Naomi Shelton (Studential)
Nicki Boddington (InterHealth)
Rachel Heels (Travellers Worldwide)
Rajeep Day (Enternships)
Richard Oliver (Year Out Group)
Richard Stuttle (Caroline's Rainbow)
Sport Lived
Susan Nash (NUS)
Wendy Johnson (Sustrans)

Thank you also to those who have shared their **gap-** adventures with us:
Alice, Tony and Rowan
Alice Hancock
Chantelle Lesforis
Chris Henry
Graham Bills
Harry Brittain
Tom Burrows

And finally, special thanks to three gappers who provided us with some excellent images to use.
Annie Rice
Pamela Sam
Rachael Gibson

Chapter 1
Tips for travellers

Tips for travellers

Let's start with a definition...

Although they're generally referred to as **gap**-*years*, it may be this is a habit, based on the history of travel throughout the centuries. Nowadays people travel to volunteer, work, study, see something new and it **doesn't** have to be for a year.

The one thing all such trips have in common is the fact that they're all about taking time out of the normal routine to do something different, challenging, fulfilling, memorable - so that is our definition of a **gap**-.

Who goes on a gap-?

Some stats: **Gapadvice.org** estimates the figures for the total number of people taking some form of **gap**- in 2009 as: 230,000 young people, 90,000 career breakers and 200,000 retired people.

We've known for several editions now that the biggest increases in numbers are among career breakers and mature travellers and, despite the last year having been so unsettled, this still seems to be the case.

Industry professionals say that they are now seeing many young professionals taking extended career breaks, and even couples whose children have flown the roost taking the chance to go and see the world.

So the answer is people of all ages, all walks of life, able-bodied and disabled go on a **gap**-.

Why take a gap-?

There are as many reasons to take a **gap**- as there are different opportunities on offer.

Time out before further study? A break from the daily work routine? A memorable experience? To give something back? To learn something new? All are valid reasons.

The benefits of taking a **gap**-year are considerable. Those who have taken a structured trip are likely to arrive at university refreshed and focused and research shows they are more likely to finish their chosen course.

And if you feel like you're fed up with the daily grind of a nine-to-five job, a career break can help you get out of your rut. Working full time for even just ten years means roughly around twenty thousand hours of sitting in an office staring at your computer screen.

A career-break will help you gain new perspective on life and work and will be an experience you remember for the rest of your life.

visit: www.gap-year.com

Studential, a website helping UK students with advice around their university applications, told us how a well-organised **gap-**year can be a great idea either before or after higher education.

"There are many reasons for taking a year out, but you to make best use of your time you should view a **gap-**year as a chance to achieve something.

"For example, there are many **gap-**year volunteer projects where young people can help out with tasks such as teaching sports, looking after orphans, and caring for wildlife. You can also register for a learning programme abroad, where you can gain a qualification in sports, languages and other activities. All of these will look great on your CV when you start looking for a job after university, and make you stand out from all the other applicants.

"Some people find that taking a year out will help them in some way with their higher education – if you did not get the A level grades you were expecting and missed out on a place at university, you can retake exams to bump up your marks and get into where you want to next year.

"It's also a good way of saving up some cash to help fund your student life, by getting a full or part-time job. With university tuition fees in the UK now at a maximum of £3,145, and with living expenses on top, more students are opting to work in order to pay off some of the costs before they even start their degree."

Beat the recession

Since the publication of the 2010 edition of the **gap-year guidebook**, there have been mixed messages about whether we are through the worst of the global economic recession – or about to suffer a 'double-dip'.

The last 12 months have been far from easy for most people and the short-term future remains uncertain. The UK is facing an unsavoury combination of high inflation and high unemployment, and some economists are reading the signs as a potential return to recession.

Encouragingly however, research is showing that the number of people who travelled abroad to take part in a **gap-** placement in 2009-10 has held up well. Data from Year Out Group showed that 50,000 placements were arranged in over 90 countries across the globe, still significantly higher than pre-recession figures.

More than three-quarters of **gap-**years were booked by those aged between 17 and 24, with youngsters looking to add some key skills to their CV to boost their chances in what is reported to be the most difficult graduate job market in recent history.

A report released by the Higher Education Statistics Agency showed more than one in ten students who left university in 2009 failed to find work after six months – the highest unemployment rate for ten years – with another report showing an average of around 70 applications for every graduate job.

With the traditional route of going straight to university after finishing A levels not proving as dependable as in previous years, it is little wonder that more youngsters are considering vocational training or work experience on a **gap-**

year abroad, allowing them to gain the hands-on experience which employers are looking for.

Year Out Group also reported a small increase in **gap-** trips taken by among those aged between 25 and 40, suggesting that the popularity of taking a career break or sabbatical was rising.

These figures obviously don't include those who went with non-YOG-affiliated **gap-** organisations, or those who organised their **gap-** independently, so the increase could have been even greater.

Gapadvice.org suggests the figure for UK citizens taking a **gap-** could add up to more than half a million people: 520,000.

Planning your gap- the first steps

What do you want to do?

The beauty of the modern **gap**-year is the amount of choice and variety on offer: each is as unique as the individual participant, and each is an opportunity to create a tailored programme to meet their own personal ambitions.

Knowing your own personality, your interests, your strengths and weaknesses will help you. Are you someone who likes to get stuck into something for a while or do you want to be on the move a lot?

If you're not confident about coping alone with unfamiliar situations you might want a more structured, group setting. On the other hand if you know you need time away from the crowds, you're bound to want to build in some independent travel.

The most popular choice of activity for a **gap-** or career break is volunteering, with teaching placements in particular having risen by 20% in the last few years.

Or perhaps you want to explore things you've always wanted to pursue but never had time. It could be anything from a spiritual retreat to meditation and yoga, art, photography, a new language or particular places and cultures.

Maybe you're particularly concerned about the state of the world and would like to do your bit environmentally or contribute to helping disadvantaged people? The possibilities are endless and many gappers end up constructing a programme that combines several elements.

Those with a full year at their disposal will perhaps have time for more than one activity, and might want to combine a structured element to their gap with some travel. The increase in cheap flights and wider access to previously unreachable destinations has made this even more possible.

Choosing the activity, destination and organisation most suited to the individual can be a difficult and time-consuming task. However, proper planning and research is crucial and will help ensure you get the most out of your time; a **gap-** or career break can easily be wasted without planning ahead.

visit: www.gap-year.com

It is also important that you are aware of your responsibilities. Dropping out of a placement or programme before it has finished can be disruptive not only to you but also to others directly and indirectly involved.

But don't worry if all this sounds a bit heavy: the planning and preparation stage can be almost as much fun as the trip itself. And of course, this is where **the gap-year guidebook** comes into its own...

> Alice Hancock took a **gap**-year between her A levels and studying English at Cambridge University; she told us that adding some structured work experience to her time abroad helped her get more out of her travels.
>
> "I decided in my lower sixth year to take a **gap**-year between school and university as I felt that I needed a break before plunging myself into university life. I also think it was important in terms of maturity – having to look after yourself, your money, travel, health, insurance and so on.
>
> "I spent three months in Chennai, India, working on a newspaper in order to get experience in the media and also because I was intrigued to experience India.
>
> "I considered charity work and volunteer placements but ideally I wanted some solid, usable experience. I had always wanted to travel so it was never a question of not going abroad but more to do with finding a placement that I wanted to do and felt would be relevant and interesting.
>
> "Experience is the main benefit of taking a **gap**-year. For me, it has been more specific in that I got the experience of working on a newspaper. I also developed my inter-personal skills. Travelling does mean you have to be confident in yourself. It also definitely demands that you improve your negotiating ability."

Where do you want to go?

Year Out Group's most recent research has found that currently the most popular countries for a structured **gap-** are: South Africa (1st place), Kenya (2nd – up from 12th place in 2008) and Canada (3rd).

Richard Oliver, Chief Executive of Year Out Group, told us: "South Africa offers a wide variety of worthwhile projects ranging from conservation work in the game parks, volunteering in health centres and orphanages including HIV/Aids awareness programmes and a variety of teaching placements.

"These can last from a few weeks to a whole year. South Africa is also seen as a comparatively safe destination and the exchange rate for the rand is still good value."

If you want to visit several places you can let a cheap round-the-world ticket decide the framework for you. Otherwise you need to get your route clear in your mind.

Do you feel attracted to a particular area or to a particular climate? Unexplored territory or the popular backpacker places you've heard about? If you're unsure, try connecting with people who've been, through our messageboard: **www.gap-year.com**

Heading for unknown territory off the backpacker routes in search of something more unusual will usually mean higher costs, perhaps a longer wait for visas and less efficient transport systems – therefore more preparation and travelling time. A bit of netsurfing, a check with any contacts who know a country and a chat with a travel agent will help you get a better idea of what this might mean.

Then there's the risk factor. Obviously family and friends will want you to avoid danger zones. The political situation in some places around the world is serious, unstable and can't be ignored.

You want your **gap-** travels to be stimulating, fun, to let you experience different cultures and meet new people, but do you really want to end up in the middle of a war zone with your life in danger? Foreign news correspondents and war reporters with large back-up organisations prepare properly, with proper insurance and safety and survival courses - and it makes sense for gappers too!

visit: www.gap-year.com

A good starting point is the Foreign Office website (**www.fco.gov.uk**) where you can find country profiles and assess the dangers and possible drawbacks to places you're thinking of. The FCO updates its danger list regularly as new areas of unrest emerge, but it's not, and never can be, a failsafe.

How long have you got?

Now you have at least a rough idea of where you want to go and what you want to do. The next step is to consider how long you might need to get it all in. How much time you can spare depends on *when* you're taking your gap.

That's going to be dictated by when you have to be back for starting university or college or, for career breakers, how much time your employer's prepared to let you have, or even whether you're willing to risk quitting your job for more **gap-** time.

Some gappers just get a round-the-world ticket and take off for a year; others work for a while, go away on a placement, come back and earn some more then go again. Or you can work while you're away to finance the next stage of your trip.

The essential point here is to be realistic about including time to raise the money as part of your gap and, if minimising your carbon footprint is important to you, how much extra time you're going to allow for avoiding planes where you can so you can use more environmentally-friendly, and probably slower, local transport.

Maybe you'll have to refine or cut back the list, but remember, you don't have to spend a whole year on a gap, it can be as short or as long as you want to make it.

How much do you want to spend?

Estimates vary widely, but the average cost for a full year's gap is £5000 for young people, around £6000 for mature travellers and up to £9000 for career breakers.

Much depends on where you're going and what you plan to do, and these days, if you care about the planet, climate change and ethical travel, you need also to include the costs of carbon offsetting.

Some people work for a while to raise money for, say, a three-month activity, and then come back to earn some more so they can go off again and do something different.

Travel guides are useful for copious information on towns, travel routes and budget hotels in the countries they cover. They'll help you work out some rough costs but remember some details will have changed when you get to where you are going.

You can also begin to contact gap organisations specialising in volunteer projects, and/or work and study placements that interest you to find out more about their charges. See our section later on in this chapter on finance and our special chapter for career breakers and mature travellers to give you some ideas on how to raise the money for your gap.

the gap-year guidebook 2011

Before you go, know where you're going

The more you know about your destination, the easier your trip will be: India, for example, is unbearably hot and humid in pre-monsoon April to June, Australia has seasons when bush fires are rampant and then there are the cyclone seasons in south Asia and rainy seasons in South America - and the consequent risk of flooding!!

It's also worth finding out when special events are on. It could be very inconvenient to arrive in India during Diwali - when everyone's on holiday and all the trains are full! Similarly Japan - gorgeous in cherry blossom season but avoid travelling in Golden Week.

Check out **www.whatsonwhen.com** - it's a great site, which lists all sorts of events around the world.

Before visiting any country that has recently been politically volatile or could turn into a war zone, check with the FCO for the current situation. Logon to **www.fco.gov.uk** for up-to-date information.

Note: If you're from a country that qualifies for a Visa Waiver for the USA (and that includes UK citizens) you must now register online your intent to visit the USA and you *must* receive travel authorisation. Authorisation still doesn't guarantee you'll be granted entry and you may still be asked to go to the US embassy for an interview, but you have to go through the process before you can do anything else. You'll find the details here:

http://travel.state.gov/visa/temp/without/without_1990.html

If you're intending to visit for longer, or are planning to work, you will need the correct visa (see Chapter 7 - Working Abroad).

Sort the paperwork

If you need to get yourself a passport for the first time, application forms are available from Post Offices or you can apply online. But remember: Passport interviews are a new part of the process and are required by all applicants, aged 16 or over, who are applying for a passport for the first time.

You can call 0300 222 1000 to make an appointment or for other enquiries about this, but remember also that first time applicants can't use the fast track service.

There are 68 interview offices around the country and you have to go to the correct one for where you live - see the map on the IPS (Identity and Passport Office) website:

http://maps.direct.gov.uk/LDGRedirect/MapAction.do?ref=passportinterviewoffices

The standard adult ten-year passport currently costs £77.50 and you'll need your birth certificate and passport photos. It should take no more than a month from the time you apply to the time you receive your passport, but the queue lengthens coming up to peak summer holiday season.

You can use the Passport Office 'Check and Send' service at selected Post Offices throughout the UK or send it direct. The 'Check and Send' service gets

visit: www.gap-year.com

your application checked for completeness (including documentation and fee) and is given priority by the IPS - they are usually able to process these applications in two weeks.

If your passport application is urgent and you're not applying for the first time, you can use the guaranteed same-day (Premium) service or the guaranteed one-week (Fast Track) service. Both services are only available by appointment at one of the seven IPS offices around the UK (phone the IPS Advice Line on 0300 222 0000), and both are more expensive (£129.50 for Premium, £112.50 for Fast Track).

The services are only available for renewals and amendments. And although you'll get a fixed appointment you'll almost certainly have to wait in a queue after this for your passport.

The IPS website is very helpful:
www.ips.gov.uk/passport/index.asp
London Passport Office,
Globe House, 89 Eccleston Square,
London SW1V 1PN

Leave someone in charge at home

Make sure you have someone reliable and trustworthy in charge of sorting things out for you - especially the official stuff that won't wait. Get someone you really trust to open your post and arrange to talk to them at regular intervals in case something turns up that you need to deal with.

However, there are some things you just have to do yourself, so make sure you've done everything important before you go. This particularly applies to any regular payments you make - check all your standing orders/direct debits and make sure to cancel any you don't need; and that there's money in your account for any you do need.

If you have a flat or house you're planning to sub-let, either use an accommodation agency or make sure someone you trust will keep an eye on things - it may be necessary to give them some written form of authority to deal with emergencies. There's more on all this in Chapter 2 - Career Breaks and Mature Travellers.

What to take

Start thinking early about what to take with you and write a list - adding to it every time you think of something. Here's a general checklist to get you started:

the gap-year guidebook 2011

- Passport and tickets
- Padlock and chain
- Belt bag
- Daypack (can be used for valuables in transit/hand luggage on plane)
- First aid kit: including any personal meds: split between day pack and rucksack/case
- Notebook and pen
- Camera
- Mobile phone and charger
- MP3 player - much less bulky than CDs
- Money: cards/travellers' cheques/cash
- Torch/candle
- Sheet sleeping bag
- Universal adapter
- Universal sink plug
- Spare specs/contact lenses
- Guidebook/phrasebooks - if doing several countries trade in/swap with other travellers en route
- Spare photos for ID cards etc if needed
- Photocopies of documents/emergency numbers/serial numbers of travellers' cheques
- Clothes and toiletries etc

Some of these checklist items will be more relevant to backpackers and people on treks, than to people on a work placement or staying in a family home. The list can be modified for your own particular plans.

Handy items

We asked Becci Coombes from **GirlsTravelClub.co.uk**, a **gap-**year veteran, for her tips and advice on packing for your trip.

"The key to a well-packed rucksack is not to fill it up," Becci told us, "but leave plenty of room for your necessary holiday purchases. When you are packing, lay everything out you think you are going to need, then halve it, before halving it again!"

Here is a list of some handy items Becci has found useful that you might never have considered…

- Dental floss. Have you ever thought about how handy fifty metres of strong string (albeit minty-flavoured) all neatly packaged in a cute little box with a handy integral cutter could be? Many times I have used it for hanging mozzy nets, as an emergency bootlace, as a strong sewing thread, and it also makes a great washing line for drying your swimming gear.

- Forget those universal sink plug things; when you fill the sink up with water then try and actually wash something in it, the plug will either be knocked out by your vigorous sock-washing or just float about annoyingly as all your precious hot water drains away. A squash ball is much more useful; you can wedge firmly into the hole and then use to play squash afterwards.
- Micropore medical tape is marvellous stuff for the thrifty packer. Not only can you use it as an emergency plaster on blisters and little cuts, you can hold dressings on with it or put it on tiny splinters to yank them out of your thorn-ravaged flesh.
- Clear ziplock bags in different sizes. You can use them for storing wet swimming costumes; keeping those less-than-pleasant socks from tainting the rest of your gear, and also keep any maps nice and dry as you tramp through unexpected downpours looking for shelter in a pub.
- Bin bags also come in handy in many more ways than you'd think. Aside from using them for litter, you can always use one as a rucksack cover; an emergency poncho in a downpour; or an insu stranded and cold overnight, just cut a head hole and sit under it, keeping your arms nice and warm next to your body. Fill one with dry leaves as a mattress to insulate you from the ground damp as well; on one of our Travelskills courses we stuffed them really full and used them as beanbags, and they were surprisingly comfy!

Bin bags too come in handy in many more ways than you'd think. Ok, you can use them for litter, but in the aforementioned downpour you can always use one as a rucksack cover. In another make a head hole and two armholes in the "bottom" end, turn upside down and use as an emergency poncho. Likewise, if you are stranded and cold overnight, just cut a head hole and sit under it, keeping your arms nice and warm next to your body. Fill one with dry leaves as a mattress to insulate you from the ground damp as well; on one of our Travelskills courses we stuffed them really full and used them as beanbags, and they were surprisingly comfy!

I always make sure I've got a few elastic bands about my person as they are always being used for different purposes. Roll up your biggest items of clothing and secure with a couple of bands so they take up less space, and also put a couple round your flip-flops to keep them nice and tidy. Hang towels from trees by securing round one corner.

Cobber cooling neck wraps are also an amazing bit of kit. Whereas in hot weather blokes can just whip their shirts off, this isn't really an option for girls so I can highly recommend the Cobber. It's based on the old idea of an Australian Stockman's Fridge, where you put whatever you want to keep cool in a puddle full of water and then cover it with a wet cloth. As the water evaporates from the cloth it wicks the heat away from your can of lager/chocolate milk, thus keeping it cool. To replicate this action, the cobber is made of cotton and filled with reusable non-toxic crystals. You soak it in water for about 30 minutes, the crystals swell up into a gel and then you tie it round your neck where it wicks the heat away from your carotid artery and

the gap-year guidebook 2011

keeps you cool. They last about three days before you have to soak them again, and you can also use them as a hot/ice pack.

I tend to keep my most useful bits and pieces in a plastic lunchbox, just because damp plasters/matches/Twixes aren't half as much fun as dry ones, and I have found the box very handy for all sorts of bits and pieces. Again, it can be used for collecting water from streams, as an ingenious receptacle for emergency cornflake consumption or, well, as a lunchbox. Lastly, and most importantly for us girls, my mum's top piece of travel advice is only pack very good quality chocolate with a high cocoa content, as it doesn't melt when it gets hot, it just bends!

There are mixed views about those security wire mesh covers you can buy for rucksacks. Some prefer a simple padlock and chain and say the security mesh covers are an open invitation to a thief armed with wire cutters, since they imply you're carrying something valuable. Others say the point is that they're slash proof, and so useful as a short-term deterrent against thieves armed with a knife when you're doing something where you might be distracted - like making a phone call.

One traveller we know has an ingenious solution: on the grounds that the mesh, padlock and chain methods advertise you as having something worth stealing he attaches a small bell to his backpack - he reckons it's a great deterrent since it makes the thief feel conspicuous and tells its owner someone's messing with his stuff!

- We've come across a really useful, newly-launched, credit-card sized gadget called Traakit - a GPS-style tracker device which enables family to locate travelling loved ones via the internet, without making endless phone calls, when they're on a **gap-**.

David Clayton, whose Newmarket-based company, Radaw, developed the device (launched in May 2009), told us his nephew, Harry, is carrying one while **gap-** travelling in Australia. But perhaps even more useful, particularly for anyone travelling alone, is that Traakit can also be very easily set to secure belongings inside a 'virtual fence' so they can be left in a hotel or hostel room while you're off exploring wherever you are. If the secured items are moved outside the co-ordinates Traakit automatically sends a text to the owner's mobile phone, as well as an email alerting them and giving the items' new location. It costs £273.50 (including vat and delivery) to buy plus approximately £14 per month service charge, or it can be rented for around £50 per month. For more see: www.traakit.co.uk

- Water purifying tablets - useful but won't deal with all the possible waterborne parasites. Sometimes boiling water and adding iodine are also necessary. It's best to stick to bottled mineral water if available - even for brushing your teeth - but always check that the seal is intact before you buy. That way you will be sure it's not a mineral water bottle refilled with the local dodgy supply.

Lifesaver Systems (see directory page 58) produces a bottle that converts even the nastiest stuff into drinkable water without the use of chemicals. It's not cheap but being ill through drinking bad water while travelling can be expensive or even life threatening.

visit: www.gap-year.com

Remember it's easy to get dehydrated in hot countries so you should always carry a bottle of water with you and drink frequently - up to eight litres a day.

Less is best

As airlines struggle with rising fuel costs, and diminishing passenger numbers, they are becoming increasingly inventive in dreaming up extra charges. Excess and overweight check-in baggage is one particularly fruitful area – and it's confusing as the rules vary from airline to airline. This makes it even more crucial to think very carefully about what you need to take - and what you could do without.

Basically, some charge per piece and others by weight, but that's not all. Some carriers limit you to one check-in piece, others, like BA, allow two. It can also depend on your route and your destination. Weight limits vary from as little as 20kg per bag to 30 k. Charges can even be different on outward and return journeys, with some carriers charging as much as €30 per kilogram over the permitted weight, or £90 per extra bag. It won't take much to wipe out all the money you've saved by searching for the cheapest available flights!

Inevitably if you fly business or first class the allowances are more generous but the above assumes that most people on a gap will be flying economy.

the gap-year guidebook 2011

Packing tips

- Pack in reverse order - first in, last out
- Heavy items go at the bottom
- Pack in categories in plastic bags - easier to find stuff
- Use vacuum pack bags for bulky items
- Store toilet rolls and dirty undies in side pockets - easy for thieves to open and they won't want them!
- Take a small, separate backpack for day hikes etc. You can buy small, thin folding ones
- Keep spares (undies, toothbrush, important numbers and documents) in hand luggage
- Take a sleeping bag liner - useful in hostels
- Take a sarong (versatile: can be a bed sheet, towel, purse, bag...)
- Travel towels are lightweight and dry fast
- Remove packaging from everything but keep printed instructions for medications
- Shaving oil takes less space than cream
- Put liquids in squashy bottles (and don't carry liquids in hand luggage)
- Fill shoes, cups etc with socks and undies to save space
- Tie up loose backpack straps before it goes into transit

Now sit down and rationalise - cross off everything you don't really need. Pack enough clothes to see you through - about five changes of clothing should last you for months if you choose carefully. Don't take anything that doesn't go with everything else and stick to materials that are comfortable, hard-wearing, easy to wash and dry and don't crease too much. Make sure you have clothes that are suitable for the climates you are visiting and don't forget that the temperatures in some dry climates can drop considerably at night!

You can find very lightweight waterproofs and thermals that can be rolled up easily.

Tip: Remember most places have cheap markets, not to mention interesting local clothes, so you can always top up or replace clothes while you are travelling.

Relax, you can't prepare for every eventuality if you're living out of a rucksack. The best way to know what you need is to ask someone who's already been on a gap what they took, what were the most useful things, what they didn't need and what they wished they had taken.

Maps, directions and vital information

You won't need anything too elaborate: the maps in guidebooks are usually pretty good. A good pocket diary can be very useful - one that gives

visit: www.gap-year.com

international dialling codes, time differences, local currency details, bank opening hours, public holidays and other information.

Take a list with you of essential information like directions to voluntary work postings, key addresses, medical information, credit card numbers (try to disguise these in case everything gets stolen), passport details (and a photocopy of the main and visa pages), emergency contact numbers in case of loss of travellers' cheques and insurance and flight details - and leave a copy with someone at home.

Another way of keeping safe copies of your vital documents (even if everything you have is lost or stolen) is to scan them before you leave and email them as attachments to your email address.

However, it is well known that you shouldn't send sensitive information via email and it's not clear whether that advice also applies to attachments, given that they're all stored on a remote server, so you might prefer one of the many online secure data storage options, for example:

www.passportsupport.com/about/
www.omneport.com/

Or you could even put it all on a memory stick, which has the advantage of being small and easy to conceal and carry.

Those of you lucky enough to have a smart new phone or an MP3 player onto which you can download apps will be able to input a mass of information and effectively 'carry' maps, timetables, hostel finders, information lists, and photographs of your valuable documents with you in one small, slim device.

The FCO's Locate service is free but only available to UK citizens. You fill in a simple registration form online giving your contact details and travel plans. You can also log in and update your details while you're travelling. The information's on a secure site, which is accessible only to embassy staff and the FCO's consular crisis group. If there's an unexpected crisis where you happen to be it means your friends and family can check whether you're okay and the nearest British Embassy can text you warnings and alerts.

Where to buy your kit

Some overseas voluntary organisations arrange for their students to have discounts at specific shops, like the YHA. The best advice on equipment usually comes from specialist shops, although they may not be the cheapest: these include YHA shops, Blacks, Millets and Camping and Outdoors Centres.

Take a look at **www.gap-yearshop.com** for a specialist outlet selling over the internet.

Rucksacks

Prices for a well-stitched, 65-litre rucksack can vary greatly. Remember, the most expensive is not necessarily the best, get what is most suitable for your trip.

the gap-year guidebook 2011

A side-opening backpack is easier than a top-opening one. You can get all sorts of attachments but if you don't need it why pay for it? A good outdoor store should be able to advise you on exactly what you need for your particular trip. Most of these stores have websites with helpful hints and lists of 'essential' items.

You should be able to leave your rucksack in most hostels or guest houses, if you are staying for more than a day, or in a locker at the train station. Always take camera, passport, important papers and money with you everywhere, zipped up, preferably out of view.

Tip: If you're thinking of buying second-hand make sure you check that all fastenings work and that the frame is the right size for your height and weight.

Footwear

It's worth investing in something comfortable if you're heading off on a long trip. In hot countries, a good pair of sandals is the preferred footwear for many and it's worth paying for a decent pair, as they will last longer and be comfortable. If you're going somewhere cheap you could just pick up a pair out there but you're likely to be doing a lot more walking than usual, so comfort and durability are important.

Some people like chunky walking boots, others just their trainers, but it's best to get something that won't fall apart when you're halfway up a mountain. Take more than one pair of comfortable shoes in case they don't last, but don't take too many – they'll be an unnecessary burden and take up precious space in your rucksack.

Sleeping bags

Go to a specialist shop where you can get good advice. Prices vary widely and you can sometimes find a four-season bag cheaper than a one-season bag –

visit: www.gap-year.com

it's mostly down to quality. You need to consider:

- Can you carry it comfortably and still have the energy to do all you want to do?
- Hot countries - do you need one? You may just want to take a sheet sleeping bag (basically just a sewn-up sheet).
- Colder countries: What will you be doing? Take into account weight and size and the conditions you'll be travelling in – you might want to go for one of those compression sacs that you can use to squash sleeping bags into. For cold countries, you need heat-retaining materials. You can usually – but not always – rent down-filled bags for treks in, say, Nepal.

First aid kit

Useful basics:

- Re-hydration sachets (to use after diarrhoea)
- Waterproof plasters
- TCP/TeeTree oil
- Corn and blister plasters for sore feet
- Cotton buds
- A small pair of straight nail scissors (not to be carried in your hand luggage on the plane)
- Safety pins (not to be carried in your hand luggage on the plane)
- Insect repellent
- Antiseptic cream
- Anti-diarrhoea pills (only short-term; they stop the diarrhoea temporarily but don't cure you)
- Water sterilisation tablets
- Antihistamine cream
- Your own preferred form of painkiller

You can get a medical pack from most chemists, travel shops or online from MASTA (**www.masta.org**).

Homeway (see **www.gap-yearshop.com**) also specialises in medical kits for travellers: the contents vary from sting relief, tick removers, blister kits, sun block and re-hydration sachets to complete sterile medical packs with needles and syringe kits (in case you think the needle someone might have to inject you with may not be sterile).

You can also buy various types of mosquito net, water purification tablets and filters, money pouches, world receiver radios, travel irons and kettles. Not to mention a personal attack alarm.

Tip: If you take too much kit though, you'll need a removal van to take it with you!

the gap-year guidebook 2011

Cameras

Picture quality on many mobile phones is now so good that you may not need to take a camera as well, especially if you're going to be uploading your pictures onto one of the many photo sharing websites now available.

If you do want the back-up of a camera check with your local photographic dealer about what will best suit your requirements. Make sure you get a camera case to protect from knocks, dust and moisture and don't buy the cheapest you can find. Cheap equipment can let you down and you need something that doesn't have software compatibility/connection problems.

Here are a few other tips:

- Digital cameras use lots of power (especially if using flash). Take plenty of batteries with you or take rechargeable batteries and a charger (you'll save money in the long run but check they're usable in your particular camera).
- Don't risk losing all your photos! Back them up as you travel. Maybe visit an internet cafe occasionally and upload your best photos to a site such as Photobucket.com (which is free). Upload them onto your Facebook, myspace (or similar) site. Or even send them to your home email account.
- Don't walk around with your camera round your neck. Keep it out of sight whenever possible to reduce the risk of crime.
- Remember certain countries charge extra for using a camcorder at heritage sites, safari parks and monuments, but often they don't charge for still cameras.

Looking after yourself...

Health

Note: Although we make every effort to be as up-to-date and accurate as possible, the following advice is intended to serve as a guideline only. It is designed to be helpful rather than definitive, and you should always check with your GP, preferably at least eight weeks before going away.

It's not only which countries you'll be going to, but for how long and what degree of roughing it: six months in a basic backpacker hostel puts people at higher risk than two weeks in a five-star hotel.

Before you go you should tell your doctor:

- Your proposed travel route
- The type of activities you will be doing

Ask for advice, not only about injections and pills needed, but symptoms to look out for and what to do if you suspect you've caught something.

Some immunisations are free under the NHS but you may have to pay for the more exotic/rare ones. Some, like the Hepatitis A vaccine, can be very expensive, but this is not an area to be mean with your money - it really is worth being cautious with your health.

Also, many people recommend that you know your blood type before you

visit: www.gap-year.com

leave the country, to save time and ensure safety. Your GP might have it on record - if not, a small charge may be made for a blood test.

If you're going abroad to do voluntary work, don't assume the organization will give you medical advice first or even when you get there, though they often do. Find out for yourself, and check if there is a medically-qualified person in or near the institution you are going to be posted with.

People who've been to the relevant country/area are a great source of information. Some travellers prefer to go to a dedicated travel clinic to get pre-travel health advice. This may be especially worthwhile if your GP/practice nurse does not see many travellers.

Here are some options:

www.welltravelledclinics.co.uk is a UK travel clinic company, and part of the Liverpool School of Tropical Medicine

www.e-med.co.uk has a useful free travel service, which you can email for advice on immunisations, anti-malaria medication and what to watch out for.

www.fitfortravel.scot.nhs.uk
www.travelhealth.co.uk

Department of Health website

www.nhs.uk/LiveWell/TravelHealth/Pages/Travelhealthhome.aspx

For safety advice try the Foreign and Commonwealth Office:

www.fco.gov.uk/travel

Another good idea is to register with an organisation such as Medic Alert, a non-profit making charity providing a life-saving identification system for individuals with hidden medical conditions and allergies.

The MedicAlert service is particularly helpful for those who wish to travel. The MedicAlert Emblem contains the international sign of medicine, and is recognised around the world. MedicAlert also has a 24-hour emergency number which can be accessed by medical personnel anywhere in the world and has a translation service in more than 100 languages.

As a MedicAlert Member, you wear a bracelet or necklet (known as an emblem) engraved with a personal identification number, main medical conditions and an emergency telephone number. Each tailor made Emblem bears the internationally recognised symbol of the medical profession.

In an emergency, medical personnel have immediate access to vital information on the back of the MedicAlert disc. By phoning the emergency number, they can also gain further medical and personal information such as your name and address, doctor's details, current drug therapy and next of kin details.

Membership to the service, including a tailor-made emblem, starts at £19.95 plus the first year's membership at £25.

Dr George Sikharulidze at MedicAlert told us: "Many people with a hidden medical condition rely on a MedicAlert Emblem whilst travelling. Over the years, we have had many calls from medical staff overseas who are treating one of our members in an emergency. Within seconds, vital information can be relayed to medical staff and important treatment can commence."

the gap-year guidebook 2011

Accidents/Injuries

Accidents and injuries are the greatest cause of death in young travellers abroad. Alcohol/drug use will increase the risk of these occurring. Travellers to areas with poor medical facilities should take a sterile medical equipment pack with them. Make sure that you have good travel insurance that will bring you home if necessary.

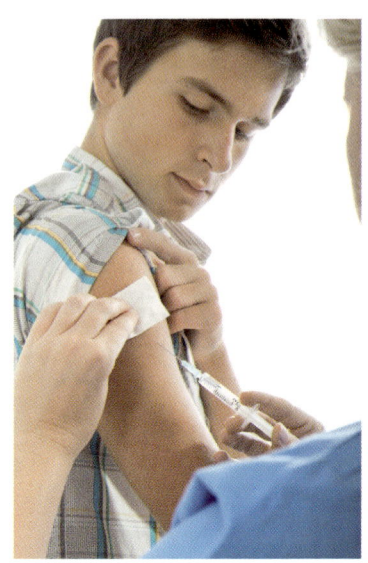

AIDS

The HIV virus that causes AIDS can be contracted from: injections with infected needles; transfusions of infected blood; sexual intercourse with an infected person; or possibly cuts (if you have a shave at the barbers, insist on a fresh blade, but it's probably best to avoid the experience altogether). It is not caught through everyday contact, insect bites, dirty food or crockery, kissing, coughing or sneezing. Protect yourself: always use condoms during sex, make sure needles are new and if you need a blood transfusion make sure blood has been screened, and don't get a tattoo or piercing until you're back home and can check out the tattoo shop properly.

Remember that AIDS is a fatal disease and though medical advances are being made there is no preventive vaccination and no cure.

Asthma and allergies

Whether you are an asthmatic or have an allergy to chemicals in the air, food, stings, or antibiotics, ask your GP for advice before you go. You will be able to take some treatments with you.

Allergy sufferers: if you suffer from severe shock reactions to insect bites/nuts or any other allergy, make sure you have enough of your anaphylactic shock packs with you - you may not be able to get them in some parts of the world.

Chronic conditions

Asthmatics, diabetics, epileptics or those with other conditions should always wear an obvious necklace or bracelet or carry an identity card stating the details of their condition. Tragedies do occur due to ignorance, and if you are found unconscious a label can be a lifesaver. See **www.medicalert.org.uk** for information on obtaining these items.

You should also keep with you a written record of your medical condition and the proper names (not just trade names) of any medication you are taking. If you are going on an organised trip or volunteering abroad, find out who the responsible person for medical matters is and make sure you fully brief them about your condition.

Contraceptives

If you are on the pill it is advisable to take as many with you as possible. Remember that contraceptives go against religious beliefs in some countries, so they may not be readily available. Antibiotics, vomiting and diarrhoea can inhibit the absorption of the pill, so use alternative means of contraception until seven days after the illness.

Condoms: unprotected sex can be fatal, so everyone should take them, even if they are not likely to be used (not everyone thinks about sex the whole time). Keep them away from sand, water and sun. If buying abroad, make sure they are a known brand and have not been kept in damp, hot or icy conditions.

Dentist

Pretty obvious but often forgotten: get anything you need done to your teeth before you go. Especially worth checking up on are wisdom teeth and fillings - you don't want to spend three months in Africa with toothache.

Diabetics

Wear an obvious medical alert necklace or bracelet, or carry an ID card stating your condition (preferably with a translation into the local language). Take enough insulin for your stay, although it is unlikely that a GP will give you the amount of medication needed for a full year of travelling - three to six months is usually their limit, in which case, be prepared to buy insulin abroad and at full price. Ring the BDA Careline to make sure the brand of insulin you use is available in the particular country you are planning to visit. Your medication must be kept in the passenger area of a plane, not the aircraft hold where it will freeze.

Diabetes UK,
10 Parkway,
London NW1 7AA
www.diabetes.org.uk
Careline: +44 (0) 845 120 2960, weekdays 9am-5pm.
Email: careline@diabetes.org.uk

Diabetes UK produces a general travel information booklet as well as specific travel packs for about 70 countries.

Diarrhoea

By far the most common health problem to affect travellers abroad is travellers' diarrhoea. This is difficult to avoid but it is sensible to do the best you can to prevent problems. High-risk food/drinks include untreated tap water, shellfish, un-pasteurised dairy products, salads, peeled/prepared uncooked fruit, raw/undercooked meat and fish. Take a kit to deal with the symptoms (your doctor or nurse should be able to advise on this). Remember to take plenty of 'safe' drinks if you are ill and re-hydration salts to replace lost vitamins and minerals.

the gap-year guidebook 2011

If vomiting and/or diarrhoea continue for more than four to five days or you run a fever, have convulsions or breathing difficulties (or any unusual symptoms), get someone to call a doctor straight away. Seek advice on the best doctor to call; the British Embassy or a five-star hotel in the area may be able to offer some advice here.

Eyes

Contact lens wearers should stock up on cleaning fluid before going, especially if venturing off the beaten track; but if you're going away for a long period it might be worth switching to disposable types so there's less to carry - ask your optician for advice.

Dust and wind can be a real problem, so refreshing eye drops to soothe itchy eyes and wash out grit can be really useful. If you wear contact lenses, your optician should be able to offer you a range of comfort drops which will be compatible with your lenses.

Also most supermarket pharmacies, plus travel and camping shops, sell plastic bottles of mildly medicated hand cleanser that dries instantly. They're small and light to carry and you only use a small amount each time so it's worth packing a couple. They're really useful for cleaning hands before putting in contact lenses if the local water supply is suspect. It's also worth making sure you have glasses as a back-up, as it's not always possible to replace lost or torn contacts.

If you wear glasses consider taking a spare pair - they don't have to be expensive and you can choose frames that are flexible and durable. Keep them in a hard glasses case in a waterproof (and sand proof) pouch.

Malaria

This disease is caught from the bite of an anopheles mosquito and mosquitoes are vicious and vindictive. Highest risk areas are tropical regions like sub-Saharan Africa, the Solomon Islands and Vanuatu (Pacific), the Amazon basin in South America and parts of Asia. There's no jab, but your GP will give you a course of pills to take.

The most dangerous form of malaria is falciparum, which is particularly common in sub-Saharan Africa (places like Ghana, Gambia, DR Congo). It can cause liver, kidney, stomach and neurological problems and if left untreated, can be fatal.

One bite from a mosquito is enough. The parasite gets to your liver within 30 minutes and will reproduce there rapidly, infecting the blood stream. Once the parasites are in your blood stream you start to notice symptoms. Some versions can remain dormant in the liver, leading to repeat episodes of the illness.

The best protection is to try (as much as possible) to avoid being bitten. Here are tips for how:

- Use insect repellent, preferably containing either at least 30% DEET (diethyltoluamide), or extract of lemon eucalyptus oil.
- Keep your arms and legs covered between dusk and dawn and use a 'knockdown' spray to kill any mosquitoes immediately.

- Mosquito nets are useful, but they can be hard to put up correctly. It is often worth carrying a little extra string and small bits of wire so that the net can be hung up in rooms that don't have hanging hooks. Ideally the net should be impregnated with an insecticide, you can buy nets that are already treated from specialist shops and travel clinics (see www.gapyearshop.com).
- For some places, dual-voltage mosquito killer plugs are a good idea. Tests carried out for *Holiday Which?* by the London School of Hygiene and Tropical Medicine found four that gave 100% protection - Boots Repel, Jungle Formula, Lifesystems and Mosqui-Go Duo. They also tested hand-held electric buzzers which claim to frighten off mosquitoes and found that they did not work on the anopheles mosquito.
- Another good idea is to spray clothes with permethrin - which usually lasts up to two weeks, although Healthguard has a product, called AM-1, which works for three months or 30 washes. Visit www.healthguardtm.com to find out more or call them on +44 (0)20 8343 9911.

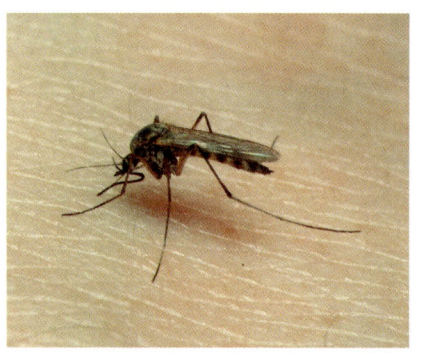

The pills can be expensive, and some people, particularly on long trips, stop taking their pills, especially if they're not getting bitten much. Don't. Malaria can be fatal.

No one drug acts on all stages of the disease, and different species of parasites show different responses. Your GP, practice nurse or local travel clinic should know which one of the varied anti-malarials is best for you, depending on your medical history (eg for epileptics or asthmatics, for whom some types of anti-malarials cannot be prescribed) and the countries you are visiting. Visit your GP or travel clinic at least eight weeks before you go to discuss the options.

It's also worth doing a little research of your own before going to your GP or practice nurse. A useful website is www.malariahotspots.co.uk All the anti-malarial tablets have various pros and cons, and some of them have significant side effects. If you're going to an area where you have to use the weekly mefloquine tablets, MASTA recommends that you start taking the course two and a half to three weeks before departure. Most people, who experience unpleasant side effects with this drug, will notice them by the third dose. If you do have problems, this trial will allow you time to swap to an alternative regime before you go.

If you are in a malaria-risk area, or have recently been in one, and start suffering from 'flu-like' symptoms, *eg* fever, muscle pain, nausea, headache, fatigue, chills, and/or sweats, you should consider the diagnosis of malaria and seek medical attention immediately.

A traveller with these symptoms within several months after returning from an endemic area should also seek medical care and tell their doctor their travel history. The correct treatment involves the proper identification of the type of malaria parasite, where the traveller has been and their medical history.

Sunburn

Wherever your **gap**-year takes you, the advice from Cancer Research UK's SunSmart campaign is to enjoy your time in the sun safely. This means not getting caught out by sunburn which, as well as being unsightly, is a clear sign that skin cells have been damaged. Over time, this damage can build up and may ultimately lead to skin cancer.

So while everyone needs some sun in their lives, too much can be harmful. The facts are worrying – skin cancer is one of the most common cancers in the UK and the number of people who develop it is increasing faster than any other type of common cancer. Every year over 10,300 people are diagnosed with malignant melanoma – the most lethal type of skin cancer - and almost 2,000 die from the disease. It is diagnosed in a disproportionately high number of younger people, being the second most common cancer in young adults (aged 15-34) in the UK.

And as well as causing skin cancer, too much UV can cause premature ageing, making skin look old and leathery before its time.

But the good news is that most cases of skin cancer can be prevented.

When you're out in the sun, the most important thing is to make sure you don't burn. Get to know your skin type and how it reacts in the sun. As a general rule, the lighter your skin, the more careful you should be in the sun.

When your risk of burning is high, often during the hottest part of the day, spend time in the shade, cover up with a T shirt or a towel and regularly apply plenty of sunscreen (at least factor 15 – but the higher the better) to protect your skin.

Whatever your skin type the message is simple - don't let sunburn catch you out.

Anyone can develop skin cancer but some people have a higher risk and need to take more care, including those with fair skin, lots of moles or freckles, a history of sunburn or a family or personal history of skin cancer.

SunSmart is the UK's skin cancer awareness campaign, funded by the UK health departments. To identify your skin type, find out more about skin cancer, how to enjoy the sun safely, and the dangers of using sunbeds visit **www.sunsmart.org.uk**.

visit: www.gap-year.com

Tick borne encephalitis

Ticks are second only to mosquitoes for carrying diseases to humans and immunisation is recommended for people who intend to walk, camp or work in heavily forested regions of affected countries between April and October when the ticks are most active. Your doctor or practice nurse can advise if you should have this immunisation for your travel destination.

We got in touch with the good people of Tick Alert to get their expert advice. Here's what they had to say:

TBE is a viral disease contracted via the bite of an infected tick which is endemic in 27 countries in Europe. It leads to an annual average of 10,000 cases needing hospital treatment. Two in every 100 TBE sufferers will die from the disease.

The map on the previous page shows the latest countries and regions identified by the International Scientific Working Group on TBE to be a risk for the disease. This group of the world's leading experts on TBE says new areas are being discovered all the time.

TBE symptoms

TBE is a viral disease that attacks the central nervous system and can result in serious meningitis, brain inflammation and death. TBE incubation is six to fourteen days and at first can cause increased temperature, headaches, fever, cough and sniffles, symptoms similar to a cold or flu. The second, more

the gap-year guidebook 2011

dangerous phase of TBE can lead to neck stiffness, severe headaches, delirium and paralysis. There is no specific treatment for TBE.

How to protect yourself

- Use an insect repellent that is effective against ticks.
- Avoid wearing shorts in rural and wooded areas, tuck trousers into socks, or cover all exposed skin with protective clothing (though not always practical in summer).
- Inspect your skin for ticks and remove any found as soon as possible with fine-tipped tweezers or a tick-removal tool. If using a special tool, follow instructions for use. If you are using fine-tipped tweezers, grasp the tick firmly and as close to the skin as possible. In a steady motion, pull the tick's body away directly outwards without jerking or twisting. Make sure you get the tick's head out as sometimes the head can remain embedded.
- Also, avoid unpasteurised milk which may also be infected with the TBE virus in endemic regions.

Vaccinations

Ones to consider:

- Hepatitis (A&B)
- Japanese Encephalitis
- Meningitis
- Polio
- Rabies
- Tetanus
- Tuberculosis
- Typhoid
- Yellow Fever

Ask your GP for advice on vaccinations/precautions at least six to eight weeks before you go (some may be available on the NHS). Keep a record card on you of what you've had done. Certain countries won't admit you unless you have a valid yellow fever certificate.

Seeking medical advice abroad

You can expect to be a bit ill when you travel just due to the different food and unsettled lifestyle (painkillers and loo paper will probably be the best things you've packed).

visit: www.gap-year.com

While you're away:

- Keep a record of any treatment, such as courses of antibiotics, that you have when overseas and tell your doctor when you get back;
- Be wary of needles and insist on unused ones; it's best if you can see the packet opened in front of you, or you could take a 'sterile kit' (containing needles) with you; and
- If you don't speak the language, have the basic words for medical emergencies written down so you can explain what is wrong.

Is a gap-year safe?

Accidents can happen anywhere and so can earthquakes, floods, cyclones and other random events.

But there are some risks you can avoid by being alert, informed and prepared. You should take personal safety seriously and not put yourself in danger by agreeing to anything, about which you have misgivings, just because you don't want to risk someone thinking that you're stupid or scared.

Tip: There's one rule: If in doubt - don't

The Foreign Office estimates that of the approximately 250,000 young people who take a **gap-** each year, around 75,000 are prone to a reckless spirit that it calls the 'Invincibles'.

This concern prompted the UK's first-ever Gap-Year Safety Conference in London in June 2009. It brought together figures from the **gap-** industry, the FCO, British Standards and the British Safety Council to highlight the need for improved safety standards, including third party providers in Third World destinations.

Two useful initiatives offered by the UK's Foreign Office that have been running for some time are its Know Before You Go campaign, in which we at **www.gap-year.com** and **the gap-year guidebook** are partners, and Locate.

The FCO deals with an estimated 3.5 million enquiries, and supports around 85,000 Brits in difficulty each year. While support includes visiting those who have been admitted to hospital or arrested, to rescuing British citizens from forced marriages abroad, the FCO launched its service because it had found that the most common problems it was being called in on were the most preventable ones, such as inadequate or no insurance or lack of proper medical precautions.

Locate helps the FCO to track down Britons in the event of a crisis abroad. Again the need was revealed by a survey, which found that two thirds of us don't actually know where our travelling loved ones are and over half of us go abroad without leaving details of our trip with friends and family.

While the FCO deals with all travellers - not only those on a **gap-** - we agree with the message about being as prepared as possible before you go and that's what this guidebook is for.

We at **gap-year.com** also recommend that you consider taking a gappers' safety course before you go, to teach you how to recognise danger (from

the gap-year guidebook 2011

people as well as natural disasters), and how to look after yourself in a bad situation - it could be the thing that saves your life.

What the experts say:
Mind the Gap Year

Planning a **gap**-year can be a very exciting time. In order to get the most out of your **gap**-year and enjoy it to the fullest you need to plan and prepare for every eventuality. Staying safe is the key to having a good time.

These days research comes in many different forms, books, websites, fairs and courses. Safety courses have increased in popularity in the last few years particularly with celebrities such as Ewan McGregor and Charlie Borman taking part and training before their well-known motor cycle trips.

There are a number of different courses run by various companies across the country ranging from two hours to two days, the one thing they all have in common is that they are run by instructors with first-hand experience, a priceless tool.

Why attend a course? Why not? Attending a specialist Gap Safety course can be a vital tool in the planning and preparation of your trip, increasing self-awareness and enabling you to recognise danger and get yourself out of tricky situations.

Most of the courses follow a similar format, covering:-

Before you go – research, cultural differences, preparation, Insurance, documents and money

What to take – The clothing you will need, first aid kits, gadgets, electrical items, security of your belongings and tips on economical packing

Over there – Accommodation, food and water, transport, local authorities and awareness of a new environment and laws

Medical Issues – Emergency first aid, staying healthy, self-defence, climate, bites, bugs and vaccinations

Many of the courses will also run a 'for girls by girls' session

Make sure you know enough about what you want to do and where you want to go, talk to other travellers (there are many message boards online). If you're travelling with an organisation, check them out; ask to speak to others that have done the same trip.

Ensure you have adequate travel insurance to cover everything you want to do including working both paid and voluntary plus any activities you have in mind to do.

Make sure you have copies of all of your documents, try an online document safe. Ensure you have telephone numbers of people to contact in an emergency; Emergency medical assistance company, someone at home and if possible someone in the same country.

Travelling to unknown countries can be a great culture shock so a little

visit: www.gap-year.com

preparation beforehand will ensure that you make the most of all of your opportunities without missing out.

Mind The Gap Year are specialists in safety, planning and preparation, for more information visit www.mindthegapyear.com

The point is that as long as you have done all you could to be well prepared with travelling essentials and knowledge, then you should go for it!

Personal safety and security checklist

We asked our friends at GapAid, a charity established to help provide ensure youngsters are better-prepared on their **gap-years** and aware of the potential dangers and how to deal with them, for their advice.

- Make sure you keep in touch with friends and family back home, fellow travellers, the hostel or hotel you are staying in and the British Consulate, by making sure that people are aware of where you are, who you are with and when you will be back, if something goes wrong people will know and can start to help.

- Be culturally aware, polite and respectful; read up on local customs and dress and do not break these rules, you maybe the centre of attention as a westerner but at least if you are dressed correctly it will help. It might be worth having a sarong or scarf in your bag; this can be used as a skirt or shawl should you need it.

- Don't drink too much or stay out to late, it is not like being at home and you will make yourself unnecessarily vulnerable.

- Hanging the "Do Not Disturb" sign on your hotel door when you go out should help deter thieves.

- Having waterproofed documents (either laminating or in a secure plastic wallet), there is always a chance you will get caught in the rain or need to cross a river if trekking, this way you valuables and documents will stay dry.

- Walk with confidence and never use your guidebook, get out your map or start counting money in the street, find a café, sit and relax and read in peace, don't make yourself a target. Keep a small amount of change for food and drinks in a separate wallet so you don't have to keep going through your notes.

- If you have a 'weak' stomach avoid street stalls, eat in busy restaurants (where the locals are) and try and eat vegetarian if possible although saying this salads can be some of the worst.

the gap-year guidebook 2011

- If travelling alone, you are most vulnerable when you are sick (sometimes you feel like you have to travel that day) but my best advice would be don't. If you feel ill (like being drunk) don't travel and if you do make sure you are with another person you know well.
- Don't be afraid of approaching other backpackers - this is easier in non-Western countries when you can generally tell who is a traveller and who isn't. Not only might you make new friends but also it's great to share experiences and good times as sometimes travelling can be very lonely.
- Talk to locals: the best way to get insight before you travel is to talk to trusted people who live there. Networks are springing up all over the place offering unique local insights based from food lovers, or culture vultures, try Tripbod: www.tripbod.com
- Whatever happens, however bad - remember people are generally good and you will find people (other backpackers, locals, hostel owners etc) who will go out of their way to help you and make sure that you are safe and ok.
- If you are in trouble, whatever the local police tell you, contact the local British embassy or consulate - most of them are incredibly helpful and they will have dealt with situations like yours before and will know what you should do, make sure that you have several copies of their contact details to hand.

Tip: It can help to arrive with some local currency in notes and coins. You can often change travellers' cheques in banks at airport arrivals halls.

Remember, anyone can get lost. When you are on the road don't panic. Always agree meeting places before you go somewhere and play safe by having a back-up plan. Then if you don't turn up reasonably on time someone will be alerted to raise the alarm.

Before you do anything or go anywhere think about the consequences – this isn't about not having a good time, or being boring - it's about getting through your **gap-** without taking foolish risks.

In many places, though, you'll find people are very hospitable and curious about you and you might find their unabashed and quite frank questions intrusive. While you have to be sensible about how much information you give, equally try not to be too suspicious about their motives. What feels like an invasion of your personal space, or probing questioning, doesn't automatically mean anything sinister - remember the British in particular can be quite reserved so you'll notice the contrast. It's all a question of balance and courtesy.

Caroline's Rainbow is a charity set up to promote Travel Safety Awareness amongst young travellers. We asked them for their advice: "**Gap**-years provide amazing opportunities to meet new people, enjoy exhilarating adventures, experience different cultures and create lifelong memories. To make sure your gap year trip is memorable for all the right reasons though, it is important that you do your research and are aware of safety issues whilst travelling.

"Taking the time before you travel to research the countries you'll be visiting, brush up on local customs, research general travel safety tips and perhaps learn a few phrases in the local language could not only help to keep you safe

visit: www.gap-year.com

and prevent you from inadvertently causing offence. The more you know will also add to the enjoyment of your trip in the long run.

"Who wants to be stranded in an unfamiliar place late at night wishing they'd taken a few minutes to check transport times or distances to the nearest hostel? Or who fancies getting a hefty fine or worse for inadvertently breaking local laws such as chewing gum in Singapore or wearing camouflage clothing in Barbados? Spending a few hours researching such issues before you travel will ensure a much safer and more enjoyable trip once you're on the road.

"So what are the main travel safety issues you should be aware of? Firstly, travel safety awareness begins long before you pack your bag and head off on your great adventure – you should research local customs, laws and cultures before you travel; Caroline's Rainbow Foundation's Global Guide is a great place to start www.carolinesrainbowfoundation.org.

"Visit your doctor for relevant vaccinations and medications a few months prior to departure; and arrange adequate travel insurance, being sure to check carefully for any restrictions or exemptions. It is also a good idea to make two copies of all your travel documents, leave one copy with someone at home and take a spare copy with you in case the originals are lost or stolen.

"Pre-trip preparation can really make a big difference to the safety and enjoyment of your trip. But travel safety awareness is about much more than just pre-trip planning. When you're on your travels and having the time of your life it's easy to become complacent and let your guard down.

"However, regardless of how comfortable you may feel in your surroundings, it is vital to remember that you are in a foreign country and you must appreciate the impact your decisions, actions and behaviour may have upon the local people and the possible repercussions this may have.

"It is also essential to make personal safety a priority, you should keep thinking ahead all the time while travelling. When choosing accommodation don't just look for the cheapest room, consider it's location, check the locks work and also check the fire evacuation procedures.

"When considering what clothing to wear be mindful of the impact your choices could have. Be mindful of the value cameras, phones and other accessories may have to local people. Don't flaunt your belongings and don't carry lots of money around with you and most importantly, remember that nothing is worth more than your life. Belongings can be replaced and if challenged, letting go could save your life.

"Further information and advice about staying safe on your travels can be found at: **www.carolinesrainbowfoundation.org**"

If you are offered strange drinks or drugs be sensible and think about your safety first. One of the biggest dangers in accepting a drink is that someone can slip in the so-called 'date rape' drug (Rohypnol). It doesn't taste of anything and you won't know you're taking it. Combined with alcohol, it can induce a blackout with memory loss and decrease your resistance, leaving you open to attack.

About ten minutes after ingesting the drug, you may feel dizzy and disoriented, simultaneously too hot and too cold, or nauseous. You might have difficulty

the gap-year guidebook 2011

speaking or moving and then pass out. Victims have no memory of what happened while under the drug's influence.

If you are tempted to try the local variety of cannabis in the belief that it is relatively harmless, remember that this isn't a view shared by everyone at home, never mind in other countries. Know what the local drug laws are and don't take risks. In many places in south Asia and south-east Asia, for example, it is illegal and possession carries stiff penalties in prisons where conditions are not remotely like they are in the UK. It's a shame to have to add this, but don't assume that a friendly Brit (who may or may not be a traveller) you might meet in a bar, on a beach, up a mountain *etc*, is any more trustworthy, genuine and agenda-free than a local. It's great to make conversation, break down barriers and feel 'at home' in a place - just exercise a degree of caution with any stranger!

If someone keeps pestering you with unwanted sexual advances after you have said no, get to somewhere where there are other people within earshot. Only use violence as a last resort - it's not worth fighting back against violent muggers. They're likely to be stronger than you and may be carrying a gun or a knife. Try to remain as calm and confident as possible - that way you'll be more likely to recall those useful tips you learnt on the training course you attended before you left.

Tip: Try to always carry a supply of small change and small notes in a pocket (trousers or jeans with deep pockets can be very useful) and not reveal that you are carrying larger notes.

Do not keep all your money in one place; distribute it between, say, a small daytime backpack, your rucksack or suitcase and a hidden belt bag so that if you are robbed, you still have some money in reserve.

If someone tries to snatch your bag throw it at them - it keeps as much space as possible between you and them and puts them off guard, giving you time to get away. Stick close to other people while you get back to base. Money pouches worn around the waist under clothes are really good, though thieves have become much more expert at spotting them and removing them without you knowing, so it's a good idea to pass the straps through your belt loops.

Tip: One solution could be to buy some stick-on Velcro™ (or the stitch-on variety - more time-consuming but ultimately more secure) and attach a strip to the waistband inside all your trousers with the matching strip on the back of the belt bag.

If you have money, a camera or a passport stolen abroad (and the chances of this are high), report the theft immediately to the nearest police station and make sure you have some written record from them, giving the date that you did so, with all relevant details.

Police in popular budget destinations may have had to deal with hundreds of insurance scams in the past and may not be sympathetic. Dress smartly (and cover up; going in a bikini is not a good idea), stay polite and calm, but firm.

It is very unlikely anyone will catch the thief or get your stuff back - all you need is a record of the police report for your insurance claim. Ask someone back home to notify insurers and post or fax a copy of the police notification

visit: www.gap-year.com

home. Many insurers will not pay up for loss or theft unless the police are notified (some policies won't pay out if you don't do this within 24 hours).

This also applies if you are involved in any accident likely to result in an insurance claim. Keep records of everything that might be important – better to throw it away later than not to have it when needed.

In-country advice...

Responsible travel, respect, behaviour and dress codes

Your first impression of some countries will be a swarm of people descending on you, pestering you to take a taxi or buy something - at night when you're tired from a long plane trip it can be quite scary. If you're not being met by anyone, check whether there's a pre-pay kiosk in the airport and pay for a ticket to your ultimate destination. That way the taxi driver can't take you on a detour since they won't get their money until you're safely delivered and your 'chit' has been signed.

Some people advise that, if you arrive alone in the middle of the night (which is often the case on long-haul budget flights), it might be safer to wait until daylight before heading onwards. That's not a pleasant prospect in most airports, but it may occasionally be the sensible option.

In many countries of the developing world, where there are no social security or welfare systems, life can be extremely tough and leave people close to despair. That's likely to be even more the case, in the face of growing food shortages and escalating fuel and food costs as a result of the ongoing global recession. What may seem like a cheap trinket to you may be enough to buy them a square meal for which they are desperate enough to steal from you violently, so it is sensible not to wear too much jewellery.

Equally, wandering around discarding uneaten food is a particularly tactless thing to do, when large numbers of people may not know where their next meal is coming from.

Bear in mind that, in most places, even the so-called First World, rural communities are usually far more traditional and straight-laced than city ones and casual western dress codes and habits can offend.

If you don't want to find yourself in real trouble, do some research. Each culture or religion has its own codes of behaviour and taboos and, while no one would expect you to live by all their rules, as an ethical and responsible traveller, showing respect for the basic principles is a must as a guest in their country, not to mention being a sensible precaution if you want to stay safe.

Also remember that a country's native people are not just part of the landscape, they are individuals who deserve respect and courtesy, so if you want to take a photo of them - ask first, or at least be discreet!

These are the sorts of things you should bear in mind: in most Asian and African countries don't wear a bikini top and shorts in city streets if you don't want to attract the wrong kind of intrusive male attention. In any case an all-over light cotton covering will better protect you from sunburn and insect bites.

the gap-year guidebook 2011

Men and women should dress modestly, particularly, but not only, in Muslim countries. Women especially should wear long sleeves and cover their legs. Uncovered flesh, especially female, is seen as a 'temptation' and you'll be more comfortable, not to mention finding people more friendly and welcoming if they can see you're sensitive to local customs.

You should also remember that, in Buddhist countries, the head is sacred and so it is unconventional to touch it.

Before entering temples and mosques throughout India and south Asia, you must remove your shoes. There are usually places at the entrances, where you can leave them with attendants to look after them. Women are also expected to cover their hair - and in Jain temples wearing or carrying anything made of leather is forbidden. Even in parts of Europe you'd be expected to cover your head and be dressed respectfully if you go into a church.

Open gestures of affection, kissing or even holding hands between married couples can be shocking to some cultures. This is particularly true of India, though it seems to be relaxing a little in the cities. However, you will often see men or boys strolling around hand in hand or with arms around each other's shoulders in India - don't misinterpret: they are friends, *not* gay couples!

Remember also, that if you are speaking English with a local inhabitant, they may not understand or use a word with the same meaning as you do. Particularly in the area of emotional relationships and dating, remembering this and understanding the local religion, customs and morality can save a lot of misunderstanding, misery and heartache.

Sitting cross-legged, with the soles of your feet pointing towards your companions, is another example of a gesture regarded as bad manners or even insulting in some places and actually if you think about it, it's pretty logical if you're in a place where people walk around less than clean streets either barefoot or in sandals.

Since daily life and faiths are often closely interlinked, it helps to know a little about the major philosophies of life in the countries you visit so, to get you started, here's some very basic info about some of the main belief systems out of the many hundreds around the world. We use the term belief systems because, arguably, some of these are closer to being philosophies of life than to religions or faiths in the sense most people would understand them:

Bahá'i

God: a single God known through God's creation and prophets.

Foundation text: Bahá'is believe that all religions are different approaches to faith in a single God. So no core text, but Bahá'ís believe in unity, equality and human rights for all. The founder, Bahá'u'lláh, taught that world unity is the final stage in the evolution of humanity. There is no conversion and no requirement for followers to renounce their previous faith. Bahá'i originated in Iran, and is the world's youngest, and widely considered to be its fastest-growing, religion.

Place of worship: can be anywhere, but there is a stunning modern, pink

visit: www.gap-year.com

marble building, the Lotus Temple, in Delhi.

Holy day: the main one is 29 May, which commemorates the founder's teachings and his death on that day in 1892.

Shinto

The official religion of Japan, it has no specific God, no founder and no specific core texts.

Beliefs: a three-level universe; the Plain of High Heaven; the Manifested World; and the Nether World, but with the invisible worlds seen as an extension to the visible world. Kami (gods and spirit beings which include the ocean, the mountains, storms and earthquakes) allow believers to regard the whole natural world as both sacred and material. Ethics start from the basic idea that human beings are good, and that the world is good. Evil enters the world from outside, brought by evil spirits. Shinto has no moral absolutes and assesses the good or bad of an action or thought in the context in which it occurs: circumstances, intention, purpose, time, location, are all relevant in determining whether an action is bad. Harmony depends on the group being more important than the individual.

Place of worship: shrines: an enclosed sacred area with a gate, an area for ablutions and a main sanctuary. There is an emphasis on ancestral spirits and on the importance of gratitude for the blessings of the kami. There are many special prayers and rituals marking the various stages through life from birth to death.

Festivals: the main one is *Oshogatsu* (New Year) but there are festivals throughout the year marking spring and autumn as well as coming of age (*Seijin Shiki* or Adults' Day) and *Schichigosan* (when parents give thanks for their children's lives and pray for their future).

Taoism

God: *Tao* means 'the Way' and is a philosophy of living, but there is a concept of the Eight Immortal Beings (*Psa Hien*) who are the protectors of various aspects of life.

Core text: the *Tao Te Ching* (the Book of the Way, known in the West as the *I-Ching*) written by Lao Tzu.

Place of worship: everywhere - the Way is essentially a philosophy for living a life in balance.

Core beliefs: *Tao* is 'The Way' and the first cause of the universe, *Te* is the virtue of the person who lives in accordance with *Tao*. Taoists follow the art of *wu wei*, (ie to let nature take its course, but also to be kind to others because it will be returned) and the essential aim of Taoism is to achieve a world in equilibrium (a balance of Yin and Yang, the extremes of the universe such as the sun and moon, heaven and earth, chaos and order). There is no rigid division between body and spirit.

Mechanisms for achieving balance include meditation, breathing exercises, use of acupuncture, practising Tai Chi, and *Feng Shui*.

Confucianism

God: like Taoism, in China Confucianism is a philosophy for living life and therefore there is no concept of a God.

Place of worship: everywhere.

Core beliefs: based on the teachings of Confucius, who was a philosopher, moralist, statesman and educationist. The *Jen*, the essence of his teaching can be loosely translated as 'social virtue'. Like Taoism it strives for balance and harmony - by behaving towards others as one would want them to behave towards oneself. Confucius is believed to have met Lao Tzu and, by some accounts, to have been his disciple. His main concerns were with good order in human beings' principle relationships and with good government expressed in the values: *Li* (ritual, propriety, etiquette); *Hsiao* (love within the family, love of parents for their children and of children for their parents); *Yi* (righteousness); *Xin* (honesty and trustworthiness); *Jen* (benevolence, humaneness towards others); and the highest Confucian virtue, *Chung* (loyalty to the state *etc*).

Shamanism

In Latin America, particularly the area around the Peruvian Amazon basin, the traditional holistic belief system is called shamanism though the shamanistic tradition is not found only in Latin America.

Within the shamanist system, as in other traditional systems around the world, diet is important for both physical and spiritual wellbeing. Shamans are found in many communities and act as a link to the spirit world, healing specific illnesses, both mental and physical, as well as officiating at important life moments, such as birth and death. Plants are the starting point for seekers of physical and spiritual health and the shaman will help select the one that is appropriate for an individual's needs.

Many shamans have expert knowledge of the plant life in their area, and a herbal regimen is often prescribed as part of the treatment. They often say they learn directly from each plant how to harness their effects and healing properties only after obtaining permission from its abiding or patron spirit. Each plant is believed to have a spirit and each is linked to treating a specific condition of the mind or body.

visit: www.gap-year.com

It's possible to join programmes in the Amazon basin but - a note of warning - there's a spiritual as well as dietary aspect to the treatment, sometimes using plants with hallucinogenic properties, which can be a test of mental strength and stability. Misuse and abuse of these powerful plant-based 'medicines' can have dangerous and even fatal consequences.

Humanism

Humanists are agnostic or atheist since they believe it is impossible to prove the existence of God and that it is possible to be good without the need for a God.

The essence of humanist practice is that it is about rational behaviour, rejecting both a supernatural being involved in human affairs and the idea of an afterlife.

Core texts: there are none, nor are there any declarations of faith. Humanists regard themselves as independent thinkers who have arrived at a set of moral and ethical values and behaviours, which are shared. They include accepting responsibility for one's actions and behaviour and that it is important to try to live a full and happy life and to help others do the same. They value human rights, freedom of communication, freedom from want and fear, education should be moral but free of bias from the influence of powerful religious or political organisations and that no doctrine, religious or political, economic or moral should be immune to critical scrutiny.

Zoroastrianism

God: Ahura Mazda.

Foundation text: the *Avesta*. There are few rules in Zoroastrianism, whose basic concepts are truth and purity and can be summed up as 'good thoughts, good words and good deeds'. Men and women are considered equal and with a responsibility for their own behaviour. The main thrust is to be the best one can be so there is a strong emphasis on education and on free will. Zoroastrianism is named after its founder the prophet Zarathustra and originated in Persia (now Iran). Many followers fled to India (where they are known as Parsis) following the Mongol invasion of Persia and its subsequent conversion to Islam.

Place of worship: Fire temple - the eternal flame is seen as a symbol of purity, but it is *not* worshipped. It is incorrect to call Zoroastrians fire worshippers.

Main festival: Noruz - New Year (around 21 March).

Islam

God: Allah.

Foundation text: the *Qur'an* transmitted by the Prophet Mohammed (the Messenger, Rasul, of God). It is customary when referring to the Prophet to add the words "peace be upon him".

Place of worship: Mosque. It is also a place of learning and teaching. The five pillars of Islam: *Shahada* (declaration of faith); *Salat* (prayers five times a day); *Zakat* (charity tax for the poor); *Sawm* (fast during Ramadan); and *Haj* (pilgrimage to Mecca).

Holy day: Friday.

Main festival: Ramadan - a month when Muslims fast from dawn to dusk.

Greeting: *As Salaam aleikum* (Peace be upon you); reply *Wa aleikum salaam*.

Prohibited food and drink: pork, alcohol.

Jihad: literally means struggle - it does not mean holy war, though the term has been inaccurately used in that way by many people, Muslim and non-Muslim. The struggle is primarily a personal one against one's own faults and weaknesses.

Judaism

God: *Yhwh* (pronounced Yahweh).

Foundation texts: the Old Testament of *The Bible* and the *Torah*.

The Talmud: an explanation of the *Torah*, teachings and discussions of Jewish scholars.

Place of worship: the Synagogue, also used as a place of learning and teaching.

Holy day: Sabbath (sunset Friday to sunset Saturday).

Main festival: Yom Kippur - the day of atonement when Jews must seek forgiveness from those they have wronged.

visit: www.gap-year.com

Prohibited food: pork.

Zionism: an international political movement launched in 1897, by Austrian journalist Theodor Herzl, with the aim of establishing, in law, a Jewish homeland in Palestine. To be a Jew is not automatically to be a Zionist.

Hinduism

God: Brahman - represented by the 'Om' symbol, the creator and destroyer of life and the universe. The multiplicity of other 'gods' such as Brahma, Vishnu and Shiva, (the Trimurti) Parvati, Kali, Durga, Ganesha, to name but a few of the many Hindu deities, represent different paths to follow reflecting the variety of human life and the sense of personal responsibility for one's own actions.

Foundation literature: the *Vedas*, the core text representing an oral tradition coming direct from God.

Main festival: Diwali is the main one but there are many more. Place of worship: temples to the many different deities are widespread and can be anything from tiny street shrines to huge, elaborately carved ancient monuments. People also have shrines in their homes. Many rivers, not only the Ganges, are also sacred.

Holy days: far too many to list. There is no specific day for prayer.

Prohibited food: beef (cows are sacred) but various peoples follow specific dietary requirements, from total vegetarianism through to eating of non-prohibited meats and fish, depending on the region they're from and their caste.

Essence of Hinduism: life is seen as an endlessly-repeating cycle of death and rebirth. Essentially the aim is to reach *moksha* and therefore release from the cycle of reincarnation. Karma is the accumulated result of a person's past action and determines the form in which they will be re-born. Dharma is the path of righteousness and duty, following which the individual can hope to improve their karma until they eventually reach *moksha*. This means that, as for other faiths, Hinduism is interwoven into the fabric of daily life and there is an emphasis on personal responsibility for one's behaviour, and therefore on modesty in dress and actions.

Buddhism

God: there is no name or central concept of a God. Buddhism is essentially a philosophy and a way of life leading to the goal of attaining nirvana - the release from the struggle to survive and from passion, aggression and ignorance.

Place of worship: although there are many shrines to the founder of Buddhism, Siddharta Gautama, he is not worshipped as a god nor is he seen as one. The nature of Buddhism does not require a place of worship

the gap-year guidebook 2011

and the *stupas* (characteristic round towers) are sacred buildings housing relics or the remains of a saintly person. There is, however, a tradition of monastic communities, particularly found in the foothills of the Himalayas, in Thailand and in Tibet.

The essence of Buddhism: a philosophy for living summed up by the Four Noble Truths and the Noble Eightfold Path. The four truths were contained in the Buddha's first sermon and explain that suffering is part of life (the first truth) caused by the struggle to survive and by craving and aversion (second truth). That suffering can be overcome and we can become happy and free with more time to help others (third truth). The fourth truth is the way to achieve this - by following the Eightfold Path.

The Eightfold Path: Right View; Right Intention; Right Speech; Right Discipline; Right Livelihood; Right Effort; Right Mindedness; and Right Concentration.

Affirmation: Buddhists take five vows: to refrain from killing living beings; taking that which is not given; from sexual misconduct; from false speech; and from alcohol and drugs which confuse the mind.

Jainism

God: Jains believe in karma and there is no room in the belief system for a creator God. To follow the Jain faith is to follow a very rigorous and difficult way of life.

visit: www.gap-year.com

Place of worship: there are many ancient, beautiful and very ornate temples in India, particularly in Gujarat, but they are not quite places of worship in the sense generally understood.

The essence of Jainism: all beings, including inanimate objects, such as stones and earth, are alive and feeling. Consequently this is a strictly non-possessive and non-violent code of living.

Followers are divided into *sadhus* (monks), *sadhivas* (nuns), *shravak* (laymen) and *shravika* (lay women). The essence of Jainism is to strive for liberation of the self through right faith, right knowledge and right conduct (not unlike the Zoroastrian good thoughts, good words and good deeds).

The five great vows (*Maha-vratas*): right conduct includes not harming any living thing, not stealing, chastity, detachment from people, place and material things. Jains wear only white, usually with a mask over the nose and mouth to avoid inhaling insects. They also carry a soft brush to sweep any place they plan to sit to avoid harming any living thing.

Main festival: *Paryshana Parva* (August/September), which ends with people wishing each other *Michhami-Dudakam*, meaning: 'Forgive me if I have done anything wrong or hurt your feelings knowingly or unknowingly.'

Sikhism

God: Sikhism recognises one universal God of all nations, who has no name.

Place of worship: *Gurdwara* - this is both a temple and a community centre, a symbol of equality and fraternity. Many *Gurdwara* community kitchens, known as *Pangat*, or *Guru-Ka-Langar*, produce a daily meal to feed thousands of destitute people in their neighbourhoods. It's a religion firmly rooted in the world and so encourages work, enterprise and wealth.

Foundation text: the *Guru Granth Sahib*. The essence of Sikkhism: the religion evolved in India at a time of considerable spiritual confusion, following the *Mughal* (Muslim) invasion into largely Hindu India. Sikkhism is open to anyone and is a faith rooted in optimism and in equal status, though with different roles, between men and women. Sikh unity and personality is based on the five Ks - *Kesha* (long and uncut hair); *Kangha* (a comb); *Kara* (a steel bracelet); *Kaccha* (special shorts worn as underwear) and *Kirpan* (the sword).

Prohibited: alcohol, tobacco, eating meat, and adultery.

Holy day: there is a daily service, called the *Granthi*, in the *Gurdwara* and Sikhs are expected to start their day with prayer, though they can visit the *Gurdwara* at any time of the day to pray. However what matters most is the way they live their daily lives.

Festivals: Vaisaki – harvest festival (around 13 April) and the celebration of the birth of the *Khalsa* (the brotherhood of those pure in word and deed).

For more information, or if you are interested in finding out about other religions, try: www.bbc.co.uk/religion/religions

the gap-year guidebook 2011

Communication
Keeping in touch

Spare a thought for those you're leaving behind - friends as well as family. Not only will they be worried about your safety, but they may actually be interested in your travels - most are probably jealous and wish they could go too.

It's not just about keeping them happy: make sure you tell them where you are and where you are going - that way if something does happen to you, at least they know where to start looking. Backpackers do go missing, climbers have accidents, trekkers get lost; at least if someone is concerned that you have not got in touch when expected, they can then alert the police. If you've promised to check in regularly with close family *make sure you do*, especially when you move on to another country. Of course, if you don't stick to what you agreed, don't be surprised if the international police come looking for you.

You can use a BT Chargecard to phone home from abroad from any phone - just call the operator and quote your pin number (having set it up before you left). The calls are charged to your BT phone account back home and are itemised on the bill; weekly limits can be set in advance. There are different types of Chargecard accounts you can set up, including limiting card use to one number or a set of numbers. For further details on BT Chargecards see:

www.payphones.bt.com/callingcards/prices/index.htm

While you probably can't wait to get away, you may be surprised how homesickness can creep up on you when you're thousands of miles away. Getting letters or emails can be a great pick-me-up if you're feeling homesick, weary or lonely, so, in order to ensure a steady supply of mail, distribute your address(es) widely to friends and family before you go. If you're not able to leave behind an exact address then you can have letters sent to the local Poste Restante, often at a main post office, and collect them from there. Also, parcels do usually get through, but don't send anything valuable.

Keeping a diary/sketchbook to record places, projects, people, how you're feeling and the effect things are having on you, can help when you get an attack of the homesick blues or just feel a bit down.

Mobile phone basics

Make sure you've set up your account to allow you to make and receive calls and text messages in all the countries you'll be travelling to (and emails if you've got a WAP phone).

Try to limit use of your mobile to emergencies - they usually cost a fortune to run abroad as you pay for all the incoming calls at international rates too.

It's worth insuring the handset, as mobile theft is common and if it's the latest model, try not to flash it around.

But don't rule out using your mobile phone as **gap-** kit; it might save your life if you break your leg halfway up a mountain and need to call for help (make sure you keep the battery charged).

If you are staying in one country for several weeks, consider getting either a

visit: www.gap-year.com

cheap local mobile phone or a local SIM card for your UK mobile. Don't forget to alert friends back home to the new number. Local texts and calls tend to be very cheap and incoming calls from abroad are free, which avoids the massive charges when using your UK mobile.

Snail mail

Aerogrammes are a cheap way of writing from most countries. Registering letters usually costs only a few pence (or equivalent) from Third World countries, and is definitely worthwhile. Postcards are quick, cheap and easy - though not very private.

www.pc2paper.co.uk - This website allows you to send letters worldwide from the internet and store addresses in your account. You type your message and they then convert it into an actual letter and post it for you. The costs vary depending on weight and size.

Email

If you can get to a cybercafé or internet kiosk in an airport, hotel, university, office or home when you're abroad, you can simply log in to your mailbox (remember you'll need your User ID and password if these are part of the package). If you think getting to a cybercafé is going to be hard, there are always WAP phones (you need to register your email address before you leave).

Air Mail (**www.airmail.co.uk**) will forward emails to you as text messages sent to your mobile, and you can send emails by simply sending them a text message, which they will forward as an email. Check their website for their up-to-date tariff. In practice, however, if there are no internet facilities in the area then the chances are there won't be a mobile phone signal either, and you may have to resort to more traditional methods of communication.

Having said that, thousands of cybercafés now sprinkle the globe, and internet connections can be difficult in Delhi but perfectly okay in Bolivia, so you'll probably find somewhere that you can email home at some point.

Internet Cafes

Dongles, wi-fi and net access via mobile phones may be great news for **gap**-travellers in out-of-the-way places and in emergencies, but you could say they also could take away one of the less talked about pleasures of a **gap**-.

Thanks to an interesting series of documentaries on the BBC World Service we've a whole new perspective on internet cafes.

the gap-year guidebook 2011

They're much more than just a place to upload your latest batch of photos, check in with the folks at home and pick up the footie results along with your e-mail.

In many places they're a lifeline for local people – to small farmers or traders, to families separated by war, poverty or natural disaster or a way of bringing education to children in isolated villages across the developing world – and, like any other kind of café, a place of crucial social interaction.

"Internet Hobo" Nick Baker travelled the world of internet cafes for the BBC World Service, guided to his next destination only by those he meets along the way.

In only the first three episodes Nick found himself in New York, where internet cafes are the preserve of students, then in Yunming in southern China he found online gamers and novelists, and finally in Accra, in Ghana, he discovered less socialising and more people doing serious business.

And that is partly the point – the internet has allowed many people in communities with little or nothing in the way of energy supplies, roads and other basic infrastructure so many of us take for granted to leapfrog a stage in development and improve their economic circumstances.

It could be farmers across parts of Africa checking the latest crop prices or weather forecasts or children picking up basic literacy online but equally having to go to an internet café means people get to meet other people and share their experiences.

For a traveller, though, it's as much about the café as it is about the internet so for an inquiring gapper hoping to learn more about the lives of the ordinary people in whose country they're travelling they're an opportunity not to be missed.

Equally if you are travelling independently and following your whims where better than to check with other backpackers for decent places to stay or get an idea of local customs and prices for food, transport, entertainment, whatever.

So even if you're travelling with the latest in e-technology it's worth taking your netbook or laptop to an internet café for a wi-fi hook-up. You'll get as much info from the people as you can from the machine!

Perhaps we should also include one note of caution - look for cafes with open spaces not curtained booths. Very often, particularly in very traditional societies where there is only minimal contact permitted between unmarried boys and girls, internet cafes with computers in closed booths are often male-only territory – and a place to check out the latest in "adult" entertainment... Not a good place to go if you're a female gapper just wanting to check her e-mail and say hi to mum!

Online journals

Another easy way to keep everyone up-to-date is to set up a travel blog – as many people now do. You can also sign up to Facebook or MySpace before you go (if you haven't done so already). On Facebook, your photos and comments will be available only to your 'friends' (unless you relax the privacy settings for a particular album) but there is the added advantage of being able to send messages and pictures to specific people without having to remember their email address, providing, of course, they too have a Facebook page.

Other sites you might like to check out are:
www.travelblog.org
www.yourtraveljournal.com
www.offexploring.com
www.fuzzytravel.com
www.twitter.com/
www.travoholic.com/articles/flashpacking.htm

If you're interested in cities have a look at the urban travel blogsite:

www.gridskipper.com/

And finally... back to earth

We've talked to enough people who've already taken a **gap-** to know that returning home can be a shock to the system.

Returning to ordinary life takes time. It doesn't matter when you took your **gap-**, you're likely to still go through the same sequence of feelings over the three months it generally takes to readjust.

How you respond, though, will depend on what you are returning to - if you went between school and university you might find yourself switching courses or storing up something else to explore later. Or you might be quite content to take up your course with renewed enthusiasm after a travelling break from study.

It's different again for people mid-career or over-50 mature travellers, but the pattern of adjustment is pretty much the same.

InterHealth, who provide a full range of health services and pre-travel health preparation, describe the feeling as reverse culture shock.

"Reverse Culture Shock is a common response experienced by people returning home from another culture. It can often be worse than culture shock as it's often unexpected. Returning home should be the easiest part of the trip, and sometimes it is, however, your trip may have changed you, your values and expectations. Sometimes it may be difficult to acknowledge that you have changed and home is still the same. Your family and friends may have unrealistic expectations of you. This may be hard on you but it will also be hard on them.

"You may feel a major loss upon returning home, almost as if you have been bereaved. There may also be a communication barrier between yourself and your family and friends back home. You may not be able to express the magnitude of what you have been through abroad.

"Your view of your home country may have changed in the light of your overseas experience, and you might find yourself rejecting some of your old values and ways of living. This may cause conflict between you and your friends and family who may be affected by your lifestyle change.

"You may try to re-adapt to your old lifestyle and re-connect with your old friends but find it hard to do so. Situations and relationships back home are bound to have changed in your absence; especially if you have been away for a long time. You may feel that you no longer belong and that joining in is hard.

"If you have returned home without an immediate plan for the future you may feel as though there is a lack of purpose to your life, which sorely contrasts to when you were abroad and perhaps carrying out an important role."

All of the above can leave you feeling isolated, anxious, or depressed. It is important to remember that you are not alone in these thoughts, and that things can be done to help.

InterHealth recommends you stay away from any rash behaviour as you try to adjust.

"It is important not to engage in maladaptive coping strategies, such as:

- Drug or alcohol abuse
- Risk-taking behaviour (*eg* risky sex or dangerous driving)
- Social withdrawal
- Leaving again shortly after your return home

"These behaviours not only affect you, but also your family, friends, and colleagues.

"Everyone is different, and nobody knows you like you do. However, here are some tips that you might find useful:

- Prepare: prepare yourself before you go by learning more about reverse culture shock
- Keep in touch: keep in touch with your friends and family while you are away
- Give yourself closure: say a proper goodbye to your friends and colleagues
- Take a break: when you get home, take at least a few days off
- Write: writing can be a cathartic experience and can help order your thoughts. If you have experienced some life-changing or difficult events, write about them
- Avoid indulgences and rash behaviour: avoid self-indulgence in alcohol, drugs, and food – these comforts make you feel good in the short term but are guaranteed not to help your recovery process. Also try to avoid making rash decisions; you may feel bored and want to accept the first offer that comes your way, but it is best to be patient and let your emotional state settle

"Usually you will settle down quickly, depending on certain factors such as the effectiveness of your coping strategies and the extent of your overseas experiences. The experiences from your international assignment are likely to become incorporated into your values and the way you live. You may find yourself drawing on them to inform your decisions and thoughts, and when advising others.

"If, after a few months, you have not settled after your return we recommend

visit: www.gap-year.com

you talk to a trustworthy friend or a psychological health professional. You can email **phs@interhealth.org.uk** for further advice."

The length of time you've been away makes no difference to the feelings you go through on your return and even after six months you may still need time to adjust.

We've talked to people who've taken a two week leave of absence from work through their company's charitable foundation and to people who've spent a year or more away. They all report coming back and finding themselves looking at everything through fresh eyes and questioning the importance of various aspects of homelife that they've previously taken for granted.

On average, it seems to take about three months on average between stepping off that last plane after a **gap-** and getting back into life's routines To start with, a commonly-reported phenomenon is the odd sensation of the body decelerating while the brain's still on the move. So, after the first three weeks of initial euphoria and sharing, be prepared to come down to earth with a bump.

Here's one gapper's comment: "There is no feeling quite like it, I keep thinking about my next trip to keep me going!"

What do you do now?

This one depends on what you had planned before you left and whether the option's still there - and if you still want to do it - once you're back.

Some people advise that, if you can manage it, putting aside some money for about three months of living expenses for your return, as part of pre-**gap** preparations, takes the pressure off if you're going to be job hunting. But if taking time out isn't an option, don't panic.

the gap-year guidebook 2011

If you already have work to go back to you may have to combine the post trip elation with a fairly quick return to the 'rat race'. And you'll need to think about how you interact with your colleagues. How much do you say about your trip? A spokeswoman for one major UK employer, which supports its staff in taking time out, and also has a foundation on whose projects they can do voluntary work, had this advice:

"When you are returning to work it is important to have a plan. Returning to work after 18 weeks or more can prove difficult on both a psychological and logistical level.

"Keep your line manager up-to-date with the timings of your return to work. This will ensure that they can factor you into their resource planning and also help you integrate back into the working environment.

"Do not rule out a degree of retraining when you return to work. Refreshing your skills will benefit most people in the work place, and, if you have been away from work for a long period of time, you should use the opportunity to familiarise yourself with new systems, procedures and practices.

"When you return to work take into consideration reverse culture shock. Whilst you might be keen to talk about your travels for many months to come, your colleagues may not be so keen to listen."

Karen Woodbridge, Director of Suffolk-based Hornet Solutions (an Independent HR/Employment Law Consultancy), also offers some important advice:

"Remember the old adage 'Out of sight, out of mind'. Your colleagues have been getting on with business whilst you've been away. There may even have been changes of personnel, for example your old team members or boss may have left the company. There certainly will be new alliances and different company politics. Don't expect people to remember that you were a 'star performer' before you left. That role may well be occupied by someone else now.

"So, in many ways it will help if you think about returning to your old position as if it were a brand new job, *ie* expect things to be new, to have changed and realise that it will be up to you, once again, to find out how everything works and prove yourself. Realising you may face these challenges and planning how to overcome them will help you to more successfully integrate and adapt to your return at work."

If you have to start earning as soon as you get back and your old job wasn't kept open for you, you can always consider temporary work. These positions are often available immediately and can be flexible enough to enable you to carry on with your permanent job search. And you never know, once working in a company, opportunities often come up that you'd never have expected.

However, when looking for that new permanent role, Karen Woodbridge says: "You need to carefully consider how to put together your CV. Unfortunately many people use the phrase 'travelling' to cover gaps; they may be using this term to hide an unsuccessful job which ended in their dismissal or possibly even time spent in prison! Consequently, recruiters can be cynical whenever they see 'travelling' on a CV, which may result in your CV, with its genuine period of travelling, being rejected before you are even given a chance to explain.

visit: www.gap-year.com

"The way to tackle this is to expand on your experience. Highlight all the positive things you did, discovered or learnt in your time away. Within the confines of the space (and CVs should usually be no more than two pages) make your experience seem very real and highlight how it has increased the contribution you can make to the role for which you are applying. I would also highlight the additional benefits your travelling experience will bring to your new employer on your covering letter. But remember, in a job search situation it's the benefits to the employer that will count, not how much fun you had."

How is it now? Deciding what next

While taking up the threads of life, you've no doubt been trying to process everything you've learned from your **gap-** experience.

How do you feel? What's changed? What's been confirmed? Where to now? Is there something new you want to do next as a result? How to go about it? You'll almost certainly still be in touch with friends you made on your travels, maybe even had a couple of after **gap-** reminiscence meetings. Others may still be travelling and keeping you restless!

You may also still be in touch with the projects you worked on. It's a fairly common feeling to want to keep a link to something that's been a life changing, learning experience. Is this you?

The best piece of advice on dealing with the consequences of any life changing experience is to be patient and give it time. Nothing but time can make things settle into some kind of perspective and help you work out whether you are in the grip of a sudden enthusiasm or something deeper and more long-lasting.

The first reaction most people report is that it's whetted their appetites to hit the road again. But at the same time you need to be sure you're doing it for the right reasons. As one gapper told us: "There seemed to be a lot of lost souls who were running away from reality at home rather than going travelling for positive reasons. The problems will still be there when they get back home, and in many cases putting them off will only make things worse."

Change of direction?

In time you'll know whether your urge to travel has also become an urge to keep the links with the communities you visited now you're back.

What level of involvement do you want? Is it going to be something local like fundraising - doing local talks, letters to newspapers - or are you seriously looking to change career?

If you have come back with the germ of an idea for a career change as a result of a volunteer placement, for example, there's nothing to stop you slowly exploring the options and possibilities.

Have a look at your CV. Try to talk to people working in the field you're considering moving into. Armed with some basic information, you could also consider talking through issues such as what transferable skills you have to add to your volunteer experience, what training you might need and how

the gap-year guidebook 2011

affordable it is, with a careers counsellor or recruitment specialist – preferably with an organisation that specialises in aid/charity or NGO positions.

Try these links:
www.totaljobs.com/IndustrySearch/NotForProfitCharities.aspx
www.cafonline.org
www.charitypeople.co.uk/
www.peopleandplanet.org/ethicalcareers/

To keep you going you should also never underestimate the power of synchronicity. You may find unexpected connections and information come your way while you're getting on with other things. If it's meant to be, you'll find ways to make it happen.

Preparation

Tips For Travellers

Being Safe

Adventure First Aid
15 Laskeys Heath,
Liverton,
Newton Abbot, TQ12 6PH UK

E: info@adventurefirstaid.co.uk
T: +44 (0) 1626 821 360
www.adventurefirstaid.co.uk

Travel first aid and crisis management courses over two days, delivered by experienced professional trainers.

British Red Cross
44 Moorfields,
Barbican,
London, EC2Y 9AL UK

E: information@redcross.org.uk
T: +44 (0) 844 871 1111
F: +44 (0) 207 7562 2000
www.redcross.org.uk

The Red Cross (Charity No. 220949) offers first aid courses around the UK lasting from one to four days depending on your experience and the level you want to achieve.

Ecobrands
3 Adam & Eve Mews,
South Kensington,
London, W8 6UG UK

E: info@ecobrands.co.uk
T: +44 (0) 207 460 8101
F: +44 (0) 207 565 8779
www.ecobrands.co.uk

Pharmaceuticals for the traveller, available to buy online.

Gap Aid
PO Box 734,
Oxford, OX1 9EY UK

E: ally@gapaid.org
T: +44 (0) 7903 285 314
www.gapaid.org

Providing essential information for those considering a year out, from help with financial planning and insurance cover, to what to pack and where to go - GapAid's website helps you prepare for an adventure of a lifetime. Read, Research, then Travel.

Gapyear Trackers
Suite 246, 79 Friar Street,
Worcester, WR1 2NT UK

E: sales@gapyeartrackers.com
T: 0800 1577911
www.gapyeartrackers.com

A Gap Year GPS Tracker can be discreetly carried by the traveller, providing a sense of reassurance and peace of mind for family and friends back home.
Should the traveller get lost, separated from their group or be involved in an emergency, their location will be known.
Please contact us for further details.

the gap-year guidebook 2011

Go Gap Year
Consular Directorate,
Foreign and Commonwealth Office,
Old Admiralty Building,
Spring Gardens, SW1A 2PA UK

E: feedback.consular.services@fco.gov.uk
T: +44 (0) 20 7008 1500
F: +44 (0) 20 7008 0152
www.gogapyear.com

Run by the Foreign and Commonwealth Office of the UK government, this website offers safety advice for gap-year travellers.

InterHealth Worldwide
111 Westminster Bridge Road,
Lambeth, SE1 7HR UK

E: info@interhealth.org.uk
www.interhealth.org.uk

InterHealth provide services such as travel health advice, *eg* on immunisations, and support people worldwide.

Intrepid Expeditions
3 Chapel Court Cottages,
Broadclyst,
Exeter, EX5 3JT UK

E: nigel@intrepid-expeditions.co.uk
T: +44 (0) 800 043 2509
www.intrepid-expeditions.co.uk

Runs many different survival courses, including a first aid course, ranging from two to 14 days.

Lifesaver Systems
Old Bakery,
7 Tuddenham Avenue,
Ipswich, IP4 2HE UK

E: info@lifesaversystems.com
T: +44 (0) 1473 232656
www.lifesaversystems.com

All-in-one filtration system, in a bottle, which will turn the foulest water into safe drinking water without the use of chemicals.

Lifesavers (The Royal Life Saving Society)
River House, High Street,
Broom,
Alcester, B50 4HN UK

E: lifesavers@rlss.org.uk
T: +44 (0) 1789 773 994
F: +44 (0) 1789 773 995
www.lifesavers.org.uk

Contact them for information about qualifications in life saving, lifeguarding and lifesupport.

Mind The Gap Year
19-21 West House,
West Street,
Haslemere, GU27 2AB UK

E: info@mindthegapyear.com
T: +44 (0) 845 180 0060
www.mindthegapyear.com

We are a tailor-made combination of insurance and services for the gap-year traveller, promoting how to stay safe and prepare for your travels.

Objective Travel Safety Ltd
Bragborough Lodge Farm,
Braunston,
Daventry, NN11 7HA UK

E: office@objectiveteam.com
T: +44 (0) 1788 899 029
www.objectivegapyear.com

A fun one-day safety course for travellers, designed to teach them how to think safe and prepare for challenges they may face.

Remote Trauma Limited
2 Bridle Close,
Surbiton Road,
Kingston Upon Thames, KT1 2JW UK

E: admin@remotetrauma.com
T: + 44 (0) 844 800 9158
F: + 44 (0) 844 800 9158
www.remotetrauma.com

Specialist medical support and first aid training.

St John Ambulance
National Headquarters,
27 St John's Lane, Clerkenwell,
London, EC1M 4BU UK

T: +44 (0) 8700 10 49 50
F: +44 (0) 8700 10 40 65
www.sja.org.uk

The St John Ambulance Association runs first aid courses throughout the year around the country. Courses last a day and are suitable for all levels of experience.

Suffolk Sailing
Unit 75, Claydon Business Park, Gipping Road,
Great Blakenham,
Ipswich, IP6 0NL UK

E: liferafts@suffolk-sailing.freeserve.co.uk
T: +44 (0) 1473 833010
F: +44 (0) 1473 833020
www.suffolk-sailing.co.uk

Although mainly suppliers of sailing safety equipment, Suffolk Sailing does offer a one-day RYA/DOT Basic Sea Survival Course for Small Craft.

The Instant Mosquito Net Company Ltd
25 Berkeley Close,
Rochester, ME1 2UA UK

E: steven.spedding@mosinet.co.uk
www.mosinet.co.uk

Fully portable, self supporting mosquito net. Lightweight, easy to use and folds into its own carry bag.

The Year Out Group
Queensfield,
28 King's Road,
Easterton, SN10 4PX UK

E: info@yearoutgroup.org
T: +44 (0) 1380 816696
www.yearoutgroup.org

See main entry under volunteering.

TravelPharm
Unit 10 D, Mill Park Industrial Estate,
White Cross Road,
Woodbury Salterton, EX5 1EL UK

E: info@travelpharm.com
T: +44 (0) 1395 233771
F: +44 (0) 1395 233707
www.travelpharm.com

Provides travellers with a range of medication and equipment at very competitive prices to make your journey both healthier and safer!

Ultimate Gap Year
5 Beaumont Crescent,
Earl's Court,
London, W14 9LX UK

E: info@ultimategapyear.co.uk
T: + 44 (0) 20 7386 9101
www.ultimategapyear.co.uk

Personalised safety training suitable for anyone embarking on a gap-year. Training held at homes throughout south-east England.

YSP - Your Safe Planet Ltd
Bridgefield House,
Spark Bridge,
Ulverston, LA12 8DA UK

E: enquiries@yoursafeplanet.co.uk
T: +44 (0) 141 416 4622
www.yoursafeplanet.co.uk

Website linking travellers to trusted local people worldwide, giving you access to local knowledge before you go.

Communication

0044 Ltd
2 Chapel Court,
Holy Walk,
Leamington Spa, CV32 6EX UK

T: +44 (0) 870 950 0044
www.0044.co.uk

Their global SIM card could save you money on international calls.

Aether Mobile Ltd

E: customersupport@aether-mobile.com UK
T: 07872228000/08712870010
www.aether-mobile.com

Get your SIM now and cut your mobile phone calls by up to 80% when abroad and get free incoming calls in 65 countries.

CommsFactory
Oaklands, Shirlheath,
Kingsland,
Leominster, HR6 9RH UK

E: info@commsfactory.co.uk
T: +44 (0) 1568 708 034
www.commsfactory.co.uk

Produces foreign language and communications materials for emergency services and adventure travellers including the Lost For Words card.

Internet Outpost
PO Box 4640,
Cairns, QLD 4870 Australia

E: info@internet-outpost.com
F: +61 7 4041 4600
www.internet-outpost.com

Internet access and more available to travellers throughout Australia, New Zealand and Indonesia. Some of the facilities you have access to are:
CD Burning, Printing, Microsoft Word, Microsoft Excel, Faxing, Scanning, Photocopying

My Mate Back Home
PO Box 7143,
Westbourne,
Bournemouth, BH4 0EA UK

E: admin@mymatebackhome.com
T: +44 (0) 1202 540942
www.mymatebackhome.com

A company that looks after your mail and makes sure that it gets to you, anywhere in the world.

PocketComms Ltd
The TechnoCentre, Coventry University Technology Park,
Puma Way,
Coventry, CV1 2TT UK

E: sales@pocketcomms.co.uk
T: +44 (0)845 6029869
www.pocketcomms.co.uk

A universal language system in pictorial form.

Sim4travel Ltd
SCN Ltd t/a SIM4travel,
4 Royal Mint Court,
London, EC3N 4HJ UK

T: +44 (0) 207 107 9700
www.sim4travel.co.uk

Stay in touch for less overseas. Use your own mobile and save up to 80% off standard call charges.

What to take

Adventure Centre
240 Manchester Road,
Warrington, WA1 3BE UK

E: tents@cheaptents.com
www.cheaptents.com

Top quality camping equipment available to buy at discount prices.

Attwoolls Camping & Leisure
Attwoolls,
Bristol Road,
Whitminster, GL2 7LX UK

E: camping@attwoolls.co.uk
T: +44 (0) 1452 742233
F: +44 (0) 1452 742213
www.attwoolls.co.uk

A huge showroom south of Gloucester stocking tents, camping equipment, accessories and skiing equipment. You can also buy online.

Coleman The Outdoor Company
Coleman (UK) Ltd,
Kestrel Court Harbour Road ,
Portishead Bristol, BS20 7AN UK

E: customerservices@colemanuk.co.uk
T: +44 (0) 1275 390510
F: +44 (0) 1275 390518
www.coleman.eu

Coleman offer outdoor products and camping accessories from tents and sleeping bags to kayaks and lanterns.

Cotswold Outdoor Ltd
Unit 11, Kemble Business Park,
Crudwell,
Malmesbury, SN16 9SH UK

E: customer.services@cotswoldoutdoor.com
T: +44 (0) 844 557 7755
www.cotswoldoutdoor.com

Huge retail outlet for camping equipment, clothes, maps, climbing gear, footwear and more.

Craigdon Mountain Sports
Head Office, Unit 2, Burghmuir Circle,
Blackhall Industrial Estate,
Inverurie, AB51 4FS UK

E: sales@craigdonmountainsports.com
T: +44 (0)1467 624900
F: +44 (0)1467 629694
www.craigdonmountainsports.com

Scotland's premier independent outdoor retailer stocking a wide range of clothing and equipment.

Go Outdoors
Head Office, Hill Street,
Bramall Lane,
Sheffield, S2 4SZ UK

E: enquiries@gooutdoors.co.uk
T: 08450 020 888
www.gooutdoors.co.uk

Offer a wide choice of outdoor accessories and equipment, from tents, rucksacks, sleeping bags to clothing and brand labels.

Itchy Feet Ltd
4 Bartlett Street,
Bath, BA1 2QZ UK

www.itchyfeet.com

This company stocks a wide selection of equipment for all your travel needs. Also has a London branch.

Nikwax Ltd
Unit F,
Durgates Industrial Estate,
Wadhurst, TN5 6DF UK

E: enquiries@nikwax.co.uk
T: +44 (0) 1892 786400
F: +44 (0) 1892 783748
www.nikwax.com

To clean and waterproof all your gear, extend its life and maintain high performance with low environmental impact - Nikwax it!

Nomad Travel & Outdoor
Unit 34, Redburn Industrial Estate,
Woodall Road,
Enfield, EN3 4LE UK

E: orders@nomadtravel.co.uk
T: +44 (0) 845 260 0044
www.nomadtravel.co.uk

As well as the usual stock of clothing, equipment, books and maps their stores also hold medical supplies and have in-store clinics.

Páramo Directional Clothing Systems
Unit F,
Durgates Industrial Estate,
Wadhurst, TN5 6DF UK

E: info@paramo.co.uk
T: +44 (0) 1892 786 444
www.paramo.co.uk

Waterproof clothing, reversible shirts, windproofs, fleeces and other outdoor clothing.

Park Lane College
Leeds City College,
Park Lane Campus,
Leeds, LS3 1AA UK

E: course.enquiry@parklane.ac.uk
T: +44 (0) 845 045 7275
www.leedscitycollege.ac.uk

Waterproof clothing, reversible shirts, windproofs, fleeces and other outdoor clothing.

Vango
2 Kelburn Business Park,
Port Glasgow, PA14 6TD UK

www.vango.co.uk

Evergrowing range of tents, sleeping bags, rucsacks and outdoor accessories.

Yeomans Outdoors
Centenary House, 11 Midland Way,
Barlborough Links,
Chesterfield, S43 4XA UK

T: +44 (0)1246 571270
F: +44 (0)1246 571271
www.yeomansoutdoors.co.uk

Stocks a wide range of tents, camping equipment and outdoor clothing.

Chapter 2
Finance

2 Finance

How much will you need?

It all depends on what you're doing and for how long. Estimates put the average **gap**-year at costing between £3000 and £8000.

What do you need to pay for?

A **gap-** needn't break the bank, but it helps if you start by making yourself a list of all the things you might need to pay for, and then research how much it all comes to. Then you can start looking at ways you can save some money by shopping around and keeping costs down. Here's a checklist to help you get started.

Before you go:

- Passport
- Visas and work permits (check the FCO website for the relevant embassy - **www.fco.gov.uk**)
- Insurance
- Flights
- Fees for placements/organised treks etc
- Special equipment if needed
- Vaccinations - they're not all free - and a travellers' medical pack

In country:

- Accommodation (if travelling independently)
- Transport (if travelling independently)
- Food
- Entertainment
- Shopping - gifts and souvenirs
- Emergency fund

Raising the money

There's no doubt it's going to be harder to raise money for **gap-** travel during a recession, when the competition for even low-skilled or part-time work is likely to be intense.

Changing Worlds, a leading **gap**-year company with charitable aims, has been providing opportunities for those wanting the challenge of living and working

visit: www.gap-year.com

abroad for over a decade – so we asked them for their advice to gappers looking to raise some money for their life-changing trip.

"Of course there is no simple answer as everyone is different. For the lucky few parents, grandparents, god - parents or whoever step in and help out in a major way.

"Realistically however most people have to go out and earn the money. It might mean working full-time at a local supermarket, supporting the family business or adding your name to the baby-sitting list in your neighbourhood.

"The nuts and bolts of it are that you need the funds and you have got to earn the money somehow. Remember what you are about to embark upon is 'a once in a lifetime' thing so grit your teeth, be prepared to put in the hours and everything will be fine.

"To help raise the funds people have done some extraordinary things… Falling out of aircraft from an outrageous height, dangling from a long piece of rubber hose over a car park, organising a disco for lots of screaming kids, setting up a car boot sale on a Sunday morning, bouncing on a trampoline for a ridiculous number of hours – just some successful ideas we know have been used in the past.

"Auctions, fashion shows, garage sales, raffles, fetes and parties on your behalf can also be useful sources of funding. And whatever you do write about it and take some photos.

"Do look for sponsorship, and think locally. One of our gappers from a couple of years ago, Kathryn wrote to her local TV company about her plans to go to India. She was lucky; the response was positive and she got some airtime. As a result businesses and companies in her region offered to help raise funds in return for a written report on her return to the UK. This was an exceptional case and Kathryn was very lucky.

"Pick up your Yellow Pages and thumb through it for possible opportunities. Who might be

the gap-year guidebook 2011

interested in you and your travels? Community groups, charities, and religious organisations may be willing to help in some way.

"Local businesses will be interested in helping out if they think they can get some mileage out of it. It supplies them with positive publicity and their contributions are tax deductible so they win and so can you! Put pen to paper, lick a few stamps and see what responses you get.

"Seek some support from your local newspaper. The media are always hungry for human-interest 'feel good factor' stories so supply them with one – and a photo of you smiling complete with rucksack on your back and travel guide to hand! Give your business sponsors the free advertising they deserve."

If you are planning to do a training course during your **gap**-year, you may be eligible for funding via a Career Development Loan. A CDL is a deferred repayment bank loan to help you pay for vocational learning or education. The Department for Children, Schools and Families pays the interest on your loan while you are learning and for up to one month afterwards. You can get more info from the National CDL enquiry line: 0800 585 505; or by visiting the government website:

www.direct.gov.uk/en/EducationAndLearning/AdultLearning/FinancialHelp ForAdultLearners/CareerDevelopmentLoans/index.htm

Money savers

The International Student Identity Card (ISIC) gives you more than 40,000 travel, online and lifestyle discounts. It costs £9, is accepted in the UK and worldwide. There's also a 24/7 worldwide free call helpline for medical and legal assistance.

Many leading airlines also offer exclusive student/youth fares to ISIC (and IYTC) holders. Your travel agent can help you find the right one and advise if any age restrictions apply.

Your ISIC sees you right through the academic year: it's valid from each September, for up to 16 months, in other words until December the following year! You need to qualify for the year in which you'll hold the card:

- If you're a full-time student (15 hours weekly for 12+ weeks) at a secondary school, sixth form or further education college, language school, The Open University (60 points or more) or any UK university.
- If you've got a deferred/confirmed UCAS placement then you can grab an ISIC for your year away.

If you're neither of the above, but under 26, you can get an International Youth Travel Card (IYTC) with a similar range of benefits. You can get the cards online at: **www.ISICcard.com** (mail order forms are also available from this site); or by phoning: 0871 230 8546.

visit: www.gap-year.com

For budget flights and student discounts, you can check out the internet and we've included some hints in Chapter 4 – Travelling and Accomodation.

If you're travelling independently, cut the cost of accommodation by: staying in the guest houses attached to temples and monasteries; camping or staying in a caravan park; as a guest in someone's home; sharing a room; or using budget hotels or hostels, but be careful to check for cleanliness and proper exits in case of emergency.

If you're a mature traveller, perhaps you could investigate a house swap for part of your time away, but see also Chapter 3 - Career Breaks and Mature Travellers for other ideas.

International sim card: if you have your mobile phone overseas enabled you'll pay for the roaming and on top of that all your calls are routed via your home country so you're paying two-way international rates (you pay for calls you receive as well as ones you make) and that's pretty hefty!

It's cheaper to get an international sim card: here's a link to a site where you can buy one: **www.0044.co.uk**

This company also sells global phone cards, that can be used in 50 countries around the world, to make calls from 3p per minute from a landline.

However, at least one provider has recently abolished their roaming charges, making mobile calls from overseas no more expensive than UK based ones. Check with your service provider before you go.

Buy second-hand: rather than spend a fortune on a backpack, do you know someone who's just returned from a trip and might be willing to lend or sell you any equipment they no longer need? Check the classified ads in your local paper, buy on eBay (or similar) or try the **www.gap-year.com** message board.

Make sure that whatever you buy is in clean, sound condition, that the zips work, there are fittings for padlocks, and it's right for your body weight and height. If it's sound but a bit travel-worn, so much the better - you'll look like a seasoned traveller rather than a novice!

Fundraising ideas:

Chantelle Lesforis

I went on a six-month placement with Changing Worlds to Africa in 2009, between my A Levels and university. I wanted to raise the funds for the trip myself, and although it was difficult I mostly managed to do so.

One of my best ideas was to arrange a quiz night at my college. After inviting everyone I know, I had a total of 13 teams and around 75 people, including friends, teachers, neighbours, members of the family, work colleagues and my parents work colleagues. Remember, don't be afraid to ask because it will make you more money.

I also arranged a raffle, with all prizes donated from friends, family and local businesses. My advice here would be to target gyms as these are

the gap-year guidebook 2011

likely to give free day/week/month passes. Also get in touch with local salons who may also offer a free hair cut/blow dry. Tony and Guy also made me up a goody bag of hair treatments.

Overall, I raised over £600 on the quiz night and raffle, which was a great start to my fundraising.

I also decided to ask local businesses in my area for gift donations. I started off by sending them a letter, explaining a bit about myself and the placement I was going on. I wanted to show that I would be making good use of any money that they were kind enough to send me.

I found that the key to sending the letters is to find out who to write to. This can be obtained by ringing the company and making an enquiry to find out the manager's or the fundraising co-ordinator name.

The companies that you target are also important – try to keep them reasonably local so that they can relate better to your plea. It is also good to approach the companies that you think might take a particular interest in your project. For example, I approached the Co-operative, who promote the use of fair trade produce, and as a result received a gift donation of £200.

Money security

Take a mix of:

- Cash
- Travellers' cheques
- Credit card
- Travel money cards

Cash: carry small change in pockets, not big notes. Distribute it between a belt bag, day pack and your travel bag so you have an emergency stash.

Travellers' cheques: record serial numbers and emergency phone number for the issuer in case of theft. You sign each one when you get them from the bank but then there's a space for a second signature. Don't sign this second box until you're cashing it - if you do and your cheques get stolen, they can be cashed and you invalidate the insurance cover. Only cash a couple of travellers' cheques at any one time - get a mix of larger and small change denominations – often street traders and snack stalls, or taxis and rickshaws, won't have change for a large note and it makes you vulnerable - you seem rich.

Hotel currency exchanges are more expensive, local banks can take a long time and require ID. If you can find a Thomas Cook centre they're the most efficient and speedy we've found. Street rates can be cheaper but be very careful. A lot of street money changers are trading illegally - don't hand over the cheque until you have your money and have counted it.

Credit card: essential back-up. The problem with a credit card is losing it or having it stolen - keep a note of the numbers, how to report the loss of the

visit: www.gap-year.com

card and the number you have to ring to do so.

Both Visa and Mastercard are useful, in an emergency, for getting local currency cash advances from a cash dispenser at banks abroad. Remember, if you're using your credit card to get money over the counter then you're likely to need some form of ID (eg passport).

If you are paying for goods or restaurant meals by using your card, you should insist on signing bills/receipts in your presence and not allow the card to be taken out of your sight. This way you'll have no unpleasant surprises or mysterious purchases when you see your card statement.

Travel Money Cards: pre-pay travel cards are now a well-established alternative to travellers' cheques and can be used at an ATM using a pin number. The idea is that you load them with funds before you leave, but beware - like credit and debit cards, most charge for every reload and for cash withdrawals. To find out more check out the following:

www.iceplc.com/cashcard/

www.travelex.com/ae/personal/CP_default.asp?content=cp

www.postoffice.co.uk/portal/po/jump1?catId=19300207&mediaId=26800661

Wiring money

If you find yourself stranded with no cash, travellers' cheques or credit cards, then having money wired to you could be the only option. Two major companies offer this service:

MoneyGram - www.moneygram.com

Western Union - www.westernunion.com

Both have vast numbers of branches worldwide - MoneyGram has 180,000 in 190 countries and territories and Western Union has 379,000 agent locations in 200 countries and territories.

The service allows a friend or relative to transfer money to you almost instantaneously. Once you have persuaded your guardian angel to send you the money, all they have to do is go to the nearest MoneyGram or Western Union office, fill in a form and hand over the money (in cash).

It is then transferred to the company's branch nearest to you, where you in turn fill in a form and pick it up. Both you and the person sending the money will need ID, and you may be asked security questions so you need to know what the person sending the money has given as the security question *and* its answer. Make sure they tell you the spelling they've used and that you use the same.

Older travellers with more assets will have specific financial concerns and perhaps more sources of funds than younger gappers, and we've included some detail in Chapter 3 - Career Breaks and Mature Travellers.

Sticking to a budget

It sounds obvious but you can get a good idea of costs before you go from a gapper who's been there recently. Message boards like the one on

the gap-year guidebook 2011

www.gapyear.com are a good place to find such people. You can also get an idea of how far your money will go if you check an online currency converter like www.xe.com

As a general rule you'll find your money will stretch quite a long way in most of the less developed parts of the world, and once you're in-country you can find out fairly easily from other travellers/locals the average costs of buses, trains, meals and so on.

Having said that, the global recession and rises in oil and food prices have had an impact on most countries' economies. They've particularly hit costs in the less developed world and the signs are that it may take some time for things to settle down. As you're planning some months ahead of your trip it may be sensible to add a little extra for potential inflation when you're working out your minimum and maximum spend per day. The trick then is to stick to it.

Here are some tips:

Shopping: you're bound to find a zillion things that will make good souvenirs/gifts - best advice, though, is to wait. You'll see lots more wherever you are and the prices for the same goods in popular tourist and backpacker destinations will be much higher - and possibly of lower quality - than they will be in smaller towns and villages.

Do your buying just before you move on to the next destination, or return home, so you won't have spent too much money at the start of your trip, won't have to carry it all around with you and also by then you'll have an idea of what's worth buying and for how much. Another advantage of buying locally is that more of what you pay is likely to benefit the local community, and craftspeople, rather than the middle links in the chain.

If you buy souvenirs/gifts mid-trip, you could consider posting them home to save carrying them around with you but don't risk sending anything too valuable, and make sure you know what's permitted to send (and what's not) since you'll almost certainly have to fill in a customs declaration slip, which will be stuck to the outside of the parcel.

Bargaining: make sure it's the custom before you do, and try to find out roughly what it should cost before you start. Also try to look at yourself through local eyes - if you're wearing expensive jewellery and clothes and carrying a camera or the latest mobile phone you'll find it much harder to get a real bargain.

Whatever you do, smile and be courteous. The trader has to make a living, usually in pretty harsh economic conditions, and you're a guest in their country. Not only that, but if you're a responsible traveller then ethically you should be offering a fair price, not going all-out to grab a bargain you can boast about later.

Don't give the impression you really, really want whatever it is. Don't pick it up - leave that to the market trader, then let them try to sell it to you. They will tell how much they want and it's likely to be inflated, so you offer a price the equivalent amount below the figure it should be and that you're willing to pay.

visit: www.gap-year.com

If they start the process by asking you how much you're willing to offer then mention that you've asked around local people so you know roughly what it should cost, before you name a price a little below what you're prepared to pay. From this point on it's a bit like a game of chess and it can be very entertaining - so don't be surprised if you collect an audience!

You might be told a heart-rending story about family circumstances or the trader's own costs, but you can counter that by saying that however much you like the article, you're sorry but it's outside your budget. Gradually you'll exchange figures until you reach an agreement. One technique is to pretend you're not that bothered and start to walk away, but be prepared for the trader to take you at your word!

Not getting ripped off by cabbies: find out beforehand roughly what the local rate is for the distance you want to go. Then it's much the same principle as bargaining in a market. It's generally cheaper not to let hotels find you a cab - they often get a rake-off from the fare for allowing cabbies to park on their grounds so it will cost you more.

Agree a price before you get into the vehicle and if you're hiring a car and driver for a day (which can often work out cheaper especially if you're sharing with friends) usually you'll be expected to pay for a meal for the driver so make sure you agree that the price of a stop for food is included in the deal.

In India, there's a system of pre-pay kiosks, particularly at airport exits, where you can buy a chit - a paper that states a fair, and usually accurate, price for the journey. The driver can't cash it until you're safely at your destination, can't charge you more than is on the chit, and it has to be signed - usually by your hotel/accommodation before it can be cashed. So you can be sure you'll not be taking any long detours to bump up the cost. It's worth asking whether there are similar systems wherever you are.

Tipping: it's a bit of a minefield and you need to find out what the fair rate is. A tip should be a thank you for good service, so, for example, if you're in a restaurant and there's already a percentage on your bill for service you shouldn't pay more, unless of course you feel your waiter deserves it! Remember if you over-tip you raise expectations higher than other travellers - and locals - may be able or willing to pay.

Finding and affording a guide: find out if there's a local scheme for licensing/approving guides and what the 'official permit' looks like. Nearly always there will be any number of 'guides' at the entrances to any interesting place you might want to visit. Some will be official - others will be trying their luck. You'll usually find out when you pay the entrance fee.

Insurance

Your insurance needs to be fixed before you go, but the range of policies is vast - and they all cover different things. It can be a daunting area for gappers, so we asked the experts at Downunder Worldwide travel Insurance for their input. They told us:

"Going away on a long trip is one of the most exciting things that you can do on your **gap**-year and your head will be full of all the wonderful possibilities

the gap-year guidebook 2011

that this may bring. However things do go wrong and accidents do happen and when they do you are on your own unless you have travel insurance.

"The local British Embassy or Consulate will be very sympathetic and as helpful as they can be but they will not pay the bills - that is up to you. With some medical emergencies costing over £200,000, unless you are Bill Gates, you will need help. This is where your travel insurance policy comes into its own."

The basic things to check for are:

- Medical costs
- Legal
- Passport loss
- Ticket loss
- Cash loss
- Luggage
- Flight cancellation
- Missed flights
- Working abroad
- Hazardous sports
- Specific medical conditions

Other things you should ask:

- Is there a 24-hour helpline?
- Can you cover yourself for an unexpected return home so that you can continue your **gap-** later without losing your cover?
- Are there any special declarations you need to make on the health conditions of immediate family?
- Are there any conditions and requirements regarding pre-existing medical conditions?
- Are there any age restrictions or extra age-related costs on the policy? This is particularly important for mature travellers.

Some banks provide cover for holidays paid for using their credit cards, but their policies may not include all the essentials you'll need for a **gap**-year.

Banks also offer blanket travel insurance (medical, personal accident, third party liability, theft, loss, cancellation, delay and more). You may be able to get reductions if you have an account with the relevant bank or buy foreign currency through it.

Who to choose?

You don't have to buy a travel insurance policy as part of a travel package through a travel company and there is intense competition between insurance

visit: www.gap-year.com

companies to attract your attention. It may be tedious but the best advice is shop around, check out the internet, talk to a broker and read the small print very carefully.

Medical insurance

If you're going to Europe you can get a European Health Insurance Card (EHIC), which allows for free or reduced cost medical treatment within Europe, should you need it. You can apply online: www.ehic.org.uk

Your card is valid for three to five years and should be delivered to you in seven days. Or you can telephone EHIC applications, Newcastle on Tyne, on 0845 606 2030. The EHIC card only covers treatment under the state scheme in all EU countries, plus Denmark, Iceland, Liechtenstein, Norway and Switzerland. You can also pick up application forms at your post office.

However, our friends at Downunder Worldwide had a few words of warning:

"There's a misconception – and in some cases a costly misconception – that all EU citizens get the sort of free health care we are entitled to on the NHS.

"Most people have heard of the EHIC form, which provide proof of EU citizenship and entitle the bearer to medical treatment. But read the small print and you will see that under the reciprocal agreement the NHS is only bound to provide reduced-cost care and that you are only entitled to the same level of treatment as a citizen of that country.

"That might put you out of pocket a bit if you sprain your wrist – although chances are the clinic won't bother to log minor treatments. But when you have fractured one of your lower vertebrae, it's a different matter and you will have to pay to be repatriated by air ambulance – which can cost up to £30,000."

Countries with no health care agreements with the UK include Canada, the USA, India, most of the Far East, the whole of Africa and Latin America.

Wherever it happens, a serious illness, broken limb, or even an injury you might cause someone else, can be very expensive.

Medical insurance is usually part of an all-in travel policy. Costs vary widely by company, destination, activity and level of cover. Make sure you have generous cover for injury or disablement, know what you're covered for and when you've got the policy read the small print carefully. For example, does it cover transport home if you need an emergency operation that cannot be carried out safely abroad?

Some policies won't cover high-risk activities like skiing, snowboarding, bungee jumping *etc* so you'll need to get extra, specific, cover and an insurance broker can help with this. Companies may also make a distinction between doing a hazardous sport once and spending your whole time doing them. Some insurance policies also have age limits.

If you have a medical condition that is likely to recur, you may have to declare this when you buy the insurance, otherwise the policy won't be valid. Also, check whether the policy covers you for the medical costs if the condition does recur, as some will not cover such pre-existing conditions.

Already covered?

If you're going abroad on a voluntary work assignment you may find that the organisation arranging it wants you to take a specified insurance policy as part of the total cost. You may also find you have a clash of policies before you even start looking for the right policy.

For example, if your family has already booked you a one-year multi-travel insurance policy to cover travel with the family at other times of the year, you may find you are already covered for loss of life, limb, permanent disablement, some medical expenses, theft and so on. These multi-trip policies can be basic as well as quite cheap, but it's essential to check the small print of what the policy covers as it's possible that there may be a clause compelling the insured to return to the UK after a short period of time.

A lot of these policies only cover for trips of up to 60 days at a time, at which point travellers had to return to the UK. In other words, great for a holiday or

visit: www.gap-year.com

two or for a business traveller but no use at all if you plan to be out of the country for the whole year.

In this case you can start by finding out (through the broker or agent who sold you the policy) if any additional cover can be tacked on to your existing policy, though this can be expensive and most off-the-shelf policies won't do it.

Try to find a policy that doesn't already duplicate what is covered by an existing policy (they don't pay out twice), but some duplication is unavoidable and it's obviously better to be covered twice than not at all.

Making a claim

Read through the small print carefully before you travel and make sure you understand exactly what to do if you need to make a claim - most policies will insist that you report a crime to the police where this is possible (often within a certain time period), and that you send in the police report with your insurance claim. What you don't want to happen is to have a claim dismissedbecause you don't have the right paperwork to back it up.

Insurers won't pay you money unless you have complied with all their rules and many travel policies impose conditions that are virtually impossible to meet. For example, some policies demand that you report not only theft of items but also loss of items. Fine, but the police are likely to be pretty reluctant to write a crime report because you think you may have accidentally left your camera in the loo!

If you do have anything stolen and you have to get the local police to give you a report, it's a good idea to dress reasonably smartly when you visit them, be prepared to wait and try to be pleasant and polite no matter what!

The Foreign Office website (**www.fco.gov.uk/travel**) has a good page about insurance and is worth checking out for advice and links. In addition to a list of what your travel insurance should cover, which is similar to the one at the start of this chapter, it suggests the following extras, which are not always included:

- Legal expenses cover - this can be useful as it will help you to pursue compensation or damages following personal injury while you're abroad - very important in countries without a legal aid system

- Financial protection if your airline goes bankrupt before or during your trip - given the state of the airline industry this may be worth serious consideration for at least the next couple of years.

A spokesman for the Association of British Insurers told us: "The vast majority of travel insurance claims are settled quickly. However, the best way to avoid potential problems is to read the policy before you go, and ensure that you fully understand what you are covered for, and the terms and conditions. If anything is unclear, contact your insurer.

"Take a copy of the policy with you and make sure you know how to claim, especially any emergency contact numbers that you may need."

Downunder Worldwide also added that it is worth noting the excess on your policy – something that is often overlooked.

"Almost all policies have an excess attached to different sections of cover. That amount is deducted from the claim, normally for each person covered and for each relevant section of the policy. If you make a number of claims whilst you are travelling this can add up so think about taking out an excess waiver so that you have to contribute nothing. It may cost a little more but could save you a small fortune.'

And pre-existing medical conditions can be another added complication:

"If you don't declare a pre-existing condition, the entire policy will probably be invalidated. **If you are in any doubt, talk to the insurer before you buy.** Note also that, if you have an existing injury that is exacerbated by a second accident while you are travelling, cover for this may also be excluded. "

What to do if you get an emergency call to come home

We all hope there'll be no family crises while we're away on our **gap-** but it does occasionally happen that someone close is taken seriously ill, or even dies, and then all you can think about is getting home as quickly as possible.

We've talked to a couple of insurers about this and they reinforce our advice to *always* read the policy carefully before you set off on your travels.

Generally speaking, your **gap-**year travel policy ceases once you return home, but some insurers offer extra cover for one extra trip home (or more, up to four, but the price rises with each one) without your policy lapsing. In a backpacker/adventure policy of three to 18 months, one home return is in the region of £5 and four would be around £24 extra on your policy.

Most insurers are used to dealing with sudden early returns and have a 24-hour emergency assistance company to help you through the whole process.

You need to let them know anyway so you can set the ball rolling for claiming for the cost and they can deal with getting you from your **gap-** location to the airport, or, if you have one, you can use the help of your placement provider's in-country reps, or even a combination of the two, so *you* don't have to deal with transport hassles when all you can think about is getting home quickly.

However, there are often restrictions. First off, your family emergency has to affect an immediate relative - so husband, wife, mum, dad, grandparents, sisters and brothers, children, grandchildren - but *not* aunts, uncles and other extended family. It has to be serious injury, illness or death of a relative - family feuds and divorces do not count!

If you have home return extra on your policy you're covered for one extra flight home; you're *not* covered for an additional flight back to resume your **gap-**. But, if you have a return ticket, as most gappers do, the best way to go is to use your existing return, if the airline will reschedule, claim for it, then book another return flight. It's often cheaper to book a return flight than an extra one-way only.

If your ticket cannot be changed and you need to purchase a new ticket for your return journey, this can be arranged via a flight-ticketing agent or direct with the appropriate airline (subject to availability of flights and seats).

Websites such as Expedia and ebookers offer a wide selection of flights including single leg and one way tickets, which you can buy online and

visit: www.gap-year.com

allocated e-tickets, or collect them from the airline sales desk at the airport.

During peak travel or holiday times you might find the quickest way to get home may be to go to the airport and wait to pick up a 'no show' seat on standby.

Overall, say Downunder Worldwide, the key is to read everything carefully – and have reasonable expectations from your insurer.

"Travel insurance is intended to cover emergencies, not make life more comfortable. All insurers have their favourite examples of customers who have unrealistic expectations – the sort of people who try to claim for a massage because their legs are aching after a day on the ski slopes."

Finance

Insurance

ACE European Group Ltd
Customer Services, PO Box 1018, Ashdown House,
125 High Street,
Crawley, RH10 1DQ UK
E: ace.traveluk@ace-ina.com
T: +44 (0) 1293 726 225
www.aceinsure.com/backpacker/

Offers gap year/backpacker/student traveller insurance for ages 14 to 44 and traveller plus insurance for 45-55 years.

Best Backpackers Insurance
4A Gemini House,
Hargreaves Road,
Swindon, SN25 5AZ UK
T: +44 (0) 8450 264 264
www.bestbackpackersinsurance.co.uk

Including "Back Home" visits without your policy lapsing.

Blue Insurances Ltd
Suffolk House,
Trade Street,
Cardiff, CF10 5DT UK
E: info@multitrip.com
T: +44 (0) 871 231 3222
www.multitrip.com/backpacker-insurance.asp?AffiliateNo=BL09719

Multitrip.com is a domain name of Blue Insurances, offering comprehensive backpacker/long stay cover at very competitive prices. Cover starts from as little as £23.99.

Boots UK Limited
1 Thane Road West,
Beeston,
Nottingham, NG90 1BS UK
T: +44 (0) 845 125 3840
www.bootsinsurance.com

Website has area dedicated to gap-year insurance and offers policies from three to 12 months.

BUPA Travel Services
Thames Side House,
South Street,
Staines, TW18 4TL UK
E: morrisla@bupa.com
T: +44 (0) 1784 891 331
F: +44 (0) 1784 891 140
www.bupatravel.co.uk

Offers Explorer to travellers taking a gap-year or career break, whether planning a three month jaunt or a trip of over a year.

Club Direct Ltd.
Advertiser House,
18 Bartlett St,
Croydon, CR2 6TB UK

E: customer.services@clubdirect.com
T: 0800 083 2466
www.clubdirect.com

Affordable backpacker travel insurance for those who plan to travel abroad for an extended period.

Columbus Direct
Advertiser House,
19 Bartlett Street,
Croydon, CR2 6TB UK

E: admin@columbusdirect.com
T: +44 (0) 870 033 9988
www.columbusdirect.com

Offers backpacker insurance for anywhere in the world from four weeks to a year. Also offers ski travel insurance and adventure travel insurance.

Direct Travel Insurance
Shoreham Airport,
Shoreham-by-Sea, BN43 5FF UK

E: presscontact@direct-travel.co.uk
T: +44 (0) 845 605 2700
F: +44 (0) 845 605 2710
www.direct-travel.co.uk

Premiums for basic or comprehensive policy, designed for travellers up to and including 36 years of age.

GAP YEAR
and working holiday
TRAVEL INSURANCE
book online for a
10% DISCOUNT
Premium paid will depend on individual circumstances

DOWNUNDER
WORLDWIDE
TRAVEL INSURANCE

Downunder Insurance Services Ltd offer excellent cheap yet comprehensive travel insurance.

3 months	Worldwide	fr **£52**
12 months	Australia and New Zealand	fr **£120**

CALL US on **0207 402 9211**
BOOK ONLINE FOR A 10% DISCOUNT
www.duinsure.com

Downunder Insurance is authorised and regulated by the Financial Services Authority. Our FSA Register number is 306618. This can be checked at www.fsa.gov.uk/register.

Dogtag Ltd
6 Magellan Terrace,
Gatwick Road,
Crawley, RH10 9PJ UK

E: enquiries@dogtag.co.uk
T: +44 (0) 8700 364824
www.dogtag.co.uk

Insurance offered for 'action minded' travellers.

Downunder Worldwide Travel Insurance
Downunder Insurance Services Ltd, PO Box 55605,
Paddington,
London, W9 3UW UK

E: travel@duinsure.com
T: +44 (0) 800 393 908
www.duinsure.com

Save up to 60% on High Street prices plus a further 10% discount if you book online. Comprehensive travel insurance for the adventurous traveller. Working holidays covered plus over 80 adventurous sports or activities. Medical emergency and money back guarantee.

Endsleigh Insurance Services Ltd
Endsleigh Park,
Shurdington Road,
Cheltenham Spa, GL51 4UE UK

T: +44 (0) 800 028 3571
www.endsleigh.co.uk

Endsleigh has tailored gap-year cover to suit you, with over 100 sports and activities covered as standard!

Essential Travel Ltd
Princess Caroline House,
1 High Street,
Southend on Sea, SS1 1JE UK

T: +44 (0) 870 343 0024
www.insurance.essentialtravel.co.uk

Backpacker travel insurance policies for people aged under 45 available, and only for trips of up to 12 months.

Flexicover Direct
109 Elmers End Road,
Beckenham, BR3 4SY UK

E: info@flexicover.co.uk
F: +44 (0) 845 223 4508
www.flexicover.co.uk

Gap-year travel insurance for those aged 18-45.

Gibbs Denley
Crystal House,
Buckingham Business Park,
Swavesey, Cambridge, CB24 4UL UK

E: info@course-u-can.com
T: +44 (0) 1954 233698
F: +44 (0) 1954 231708
www.course-u-can.com

A travel insurance policy specifically designed for students visiting the UK and Europe.

the gap-year guidebook 2011

TAKING THE PLUNGE?
– GET SOME DECENT TRAVEL INSURANCE

- Cover designed for independent travellers
- Lots of adventurous activities covered as standard
- Period of cover can be extended while you are away
- Includes repatriation if medically necessary
- 24/7 specialist medical emergency services

roundtheworld**Insurance**

www.roundtheworldinsurance.co.uk
Telephone: 01273 320 580

ABTA J4916 / Y1114 | IATA Accredited Agent | ATOL PROTECTED 9828

Round the World Insurance is brought to you by round the world flight specialists, Travel Nation (www.travelnation.co.uk) who are an appointed representative of Campbell Irvine Limited who are authorised and regulated by the Financial Services Authority

Globelink International Ltd.
84 Cannon Street,
Little Downham,
Ely , CB6 2SS UK

T: +44 (0) 1353 699082
www.globelink.co.uk

They provide cover for backpacking and gap-years for up to 15 months in length, but extensions are available.

Go Travel Insurance
West Wing,
Miles Gray Road,
Basildon, SS14 3GD UK

T: +44 (0) 844 482 0880
www.gotravelinsurance.co.uk

Go Travel Insurance offers a flexible backpacker policy for ages 18 to 65.

Insure and Go
Maitland House,
Warrior Square,
Southend on Sea, SS1 2JY UK

E: information@insureandgo.com
T: +44 (0) 844 888 2787
www.insureandgo.com

Gap-year travel insurance for people aged under 36, also a policy for those over 36 and looking for longer trips.

JS Travel Insurance
Towerpoint,
44 North Road,
Brighton, BN1 1YR UK

T: +44 (0)1273 666 364
www.jsinsurance.co.uk

Provides comprehensive gap-year travel insurance.

Mind The Gap Year
19-21 West House,
West Street,
Haslemere, GU27 2AB UK

E: info@mindthegapyear.com
T: +44 (0) 845 180 0060
www.mindthegapyear.com

We are a tailor-made combination of insurance and services for the gap-year traveller, promoting how to stay safe and prepare for your travels.

MRL Insurance Direct
6 Magellan Terrace,
Gatwick Road,
Crawley, RH10 9PJ UK

T: +44 (0) 845 676 0689
www.mrlinsurance.co.uk/backpacker-insurance.aspx

Gap Year polices of between two and 12 months for under 45s. Over 60 activities including scuba diving and bungee.

Navigator Travel Insurance Services Ltd
19 Ralli Courts,
West Riverside,
Manchester, M3 5FT UK
E: enquiries@navigatortravel.co.uk
T: +44 (0) 161 973 6435
F: +44 (0) 161 973 6418
www.navigatortravel.co.uk

Offers specialist policies for long-stay overseas trips, with an emphasis on covering adventure sports. These policies also cover casual working.

Right Cover Travel Insurance
2nd Floor,
31 Springfield Road,
Chelmsford, CM2 6JE UK
E: enquiries@rightcover.com
T: +44 (0) 1245 272372
www.rightcover.co.uk

Offers budget cover suitable for students or backpackers.

Round the World Insurance
Travel Nation Ltd, 8th Floor, Intergen House,
65-67 Western Road,
Hove, BN3 2JQ UK
E: info@roundtheworldinsurance.co.uk
T: +44 (0)1273 320 580
www.roundtheworldinsurance.co.uk

Specialist travel insurance designed for people on round-the-world or multi-stop trips.

Sainsbury's Travel Insurance
33 Holborn,
Holborn,
London, EC1N 2HT UK
T: +44 (0) 845 300 3190
www.sainsburysbank.co.uk/insuring/ins_gapyear_trv_dive.shtml

They have a policy specifically for gappers.

Snowcard Insurance Services Limited
Lower Boddington,
Daventry, NN11 6XZ UK
E: assistance@snowcard.co.uk
www.snowcard.co.uk

Travel and activity insurance including long stays up to 18 months.

World Nomads Ltd
One Victoria Square,
Birmingham, B1 1BD UK
www.worldnomads.com

Offers an insurance package specifically targeted at independent travellers.

Worldtrekker Travel Insurance
PO Box 5317,
Southend on Sea, SS1 1WY UK
E: info@preferential.co.uk
T: +44 (0) 871 221 4008
www.preferential.co.uk/worldtrekker

Offering four levels of cover from Standard to Ultra, to residents of the UK or Channel Islands only.

Worldwide Travel Insurance Services Ltd
The Business Centre, 1-7 Commercial Road,
Paddock Wood,
Tonbridge, TN12 6YT UK

E: sales@worldwideinsure.com
T: +44 (0) 1892 83 33 38
F: +44 (0) 1892 83 77 44
www.worldwideinsure.com

This company offers travellers insurance from two to 18 months for long-haul travellers and backpackers, which also covers working overseas.

Chapter 3
Career Breaks & Older Travellers

3 Career breakers and older gappers

> **The benefits of being an older gapper:**
> - You're fit and healthy
> - You have a lot of professional experience
> - You have good people skills
> - Taking a career break can add new skills to your CV
> - You're retired but you have skills and wisdom to offer to people who may need them
> - You can afford the time and cost
> - You want to give something back
> - You're never too old to learn something new

Are you an extravagapper? A flashpacker? These are just a couple of the latest terms to describe the more mature member of the **gap-** community!

Extravagappers are apparently newly-redundant city professionals with generous redundancy packages, who are taking the opportunity of a career break rather than plunge back into a possibly demoralising, recession-hit job market.

Wikipedia describes Flashpackers as: "...backpacking with flash, or style. ... travellers who adhere to a modest accommodation and meal budget, while spending freely, even excessively, for activities at their chosen destination…"

But also: "...tech-savvy adventurers who often prefer to travel with a cell phone, digital camera, iPod and a laptop."

However, regardless of the definitions or their degree of affluence, older travellers generally have different considerations from younger ones when making their plans. These include the effects of taking a **gap-** on careers, what to do about the house and mortgage, financial issues and whether or not to take the children, if this applies.

Taking a career break for one month to a year is the fastest-growing sector of **gap-**year activity and there's some anecdotal evidence that the global recession is increasing the numbers.

Around 90,000 people take a short sabbatical each year in the UK - in other words a '**gap**-month'. It may be worthwhile considering something like this, or perhaps a longer trip if you've been made redundant or taken early retirement.

Several organisations that arrange places for people on overseas projects, have told us that more than half of their activity is now focused on helping

visit: www.gap-year.com

place mature travellers and/or people who are taking a career break.

People are living longer and are also a lot healthier well into old age. Many, therefore, feel they want to continue to use their skills in places where they will do some good.

This, coupled with the issues of the retirement age being put back and worries about inadequate pension provision, has also prompted many older people to think about extending their working lives and perhaps also pursuing a different career altogether.

Taking a **gap-**, perhaps to volunteer in another country, is one good way of identifying skills, wisdom and knowledge gained over a working lifetime, that may be useful in another sector and this could lead to a new career.

It may be the perfect opportunity to do something you always wanted to do but couldn't while you were burdened with the responsibilities of family and mortgage.

Pre-travel prep checklist:

This list covers the extra responsibilities older people might have to consider. It only covers the basics of what you might have to organise - but we hope it will be a useful start for you to cherry-pick what's appropriate and no doubt add your own extras!

Work:

- Talk to your employer about sabbatical/career break options.

Career break:

- What do you want from it?
- What do you want to do?
- Where do you want to go?

Finance:

- Paying the bills.
- Mortgage.
- Financing and raising money for the trip.
- Insurance.
- Pensions and NI contributions.

The house: Are you going to let it? If yes, you need:

- To talk to an accommodation agency.
- Safety certificates.
- Insurance.
- To investigate tax exemption.

Storage of possessions:

- What do you want to store? And can it be stored at home?

the gap-year guidebook 2011

Children:
- Talk to the school(s) about taking them.
- Find out about education possibilities where you're going.
- If they're coming, how long will the trip be?

Safety precautions:
- Wills and power of attorney.

Arranging a sabbatical

There is no legal obligation on employers to offer employees sabbaticals/career break. However, they are often regarded as an important part of an employee's career development, and may be granted for a variety of reasons including study research travel or voluntary work which can often be related to the employee role.

"Protect your future before you pack" advises Linda Whittern of Careers Partnership (UK), a careers counselling and job search support consultancy. "You'll need to get organised long before you go - you've lots of thinking, communicating and persuading to do!

"You want your employer to hold your job open while you're away? However nice your boss is, you'll have to make a strong case why it's in the business's interests to say goodbye to you for a year and then welcome you back.

"Bring friends and family round for some wine-fuelled brainstorming on the best way to "sell" the idea to your employer. Tell the happy group lolling on your sofa they're now your company's top management team. Their job is to work out how your company benefits from letting you go temporarily (and not permanently!!!).

"Ideas to start them off …. your 'gap' lets the company cut its wages bill now without making anyone redundant *and* it saves the hassle and cost of recruiting a new person when the economy recovers (you'll be back by then, raring to take up your job again).

"You'll need to think up low-cost ways for the company to cover any work you won't be around to do. Might your temporary absence help the company restructure the workload more efficiently, to everyone's benefit? Would the new superstar relish a short spell doing your job as she zooms up the company career ladder?

"Once you've thoroughly prepared your sales pitch, organise a session with your boss to talk through your 'career development' proposals."

Gary Hughes, director at Career Sage, a dedicated outplacement service for the public sector, advises you to think of things from your employer's point of view – and put together this checklist to consider.

- Often sabbaticals can aid the retention of senior staff by allowing them scope to try something different with the security of knowing they can return to work at the end of the time away.
- Employers who grant sabbaticals usually attach various conditions, both in

visit: www.gap-year.com

respect of eligibility to apply for a sabbatical and what happens during the sabbatical itself.

- Sabbaticals are usually available only to employees in senior grades or defined disciplines and to those of who have a specified minimum number of year's continuous service with the organisation. This can differ from organisation to organisation.
- Some organisations do not even have sabbatical policies.
- It is advisable for employers to make it clear in their sabbaticals policy that the grant of a sabbatical is dependent on the employer's operational requirements at the relevant time and that no request can be guaranteed even where an employee meets all of the eligibility criteria.
- Where an employer does grant sabbaticals, it must ensure that part-time employees are afforded the same benefits as equivalent full time staff – for example, any length of service requirement must be the same as for full-time employees.
- Normally the employee will not receive pay or benefits for a sabbatical as the employee's contract is seen as suspended. However, this is dependent on each individual employer.
- It is usual for the employee to stay in touch with their employer during the period of the sabbatical.
- It is very important that a strategy for the return to work is agreed in advance of the sabbatical.
- The employer should take particular care to ensure that any guarantee of re-employment is worded clearly and unambiguously in order to avoid any disagreement or challenge at a later date.
- If the employee is lucky enough to continue to be paid for the duration of the sabbatical this means that the contract of employment remains in force which in turn means that the employee's continuity of service is preserved. However, as stated above if the employee does not get paid then the contract is deemed as suspended, continuity of service may still be preserved under certain circumstances.

What if you can't arrange a sabbatical?

Karen Woodbridge, Director of Suffolk-based Hornet Solutions (an Independent HR/Employment Law Consultancy) says: "There is no obligation in law for companies to provide career breaks so you need to think about how your company and you would respond if your request is turned down. Would you resign? If not, and you decide instead to stay with your employer, how will they regard you? Will your rejected request affect your chances of further progress within the company? Might they consider that you lack long-term commitment to them?"

One option you might consider if you can't arrange a sabbatical and are wary of just quitting is arranging a job swap with someone from another country in a similar industry. You need to consider:

- Where do you want to travel?
- Do you speak a second, third or fourth language?
- Will you need housing?
- Do you need to be paid while away?
- How long do you want to be away for?

This may be easier in an international company where there may even be opportunities to transfer to the overseas office. Many such companies offer formal secondment programmes so it's always worth exploring these first.

If the above options are not possible, and you are prepared to resign, you could investigate whether your company might agree to guarantee you a job on your return.

Even if they don't guarantee a position for you, have regular contact with the key decision makers whilst you are away by the occasional email *etc*. This will keep you in their minds and make it easier for you to approach them when you come back home, to see if they have any suitable job opportunities. Just remember, in job hunting, as in everything else, it's not *what* you know but *who*. So it's absolutely vital that you make the effort not to lose touch with your professional colleagues, networks and contacts whilst you are away. If you do, you'll regret it once you are back.

If you're not already signed up to LinkedIn, you might like to consider it. This website is the business world equivalent of Facebook. It's free to use and you can link to colleagues and business contacts and post recommendations about them and, importantly, get them to post recommendations about you.

You can even upload your CV, and indicate that you are open to job opportunities. It could also be useful to add your list of contacts gained *whilst* you're on your career break, thus adding extra value to your LinkedIn profile.

No sabbatical? Take your chances

If you're willing to quit and take your chances, what about finding work when the break's over?

What the jobs market will be like when you return is anyone's guess; however, you'll have a faster and more productive job search if you work at it before you leave.

Think now about the job you should be aiming for after the **gap-**, suggests Careers Partnership (UK). Your **gap-** is likely to develop new skills and ambitions so you might want something different from the current role.

Your target job identified, talk to the people who'll help you find future vacancies. Research the specialist recruitment consultancies in that sector (*eg* Google them), then ask to talk to consultants with *at least* two years experience of recruiting for the jobs that interest you. You want to know those consultants' best guesses about the likely state of that jobs market a year from now, what skills employers are most likely to look for in candidates and so on.

Stay in touch with the most useful of these recruitment consultants (*eg* by

visit: www.gap-year.com

sharing snippets of your **gap-** news with them). Keeping yourself at the forefront of their minds puts you on the inside track for news about developments in the jobs market.

"Don't forget to stay in touch just as closely with ex colleagues, uni tutors, careers service advisors, etc" Linda says. "They've often huge networks for you to tap into and they're very keenly motivated to help you with your job search".

Linda suggests that to maximise your chances of making the best economic use of your career break, you should structure your time thoughtfully – and be sure to highlight your new skills on your CV on your return home.

"Employers share the general view that gaps enhance graduates' 'soft skills'; some blue chip employers actively encourage applications from 'gappers'. Employers' appreciation of the value of a **gap-** is often rather superficial and short-lived, however. Many employers have little understanding of the particular skill-sets recruits/employees have developed during their career breaks. They don't actively help staff transfer these skills to the workplace.

"Realising the full economic value of your **gap-** depends on choosing the break best aligned to your career plans and then properly marketing it to prospective and actual employers."

Linda advises: "The range of **gap-** activities on offer include teaching (circa 15%); conservation/environment (circa 15%); community (circa 37%); work experience (circa 11%); travel (circa 3%); leisure sports (circa 8%); and non-academic qualifications (circa 11%).

"When planning your **gap-**, work out precisely what the value of each proposed activity/experience will be to prospective employers. Decide what evidence will persuade employers that your **gap-** experience gives you 'added value' as a recruit. Highlight this evidence on your CV and during your interview. Once recruited, ensure your line manager and the training department know about the skill-sets you have built up during your **gap-** ... and put forward schemes for further developing these skills."

Career Sage added that it can be a wise idea to try and plan your career break around the natural hiring cycles of your industry.

"If possible, you should plan your career break with an eye on typical hiring cycles," Gary Hughes told us. "Recruitment occurs all year round for most organisations. But activity levels often fall in December and early January; the weeks in and around Easter; and the weeks that coincide with school summer holidays.

"It may be harder to find jobs in these periods: decisions take longer; people are unavailable to sign-off appointments. Conversely, activity levels peak in early spring and autumn. Organisations seek employees to work on new projects; and help to grow business."

Career Sage also suggest that you should keep your CV updated and to hand while you are away to ensure you can quickly capitalise on any surprise opportunities that might come your way.

"It may be the last thing on your mind: but it is a good idea to update your CV before embarking on a break, ensuring it is ready for your return to employment. You should always keep your CV available by email. This enables you to send it to interested parties while you are away or occupied by other pursuits.

"Some employers may see a gap in your employment history and worry that you are prone to flitting from one job to the next. Your CV should make it clear that you have carefully considered your career direction; and devoted time to looking for a job in which you can grow.

"CVs can be enhanced with examples of helpful, selfless and philanthropic actions. It may be worth devoting some or all of your career break to volunteering, either in the UK or overseas. If possible, obtain a reference or agreement to give a reference from your previous employer before beginning your career break."

Finance

You've talked to your employer, perhaps also worked out what you hope to do - there are plenty of organisations to help you plan your chosen activities in the various sections in this book. The next crucial question is finance.

Obviously the amount of money you'll need depends on where you want to go, what you want to do, and how long you want to be away. At this point, drawing up a rough budget for how much it will cost would be a good idea. (See Chapter 2 - Finance, for a checklist.) Once you have this it's worth talking to your building society or bank to see whether they have any schemes that can meet your needs.

While banks often have student and graduate advisers who can advise on what to do about everything from travel insurance to suspending direct debits and deferring loan payment, they don't seem yet to have reached the stage of having advisers *specifically* for career breakers. They are, however, increasingly aware of the trend to take a career break and may well be able to use their experience of advising younger gappers to help you think the finances through.

A recent survey amongst older people in the UK revealed that a large majority are extremely pessimistic or fearful about the quality of their lives in old age. A significant number were taking the view that, if their old age was going to be so grim, why not have one last adventure? Consequently, they were using annuities and equity release or lifetime mortgages to unlock money from their homes to boost their retirement income and pay for such adventures.

This might seem like a good plan. However, there have also been many reports of schemes offering to buy people's homes and allowing them to rent them back for their lifetimes, only for them to be evicted after a few months or to find 'hidden charges' which meant they saw little money at the end of it. So beware! Read the small print *very* carefully.

Some companies offer lifetime mortgages, where you can release the value of your home and live in it without paying anything until you die, when the company will recover its money from the sale of the home.

Individual circumstances vary and if you feel you are 'asset rich but cash poor' it may be tempting to consider such options. You should only consider such a scheme with a reputable company and if the scheme includes protection against negative equity. We would strongly advise that if you are thinking of doing something like this you consult an independent financial adviser.

Graham Bills: Riding Route 66

When an old schoolfriend and I wanted to acknowledge our 42-year friendship and celebrate our 50th birthdays, we came up with the idea of riding the famous Route 66 across America on Harley Davidsons - classic mid-life crisis stuff.

It only took a couple of evenings in the pub to plan. We just picked a date, got there and set up, making the rest up as we went along. It took 16 days of riding. Although most of the original Route 66 has been replaced by interstate, we stuck to the old road as much as possible, riding through *Main Street USA* - soda fountains, gas stations and rattlesnake ranches all the way.

the gap-year guidebook 2011

Of course, the trip was worthwhile because of the fantastic time we had and the many great people we met along the way. But we also had the bonus of returning home to the UK completely refreshed and invigorated. The trip was a totally different thing for us to do and really recharged the batteries.

We were both fortunate to be in positions to be able do the trip in the first place – as we run our own businesses, getting the scheduling right was the most difficult thing.

I think it is easy to find excuses not to take risks and do the things you have always wanted to - but from my experience, I'd strongly recommend setting those aside and taking the plunge.

Maximise your funds: The chance for a good clear out

Is the garage crammed, are every drawer and cupboard stuffed? Is it all 'file and forget' or 'might come in handy' but never has? Admit it, you're one of those people who hasn't touched any of this stuff for years and you've kept saying you'd do a massive clear out. Aren't you?

But the more you add over the years, the more daunting it is and the easier it is to put off. We all do it. And how much houseroom do some of us give to all that stuff our children insist they have no space for but have sentimental attachments to?

Preparing for your year out is the perfect opportunity to de-clutter your life. Have a look at what you need to get rid of and turn into funding for your **gap-**. Consider raising some cash by selling items through online auction sites, such as eBay, holding a garage sale or a car boot sale.

You'll create space to store your precious items (the things you want to keep but not leave lying about), you'll add some cash to your travel fund, and you'll come back to a well organised home. Also, if you've decided to let your home empty (see below) you'll need less rented container space - and save yourself some money.

Consider selling the car

If you have a car it's likely to devalue in the year you are away, whether anyone is driving it or not, so you could sell it and put the money into your career break fund. Leasing out your car is not an option - most insurers will not insure drivers of vehicles leased privately from their owners.

Imaginative fundraising

If you've already settled on the kind of project you want to do and it involves raising a specific sum, as volunteer projects often do, you can hold fundraising events to help you raise the cash - the options are as limitless as your imagination!

visit: www.gap-year.com

You have an untapped resource where you work - you could try asking for a contribution from your employer. It's good PR to have a link with someone doing something for a worthy cause.

If your employer agrees, what about baking cakes to sell at coffee time or holding competitions (guess the weight/number of objects in a container) or even asking colleagues to sponsor you? Even simple things like putting all those irritating bits of small change that weigh down pockets, and cram purses, into a large pot or jar can mount up surprisingly quickly.

Pensions and National Insurance contributions

If you have an occupational pension and are taking a sabbatical you should check with your employer to see if they offer a pension 'holiday' and what that might mean to your eventual pension, but it might be possible to stop or reduce your payments while you are away. If you have been with the company less than two years, it might be possible to arrange a refund of pension contributions.

For the state pension you might want to look at two issues: During the time you're away, you will be officially classified as living abroad and you won't be paying NI. However, you should check what that will do to your contributions' record and how it might affect your eventual state pension.

You can find out if there are gaps in your record by calling the HMRC (HM Revenue and Customs) helpline (0845 915 5996) and for more information. People living abroad should call: 0845 915 4811.

Once you have that information it's worth talking to the DWP (Department for Work and Pensions). They have a help and advice service (Tel: 0845 606 0265) and you can find out what you can expect by way of state pension. A DWP adviser told us that, from 2010, to get the maximum state pension both men and women will have to have paid NI for at least 30 years.

However, another useful fact, if you're likely to reach retirement age during your **gap-** and can afford it, is that there's an incentive for deferring your state pension. For every five weeks you agree to defer, you get 1% added to your eventual pension. After a year, you can either take that as a taxable lump sum or have it incorporated into your regular pension payments. You can defer for more than a year and continue to add this interest to your eventual state pension.

The Directgov website also has a useful page on pensions for people living abroad:
www.direct.gov.uk/en/BritonsLivingAbroad/Moneyabroad/DG_4000013

Earning on your career break

It may even be possible to part-fund your career break by using your skills on volunteer and other projects.

United Nations Volunteers sometimes pay modest living or travel costs, for people with the skills they need for particular volunteer projects.

the gap-year guidebook 2011

Have a look at their website: **www.unv.org/how-to-volunteer.html**

If you wanted a 'taster' before taking the big step of leaving the country, UNV also has a scheme for online volunteers, where you can become involved in worthwhile projects, using your computer in your spare time, at home: **www.onlinevolunteering.org/en/vol/index.html**

There are also organisations that can help with funding for specific projects: The Winston Churchill Memorial Trust is one of them.

It provides grants for people wanting to travel abroad and work on special projects that they cannot find funding for elsewhere and, crucially, then use the experience to benefit others in their home communities. Applicants must be British citizens, resident in the UK and must apply by October each year.

The Trust awards travelling fellowships to individuals of all ages wanting to pursue projects that are interesting and unusual. Categories cover a range of topics over a three-year cycle. Roughly 100 are awarded each year and they usually provide funds for four to eight weeks.

The Trust emphasises that fellowships are *not* granted to gappers looking to fund academic studies, attend courses or take part in volunteer placements arranged by other organisations.

The advice is to study the WCMT website for examples of projects that have been funded, as they are very wide-ranging and will help you come up with your own ideas.

To find out more you can contact the Trust at:

15 Queen's Gate Terrace, London SW7 5PR
Tel: +44(0) 207 584 9315
Fax: +44(0) 207 581 0410
Email: office@wcmt.org.uk
www.wcmt.org.uk

Tax issues

If you go to live or work abroad, and become non-resident in the UK, you might still have to pay UK tax - but *only* on your income earned in the UK (savings, dividends, rental income *etc*). If you do need to pay, you may need to complete a Self Assessment tax return.

This website explains the tax implications for all the circumstances in which you might be abroad, whether temporarily or permanently. It's particularly useful if you're thinking of renting out your home:
www.direct.gov.uk/en/BritonsLivingAbroad/Moneyabroad/index.htm

What about the house?

Some mortgage lenders may allow a payment holiday of up to six months without affecting your scheme.

Another option might be to rent out your house. You may need to check terms and conditions for subletting with your mortgage lender, but it can be a good way of covering the mortgage costs while you are away.

As it is your home and you need to be sure it will be looked after while you are away, the above reinforces our advice that, if you decide to rent, it's worth using an accommodation agent to take care of things and make sure you comply with all the regulations.

It would also be wise to check with the Inland Revenue to see whether you are eligible for a tax exemption certificate (on your rental income), which should be given to the accommodation agent.

Many letting agencies only operate in a local area and we asked Robert Ulph, Director of Pennington's, Ipswich, Suffolk, for some guidelines. He said an agent will generally take a six-week deposit from the tenant and will make sure the house is clean and the garden sorted out before you return:

"We come across this quite regularly. We see a lot of people thinking about letting their properties because they want to go off and do something different, especially people aged 50-plus. Actually it's very simple. I would say prepare in good time and, if you let to the right people who will take care of the property and pay the rent on time, you don't have any problem at all."

Firstly, he advised only using an agent who was a member of ARLA, the Association of Residential Letting Agents. They will usually charge 10-15% of the rental for their services, but they can guide you through the preparation as well as looking after things while you are away.

When letting a house there are some rules to abide by and some safety certificates you must have if you're going to take this route. Mr Ulph said: "Generally people rent fully-furnished - otherwise think about the storage costs. But any furniture in the house which is made of foam, must comply with fire regulations. This also applies to anything, such as cushions, that you want to store. If they aren't made of fire retardant materials they cannot be stored in the house."

A second must-have is a current gas safety certificate for any appliances. You need one for the gas supply to the house, which costs around £80, and it is essential that you also have a certificate for each appliance in the house - roughly an extra £20 per appliance. A corgi-registered engineer must carry out the test and the certificate is valid for a year.

For electricity the regulations are different, and Mr Ulph said a certificate is not required *unless* you let to students or the property is a house in multiple occupancy (HMO). However, an electrician with a Part P qualification *must* carry out any new work and give you a certificate to prove that this has been done. Wiring has to be safe and if your wiring has been installed for 15-20 years it would make sense to have it checked.

A new regulation since our last edition is that landlords now have to get an Energy Performance Certificate (EPC). This new Act came into effect from the 1st October 2008 and requires all rental properties, with a new tenancy in England and Wales, to have an EPC, which can usually be organised by your lettings agent and looks similar to the energy labels found on domestic appliances such as fridges and washing machines; it will cost in the region of £95 and will last for ten years.

Another must is to tell your insurance company what you're planning. He said: "Some don't like it and you may have to take out specialised cover."

Then there is the question of what to do with your personal property and who to let to. Thorough credit and reference checks are vital to get the right tenant. Mr Ulph said: "It's important to get the right people and to be realistic. You are going to come back to some wear and tear. Don't expect the house to be exactly as you left it. Things do happen that are not the tenants' fault. But most people with proper references will take care of your property. It's a good idea to meet your tenants, then it becomes someone's home they're renting."

He said that leaving ornaments and pictures in place would also reinforce that message, but personal possessions and valuables should be packed away and stored - this can be the attic or basement (if you have one).

While this edition was being revised, an inquiry came in about insurers who specialise in cover for homes left empty. There are some but you should check them with the Association of British Insurers to make sure they're reputable.

It's also possible to arrange with a lettings agency to do a once-a-week check on your property, if you do choose to leave your home empty, but we would advise you to consider this very carefully. It may not be an option if you're going to worry while you're away!

visit: www.gap-year.com

Another possibility is a house swap

Obviously you'd have to be careful in arranging this and in satisfying yourself that you're happy with the people you're planning to swap with, but we've found a number of agencies that can help you.

The following arrange holiday swaps in many countries around the world and have plenty of advice on how to go about it. You have to sign up as a member to access some information:

www.homelink.org - annual membership is £115. It has regional websites in 30 countries and has been operating for 50 years.

www.intervac.co.uk - annual membership is £49.99.

www.homebase-hols.com/ - annual membership is £29.

Alice's adventures in India

Alice, Tony and Rowan (then aged 29, 31 and 20 months) decided they'd had enough of Peckham and the rat race so they headed off for six months in India exploring the sub continent from the Himalayan foothills right down to Karnataka in the south.

"Travelling as a family was harder than we expected, and more rewarding. I found it very hard to just relax and enjoy the experience, and put a lot of pressure on myself to achieve my own goals and make best use of the time.

"While Tony was looking forward to spending lots of time as a family, I was looking forward to a break from full time mothering! Tony and I did a lot of talking and have got much better at being clear with each other about what we want and need from each other.

"I think that, although it wasn't always comfortable, the time was incredibly valuable: I have become much better at going with the flow, and we deal with conflict much more effectively.

"All this is a function of having the time, to process, think, discuss, try things out.

"I don't think we would be where we are now if we had stayed at home in Peckham.

"We have some wonderful memories, and Rowan opened lots of doors, or rather, walked straight through them without asking: small children really bring out the best in people, and you get a much more genuine reaction.

the gap-year guidebook 2011

"I heartily recommend it. We had no specific problems relating to having such a small child, and actually there are many advantages to travelling in less developed areas with a tot.

"The environment is less formal and people were generally very warm and welcoming toward Rowan.

"He enjoyed the experience greatly, and we are lucky in that he is a great extrovert and not fazed by lots of change and newness.

"Down sides: he (Rowan) had infinitely more energy than we ever did! Travelling on long journeys seemed to leave him refreshed and ready to explore, when we just wanted to sit, have a cup of tea and zone out, which could be a strain.

"We had far less opportunities to discuss and plan: you have to be very organised, as spur of the moment planning is not nearly as easy when you are on a street corner with one eye on an escapee or screaming toddler.

"Regular sightseeing and typical traveller pastimes such as whiling the time away in coffee shops and socialising with other travellers were more or less out, as were more adventurous options like trekking.

"We had to think family, and we did sometimes feel that we were missing out, particularly on the daydreaming. I also learned the value of my support network at home, and was really missing my mummy friends at one point: we felt a bit isolated, whether among Indian families or childless travellers, we didn't quite fit.

"Looking back, I think all of this would have been much smoother a year later. He was quite a handful when we went out there, was a much better travel companion towards the end of our trip, and now, a year on, is a completely different proposition: more organised in himself, more open to reason and more able to engage in a conscious way with a different culture/environment.

"Specific suggestions I would make: Get a good sling. A "soft structured carrier" works well for any child over the age of 6 months and up to 3 years, and is practically essential: they are extremely comfortable on front and back and very lightweight and compact to pack, and pushchairs are not always a practical option given the roads.

"If you are new to a country/culture, start the trip somewhere you will feel well within your comfort zone but have a chance to get the rhythm

visit: www.gap-year.com

of the culture: a luxury hotel is less of a good idea than a well recommended family guesthouse where you have a friendly face to show you the ropes.

"We took too much stuff. If we went again I would probably take a 30l rucksack for me and Rowan with perhaps a daysack on top.

"We took lots of books and odds and ends which we really could have managed without.

"We are having issues with Tax Credits because they claim to have no record that we informed them of our trip - I would contact them in writing if we went again.

"I would probably plan a bit more of an itinerary next time. We felt a bit overwhelmed by the level of choice, and weren't sure how we were going to feel once there.

"More planning, and more discussion before we went about what we wanted out of the trip, and what we wanted when we got home."

Getting back to normal?

"I wish that we had thought more carefully about our return. We had decided that we were not going to return to London, and that was it!

"We stayed with parents, nice for the first month but there were definitely tensions. Tony got a little bit of freelance work in touring theatre which took him away from home for several weeks at a time, making it difficult for us to move forward with life arrangements, especially where we needed to discuss things.

"It took a long time to decide that we weren't ready to settle anywhere, and had more travelling to do in the UK so we've taken the plunge and bought a converted horsebox.

"This gives us a lot of geographic and economic flexibility, but it took us 4 months of house hunting, in between work commitments, to decide that this was definitely the route we wanted to go down, then another two months to locate the right thing and actually buy it, then another couple of months settling in.

"If we had thought carefully, we could have made the decision about where/how we wanted to live before we left and saved a lot of stress - being transient is quite difficult and we are much more settled now we have our own home again, but we are only now beginning to feel normal and settled again.

the gap-year guidebook 2011

> "On the other hand, having concrete plans may have got in the way of what has been quite an organic - if uncomfortable - process of integration within ourselves.
>
> "It's fair to say that since India we have a lot more confidence about what we can manage with Rowan and how simply we can live, and also have a clearer idea and more determination about what it is that we want out of life. It took time to work out what this would mean in practice, and also to realise what was possible.

Household contents - storage

Two things to think about if you really want to clear your house before renting:

- Do you really want to add this to your list of 'things to do' before you go?
- Can you afford it?

We talked to an independent storage company with sites across the UK to get some idea of what's involved.

Sydney Hyams is managing director of Archival Record Management. His company rents ten, 20 and 40ft storage containers on managed sites – ie where there are security guards and your property is safeguarded from fire, flood and theft. He advises that you would need a 20ft container for the contents of an average house. The containers are 'self service' so you would have to pack, move and unpack yourself and therefore need to add the costs of van rental and transport to the container rental costs.

You would also have to arrange your own insurance, but, said Mr Hyams, normally you can extend your household contents insurance to cover property on secured sites.

It might be worth trying local independent storage companies in your area. Philip Taylor, of Boxstore, Rogers Farm, in Boxford, Suffolk, told us that renting out property when taking a **gap-** is proving more popular each year, and that when choosing where to store your possessions, it is worthwhile shopping around for the most competitive price.

He said: "Comparing like for like, smaller independent storage companies can be anything up to 50% cheaper than the larger ones. Once your belongings are in the van, travelling up to 50-100 miles is still an option to realise these savings, especially on the longer term."

National removals and storage companies, like Pickfords, also provide container storage on managed sites and can sell you the packing materials and boxes you might need as well. Prices vary according to the distance from the storage site, size of container and length of time and some self storage companies do not charge VAT on household storage, but others do. It is worth bearing in mind that storage alone for a year would come to over £1000.

But remember, on top of that you have to add the packing, loading, removal and unloading costs at each end of your career break. On average the process

visit: www.gap-year.com

can cost £300-£400 more than an ordinary house move and prices vary depending on whether your dates fall into peak season for house removals - such as children's school holidays and the peak times of year for house sales.

There's more information here:
www.pickfords.co.uk/html/storage/removal-and-storage-company.htm

What about the kids?

There's some evidence that another growing trend is for families to take a **gap** together, particularly while the children are young.

While it's virtually impossible to get reliable figures, there's a lot of anecdotal evidence from **gap-** providers.

Phil Murray, director of gapadvice.org, says: "gapadvice.org is asked from time to time for a view on whether or not such **gap-** years are advisable. The view is that as long as the children are safe, have access to medical facilities and their education development is not harmed, family **gap-**years can have very beneficial outcomes. Children are exposed to a variety of mind-broadening situations and their overall development can be very positive.

"Some **gap-**year companies might have a minimum age limit of eight years. It certainly is important to get the support of the school if children are being removed from mainstream education for a lengthy period."

Whether to take the children out of school is really up to you as parents. Much will depend on the length of time you plan to be away and the point your children are at in their education.

Essentially you need to balance the effects of taking a child out of school against the benefits of the 'education' they will get from seeing something of the world. You also need to think through health and medical issues, but that may mean nothing more than carrying essential medical supplies with you, as all travellers are advised to do when travelling abroad.

It's also possible that you can get your child into a local school for some of the time they are away, or you can organise some basic study for them with the help of their school while you are travelling.

The official view from the Department for Education is that, ultimately, it is down to the parents, but that they should talk it through with their child's school or local education authority.

It is crucial that it's cleared with your child's school and Head teacher, who has to authorise it, if you don't want to face court action by the local authority and

the gap-year guidebook 2011

a possible hefty fine for taking a child out of school during term time But parents who have done it, even with very small children, say that it has been a very worthwhile experience and brought them closer to their kids. A few **gap-** organisations are now providing family **gap-** volunteer placements.

It's worth remembering that most children are a lot more adaptable than parents think and really don't miss all the trappings of modern civilisation once they are in a new place. If you're thinking about it, there's some good advice for parents on: **www.netmums.com/h/n/holidays/home/all/887/**

Safety precautions

You will find a great deal of advice on all aspects of planning your **gap-** in Chapter 1 - Tips for Travellers, as well as in-country advice and what to expect when you get back. Tips for Travellers is relevant to all travellers, whatever their age. We also cover the importance of getting the right kind of travel insurance and the questions you need answered in Chapter 2.

But there are some other issues that perhaps might be more important for older travellers to consider. You almost certainly have more in the way of assets than someone straight from school or university - things like a house, insurance and pension schemes; valuable personal property.

In the unlikely event of something going wrong, it makes sense to ensure your affairs are in order and to have someone you trust authorised to take care of your affairs until you can do so for yourself. It will make things that much easier for those back home, who may be coping with the trauma of a loved one in hospital overseas, if they have some idea of how you want your affairs to be handled.

You should consider two things - making a will and possibly appointing someone with legal power of attorney.

Making a will

Points to remember when making a will:

- It doesn't have to be expensive.
- It can be amended later if your circumstances change.
- You can make it clear what you want to happen to your property.
- It prevents family squabbles.
- It allows you to choose executors you can trust.

You should:

- Give yourself time to think.
- Use a professional, preferably one experienced specifically with will preparation.
- Make sure you can update it without large additional charges.
- Make sure there's an opt out from executor or probate services if you don't need them - by the time the will is needed, which could be many years away,

visit: www.gap-year.com

it may be that someone in the family, who was too young when you made it, who can deal with it.

Power of attorney

Many people choose to make an informal arrangement with a family member to take care of things at home while they're travelling, but if you were to need someone authorised to pay bills at home or liaise with your travel insurance company, it might make sense to have a proper, formal arrangement in place before you go to give them the authority to act on your behalf.

You might be able to arrange with your bank to add them as a signatory to your account, in case it should be necessary, as long as you feel comfortable that the person you choose will make the right decisions about your money if you can't.

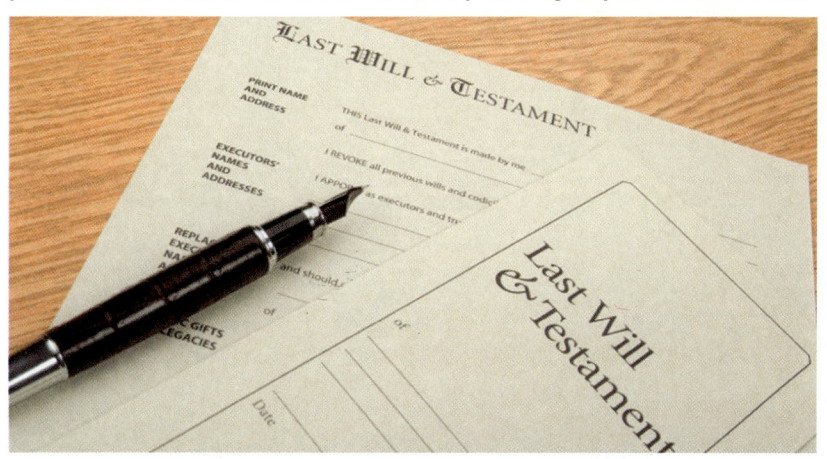

A more secure way is to appoint a power of attorney, but be warned it's a lengthy process, which can take up to five months to process. Until the documents are properly registered, whoever you appoint cannot act for you.

There's no fast track procedure on compassionate grounds and the Public Guardians' Office website says: "If there are no problems with the LPA or application, we are typically returning the registered LPA in around nine weeks from the date of receipt. If there are any problems with the LPA or application, we are currently informing the applicant within two weeks of receiving the application."

Getting it right when there are at least 30 pages of forms per person is no joke; and, if you're a couple, each one of you has to fill out a set. So to avoid delays and mistakes (with possible charging of repeat fees) it makes sense to get professional advice from a specialist.

The process is administered by the Public Guardians' Office, which charges a fee of £150. But compare that with having someone professional look after your property and personal welfare. It can cost as much as £1500 for a couple. To find out more about the new legislation go to: www.publicguardian.gov.uk

inspire

SHARE SKILLS, CHANGE LIVES!

WHY VOLUNTEER ABROAD WITH INSPIRE?

- A wide range of carefully selected projects across the world
- Proven expertise to match volunteer skills and aspirations to projects
- Flexible approach and sensitivity to volunteer needs
- Committed to ethical volunteering and sustainable development
- Supporting overseas communities, local NGOs and charities

So what are you waiting for?
Discover a new country and do your bit for the world!

Call today on 08000 32 33 50
info@inspirevolunteer.co.uk | www.i-volunteerabroad.co.uk

Career Breaks

African Conservation Experience
Unit 1 Manor Farm, Churchend Lane,
Charfield,
Wotton-Under-Edge, GL12 8LJ UK

E: info@conservationafrica.net
T: +44 (0) 1454 269182
www.conservationafrica.net

African Conservation Experience offer volunteering opportunities at wildlife conservation projects in southern Africa. You can count on our full support and more than 10 years experience. See our main advert in Conservation

Gap Year for Grown Ups
Zurich House,
1 Meadow Road,
Tunbridge Wells, TN1 2YG UK

E: info@gapyearforgrownups.co.uk
T: +44 (0) 1892 701 881
www.gapyearforgrownups.co.uk

Company specialising in career breaks and volunteer work for the over 30s, hundreds of programmes in 30 countries from two weeks to 12 months.

Inspire
Town Hall,
Market Place,
Newbury, RG14 5AA UK

E: info@inspirevolunteer.co.uk
T: 08000 32 33 50
www.i-volunteerabroad.co.uk

Choose from a wide range of projects and select a programme duration from one month onwards - regular start dates every month for gap-year students or those on a career break to tailor-make their very own experience.

JET - Japan Exchange and Teaching Programme UK
JET Desk, c/o Embassy of Japan,
101-104 Piccadilly, Mayfair,
London, W1J 7JT UK

E: info@jet-uk.org
T: +44 (0) 20 7465 6668
www.jet-uk.org

The JET Programme, the official Japanese government scheme, sends UK graduates to promote international understanding and to improve foreign language teaching in schools for a minimum of 12 months.

NONSTOP Adventure Ltd
Unit 3B, The Plough Brewery,
516 Wandsworth Road, Battersea,
London, SW8 3JX UK

E: info@nonstopadventure.com
T: +44 (0) 845 365 1525
www.nonstopadventure.com

Family owned company offering sailing, skiing and snowboarding training courses.

Raleigh
Get Out There

Expand your horizons, invest in your future

Raleigh is a unique, revealing, and unrivalled experience that you will never forget. James Ash

raleighinternational.org
020 7183 1270
info@raleigh.org.uk

Oasis Overland
The Marsh,
Henstridge, Somerset BA8 0TF UK

E: info@oasisoverland.co.uk
F: +44 (0) 1963 363200
www.oasisoverland.co.uk

Oasis Overland provide exciting and affordable adventure travel experiences, where you'll work as part of a team with like-minded travellers as you explore different cultures and regions.

Raleigh International
207 Waterloo Road,
Southwark,
London, SE1 8XD UK

E: info@raleigh.org.uk
T: +44 (0) 20 7183 1283
F: +44 (0) 20 7504 8094
www.raleighinternational.org

Develop new skills, meet people from all backgrounds and make a difference on sustainable community and environmental projects around the world.

The Career Break Guru

E: tessa@careerbreakguru.com
www.careerbreakguru.com

The Career Break Guru was created to advise and guide grown-up gappers as they dream about, plan and create their ideal trip.

The Year Out Group
Queensfield,
28 King's Road,
Easterton, SN10 4PX UK

E: info@yearoutgroup.org
T: +44 (0) 1380 816696
www.yearoutgroup.org

See main entry under volunteering.

Travel Nation
8th Floor, Intergen House,
65-67 Western Road,
Hove
East Sussex BN3 2JQ

E: info@travelnation.co.uk
T: 01273 320580
www.travelnation.co.uk

Independent specialist travel company providing expert advice and the best deals round-the-world trips, multi-stop itineraries, overland/adventure tours and Trans-Siberian rail journeys.

VentureCo Worldwide
The Ironyard,
64-66 The Market Place,
Warwick, CV34 4SD UK

T: +44 (0) 1926 411 122
F: +44 (0) 1926 411 133
www.ventureco-worldwide.com

VentureCo provides the ideal combination for career break travellers who want to explore off the beaten track, learn about the host country and give something back to the communities they stay with. Ventures last between two and 15 weeks.

the gap-year guidebook 2011

DECISIONS, DECISIONS...

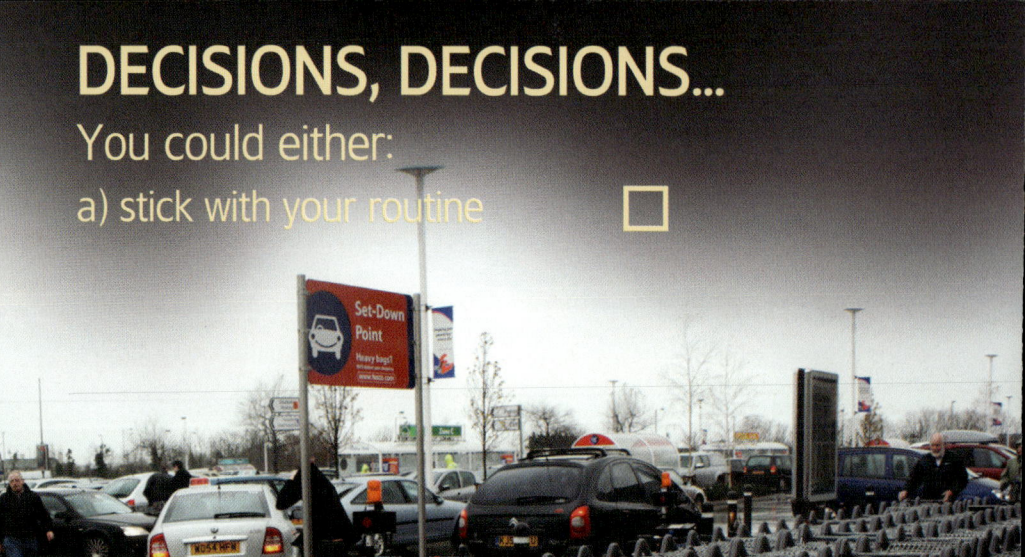

You could either:

a) stick with your routine ☐

b) break from your routine ☑

- Round the world flight specialists
- Trans-Siberian rail journeys
- Multi stop itineraries
- Travel insurance
- Adventure tours
- Hop-on / hop-off bus passes

travelNation
Round the World and Adventure Travel Experts

www.travelnation.co.uk
Telephone: 01273 320 580

ABTA J4916 / Y1114 — IATA Accredited Agent — ATOL Protected 9828

Chapter 4
Travelling and accommodation

So, you have a year to travel the globe? That's great news. The even better news is that we can help you do it safely, confidently and affordably.

As one of the world's largest provider of tourist and backpacker accommodation we have spent the past 100 years perfecting a way to help people of all ages discover this planet we call home in a fun and friendly way.

Who are we?

Hostelling International (HI) operates in 90 countries with 4,000 unique hostels in aspiring locations worldwide. No other hostel operator can match us for sheer quality or variety of accommodation. As well as 'quirkier' venues (ships, refurbished jumbo jets, ex jails and lighthouses), we have locations in every major travel hub so you can start your hostel experience as soon as you get off the plane or train!

What do we do?

We take our business very seriously (but not in a 'we don't ever have a laugh' way). Our quality management system (HI-Q) is in place to assure you that wherever your gap year takes you our network's accommodation standards will be clean, safe, comfortable and consistent. HI hostels also operate in ways sympathetic to the environment often using solar power, water saving devices, low-energy lighting and recycling initiatives.

Why choose hostelling?

Unlike sometimes bland motels, impersonal hotels or 'at-the-mercy-of-the-elements' camp sites, hostels will provide a secure roof over your head, a comfy bed for the night and communal space in which you can start making friends for life.

Hostel staff know their local areas back to front and will help you get the most out of your stay. Many hostels run excursions and organise activities – so get involved! When it's time to leave they will ensure you get on your way easily...to your next HI world location obviously!

So, are you hungry for HI hostelling yet? Let's whet your appetite...

- Relax at a poolside retreat close to Brazil's spectacular Iguacu Falls
- Enjoy the roof terrace with gob-smacking views at the stunningly modern Sydney Harbour hostel
- Spend time in a real Highland castle amidst the legends of Scotland's glens and mountains
- All aboard boat hostels in Portugal, Sweden and Hungary

visit: www.gap-year.com

- Visit an Afro-Victorian mansion in South Africa
- Experience traditional Japanese tatami rooms and food
- Rest on the shores of a peaceful lake just minutes from the Colorado river, USA
- Stay in eco-friendly wig-wams or recycled railway carriages in New Zealand's native bush

Let's go!

Now you're ready log on to hihostels.com to book your real hostel experience. Download a FREE copy of the hostel guide, intuitive travel guides and planning tools to make your dream itinerary come true. Read customer reviews, hostel ratings and top travel tips from people who have been there, done that and are now sat at home envying your every step.

Join us and say 'Hi' to the world!

Get online! Only on hihostels.com can you make multistage bookings covered by just one fee and you only pay a 5% deposit (we're nice like that). And remember when you arrive at your first HI hostel make sure you ask about membership. Joining us will add you to 4 million others who enjoy fabulous discounts, offers and services at home or abroad. For more information check out: hihostels.com/web/membership.en.htm. You can't apply for membership online (we like to meet you in person) but the website will tell you how joining the HI family will help you get the best out of your gap year.

See you all soon and happy hostelling!

Hostelling International is a non-governmental, non-profit making organization recognized by UNESCO. Registered charity no. 1117014.

the gap-year guidebook 2011

4 Travelling and accommodation

Global warming, climate change and the world's depleting energy resources continue to be a serious concern, regardless of the economic climate, and increasingly people want to know how to be environmentally friendly on their **gap-** travels. Nowhere is this likely to be more of an issue than in the types of transport you choose.

We asked our friends at SusTrans, a leading UK charity enabling people to travel by foot, bike or public transport for more of the journeys we make every day, for some advice on making more ethical travel choices on **gap**-years.

"How you make local journeys can make a huge difference to your gap year experience. As well as being cheaper, healthier and more environmentally-friendly ways to travel, walking and cycling are the best ways to become familiar with new surroundings or discover whole new parts of your home town.

"It's a good idea to plan your route before you set off, especially in a new place. Over the last fifteen years Sustrans and partners have developed the National Cycle Network - 12,600 miles of walking and cycling routes across the UK. It's easy to find routes near you at **www.sustrans.org.uk**.

"For journeys that are too far to walk or cycle, public transport is a good option. It will allow you to go further afield and meet more people as you travel. Plan your train, bus, coach or tube journeys at www.traveline.org.uk."

If you're hoping to travel to several destinations time is inevitably an issue, so it may not be practical to avoid air travel altogether, but there are ways you can minimise your carbon footprint.

If you're concerned about global warming, and want to do your bit, you can pay a small 'carbon offset' charge on your flight. If you want to know more try: **www.co2balance.uk.com/co2calculators/flight/**

The site has a calculator so you can work out how much to pay for journeys by car, train or air. It also has some simpler options - for example £50 will offset one long-haul one-way flight from London to Australia. Your money goes towards sustainable development projects around the world and there's a complete list of all current projects on the website:
www.co2balance.uk.com/carbon-offset-projects/projects-overview/

They are all managed by co2balance, but are also all independently validated and verified by international standards organisations. Projects include providing energy efficient woodstoves in east Africa, wind power in India and renewable energy projects in China.

The UK's Green Traveller website includes a list of top ten fair trade holidays worldwide and lots more advice if you want your travel to be as environmentally friendly as possible:
www.greentraveller.co.uk/node/487

visit: www.gap-year.com

To find out more about sustainable and responsible travel you could also look at the website of the International Ecotourism Society, which has a lot of tips for responsible travel both en route and in-country: www.ecotourism.org

Another option for responsible travellers is to make the journey part of your **gap-**, if you have time; for example, plan a rail route with stops along the way allowing you time to explore. There's more on this in the trains section below.

You may also be able to combine different forms of transport to get to your destination and while you're in-country. We've had a look at some other transport options and these can be found in the following pages.

Ethical travel

Thinking about the best way to get to and from your destination is one thing, but ethical travel means much more than that.

We asked Tourism Concern to explain further: "Tourism is an enormous industry and affects the lives of millions of people. Environments can be wrecked by irresponsible and unregulated diving, climbing and other outdoor activities.

"Communities have been forcibly removed from their land to make way for tourism developments across the world, from Africa to Australia. Water used for swimming pools, golf courses and twice daily power showers can dwindle supplies for the local populations. Exploitation of local workers is a problem usually invisible to a visitor's eyes. "When you start to look more closely, the issues can seem overwhelming, but the good news is that with the decisions you make today and while you're away, you are taking big steps to ensure that your trip benefits everyone."

Tourism Concern's ten tips for ethical travelling

1) Be aware: Start enjoying your travels before you leave. Think about what sort of clothing is appropriate for both men and women. If the locals are covered up, what sort of messages may you be sending out by exposing acres of flesh? But use your guidebook as a starting point, not the only source of information. Once you've arrived, find out what's going on by talking to locals, then have your own adventures.

2) Be open: Something may seem bizarre or odd to 'you', but it may be normal and just the way things are done to 'them'. Try not to assume that the western way is right or best.

3) Our holidays - their homes: Ask before taking pictures of people, especially children, and respect their wishes. Talk to local people. What do they think about our lifestyle, clothes and customs? Find out about theirs.

4) Giving constructively: Giving sweets or pens to children encourages begging. A donation to a project, health centre or school is more constructive.

5) Be fair: Try to put money into local hands. If you haggle for the lowest price, your bargain may be at the seller's expense. Even if you pay a little over the odds, does it really matter?

6) Buy local, behave local: Look at the environment you're in, try to eat locally sourced foods and buy locally produced goods. Think about resources, don't shower for 20 minutes at a time in an arid zone, just because you might at home.

7) Ask questions: Write a letter to your tour operator or venture manager about their responsible tourism policy.

8) Think before you fly: Use alternative forms of transport where possible. The more and further you fly, the more you contribute to global warming and environmental destruction. Consider flying long-haul less often but staying longer when you're there.

9) Discover Tourism Concern: A charity that campaigns against exploitation in tourism and for fairly traded and ethical forms of tourism. Their website has a wealth of information on action you can take to avoid guilt trips. www.tourismconcern.org.uk

10) Be happy: By taking any, some or all of these actions you are personally fighting tourism exploitation. Enjoy your guilt-free trip!

visit: www.gap-year.com

Getting about

Planes

The internet is invaluable when searching for ticket information, timetables, prices and special offers, whether you're travelling by air, sea, train or bus.

Because the internet gives customers so much information to choose from, travel companies have to compete harder to win your booking. The internet shows you what flexibility is possible (a lot), so you could find your decision-making turned upside down.

When booking flights, have a look at special offers for round-the-world tickets first, find out how far in advance you can book, and then plan your destinations to fit.

If one of your destinations has a fixed arrival and departure date - for example if you're signed up for a voluntary project - you could try asking for a route tailor-made for you using the prices you find on the web.

Make sure you check out the company making an offer on the web before you use internet booking procedures (does it have a verifiable address and phone number?). Remember, under EU law companies must publish a contact address on their website. So, unless the company in question is a household name, or you are able to locate a legitimate address via another source, think twice before handing over your hard earned cash.

It's important - as ever! - to read the Terms and Conditions to see what you're paying for and whether you can get your money back before you agree to buy - just as you would outside the virtual world.

What to watch out for

Once you've booked a flight online, especially if you do it through an agent such as **www.lastminute.com**, rather than direct with the airline, you may have to pay extra fees for rescheduling, not to mention date restrictions if you need to change the date. Unless you have a good, solid reason for cancelling - and most airlines define such reasons very narrowly - you also risk losing the money you've paid.

As we mention in Chapter 1, increasingly airlines are covering their additional fuel costs and taxes by adding charges for different services - like in-flight baggage storage, airport duty, seats next to each other (if you're not travelling alone) - you need to have your wits about you when you're going through the online booking forms as these extras can add a substantial amount to the final total, making that budget deal significantly more expensive than you originally thought (up to £100 at best and almost equalling the flight cost at worst).

Remember, the ads usually say 'flights from…£XXX' and that's your clue to watch out for extras.

Bargain flights: Scheduled airlines often offer discount fares for students under 26 so don't rule them out. Other cheap flights are advertised regularly in the newspapers and on the web. All sorts of travel agents can fix you up with multi-destination tickets, and student travel specialists often know where to find the best deals for **gap-**year students.

It's worth checking whether a particular flight is cheaper if you book direct with the airline - and if you are using a student travel card you may find that you have to do it this way to get the discount, rather than using one of the budget deal websites.

Above all, travel is an area where searching the internet for good deals should be top of your list - though it works best for single-destination trips rather than complex travel routes.

Fear of flying...

We all know that statistically flying is by far the safest means of transport, but that doesn't stop even the hardiest of passengers suffering a fleeting jolt of panic every time a slight bump of turbulence is felt.

So to help you feel more comfortable, Becci Coombes of **GirlsTravel Club.co.uk** has kindly put together some hints and tips to put your mind at rest.

"To start with, anxiety is perfectly understandable; after all, it's not often in our daily lives that we give complete control over our personal safety into the hands of a stranger in such extreme circumstances. However, just look at the faces of the stewardesses. They're completely relaxed and, even when busy and tired, still manage to walk about the cabin perfectly calmly without the need for a large gin and two valium. They are completely at ease with being

visit: www.gap-year.com

on an aircraft day in and day out, so I always think if they can do it, so can I!

"All planes will make odd thunking noises (when the landing gear retracts or comes down), or changes in engine noise that make it seem like the plane is decelerating. All this is perfectly normal so try not to pay any attention to it; sitting there listening anxiously to the sound of the engines won't help your general state of comfort. Put on the earphones and listen to some music instead.

"Turbulence is also completely normal. Most planes fly above extreme weather conditions, and the pilot will know if there are any patches of turbulence coming up and will advise you accordingly; planes are built to withstand these sorts of pressures, so once again, keep an eye on the faces of the stewardesses. They don't panic when turbulence happens, so you don't need to either.

"I find the homeopathic remedies aconite and arnica to be excellent for pre-flight anxiety, but by far the best remedy I have found is Bach's Rescue Remedy. A couple of squirts is incredibly helpful and will ease those dreadful butterflies. Sit upright, place your palms on your thighs, and push hard with your feet against the floor; you should breathe slowly in through the nose and out through the mouth then you will feel out the fear and tension go out of your body."

Trains

Travelling by train is one of the best ways to see a country - and if you travel on an overnight sleeper it can be as quick as a plane. India's train network is world-famous and an absolute must experience! But don't think you can't use trains in other parts of the world. What follows is just a taster.

Inter-railing - Europe and a bit beyond

If you want to visit a lot of countries, one of the best ways to travel is by train on an InterRail ticket. With InterRail you have the freedom of the rail networks of Europe (and a bit beyond), allowing you to go as you please in 28 countries.

From the northern lights of Sweden to the kasbahs of Morocco, you can call at all the stops. InterRail takes you from city centre to city centre - avoiding airport hassles, ticket queues and traffic jams, and giving you more time to make the most of your visit. Passes are available for all ages, but you need to have lived in Europe for at least six months.

Overnight trains are available on most of the major routes, saving on accommodation costs, allowing you to go to sleep in one country and wake up in another.

Supplements apply so ask when you book. You will have to pay extra to travel on some express intercity trains or the Eurostar. Most major stations such as Paris, Brussels, Amsterdam and Rome have washing facilities and left luggage.

The InterRail One Country Pass can be used for the following countries:

Austria, Belgium, Bulgaria, Croatia, Czech Republic, Denmark, Finland, France, Germany, Great Britain, Greece, Hungary, Italy, Luxembourg, Macedonia (FYR),

the gap-year guidebook 2011

Netherlands, Norway, Poland, Portugal, Republic of Ireland, Romania, Russia, Serbia, Slovakia, Slovenia, Spain, Sweden, Switzerland and Turkey.

The alternative choice is the InterRail Global Pass, which is valid in all participating InterRail countries. Available for several lengths of travel it is ideal for gappers wanting to explore several, or even all, European countries in their year out.

One Country Pass Prices

Second class prices vary by the country and range from £25 (under 26)/£39 (over 26) for three days in one month, to £65/£149 for eight days in one month in Bulgaria; to £155/£245 in France.

Belgium, The Netherlands and Luxembourg are combined as the InterRail Benelux Pass. For Greece you have the option to order a Greece Plus Pass, which includes ferry crossings to and from Italy.

Global Pass

For second class travel, over 22 continuous days, prices range from £259 (under 26) to £399 (over 26) and are valid from five days to one month. For further details on prices and how to buy an InterRail pass, visit their website: www.interrailnet.com and www.raileurope.co.uk/inter-rail/

Eurostar

The Eurostar train is a quick, easy and relatively cheap way to get to Europe. You can get from London to Calais from £59, and the trains are comfortable and run frequently. Tickets can be purchased online at **www.eurostar.com**, in an approved travel agency, or at any Eurostar train station.

Trans-Siberian Express

If you're looking for a train adventure - and you have a generous budget to play with - what about the Trans-Siberian Express? You could do a 14 day Moscow-Beijing trip. Do this as a 'full-on' or a 'no-frills' package.

You can also choose from a range of other trips lasting from nine to 26 days. On top of this you will need some money for food and drink, visas, airfare, etc.

For China, Russia and Mongolia you'll need to have a visa for your passport to allow you into each country. Contact each relevant embassy to find out what type of visa you will need (*ie* visitors or transit). It's probably easiest to arrange for all your train tickets, visas and hotel accommodation through a specialist agency, about six months before you leave. Your journey will be a lot easier if you have all your paperwork in order before you leave - although it will cost you more to do it this way.

The trains can be pretty basic, varying according to which line you're travelling on and which country owns the train. On some trains you can opt to upgrade to first class. This should give you your own cabin with shower, wash basin and more comfort - however, although you'll be more comfortable, you may find it more interesting back in second class with all the other backpackers and traders.

If you're travelling in autumn or winter make sure you take warm clothes - the trains have rather unreliable heating. If you travel in late November/December you may freeze into a solid block of ice, but it will be snowing by then and the views will be spectacular. Travelling in September will be warmer and a bit cheaper.

If you want to read about it before you go, try the Trans-Siberian Handbook by Bryn Thomas. (You can buy it on Amazon.) It's updated frequently and it has details about the towns you'll be passing through, and includes the timetables.

There are several websites you can look up, but **www.trans-siberian.co.uk** is one of the best out there. For cheaper options you could also try Travel Nation, which has a useful page of FAQs on the Trans-Siberian Moscow to Beijing rail trip: **www.travel-nation.co.uk/trans-siberian-train/faqs.htm**

India and the rest of the world

Tell anyone you're going to India and you'll invariably be told you must try a train journey! Indian trains are the most amazing adventure - with all sorts of extras - like a meal included in the price on the Shatabdi Express intercity commuter trains, or the vendors who wander the length of the train with their buckets of snacks, tea or coffee, calling their wares "chai, chai, chai" as they go.

But Indian trains get booked up weeks or months in advance, especially if you're planning to travel during any major public festival like Diwali, which is a national holiday. You need a seat or berth reservation for any long-distance journey on an Indian train; you cannot simply turn up and hop on. Bookings now open 90 days in advance. Reservations are now completely computerised and a tourist quota gives foreigners and IndRail pass holders preferential treatment. Go to: **www.irctc.co.in/**

There's also a unique reservation system. After a train becomes fully booked, a set number of places in each class are sold as 'Reservation Against Cancellation' or 'RAC'. After all RAC places have been allocated, further prospective passengers are 'wait-listed'. When passengers cancel, people on the RAC list are promoted to places on the train and wait-listed passengers are promoted to RAC.

If you want to try your hand at organising your own train travel in India you can get a copy of the famous Trains at a Glance from any railway station in India for Rs 35 (50p) or you can download it as a PDF from:
www.seat61.com/India.htm

But beware, it contains every train timetable (94 in all) for the sub-continent and it's very long!

Annie Rice spent six months travelling South America, Australasia and Asia after her A Levels and told us that the Indian train service lived up to all her pre-trip expectations.

"India is renowned world-wide for its superb train service and it didn't let us down. Opting for AC sleeper seats we paid more than triple the average local fare – but they were still rock-bottom prices and well worth the money; a comfortable night's sleep in a clean, cool environment.

"However, if you are on a very tight budget then sleeper class carriages are half the price and still provide a reasonably comfortable journey. Make sure you pack some snacks for the ride as a western stomach may not be able to handle the usual train cuisine. Trains get booked up days, even weeks in advance so be sure to book ahead, www.cleartrip.com is an excellent, secure site to do this through."

The Man in Seat 61 is possibly the most incredibly comprehensive train and ship travel website ever. It literally covers the world from India to Latin America, Africa and south-east Asia. It's not only about times, costs and booking, it goes into some detail about the kinds of conditions you can expect.

It's written by Mark Smith, an ex-British Rail employee and former stationmaster at Charing Cross. He has travelled the world by train and ship and it's a personal site run as a hobby, so he pledges it will always remain freely available. www.seat61.com

> Chris Henry writes about his career break in China, where he quickly discovered that everything works on a different scale - not least the transportation...
>
> "China is a great place to do a career break. I was a tired, worn-out hack when I left England to work on a magazine in Beijing as a features writer. By the time I returned to the UK I was a re-energised, positive journalist who loved their job once more. Think of it as travelling out as Gordon Brown and returning as Barack Obama.
>
> "In China EVERYTHING is bigger. On my way from the airport to my accommodation, I discovered Beijing has the equivalent of six M25 motorways orbiting it. It was to take me some time to get my head around the geography of the place.
>
> "On my very first afternoon in the city I decided to walk to a restaurant my guidebook recommended. On the map it was 'only' four blocks.

the gap-year guidebook 2011

Those four blocks took me three hours to walk – they were so much bigger than a block in England

"I had my first – and last - experience of a Chinese bus journey on the first day travelling to my new work. The ticket cost one Yuan – just 10 pence – but the actual ride would have cost much more if it had been a ride at a theme park. It was a white-knuckle ride for sure!

"As more and more people crowded on the vehicle, the bus conductor was shouting at everyone trying to fit them into every available nook and cranny. On the rare occasions the traffic began to move the driver accelerated as if he'd just been told his wife had gone into labour. And then there were long periods (hours, it seemed) when we sat motionless in the early morning rush hour traffic. Needless to say for the rest of my time in Beijing I walked to work.

"Walking to work was a pleasant 30-minute stroll along the streets of central Beijing as they were slowly waking up. It remains one of my favourite memories from my stay. I passed people reading newspapers at the bus stands, groups of elderly people doing exercises in the community open air gyms and others scurrying about their business.

"Every time it came to crossing the road (usually the road had at least six lanes to negotiate) I would take a deep breath, step out and hope for the best as I wove through traffic to get to the other side, without having any real understanding of where the next car was going to appear from. It sounds dangerous – and probably was – but I found that getting to grips with crossing the road was one of the first things that started to make me feel at home in the city.

"The experience of walking to work sums up so well what it is like as you learn to live and work in Beijing. All at the same time it is full of noise, smells, excitement, kindness and grumpiness. In fact, wandering the streets either by foot or bike (bike was my favourite mode of transport – Beijing is as flat as a chess board and makes for excellent cycling) is a great way to experience the city and appreciate the amazing atmosphere around the place. On minute you can by cycling past a temple, the next you're in Tiananmen and then suddenly you'll see a huge shopping centre."

Buses/Coaches

Getting on a bus or coach in a foreign country, especially if you don't speak the language, can be a voyage of discovery in itself. UK bus timetables can be indecipherable, but try one in Patagonia!

Get help from a local you trust, hotel/hostel staff, or the local police station if all else fails. In developing countries, locals think nothing of transporting their livestock by public transport, so be prepared to sit next to a chicken! That said, some buses and coaches can be positively luxurious and they do tend to be cheaper than trains.

visit: www.gap-year.com

Gapper Annie Rice told us her experiences of bus journeys in South America were surprisingly comfortable and convenient.

"The prospect of a 20-hour bus ride can be somewhat daunting and admittedly, hopping on a plane for an hour sounds much more appealing - but in South America the cross-country coach journeys are something to look forward to. You will save huge amounts of money using buses and get a good night's sleep in the process. The connections are brilliant, with strong travel links between cities and countries. Be sure to book your seat in advance then sit-back on your recliner and enjoy the view."

The 'Old Grey Dog'

Greyhound buses have air conditioning, tinted windows and a loo on board, as well as a strict no smoking policy. Greyhound offers Hostelling International members a discount on regular one-way and round-trip fares. They have a Discovery Pass, which allows seven, 15, 30 and 60 days unlimited travel. There's the usual 10% discount for ISIC and Euro 26 ID cardholders (go to **www.discoverypass.com**).

the gap-year guidebook 2011

The bus company operates outside America too, with Greyhound Pioneer Australia (www.greyhound.com.au) and for South Africa there's Greyhound Coach Lines Africa (www.greyhound.co.za). Check out their websites or contact them for information about their various ticket options.

See also www.yha.com.au (Australia) and www.norcalhostels.org (USA).
Greyhound Lines, Inc
15110 North Dallas Parkway, Suite 600, Dallas, TX 75248, USA
Tel. 972-789-7000; Fax 972-387-1874
www.greyhound.com

And...

Here's a website we found that's worth a look if you're going to South Africa. Baz Bus is a hop-on, hop-off touring bus service between Cape Town and Port Elizabeth and is billed as a backpacker favourite. **www.bazbus.com** It was founded in 1995 by a former backpacker, Barry Zeidel and has a fleet of 19-seater buses with on-board TV and even has trailers able to carry surfboards and bicycles.

You can buy passes for travel in any direction you want, and as often as you like, within the time period. You get picked up and dropped off at the door of your backpacker hostel. The travel pass starts on the first day of your travel and is valid for seven or 14 or 21 consecutive days.

We have found similar services in Australia, New Zealand and France (see directory page 107) and are keeping our eyes out for more.

Student gappers could also check out www.istc.org (International Student Travel Confederation) for useful information and advice on special travel deals and discounts - planes, trains, coaches and ferries. Other useful sources of information are:
www.statravel.co.uk
www.studentflights.co.uk
www.thebigchoice.com/Travel/

Touring

Travelling as part of a tour - usually as part of a group of like-minded gappers, on a coach especially fitted out for the task - can prove a fun, action-packed adventure. It doesn't have to mean chugging around the tourist sights, staring at the wonders of the world passing by your window. A tour can mean anything from full-on adventure trips across the desert to smaller, more intimate tours along a specific theme, such as vinyards or culinary hot-spots.

Booking a place on a tour can be a great way to meet new people and shouldn't be dismissed just because some backpackers see it as "the easy option". If you do your research and book with the right company, you'll find yourself with a small bunch of like-minded people and a tour leader who should know your destination's history and culture inside out.

A good leader will also have contacts in the local community and can get you into local hotels and restaurants - leaving you to enjoy your travels rather than worrying about finding a place to sleep the night.

visit: www.gap-year.com

Scout around for long enough and you'll find a tour to suit most tastes, from smaller groups of travellers who are serious about getting off the beaten track to meet the locals and experiencing their way of life, to younger, noisier groups looking for a fun, sociable way to explore a country or region.

TrekAmerica, for example, have been taking groups of adventurous, independent travellers around North America for almost 40 years; they told us that touring is one of the few ways you can get to truly appreciate the vastness of a country like the USA.

"Instead of simply flying over it, an overland journey from New York to LA or vice versa, fits in perfectly with any round the world ticket and lets you experience the true diversity of America; its big cities, small towns and spectacular national parks and wilderness areas.

"If a gap year is all about new and exciting experiences then an American Road trip will deliver just that. Eastern energy blends with southern hospitality and the laid-back lifestyle of the west coast, and each state line represents a whole new world of discovery.

"If long drives or endless hours on a Greyhound bus don't appeal then booking on to an organised tour is often the best option when travelling across the states. You'll not only enjoy the companionship of your fellow travellers, but you'll also benefit from the security and cost savings that a small group tour offers.

"And with the tour leader doing all the driving, you'll also arrive at each destination fresh and ready to make the most of every opportunity."

Overlanding

Overlanding involves travelling in groups on a rough-and-ready truck. Vehicles come fully equipped with a kitchen and tents - perfect for both seasoned backpackers and first timers. We asked Oasis Overlanding to explain more.

What is overlanding?

Overlanding is all about the journey and what you see and experience along the way. It usually involves travelling in a truck that's been converted to carry passengers although some shorter trips may use local transport. The truck carries food supplies supplemented by visits to local markets en route. Accommodation is generally

the gap-year guidebook 2011

under canvas or in basic hotels and meals range from cooking in a group over the camp fire to trying out a local delicacy (guinea pig and chips, anyone?).

Where can I go overlanding?

Overland trips are worldwide, you can find anything from two weeks in Peru to 40 weeks across the African continent.

Day to day

Most overland companies employ a driver and a tour leader on each trip and your group is usually made up of travellers from all walks of life and different nationalities. Together you will shop for food, cook meals and set up camp. Some days involve driving from one destination to the next, often through spectacular landscapes. Other days offer the opportunity to explore a place or to do optional activities like white water rafting or bungee jumping.

Why overlanding?

Overlanding is a fantastic way to start your **gap**-year, especially if you're travelling on your own or are a bit apprehensive about being away from home for the first time. It's also a great way to travel after working hard on your volunteering placement - overlanding takes a lot of the hassle out of travelling such as border crossings and booking accommodation.

visit: www.gap-year.com

Car

Another popular option is to travel by car. It means you have somewhere to sleep if you get stuck for a bed for the night, you save money on train fares and you don't have to lug your rucksack into cafés.

If you are considering it, you need to know the motoring regulations of the countries you'll be visiting - they vary from country to country. Check that you are insured to drive abroad and that this is clearly shown on the documentation you carry with you.

The AA advises that you carry your vehicle insurance; vehicle registration documents and a current tax disc in the car and, of course, take your driving licence with you. If you still have an old paper licence you might want to consider getting it updated to a photo licence before you go, but make sure you leave enough time for this - the DVLA isn't known for its speedy processing.

It is also advisable to take an International Driving Permit (IDP) as not all countries accept the British driving licence. In theory you don't need one in any of the EU member states, but the AA recommends having an IDP if you intend to drive in any country other than the UK – and it's better than getting into trouble and being fined for driving without a valid licence.

An IDP is valid for 12 months and can be applied for up to three months in advance. The AA and RAC issue the permits - you must be over 18 and hold a current, full, UK driving licence that has been valid for two years. You'll need to fill in a form and provide your UK driving licence, passport and a recent passport-sized photo of yourself, which you can take to a participating Post Office. Be warned, you need to allow at least ten working days for processing, so don't try and do this at the last minute.

The AA website has loads of info about the permit, and driving abroad in general, and you can download the application form here:
www.theaa.com/getaway/idp/motidp002.html

It's a good idea to put your car in for a service a couple of weeks before you leave and, unless you're a mechanic, it's also worth getting breakdown cover specifically for your trip abroad. Any of the major recovery companies such as the AA, RAC or Green Flag offer this service. Remember, without cover, if you end up stuck on the side of the road it could be an expensive experience.

The RAC recommends taking a first aid kit, fire extinguisher, warning triangle, headlamp beam reflectors and spare lamp bulbs. These are all required by law in many countries and make sense anyway. for more information telephone:

Check out their website: www.rac.co.uk

Unless you're a very experienced driver, with some off-road experience, we wouldn't advise hiring a car and driving in many places in the developing world. South-east Asian, south Asian, south American and African roads are often little more than potholed tracks, and you really have to know what you're doing when faced with a pecking order decided purely by the size of your vehicle and the sound of your horn - not to mention negotiating wandering livestock, hand-pushed carts, overloaded local buses and trucks, and pedestrians with no road sense whatsoever.

the gap-year guidebook 2011

In India, for example, this means road rules operate on a 'survival of the fittest' basis - big gets precedence and you better get out of the way if you're in something smaller. The only exception is cows, which are sacred, and if a cow decides to sit down in the middle of the road then everyone stops or goes around it. Heaven help you if you ever collide with one!

But often you'll find you can hire a car and a driver pretty cheaply for a day or two and then you'll be an ethical traveller contributing to the local economy.

In Australia, buying a cheap car to tour the country at your own leisure is a popular option. But attempting to drive around Australia in an old Ford Falcon or some clapped out old campervan is definitely a challenge. Pete Burke, the owner and founder of Traveller's Auto Barn, shares his extensive knowledge and experience of choosing the right wheels for your trip.

"Small manual diesel cars are very popular in Europe, but if that's what you are looking for in Australia, you are...WRONG, WRONG, WRONG. Why are small manual cars popular in Europe? Because taxes are very high on larger cars, because fuel is very expensive, and because the streets are very narrow.

"But, you are in Australia now. There is no significant tax difference between an old four cylinder car and a large six cylinder car. Fuel is approx half the price that it is in Europe and there is plenty of wide open space in Australia. The result? BIG cars are popular.

"My advice? Buy a car suited to the journey ahead. So, what is the journey ahead?

"Are you a couple lazily cruising the East Coast? Buying a van would be an acceptable risk. Three mates travelling either the East or West Coast and the Red Centre? Go for an Aussie made six cylinder wagon. Do you want to go off-roading on Fraser Island? Rent a four-wheel drive for the week.

"For me, mindset is the key to a successful roadtrip. Success is not driving around Australia without a breakdown - that's pure bloody luck. Success is not buying a car for $2000 and selling it for $2500 - that's a bonus.

visit: www.gap-year.com

"Success is buying a car, driving 10-20,000kms around Australia, having a few breakdowns, spending a little on repairs and selling the car in under a week.

"If your expectations are to buy a car for $2000, drive around Australia, absorb no repair costs, and then make quick profit at the end of your trip - good luck, you'll probably be disappointed.

"Of course, we've all heard of someone who has done just exactly that. But for every one who summits Everest there are hundreds who don't.

"On the flip side, if your expectation simply is to drive around Australia, and to do so more cheaply than hopping the bus – then you most likely won't be let down, as you this a much more achievable goal."

Ships

If you want to get to the continent, taking a ferry across to France or Belgium can be cheap - but why not sail free as a working crewmember on ships?

Before you leave the UK, contact the head offices of shipping companies to find out the procedures before you leave the UK and how to book a passage from a foreign port.

Or how about getting to grips with the rigging on a cruise yacht? There are numerous employers and private vessel owners out there on the ocean wave who take on amateur and novice crew. In this way you could gain valuable sailing experience and sea miles. You can also make some useful contacts on your way to becoming a professional crewmember. And have the time of your life.

Then there's the 'Classic Sailing' **gap**-year challenge. If you're over 18, in good health and have a sense of adventure, you could join other amateurs helping an expert crew to cross the ocean in a beautiful tall ship (be it a brigantine or a schooner): from the Azores to Bermuda to Charleston, South Carolina. Learn the ropes and find your sea legs! Find out more at:

www.classic-sailing.co.uk

Hitch hiking

Hitch hiking more or less died out after its heyday in the late 1960s and 1970s - partly out of safety concerns and partly as more and more young people became car owners. But with the onset of the recession it's become a regular feature of the travel pages in many national newspapers.

It costs nothing, except being a friendly and courteous passenger, and losing a bit of time waiting around for a ride, but you need to know what you're doing - and you need to know that in some countries it's illegal and that the usual sticking-your-thumb-out signal used in the UK is considered extremely rude in some countries.

There are no hard and fast rules about getting a lift, but above all you do need to think about your safety if you're going to try it - we wouldn't advise hitching alone for either men or women but on the other hand, if there are more than two of you, you might have trouble persuading a driver to stop.

If you are going to try it, make sure you know the basics. There are two useful websites:
www.hitchwiki.org/en/Main_Page
www.digihitch.com

Motorbike tours

If you're a keen biker and want to include your bike in **gap-** travel plans, there aren't many places you couldn't go. There's an excellent website by UK couple Kevin and Julia Saunders who are double Guinness Book of Records winners for their bike expeditions around the planet. The site offers plenty of advice as well as the opportunity to join expeditions with guides and team leaders: **www.globebusters.com**

Bicycles

If you're feeling hyper-energetic, you could use your pedal-pushing power to get you around town and country. This is really popular in north Europe, especially Holland, where the ground tends to be flatter. Most travel agents would be able to point you in the right direction, or you can just rely on hiring bikes while you are out there - make sure you understand the rules of the road.

With a globally growing 'green awareness', there's been a real surge in promoting cycling in the UK and abroad. Weather and terrain permitting it's a wonderful way of seeing a city, or touring a region, be it Portugal, Sweden, Provence, Tuscany…

But why confine it to Europe? There are many places where bicycles can be hired and it's a great way of getting around.

You can also participate in some amazing **gap**-year programmes, such as cycling to raise sponsorship for worthwhile charities and community projects worldwide. But charities aside, just get on your bike and enjoy a closer contact with nature and its vast range of spectacular scenery - getting ever fitter - for example, the USA's Pacific West Coast, Guatemala to Honduras, the Andes to the glaciers of Patagonia, Nairobi to Dar es Salaam, Chiang Mai to Bangkok, the South Island mountains of New Zealand…

Take a look at:

www.responsibletravel.com for cycling and mountain biking holidays; also:

www.imba.com (the International Mountain Biking Association)

and:

www.cyclehire.co.nz/links.htm (independent cycle tours in New Zealand and worldwide links.)

visit: www.gap-year.com

Accommodation

Traditionally, hostels are the first option that springs to mind, whenever gappers or backpackers are looking for cheap accommodation.

Today there is a range of hostels available, which offer clean, safe and reasonably priced accommodation, some even have 'luxury' extras, such as internet connection, games rooms and laundry facilities.

However, safety can still vary widely and gappers often rely on *Rough Guide* or *Lonely Planet* guidebooks, or the word-of-mouth recommendations from other backpackers to find a suitable one.

Use your common sense and always check where the fire exits are when arriving at a hostel, because it's too late to look if there's already a fire and you're trying to get out of the building.

If you do find you're staying in a basic, no frills-style hostel, it's wise to make sure there's some ventilation when you have a bath or shower - faulty water heaters give off lethal and undetectable carbon monoxide fumes and will kill you without you realising it as you fall gently to sleep, never to wake up again.

Use your instincts - if you think the hostel's simply not up to scratch and too risky, go and find another one.

Hostelling International are the world's largest provider of tourist and backpacker accommodation, having spent the past 100 years helping people of all ages travel the world safely, confidently and affordably. They have 4,000 unique hostels in 90 countries worldwide, in major cities, towns and travel hubs as well as 'quirkier' venues such as ships, refurbished jumbo jets, ex-jails and lighthouses.

Here's what they told us:

the gap-year guidebook 2011

"For years hostelling has been the preferred option for gap year travellers. Staying in a hostel is a unique and positive experience, much more than just somewhere to stay. With hostels located throughout the world options for affordable, safe and secure accommodation are never far away. It ís a great way of seeing the world without blowing your budget and youíll meet people of all ages and nationalities who are doing the same thing.

"Facilities at hostels will vary, but most will offer shared and private bedrooms, self-catering kitchens and communal space where you can share experiences with like-minded people. Some hostels will have private en suite rooms, swimming pools, licensed restaurants and organised activities. That's the beauty of hostelling; you never have to stay in the same type of place twice.

"Experience traditional native dwellings, modern purpose-built city hubs, castles, boats and remote eco lodges all in one adventure. Any type of building can become 'home' for as long as you want it to be. Aside from providing accommodation hostelling is much more than that, it is a concept - one of helping people to meet, discover and enjoy the world."

Camping

If you're on a budget camping or caravanning can be worth considering though they're not options for some parts of the world and, particularly with camping, you need to think about whether you really want to carry all that extra equipment.

There are quite a few blogs where you can find out what camping's really like in the developed and developing world, from the USA to Oz and from Latin America to south Asia!

visit: www.gap-year.com

Try this one for reports of travellers' journeys, camping experiences and itineraries.
www.realtravel.com

Before you decide on camping though, take a look at this website which has guides on every conceivable aspect of what's involved:
http://halpi.com/category/everything_else/camping

According to the People's Media Co, many campsites are replacing tents with huts; usually they're in places close to areas where you can hike. You'll get a bed in a hut and use of other facilities so you only need a sleeping bag or sheet sleeping bag – no need to carry a tent. There's more on:
www.associatedcontent.com/article/16737/hut_hiking_around_the_world.html

Caravans, campervans and places to park them

Renting a caravan or travelling under your own steam with a camper van is another possibility - they call them Motorhomes in the US and it's easy to see why. They do have the advantage of giving you a secure place to leave your stuff and of not having to carry it all on your back but they're plainly not an option everywhere in the world.

Check out these websites:
www.campingo.com/campsite.html
www.internationalcampingclub.com/
www.eurocampings.co.uk/en/europe/
www.rentocamp.com/
www.trav.com/Campsites/Asia
www.allstays.com/Campgrounds-Australia/
www.familyparks.com.au/
www.takeabreak.com.au/caravanparks.htm

Or how about camping Bedouin style in Jordan? There's a site about ten miles north of Petra: www.bedouincamp.net/enter.html

According to the website Associated Content, many campsites are replacing tents with huts; usually they're in places close to hiking areas. You'll get a bed in a hut, and use of other facilities, so you only need a sleeping bag - no need to carry a tent. There's more on:
www.associatedcontent.com/article/16737/hut_hiking_around_the_world.html

Temple and monastery guesthouses

The main consideration for deciding to stay in a monastery or temple guesthouse, should not be your budget, though there's no denying that it's affordable for the budget traveller. It's also pointless to pretend that a male dominated culture doesn't exist in many parts of the world and guesthouses attached to temples and monasteries are therefore excellent places for women travelling alone to stay. Indeed for anyone wanting some place to be able to relax and not be constantly on guard, or if you're seeking a peaceful sanctuary and simplicity, religious guesthouses are ideal.

Some places prefer that you have *some* link with their faith, even if only through a historic extended-family link, but there is a strong tradition of offering refuge, safety and peace in any religious community that isn't a closed order.

Historically, the religious communities and monasteries of many faiths have provided hospice and hospital services to their surrounding communities. Much of our early medical knowledge developed from here too.

Changing economics have also meant their costs have risen and many temples and monasteries have had to be practical about raising income for their communities and for the upkeep of buildings, whose antiquity makes them costly to maintain. Most are therefore open to guests regardless of faith.

Having said that, if you are considering this option, be prepared for rooms and meals to be simple, facilities to be austere and for the community to be quiet at certain times of the day. There will be daily rituals to the life of the community and, like anywhere else, it's only polite to respect their customs. Obviously it's not an option that would suit some gappers.

But a chance to think, to recharge the spiritual batteries, to learn more about oneself or a particular faith, maybe to learn yoga or meditation, is what some gappers are looking for and it can be worth considering this option as part of a **gap-** programme.

Here are a couple of weblinks to give you a start:
www.gonomad.com/lodgings/0010/davis_monastery.html
www.salon.com/travel/advisor/1999/10/07/advisor/index.html

This link is to an article that will give you the basics on staying in religious guest houses and mentions several useful guidebooks, which list such lodgings, though these are mostly in Europe:
www.smartertravel.com/travel-advice/are-monasteries-and-conventsan-affordable-lodging-secret.html?id=2613061

Hotels

If you've been on the move for several weeks and careful with the budget, you can find your spirits are flagging from coping with the often Spartan conditions in budget hotels, hostels and the like.

A couple of days of comfort in a good hotel can be a worthwhile investment as a tonic, to give you time out to sort your stuff, get some laundry done, have a decent shower and sleep in a clean, comfortable bed before you set off again.

Most hotels around the world use the familiar one to five star rating system, where five is luxury and one is likely to be a flea-pit! But the symbols used can be anything from stars, diamonds and crowns to keys, suns, dots, rosettes and letters.

As with most things in life you get what you pay for, but prices will vary wildly depending on whether you're in peak tourism season or off-peak, currency rates and the costs of living in the country you're visiting, so you may be pleasantly surprised by the rates in some of the better hotels and find you can stretch your budget without reaching breaking point.

visit: www.gap-year.com

But equally, hotel ratings are done by human beings, and they can vary wildly depending on who did them and which search engine you might have used. The best advice is to look for reviews or ratings from ordinary hotel guests who have actually stayed in the hotel - and slept in the beds!

There are several sources of independent information. Most of the travellers' guidebooks have lists of hotels within the different price ranges, but you have to bear in mind that, particularly in the tourism and hospitality industries, things can change between the time of printing and when you arrive.

If you want to check out a hotel while you're travelling, try this website: www.tripadvisor.com

What makes this site special is that it's all written by travellers from their own experiences and it pulls no punches. There are more than 15 million posts on just about every place or topic you can think of, covering destinations all over the world - including some that might surprise you, like the Middle East, (Saudi Arabia, Jordan, United Arab Emirates to name a few). You just click on a map to research the area of the world you're interested in.

It contains information on the best - and worst - of hotels, from top ranking to budget hotels as well as B&Bs, hostels and speciality accommodation. It has forums where you can ask a question and get advice on medical and safety issues, specific to the country or city you're interested in.

For example, did you know that you can quell the worst symptoms of traveller diarrhoea with neat lime juice? This was a tip we found posted by a traveller in a forum on Egypt:

"Squeeze a couple of limes and drink the juice concentrated, with no water, a few times a day. It will act as a disinfectant and also will decrease the diarrhoea …

"Lime juice is an excellent natural disinfectant. So it is a good idea to buy some limes (vegetable sellers or supermarket), wash them and have them with you. If in doubt of anything that you are going to be eating or drinking (including water or drinks with ice) cut the limes and squeeze one or two on what you are going to consume. Have [often] used this trick and it never failed."

Other websites you could try for travellers' reviews are:
www.travelpost.com/

www.cranley.com/about_cranley.htm - This site was founded by Mike Murray and Joaquim Rodrigues, two British Chartered Accountants, following extensive research on travel trends and consumer needs, as well as their own personal travel experiences across over 70 countries, which they found highlighted a need for more detailed and consistent independent on-line hotel information *and* globally consistent independent hotel ratings. They have devised their own 12-point rating system with this in mind.

Useful websites for last-minute and affordable accommodation are:

www.japaneseguesthouses.com - has over 600 *ryokans* (inns) all over Japan and an English language site where you can easily make a reservation.

'Bargain Rooms' – www.roomauction.com - you pay below the standard

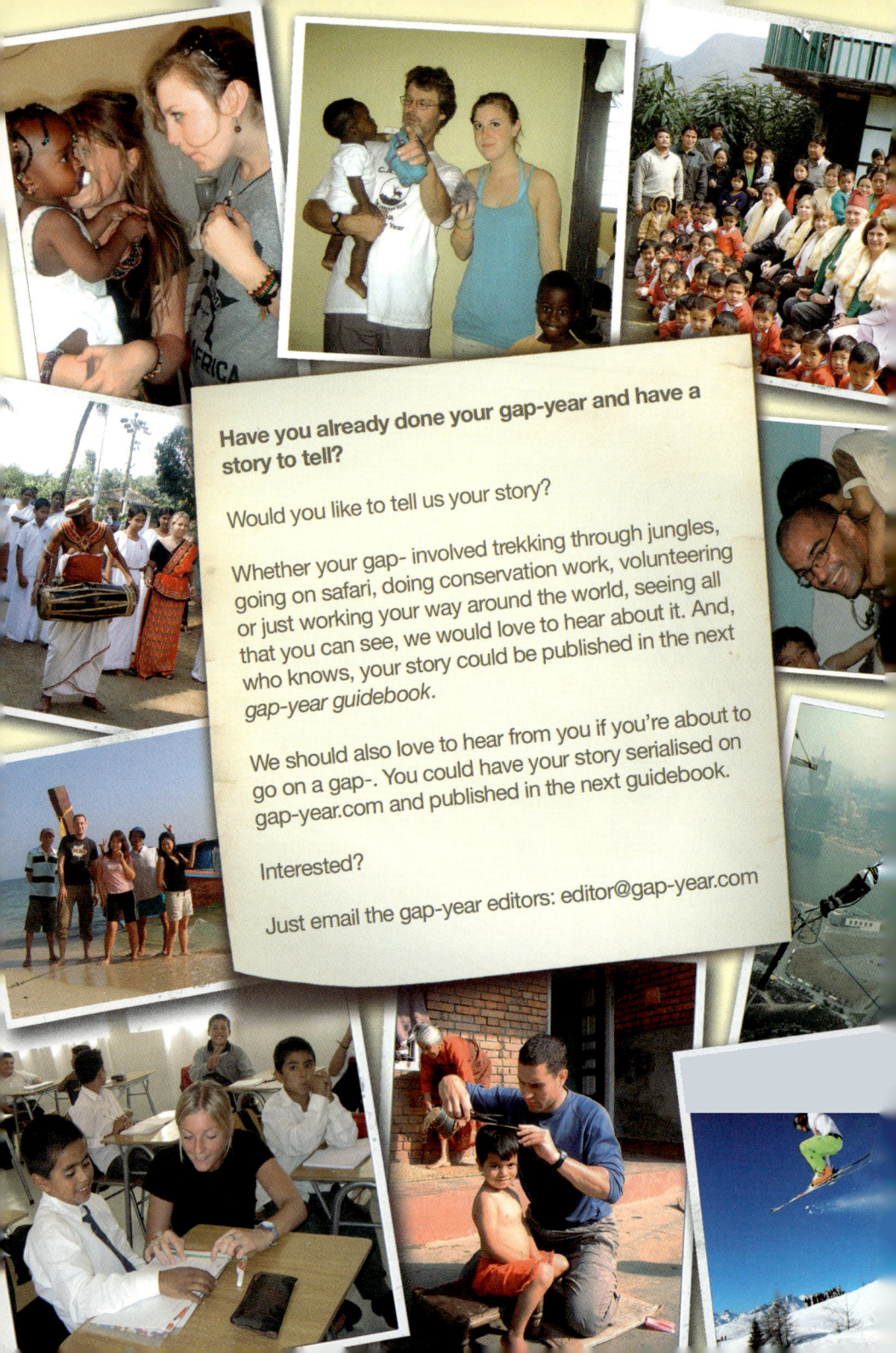

Have you already done your gap-year and have a story to tell?

Would you like to tell us your story?

Whether your gap- involved trekking through jungles, going on safari, doing conservation work, volunteering or just working your way around the world, seeing all that you can see, we would love to hear about it. And, who knows, your story could be published in the next *gap-year guidebook*.

We should also love to hear from you if you're about to go on a gap-. You could have your story serialised on gap-year.com and published in the next guidebook.

Interested?

Just email the gap-year editors: editor@gap-year.com

room rate by making the hotel a discreet offer, 'bidding' for the room.

www.laterooms.com - discount hotel rooms in UK and abroad; the low prices are genuine as they would rather see their rooms let out than not at all.

If you also have concerns about ethical tourism, whether it is the hotel's environmental impact or the conditions of its workers, the Ethical Consumer website has a report on these issues, which is downloadable as a PDF from: www.ethicalconsumer.org/FreeBuyersGuides/traveltransport/hotels.aspx
www.realtravel.com - has info on hotels and advice blogs from travellers.

Couch Surfing

This is the ultimate in finding free accommodation and, although there were safety concerns when this service first started, it's now had more than a million satisfied customers. But this not-for-profit organisation has a philosophy that's about more than that - it's about creating friendships and networks across the world.

Here's what they say on the safety issue:

"CouchSurfing has implemented several precautionary measures for the benefit of its surfers, hosts, and community. Every user is linked to the other users he or she knows in the system, through a network of references and friend links. In addition to the solid network with friend link-strength indicators and testimonials, we have our vouching and verification systems."

There's a lot more information on their website that should answer all your questions: www.couchsurfing.org/about.html

Hostelbookers.com, 52-54 High Holborn, Holborn, London WC1B 6RL
T: +44 (0) 207 406 1800
E: support@hostelbookers.com   W: www.hostelbookers.com

HostelBookers - the perfect choice for your gap-year trip
With over 18,000 properties in 3,500 destinations around the world, whatever adventure you have planned for your gap year you're guaranteed to find the accommodation you need on HostelBookers.com. What's more, we're the only independent hostel booking website that has NO BOOKING FEES, so the price you see is the price you pay.

We work closely with the properties on our site to give our customers the best value possible, which has helped to make us 8.7% cheaper than Hostelworld. In fact, we are so confident that our prices can't be beaten that we even back it up with a lowest price guarantee - find a property listed on HostelBookers.com cheaper elsewhere on the internet (for the same dates of travel and booking conditions) and we'll refund DOUBLE the difference. HostelBookers has an active Facebook following with over 20,000 fans participating in regular competitions and sharing tips and advice with fellow travellers. You can join us at www.facebook.com/hostelbookers and stay in touch whilst you're away. We also have the most popular backpacker newsletter in the world, find out what all the fuss is about on HostelBookers. So wherever you are and wherever youíre going, book with HostelBookers to ensure you have more left in your budget for your experience.

Travelling and accommodation

Accommodation

An Óige - Irish Youth Hostel Association
61 Mountjoy Street,
Dublin, 7 Ireland

E: mailbox@anoige.ie
F: +353 01 830 5808
www.anoige.ie

The Irish YHA consists of 26 hostels throughout Ireland. They have a range of hostels, from large city centre buildings to small hostels in rural settings. Online booking available.

Hostelbookers.com
52-54 High Holborn,
Holborn,
London, WC1B 6RL UK

E: support@hostelbookers.com
T: +44 (0) 207 406 1800
F: +44 (0) 207 406 1801
www.hostelbookers.com

Youth hostels and cheap accommodation in over 2500 destinations worldwide, with no booking fees.

Hostelling International
2nd floor, Gate House,
Fretherne Road,
Welwyn Garden City, AL8 6RD UK

E: office@hihostels.com
T: +44 (0) 1707 324170
F: +44 (0) 1707 323980
www.hihostels.com

Research, plan and book your trip online with Hostelling International. HI hostels are a great way to travel the world safely – explore new cultures and meet friends.

Hostelling International - Canada
205 Catherine Street,
Ottawa ON, K2P 1C3 Canada

E: info@hihostels.ca
F: +1 613 237 7868
www.hihostels.ca

Contact details for the Canadian branch of this worldwide hostel service.

Hostelling International - Iceland
Sundlaugarvegur 34,
Reykjavik, 105 Iceland

E: info@hostel.is
F: +354 588 9201
www.hostel.is

Hostelling International Iceland has twenty-five hostels all around the country, offering comfortable, budget accommodation which is open to all ages.

Hostelling International - USA
National Administrative Office, 8401 Colesville Road,
Suite 600,
Silver Spring, MD 20910 USA

E: hostels@hiusa.org
T: +1 301 495 1240
F: +1 301 495 6697
www.hiusa.org

Hostelling International USA has a network of nearly 80 hostels throughout the United States that are inexpensive, safe and clean.

the gap-year guidebook 2011

Hostelling International
Discover the real hostel experience

say **HI** *to the world*

- **Global:** access a network of 4000 hostels in 90 countries
- **Trustworthy:** stay in quality assured safe hostels
- **Unique:** boats, castles, eco lodges, mountain retreats and city hubs

With Hostelling International you can research, plan and book your trip online. HI hostels are a great way to travel the world safely – explore new cultures, meet friends and share experiences. Plus an HI membership will save you money with fantastic offers and discounts.

Visit us online: www.hihostels.com

- Book your stay and pay just 5% deposit!
- Make multi-stage bookings for only one booking fee!
- Download FREE hostel guides and planning tools
- Access top tips and customer ratings

Scottish Youth Hostel Association
7 Glebe Crescent,
Stirling, FK8 2JA UK

E: reservations@syha.org.uk
F: +44 (0) 1786 881 333
www.syha.org.uk

There are over 70 SYHA hostels throughout Scotland. You can book online but you must be a member - you can join at the time of booking. Registered Charity No. SC013138.

Swiss Youth Hostels
Schaffhauserstrasse 14,
8042 Zürich, Switzerland

E: booking@youthhostel.ch
F: +41 (0) 44 360 1460
www.youthhostel.ch

They have 58 hostels which they divide into three categories: city, countryside and mountain. They range from traditional Swiss chalets, to modern buildings, large historic houses and even one or two castles.

Youth Hostel Association New Zealand
National Office, Level 1, 166 Moorhouse Avenue,
PO Box 436,
Christchurch, New Zealand

T: +64 (0) 3379 9970
F: +64 (0) 3365 4476
www.yha.co.nz

Budget accommodation in New Zealand. Hostels open to all ages. Book online before you go.

Youth Hostels Association of India
5 Nyaya Marg,
Chanakyapuri,
New Delhi, 110021 India

E: info@yhaindia.org
T: +91 (011) 2611 0250
F: +91 (011) 2611 3469
www.yhaindia.org

Youth Hostel Association in India. Over 200 hostels which can be booked online through their website.

Car Hire

Spaceships
31 Beach Rd,
Auckland, 1010 New Zealand

E: info@spaceships.tv
F: +64 9 307 5759
www.spaceships.tv

Company offering campervan rentals in New Zealand and Australia.

Travellers Auto Barn
177 William Street,
Kings Cross,
Sydney, NSW 2011 Australia

E: info@travellers-autobarn.com.au
T: +61 2 8323 1500 (outside Australia)
T: 1800 674 374 (within Australia)
www.travellers-autobarn.com.au

There is no cheaper way to travel around Australia than in any of our campervans or stationwagons – we have offices all around Australia and all our rentals come with unlimited KM, free insurance, special discounts and lots of other things…

the gap-year guidebook 2011

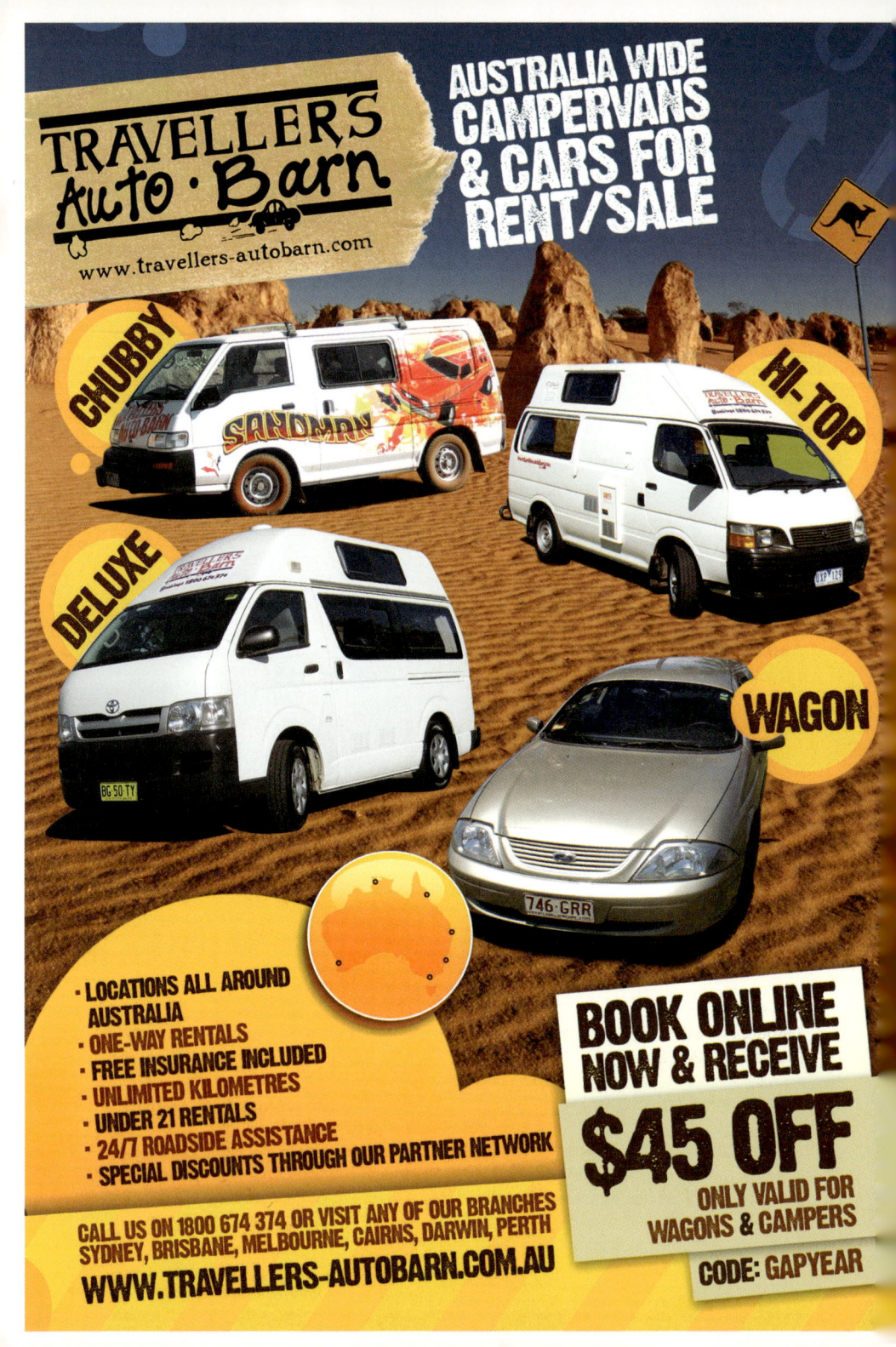

TRAVELLERS Auto·Barn
www.travellers-autobarn.com

AUSTRALIA WIDE CAMPERVANS & CARS FOR RENT/SALE

- CHUBBY
- HI-TOP
- DELUXE
- WAGON

- LOCATIONS ALL AROUND AUSTRALIA
- ONE-WAY RENTALS
- FREE INSURANCE INCLUDED
- UNLIMITED KILOMETRES
- UNDER 21 RENTALS
- 24/7 ROADSIDE ASSISTANCE
- SPECIAL DISCOUNTS THROUGH OUR PARTNER NETWORK

CALL US ON 1800 674 374 OR VISIT ANY OF OUR BRANCHES
SYDNEY, BRISBANE, MELBOURNE, CAIRNS, DARWIN, PERTH

WWW.TRAVELLERS-AUTOBARN.COM.AU

BOOK ONLINE NOW & RECEIVE
$45 OFF
ONLY VALID FOR WAGONS & CAMPERS

CODE: GAPYEAR

Getting about

British Midland Airways Ltd
Donington Hall,
Castle Donington, DE74 2SB UK

F: +44 (0) 1709 314993
www.flybmi.com

Low cost flights to Europe and America.

Cheap Flights
49 Marylebone High Street,
Marylebone,
London, W1U 5HJ UK

www.cheapflights.co.uk

This useful website does not sell tickets but can point you in the right direction to get the best deal.

EasyJet Plc
Hangar 89,
London Luton Airport,
Luton, LU2 9PF UK

T: + 44 (0) 871 244 2366
www.easyjet.co.uk

Offers cheap flights to European destinations with further reductions if you book over the internet.

Ebookers (Flightbookers Ltd)
5th Floor,
140 Aldersgate Street,
London, EC1A 4HY UK

T: +44 (0) 208 602 0830
www.ebookers.com

Cheap flights can be booked through their website.

Florence by Bike
Via San Zanobi, 120 ,
Firenze, 50129 Italy

E: info@florencebybike.it
F: +39 055 488992
www.florencebybike.it

Scooter, motorbike and bike rental company in Florence. Also sells clothing and accessories as well as bike parts.

International Rail
Chase House,
Gilbert Street,
Ropley, SO24 0BY UK

E: sales@internationalrail.com
T: +44 (0) 870 084 1410
www.internationalrail.com/interrail/interrail-passes.asp

InterRail Pass provides unlimited travel on the sophisticated European Rail network. The pass is very flexible allowing you to choose either one country or all 30 countries.

the gap-year guidebook 2011

Kiwi Experience
195 Parnell Road,
Parnell,
Auckland, 1052 New Zealand

T: +64 9 369 9410
F: +64 9 366 1374
www.kiwiexperience.com

Extensive bus network covering the whole of New Zealand. Passes valid for 12 months.

Magic Travellers Network
120 Albert Street,
PO Box 949,
Auckland, New Zealand

E: info@magicbus.co.nz
T: +64 9 358 5600
F: +64 9 358 3471
www.magicbus.co.nz

Flexible transport company for backpackers and independent travellers around New Zealand.

OzBus UK Ltd
Unit 6A, Home Farm,
Diddington, Cambridgeshire PE19 5XU UK

E: info@oz-bus.com
T: (UK) 0800 7319427 (Int) +44 1480 810080
www.ozbus.co.uk

Oz-Bus operate the only regular hop on/hop off bus service between London and Sydney for all ages of Adventure Travellers. Oz-Bus also offer The Hippie Trail, Oz-Bus Africa and Oz-Bus Down Under.

Rail Europe Ltd.
34 Tower View,
Kings Hill,
West Malling, ME19 4ED UK

E: reservations@raileurope.co.uk
T: 08448 484 064
www.raileurope.co.uk

Specializes in selling tickets and passes for travel throughout Europe by train. Available to buy online or via their call centre.

Ryanair
Satelite 3,
London Stansted Airport,
Stansted, CM24 1RW UK

www.ryanair.com

Low cost airline to European destinations – many outward flights are actually free! – but make sure you check how much the return flight will be.

Stray Ltd
31 Beach Road,
Auckland Central, New Zealand

E: enquiries@straytravel.co.nz
F: +64 (0) 9 526 2141
www.straytravel.com

Stray is New Zealand's fastest growing backpacker bus network - designed for travellers who want to get off the beaten track

visit: www.gap-year.com

Thomas Cook
The Thomas Cook Business Park,
Coningsby Road,
Peterborough, PE3 8SB UK

www.thomascook.com

General travel agent with high street branches offering flights and late deals.

Travellers Contact Point
7th Floor, Dymocks Building,
428 George Street,
Sydney, NSW 2000 Australia

E: info@travellers.com.au
T: +61 (0) 2 9221 8744
F: +61 (0) 2 9221 3745
www.travellers.com.au

A specialist travel agency for independent and working holiday travellers. We have shops in Australia, New Zealand and the UK.

Ze-Bus
203 rue des artisans,
St Jean de Luz , 64 500 France

E: info@ze-bus.com
www.ze-bus.com

Flexible transport enabling you to discover France. No fixed routes are involved as the passengers decide where to go, where to start and where to stop. Pass and tickets are valid for the entire season.

Tours

Acacia Adventure Holidays
LGF 23A Craven Terrace ,
Lancaster Gate, Bayswater,
London, W2 3QH UK

E: info@acacia-africa.com
T: +44 (0) 20 7706 4700
F: +44 (0) 20 7706 4686
www.acacia-africa.com

Acacia offers exciting and affordable overland tours and small group safaris across Africa. Enjoy game viewing, desert adventures, beach breaks, dive courses or trekking!

Adventure Tours Australia
72 The Parade,,
Norwood,
South Australia, 5067 Australia

E: marketing@adventuretours.com.au
T: +61 8 8132 8230
F: 61 (0)8 8132 1785
www.adventuretours.com.au

Adventure Tours Australia is an award winning company specialising in small group nature-based tours for the active traveller.

Adventure Tours NZ
50 Fort St,
Auckland, 1010 New Zealand

E: reservations@adventuretoursnz.co.nz
www.adventuretours.com.au

Adventure Tours NZ offer specialised small group nature-based tours for the active traveller on a budget. Go off the beaten track, see unique scenery and wildlife.

the gap-year guidebook 2011

Adventure Travellers Club P Ltd
PO Box 12205,
Nayabazaar,
Kathmandu, 12205 Nepal

E: info@nepaltravellers.com
T: +44(0)2033718994
F: +977 1 438 5484
www.nepaltravellers.com

Offers trekking and adventure tours in Nepal, Tibet, Bhutan and Indian regions. Includes camping, peak climbing, jungle safaris, river rafting and much more.

Afreco Tours
2 Manor Mews, Shalstone Manor,
Main Street,
Shalstone, MK18 5LT UK

E: info@afrecotours.com
T: +44 (0) 845 812 8222
www.afrecotours.com

Afreco Tours specialises in African safari ranger training and wildlife adventures - from four days to one year.

Africa Travel Co
PO Box 50425,
Cape Town, 8002 South Africa

E: ressa@africatravelco.com
F: +27 21 3851573
www.africatravelco.com

Specialists in trips around Africa ranging from three to 56 days.

African Horizons
PO Box 61170,
216 Mosi O Tunya Road,
Livingstone, Zambia

E: horizons@zamnet.zm
T: +260 213 323 433
www.volunteerzambia.com

Volunteer Zambia staff have over ten years experience dealing with toursim/eco-tourism and volunteer support within Zambia.

Alaska Heritage Tours
509 W 4th Avenue,
Anchorage, AK 99501 USA

E: info@AlaskaHeritageTours.com
www.alaskaheritagetours.com

At Alaska Heritage Tours we strive to give you the best of Alaska, the way you want it – with pre-packaged Alaska vacations and itineraries. Explore Alaska's top destinations.

Alpine Exploratory
9 Copperfield Street,
Wigan, WN1 2DZ UK

E: info@alpineexploratory.com
F: +44 (0) 1942 233 829
www.alpineexploratory.com

Alpine Exploratory specialises in self-guided walking and trekking tours in Europe. Full programme of guided tours also offered, as well as bespoke holidays.

visit: www.gap-year.com

Andean Trails
The Clockhouse, Bonnington Mill Business Centre,
72 Newhaven Road,
Edinburgh, EH6 4JG UK

E: info@andeantrails.co.uk
T: +44 (0) 131 467 7086
www.andeantrails.co.uk

Andean Trails is an owner run specialist adventure travel company organising small group tours to Peru, Bolivia, Ecuador, Cuba, Guyana and Patagonia.

Argentina Travel Plan
Intergen House, 7th floor,
65-67 Western Road, BN3 2JQ UK

T: +44 (0)1273 322 059

Create your own trip in Argentina. For independent travellers who don't want to do a group tour.

Australia Travel Plan
7th Floor, Intergen House,
65 – 67 Western Road,
Hove, BN3 2JQ UK

T: +44 (0)1273 32 2055
www.australiatravelplan.co.uk

Create your own trip in Australia. For independent travellers who don't want to do a group tour.

Backpacker Travel Auctions
Safari Pete,
PO Box 1465,
St Kilda South, VIC 3205 Australia

E: info@backpackertravelauctions.com
T: + 61 395 3459 80
F: +61 396 9999 01
www.backpackertravelauctions.com

Safari Pete can offer you directions to the best deals on tours around Australia and New Zealand.

Bicycling Empowerment Network
PO Box 31561,
Tokai,
Cape Town, 7966 South Africa

E: andrew@benbikes.org.za
T: +27 21 713 3634
F: +27 21 712 7492
www.benbikes.org.za

BEN, a non-profit organisation, promotes the use and sale of refurbished bicycles. They conduct Bicycle Township Tours empowering local people and winning International Responsible Tourism Awards.

Black Feather -
The Wilderness Adventure Company
250 McNaughts Road, RR#3,
Parry Sound ON, P2A 2W9 Canada

E: info@blackfeather.com
T: +1 705 746 1372
F: +1 705 746 7048
www.blackfeather.com

Company offering canoeing and kayaking trips and expeditions to remote artic locations. Offer women only trips and will do a customized trip for groups of four or more.

Borneo Anchor Travel & Tours/Sabah Divers
G27, Ground Floor,
Wisma Sabah,
Kota Kinabalu, 88000 Malaysia

E: sabahdivers2u@yahoo.com
T: +60 88 256 483
F: +60 88 255 482
www.borneoanchortours.com

They offer various wildlife, nature and adventure packages all over Sabah, Malaysian Borneo.

Brazil Travel Plan
Intergen House, 7th floor,
65-67 Western Road, BN3 2JQ UK

T: +44 (0)1273 322 059

Create your own trip in Brazil. For independent travellers who don't want to do a group tour.

BridgeClimb Sydney
5 Cumberland Street,
The Rocks,
Sydney, NSW 2000 Australia

E: admin@bridgeclimb.com
T: +61 (0) 2 8274 7777
F: +61 (0) 2 9240 1122
www.bridgeclimb.com

BridgeClimb provides the ultimate experience of Sydney, with guided climbs to the top of the world famous Sydney Harbour Bridge. Climbers can choose between The Express Climb, The Bridge Climb or The Discovery Climb.

Cambodia Travel Plan
7th Floor, Intergen House,
65–67 Western Road,
Hove, BN3 2JQ UK

T: +44 (0)1273 322 042
www.cambodiatravelplan.co.uk

Create your own trip in Cambodia. For independent travellers who don't want to do a group tour.

Cape York Motorcycle Adventures
PO Box 105,
Clifton Beach, QLD 4879 Australia

E: adventures@capeyorkmotorcycles.com.au
F: +61 (07) 4059 0801
www.capeyorkmotorcycles.com.au

Motorcycle tours in north Queensland from one to eight days duration. Private charter also available. They have their own motorbikes and a support vehicle that accompanies the longer excursions.

China Travel Plan
7th Floor, Intergen House,
65 – 67 Western Road,
Hove, BN3 2JQ UK

T: +44 (0)1273 322 048
www.chinatravelplan.co.uk

Create your own trip in China. For independent travellers who don't want to do a group tour.

visit: www.gap-year.com

Cordillera Blanca Trek
Av Interoceanica 198, Nueva Florida,
Huaraz,
Ancahas, Peru

E: info@cordillerablancatrek.com
T: +51 (0) 43 427 635
F: +51 (0) 43 966 6296
www.cordillerablancatrek.com

Offers treks in Machu Picchu, a volcanco tour and more.

Cuba Travel Plan
Intergen House, 7th floor,
65-67 Western Road, BN3 2JQ UK

T: +44 (0)1273 322 059

Create your own trip in Cuba. For independent travellers who don't want to do a group tour.

Do Something Different
Third Floor,
16 Bromells Road, Clapham,
London, SW4 0BG UK

E: contact-us@dosomethingdifferent.com
T: +44 (0) 20 8090 3790
www.dosomethingdifferent.com

Want to dog sled in the Rockies? Take a Hong Kong Island or helicopter tour? Or climb Auckland Harbour Bridge?

Dolphin Encounter
96 Esplanade,
Kaikoura, 7300 New Zealand

E: info@dolphin.co.nz
F: +64 3 319 6534
www.dolphin.co.nz

Swim or watch dolphins in Kaikoura. You do need to book in advance as there is a limit to how many swimmers are allowed per trip.

Dorset Expeditionary Society/ Leading Edge Expeditions
Lupins Business Centre,
1-3 Greenhill,
Weymouth, DT4 7SP UK

E: admin@leadingedge.org.uk
T: +44 (0) 1305 816222
F: +44 (0) 1305 775 599
www.dorsetexp.co.uk

Dorset Expeditionary Society promotes adventurous expeditions to remote parts of the world. Open to all. May qualify for two sections of the Duke of Edinburgh's Gold Award.

Dragoman
Camp Green,
Debenham, IP14 6LA UK

E: info@dragoman.co.uk
F: +44 (0) 1728 861127
www.dragoman.co.uk

Overlanding is stil the most authentic and accessible way of discovering new countries, their people and culture. Join us in Africa, South America and Asia.

the gap-year guidebook 2011

Eco Trails Kerala
Tharavadu Heritage Home, Kumarakom, Kottayam,
Kerala,
Alleppey Kumarakom, 686563 India

E: mail@ecotourskerala.com
T: +91 48125 24447
www.ecotourskerala.com

This tour company provides budget holiday tour packages in the Kumarakom and Alleppey Backwater areas.

Egypt Horse Tours
Giza,
Cairo, Egypt

E: enquiries@egypthorsetours.com
www.egypthorsetours.com

We offer Egyptian horse riding (desert and sightseeing tours). We have well kept horses to suit all abilities we welcome those who have experience with horses to work in our stables.

Egypt Travel Plan
Intergen House, 7th floor,
65-67 Western Road BN3 2JQ UK

T: +44 (0)1273 322 059

Create your own trip in Egypt. For independent travellers who don't want to do a group tour.

Equine Adventures
Long Barn South,
Sutton Manor Farm,
Bishop's Sutton, SO24 0AA UK

E: sales@equineadventures.co.uk
T: +44 (0) 1962 737647
www.equineadventures.co.uk

Horse riding tours available, in Australasia, Asia, Africa, Europe and the Americas.

Equitours -
Worldwide Horseback Riding Adventures
PO Box 807,
10 Stalnaker Street,
Dubois, USA

T: +1 307 455 3363
F: +1 307 455 2354
www.ridingtours.com

With over 30 years experience, Equitours offer tested and tried horseback tours on six continents. Rides from three to eight days (or longer) for riders of all experience.

Explore Worldwide Ltd
Nelson House,
55 Victoria Road,
Farnborough, GU14 7PA UK

E: info@explore.co.uk
T: +44 (0) 844 499 0901
F: +44 (0) 1252 391 110
www.explore.co.uk

Company organising special tours in small groups. Types of worldwide tours available are walking holidays, dog-sledding, wildlife and railway tours amongst others.

visit: www.gap-year.com

Fair Dinkum Bike Tours
PO Box 7442,
Cairns, Australia

E: dave@fairdinkumbiketours.com.au
www.fairdinkumbiketours.com.au

Offer a range of tours using local guides to cater for all levels.

Flying Kiwi
Flying Kiwi Wilderness Expeditions Ltd., T: int. +64 3 547 0171 uk 0845 224 3296
48 Forests Road, Stoke,
Nelson, PO Box 680 New Zealand

E: info@flyingkiwi.com
F: +64 3 547 0173
www.flyingkiwi.com

Flying Kiwi bus tours around New Zealand offer a unique and fun experience. Camping or cabin options are available in exciting locations and usually meals are included.

Fräulein Maria's Bicycle Tours
Dipl.Sptl.Rupert Riedl,
Meeting Point Mirabellgardens,
Salzburg, Austria

E: biketour@aon.at
T: +43 650 3426297
www.mariasbicycletours.com

Maria's Bicycle tours take you to the main attractions from the film The Sound Of Music! The tour lasts three hours with stop points along the way and operates between May and September.

Go Differently Ltd
19 West Road,
Saffron Walden, CB11 3DS UK

E: info@godifferently.com
www.godifferently.com

Company offering small-group, short-term volunteering and tailor-made holidays based on the appreciation and respect of the local environment and people.

Grayline Tours of Hong Kong
5/F, Cheong Hing Building,
72 Nathan Road,
Tsim Sha Tsui, PR China

E: sales@grayline.com.hk
T: +852 2368 7111
F: +852 2721 9029
www.grayline.com.hk

Special day tours around Hong Kong such as the Bun Festival and island hopping tour or a tour to Po Lin Monastary on Lantau Island.

Haka Tours
115 Hulverstone Drive,
Avondale,
Christchurch 7, New Zealand

E: info@hakatours.com
T: +64 3 980 4252
www.hakatours.com

Haka Tours represents the ultimate in New Zealand adventure holidays, from small group adventures to New Zealand snow tours exploring the impressive Southern Alps and the active volcanoes of the North.

the gap-year guidebook 2011

High & Wild
The Well House,
Chydyok Road,
East Chaldon, DT2 8DN UK

E: adventures@highandwild.co.uk
T: +44 (0)845 0047801
F: +44 (0)1305 852862
www.highandwild.co.uk

High and Wild plan some of the most unusual and exciting adventures to destinations worldwide.

High Places Ltd
Globe Centre,
Penistone Road,
Sheffield, S6 3AE UK

E: treks@highplaces.co.uk
T: +44 (0) 114 275 7500
F: +44 (0) 114 275 3870
www.highplaces.co.uk

Independent specialist trekking company organising tours to 22 countries.

Highland Experience Tours
Loch Ness Discovery Centre, 1 Parliament Square,
Highstreet,
Edinburgh, UK

E: info@highlandexperience.com
T: +44 (0)131 2261414
www.highlandexperience.com

Travel company offering one day and private tours around Scotland, such as a two day highland tour, a whisky tasting tour, or a tour of Scotland personalised to your own requirements.

In the Saddle Ltd
Reaside, Neen Savage,
Cleobury Mortimer, DY14 8ES UK

E: rides@inthesaddle.com
www.inthesaddle.com

Specializes in horse riding holidays all over the world, catering for all levels of experience. From ranches in the Rocky Mountain states of Montana and Wyoming, to expeditions in remote and unexplored parts of the world.

India Travel Plan
7th Floor, Intergen House,
65 – 67 Western Road,
Hove, BN3 2JQ UK

T: +44 (0)1273 322 044
www.indiatravelplan.co.uk

Create your own trip in India. For independent travellers who don't want to do a group tour.

Indonesia Travel Plan
7th Floor, Intergen House,
65 – 67 Western Road,
Hove, BN3 2JQ UK

T: +44 (0)1273 322 052
www.indonesiatravelplan.co.uk

Create your own trip in Indonesia. For independent travellers who don't want to do a group tour.

visit: www.gap-year.com

Intrepid Travel
76 Upper Street,
Islington,
London, N1 0NU UK

E: islington@intrepidtravel.com
T: +44 (0) 207 354 6169
F: +44 (0) 207 354 6167
www.intrepidtravel.com

Variety of worldwide tours on offer ranging from 'comfort' to 'intrepid'

Joint Ventures
Joint Ventures, Gwexintaba,
Lusikisiki,
Port St John's, 5120 South Africa

E: louis@jointventures.co.za
T: +27 8326 85611
www.jointventures.co.za

Their vision is: 'Bringing people together to experience the natural beauty of most extreme nature in untouched state, to enhance the outdoor activities and to empower and facilitate the lives of those living the ways of ancient civilization.'

Jungle Surfing Canopy Tours
Keydane Pty Ltd,
24 Camelot Close,
Cape Tribulation, QLD 4873 Australia

E: info@junglesurfingcanopytours.com
T: +617 409 80043
F: +617 409 80065
www.junglesurfing.com.au

Night walks in a tropical rainforest or jungle surf through the Daintree Rainforest.

Kande Horse Trails
Box 22,
The Stables,
Kande, Malawi

E: info@kandehorse.com
T: +265 (0) 8500416
www.kandehorse.com

Experience the Malawi bush on horseback. All ages and riding abilities catered for.

Kenya Travel Plan
7th Floor, Intergen House,
65 – 67 Western Road,
Hove, BN3 2JQ UK

T: +44 (0)1273 322 053
www.kenyatravelplan.co.uk

Create your own trip in Kenya. For independent travellers who don't want to do a group tour.

KT Adventure
869-HongHa-HoanKiem,
Hanoi, 084 Vietnam

E: huongali0310@yahoo.com
F: +84 4 39327297
www.vivutravel.com

KT Adventure, part of Vivu Travel, offer specialised tours in Vietnam, from adventure tours to motorbiking.

Kudu Expeditions Ltd
Unit 13, Court Farm Business Park,
Bishops Frome, WR6 5AY UK

E: info@kuduexpeditions.com
www.kuduexpeditions.com

Explore the world by motorcycle. Amazing trips, from two week multi-country tours to four month trans-continental expeditions, designed to challenge and inspire you.

the gap-year guidebook 2011

Kuoni Challenge for Charity
Kuoni House,
Deepdene Avenue,
Dorking, RH5 4AZ UK

E: info@challengeforcharity.co.uk
T: +44 (0) 1306 744477
www.challengeforcharity.co.uk

Kuoni's challenge for charity webpage lists various opportunities for people to raise money for a charity of their choice in exotic destinations.

Laos Travel Plan
7th Floor, Intergen House,
65 – 67 Western Road,
Hove, BN3 2JQ UK

T: +44 (0)1273 322 043
www.laostravelplan.co.uk

Create your own trip in Laos. For independent travellers who don't want to do a group tour.

Live Travel
154 Nelson Road,
Twickenham, TW2 7BU UK

E: phil.haines@live-travel.com
www.live-travel.com

Personalised travel plans offered as well as group tours.

Malaysia Travel Plan
7th Floor , Intergen House,
65 – 67 Western Road,
Hove, BN3 2JQ UK

T: +44 (0)1273 322 054
www.malaysiatravelplan.co.uk

Create your own trip in Malaysia. For independent travellers who don't want to do a group tour.

Melbourne Street Art Tour
110 Franklin Street,
Melbourne, VIC 3000 Australia

E: booking@melbournestreettours.com
www.melbournestreettours.com

Melbourne Street Art Tours, led by one of Melbourne's elite street art stars, gives you an overview of the Melbourne underground street art scene.

Mexico Travel Plan
7th Floor, Intergen House,
65 – 67 Western Road,
Hove, BN3 2JQ UK

T: +44 (0)1273 322 046
www.mexicotravelplan.co.uk

Create your own trip in Mexico. For independent travellers who don't want to do a group tour.

visit: www.gap-year.com

Morocco Travel Plan
7th Floor, Intergen House,
65 – 67 Western Road,
Hove, BN3 2JQ UK

T: +44 (0)1273 322 056
www.moroccotravelplan.co.uk

Follow the Berber trail through Atlas Mountain villages, sleep in Sahara Desert tents and traditional riads, munch couscous in the souqs and take it easy on the beaches of Agadir.
We'll help you build your own Morocco adventure.

Mountain Kingdoms Ltd
Old Crown House,
18 Market Street,
Wotton-under-Edge, GL12 7AE UK

E: info@mountainkingdoms.com
T: +44 (0)1453 844400
www.mountainkingdoms.com

Himalayan Kingdoms is the UK's foremost quality trekking company, running treks and tours to the great mountain ranges of the world.

Nepal Travel Plan
7th Floor , Intergen House,
65 – 67 Western Road,
Hove, BN3 2JQ UK

T: +44 (0)1273 322 045
www.nepaltravelplan.co.uk

Create your own trip in Nepal. For independent travellers who don't want to do a group tour.

Olympic Bike Travel
Adelianos Kampos 32,
Rethymnon, GR-74100 Greece

E: info@olympicbike.com
www.olympicbike.com

A variety of bike tours available for all ages. From a ride down the highest mountain in Greece, Psiloritis, to a bike and hiking tour to the Myli gorge.

On The Go Tours
68 North End Road,
West Kensington,
London, W14 9EP UK

E: info@onthegotours.com
T: +44 (0) 207 371 1113
F: +44 (0) 207 471 6414
www.onthegotours.com

Special tours such as solar eclipse tours and railways of the Raj can be arranged.

Outbike
The Adventure Collective,
PO Box 848,
Unley BC, SA 5061 Australia

T: +61 1300 948 911
F: +61 1300 948 339
www.outbike.com.au

Bike ride across Australia. Definitely a once in a lifetime experience.

Build Your Own Trip

Sail down the Nile on a Dahabiya

Trek the Annapurna Circuit

Sleep in a floating hut on the River Kwai

Piscos and Posadas in the Andes

Stay in a Swazi beehive hut

Using our unique bite-sized tours you can piece together your own trip, your way.

Choose something action packed or a little more laid back - it's completely up to you.

Offering independent travel in over 20 destinations around the world.

Travel at your own pace.

www.rickshawtravel.co.uk

RICKSHAW TRAVEL

ABTA
ABTA No. YO484

ATOL 9728 PROTECTED

Palmar Voyages
Alemania N31-77 &,
Avenue Mariana de Jesús,
Quito, Ecuador

E: info@palmarvoyages.com
T: +593 (2) 2569 809
F: +593 (2) 2506 915
www.palmarvoyages.com

Tailor-made programmes for tours in Ecuador, Peru, South America, the Andes and the Galapagos Islands.

Pathfinders Africa
11 Philips Ave,
Belgravia,
Harare, Zimbabwe

E: info@pathfindersafrica.com
T: +263 (0)4 702814
www.pathfindersafrica.com

Pathfinders Africa is an African-based expedition company that operates from Zimbabwe. Developed to meet the needs of the adventurous traveller, Pathfinders' over-riding philosophy is of friendliness and individuality.

Peregrine Adventures Ltd
First Floor, 8 Clerewater Place ,
Lower Way ,
Thatcham , RG19 3RF UK

E: sales@peregrineadventures.co.uk
T: +44 0844 736 0170
F: +44 01635 872 758
www.peregrineadventures.com

Peregrine offer small group adventure tours worldwide. They offer a vast range of tours from polar expeditions to trekking the Himalayas.

Peru Travel Plan
Intergen House, 7th floor,
65-67 Western Road, BN3 2JQ UK

T: +44 (0)1273 322 059

Create your own trip in Peru. For independent travellers who don't want to do a group tour.

Pura Aventura
18 Bond Street,
Brighton, BN1 1RD UK

E: info@pura-aventura.com
F: +44 (0) 1273 676 774
www.pura-aventura.com

Various beautiful tailor-made tours in exotic locations. Career break to fulfil a long held dream or a special diversion on your gap-year perhaps?

Rickshaw Travel
8th Floor, Intergen House,
65-67 Western Road,
Hove, BN3 2JQ UK

E: info@rickshawtravel.co.uk
T: +44 (0) 1273 320 580
www.rickshawtravel.co.uk

Rickshaw Travel is a UK based ABTA/ATOL bonded travel operator, that uses locally owned accommodation with an authentic feel that is a cut above the usual backpacker haunts.

the gap-year guidebook 2011

Ride With Us
PO Box 936,
St Albans, AL1 9GL UK

E: sales@ridewithustours.co.uk
www.ridewithustours.co.uk

Organised motorcycle holidays around western and eastern Europe that offer something for everyone regardless of their touring experience.

Saddle Skedaddle
Ouseburn Building,
East Quayside,
Newcastle upon Tyne, UK

E: info@skedaddle.co.uk
T: +44 (0)191 265 1110
www.skedaddle.co.uk

Some say there is no better way to see a country, its culture, its wildlife and its people, than by bike! This company offers off-road, road or leisure cycling.

Safari Par Excellence
UK Head Office,
Ermington Mill,
Ivybridge, PL21 9NT UK

E: info@zambezi.co.uk
T: +44 (0) 1548 830 059
F: +44 (0) 870 094 1881
www.zambezi.co.uk

Safari company with a 'no fuss or frills' ethos. They cover Zimbabwe, Zambia, Botswana, Namibia and other countries in Africa.

Sahara Travel
Sahara House,
Macetown, Ireland

E: frank@saharatravel.co.uk
F: 00353-1-4968834
www.saharatravel.co.uk

Discover spectacular landscapes and mysterious cultures on a unique Desert Safari, Camel Trek or Short Break. Spend time with the Berbers, sleep under millions of stars and explore the culture and history of North Africa.

Scenic Air AG
PO Box 412,
Interlaken, 3800 Switzerland

E: info@scenicair.ch
F: +41 (0) 33 821 64 14
www.scenicair.ch

Thinking of spending time in Switzerland? Fancy scenic flights, glacier trekking, sky-diving or other adventurous activities?

Selective Asia
69 Grand Parade,
Brighton, BN2 9TS UK

E: contact@selectiveasia.com
www.selectiveasia.com

Selective Asia offers a range of unique, privately guided tours and adventure holidays in Cambodia, Laos, Vietnam and Thailand.

visit: www.gap-year.com

South Africa Travel Plan
7th Floor, Intergen House,
65 – 67 Western Road,
Hove, BN3 2JQ UK

T: +44 (0)1273 322 047
www.southafricatravelplan.co.uk

Create your own trip in South Africa. For independent travellers who don't want to do a group tour.

Southern Cross Tours & Expeditions
MD Jones,
841-9100 Trelew,
Chubut, Argentina

T: +54 2965 428 662
www.southern-cross-patagonia.com

Palaeontology tours in South America.

Southern Regional College
College Hill,
Armagh, BT61 7HN UK

www.src.ac.uk

Palaeontology tours in South America.

Specialtours Ltd.
Specialtours at The Ultimate Travel Company,
25-27 Vanston Place, West Brompton,
London, SW6 1AZ UK

E: info@specialtours.co.uk
T: +44 (0) 20 7386 4690
F: +44 (0) 20 7386 8652
www.specialtours.co.uk

International art and cultural tours. Access wonderful private houses, art collections and gardens. Most tours are accompanied by an expert lecturer. Why not try tours such as 'Sicily in the Spring' or 'Art & Architecture in New York'.

Suntrek
Sun Plaza,
77 West Third Street,
Santa Rosa, USA

T: +1 707 523 1800
F: +1 707 523 1911
www.suntrek.com

Adventure tours arranged in the USA, Mexico, Alaska, Canada, Central and South America and Australia.

Sunvil
Sunvil House,
Upper Square,
Old Isleworth, TW7 7BJ UK

T: +44 (0) 20 8568 4499
F: +44 (0) 20 8568 8330
www.sunvil.co.uk

A range of active holidays/trips available including sailing holidays around the world and sporting breaks worldwide.

Thailand Travel Plan

Secret islands and lagoons

Giant trees & Khao Sok lakes

Elephant trekking & rafting

Remote hilltribe adventure

Combine with Cambodia, Laos

Using our unique bite-sized tours you can piece together your own trip, your way.

Choose something action packed or a little more laid back - it's completely up to you.

Independent travel through Thailand, Cambodia & Laos

Build your own trip.

www.thailandtravelplan.co.uk

ABTA
ABTA No. Y0484

ATOL 9728 PROTECTED

Thailand Travel Plan
7th Floor, Intergen House,
65 – 67 Western Road,
Hove, BN3 2JQ UK

T: +44 (0)1273 322 040
www.thailandtravelplan.co.uk

Khao Yai jungle trails and island hopping to hidden paradise. Sleep in floating huts along the River Kwai and try a real Thai homestay.

The adventure company
Cross & Pillory House, ,
Cross & Pillory Lane,
Alton , GU34 1HL UK

E: sales@adventurecompany.co.uk
T: 0845 4505316
F: 0845 4505317
www.adventurecompany.co.uk

Offers inspirational holidays and trips worldwide that venture off the well trodden tourist trails.

The Bundu Safari Company
c/o Intrepid Travel,
76 Upper Street, Islington,
London, N1 0NU UK

T: +44 (0) 207 354 6169
F: +44 (0) 207 354 6167
www.intrepidbundu.com

The Bundu Safari Company has teamed up with Intrepid Travel to offer exciting safari adventures.

The Imaginative Traveller
1 Betts Avenue,
Martlesham Heath, IP5 3RH UK

E: online@imtrav.net
www.imaginative-traveller.com

Individual, escape and volunteering tours available.

The Oriental Caravan
35 Vanburgh Court,
Kennington,
London, SE11 4NS UK

E: info@theorientalcaravan.com
T: +44 (0) 207 582 0716
www.theorientalcaravan.com

The Oriental Caravan is a truly independent adventure tour operator specialising in escorted small group travel in the Far East.

The Russia Experience
Research House,
Fraser Road,
Perivale, UB6 7AQ UK

E: info@trans-siberian.co.uk
T: +44 (0) 208 566 8845
F: +44 (0) 208 566 8843
www.trans-siberian.co.uk

The Trans-Siberian is a working train covering 9,000 km, 10 time zones, 16 rivers and some 80 towns and cities. A once in a lifetime experience.

the gap-year guidebook 2011

the world is waiting for you...
what are you waiting for ?

- Round the world flight specialists
- Multi stop itineraries
- Overland, adventure tours
- Trans-Siberian rail journeys
- Long trip travel insurance

Check out our inter-active round the world inspiration zone

travelNation
Round the World and Adventure Travel Experts

ABTA J4916 / Y1114
IATA Accredited Agent
9828 ATOL PROTECTED

www.travelnation.co.uk
Telephone: 01273 320 580

Timberline Adventures
7975 E Harvard, Suite #J,
Denver, CO 80231 USA

E: timber@earthnet.net
F: +1 303 368 1651
www.timbertours.com

Hiking and cycling tours in the USA.

Top Deck
Level 2,
107 Power Road,
Chiswick,,London W4 5PY UK

E: info@topdecktravel.co.uk
T: 0208 987 3300
F: 0208 987 3301
www.topdeck.travel

Providing unforgettable travel experiences for 18 to 30 somethings. Extended trips, festivals, ski and sailing in Europe, holidays in Egypt, Morocco, Jordan and Israel, safaris in Africa and now adventures in Australia and New Zealand.

Travel Nation
8th Floor, Intergen House,
65-67 Western Road,
Hove, BN3 2JQ UK

E: info@travelnation.co.uk
T: 01273 320580
www.travel-nation.co.uk

Independent specialist travel company providing expert advice and the best deals on round-the-world trips, multi-stop itineraries, overland/adventure tours and Trans-Siberian rail journeys. Booking agent for all of the major overland and adventure tour operators; no booking fee and you can take advantage of independent and neutral advice.

Travellers Connected.com
Queensgate House,
48 Queen Street,
Exeter, EX4 3SR UK

E: info@travellersconnected.com
T: +44 (0) 8450 291616
www.travellersconnected.com

A totally free community site for gap-year travellers. Register and contact travellers around the world for to-the-minute advice on the best places to go and best things to do.

Tribes Travel
12 The Business Centre,
Earl Soham,
Woodbridge, IP13 7SA UK

E: info@tribes.co.uk
T: +44 (0) 1728 685 971
www.tribes.co.uk

A Fair Trade Travel company with lots of exciting tours for you to choose from. Such as budget priced walking safaris to the more expensive once in a lifetime trips.

Tucan Travel
316 Uxbridge Road,
Acton,
London, W3 9QP UK

E: uksales@tucantravel.com
T: +44 (0) 20 8896 1600
F: +44 (0) 20 8896 1400
www.tucantravel.com

Budget Expeditions offer a wide range of tours at low prices.

the gap-year guidebook 2011

Vietnam Travel Plan
7th Floor, Intergen House,
65 – 67 Western Road,
Hove, BN3 2JQ UK

T: +44 (0)1273 322 041
www.vietnamtravelplan.co.uk

Meet the hilltribes of Sapa and drift along the Mekong to tropical Phu Quoi Island. Try Anchors Away in Halong Bay and learn to dive on tiny Palm Island. We'll help you build your very own Vietnam adventure.

Vodkatrain
Unit 1 St George's Court,
131 Putney Bridge Road, West Brompton,
London, SW15 2PA UK

E: europe@vodkatrain.com
T: +44 (0) 20 8877 7650
www.vodkatrain.com

Experience the Trans-Mongolian railway and the Silk Road, travelling with local people, sampling local food and travel at local prices.

Walks Worldwide
12 The Square,
Ingleton,
Carnforth, LA6 3EG UK

E: sales@walksworldwide.com
T: +44 (0)1524 242000
F: +44 (0) 1524 242657
www.walksworldwide.com

Offers different types of walking expeditions around the world, from walking across the Swedish coastal peninsulas to trekking to Everest base camp.

Wayward Bus Touring Company Pty Ltd
119 Waymouth Street,
Adelaide, SA 5000 Australia

E: reservations@waywardbus.com.au
F: +61 8 8132 1375
www.waywardbus.com.au

Wayward Bus offers tours between Melbourne and Adelaide via the Great Ocean Road and Coorong. They also go to Kangaroo Island, Kakadu and a variety of other places.

Wild at Heart Youth Adventures
Kruger Office,
Orpen Road,
Kruger Park Area, South Africa

E: info@wah.co.za
T: +27 15 7930678
www.wah.co.za

Wild at Heart Youth Safaris is a well-established South African based youth adventure company. From helping at a monkey sanctuary to working at a reptile farm there are many different opportunities available.

Wind, Sand & Stars
PO Box 4322,
Bath, BA1 2BU UK

E: info@windsandstars.co.uk
F: +44 (0)1225 320 880
www.windsandstars.co.uk

Wind, Sand & Stars is a specialist company that organises group journeys within the desert and mountain areas of Sinai, Egypt.

visit: www.gap-year.com

World Expeditions
81 Craven Gardens,
Wimbledon,
London, SW19 8LU UK

E: enquiries@worldexpeditions.co.uk
T: +44 (0)20 8545 9030
F: +44 (0)20 8543 8316
www.worldexpeditions.com

Adventure travel company offering ground breaking itineraries on every continent. They offer exciting all inclusive adventures and challenges worldwide.

Yomps
10 Woodland Way,
Brighton, BN1 8BA UK

E: info@yomps.co.uk
F: +44 (0) 20 7149 9933
www.yomps.co.uk

Yomps offer adventure travel and interesting gap-year and career break experiences.

Travel Companies

African Conservation Experience
Unit 1 Manor Farm, Churchend Lane,
Charfield,
Wotton-Under-Edge, GL12 8LJ UK

E: info@conservationafrica.net
T: +44 (0) 1454 269182
www.conservationafrica.net

African Conservation Experience offer volunteering opportunities at wildlife conservation projects in southern Africa. You can count on our full support and more than 10 years experience. See our main advert in Conservation

---

Cairns Dive Centre
121 Abbott Street,
Cairns 4870, Australia

E: info@cairnsdive.com.au
www.cairnsdive.com.au

CDC offers daily day or live aboard snorkel and dive trips to the Outer Great Barrier Reef. We also offer SSI learn-to-dive courses from beginners through to instructor level.

Goa Way
111 Bell Street,
Marylebone,
London, NW1 6TL UK

E: sales@goaway.co.uk
T: +44 (0) 870 890 7800
www.goaway.co.uk

Goaway specialises in organising travel to Goa and Kerala. You can book flights, hostels or even package tours.

Greyhound Lines Inc
PO Box 660691,
MS 470,
Dallas, TX 75266-0691 USA

E: ifsr@greyhound.com
T: +1 214 849 8100
www.greyhound.com

The most famous and largest bus company in America. Book online and join the millions of others who travel across America on the 'old grey dog'.

the gap-year guidebook 2011

Oasis Overland, The Marsh, Henstridge BA8 0TF
T: +44 (0) 1963 363400
E: info@oasisoverland.co.uk   W: www.oasisoverland.co.uk

Come and join us on one of our overland adventure trips and we promise to take you to some of the most awesome and spectacular places in the world. We believe overlanding is one of the most inspirational and rewarding forms of travel that you will experience in your life!

If you dream of travelling through Africa, South America or the Middle East, but without the routine and expense that accompanies some holidays, then look no further than Oasis Overland. Our trips are always adventurous, sometimes unpredictable and not your average package holiday.

We provide excellent value for money adventures for budget-conscious travellers. Our Overland Adventures and Expeditions last from 15 days to 40 weeks! Travelling in a custom built overland expedition truck and staying in a variety of accommodation from hostels to campsites to bush camping, you and your group will help with the day to day running of the trip such as shopping in local markets, cooking over the campfire or collecting firewood.

If you don't want to rough it quite as much, our Regional Explorer trips in Egypt, Jordan, Peru and Bolivia use local transport and simple hotels.

Along the way you can hike the Inca trail in Peru, come face to face with mountain gorillas in Uganda, explore the mighty Pyramids in Egypt or bungy jump at Victoria Falls - to name just a few!

We have been specializing in providing overland adventure travel for more than 12 years and our reliable, friendly and personal service is why our travellers come back year after year!

visit: www.gap-year.com

Inside Japan Tours
Lewins House,
Lewins Mead,
Bristol, BS1 2NN UK

E: info@insidejapantours.com
T: +44 (0)117 314 4620
F: +44 (0) 870 746 1047
www.insidejapantours.com

Specialist company offering tours of Japan, including small group tours and individual, self-guiding tours. You can also book a Japan Rail Pass online here.

Journey Latin America
12-13 Heathfield Terrace,
Chiswick,
London, W4 4JE UK

E: flights@journeylatinamerica.co.uk
T: +44 (0) 20 8747 3108
F: +44 (0) 20 8742 1312
www.journeylatinamerica.co.uk

JLA is the UK's major specialist in travel to Latin America. Its 'Open-Jaw' transatlantic tickets permit you to fly into one country and out of another.

Kumuka Worldwide
40 Earls Court Road,
Kensington,
London, W8 6EJ UK

E: adventuretours@kumuka.com
T: +44 (0) 20 7937 8855
F: +44 (0) 20 7937 6664
www.kumuka.com

Kumuka Worldwide is the leading specialist tour operator for activity holidays and adventure holidays in small group travel, around the world.

Mountain Beach Mountain Bike Holidays
13 Church Street,
Ruddington, NG11 6HA UK

E: andy@mountain-beach.co.uk
www.mountain-beach.co.uk

Find the mountain biking holiday of your dreams with Mountain Beach.

Neilson Active Holidays Ltd
Locksview,
Brighton Marina,
Brighton, BN2 5HA UK

E: sales@neilson.com
T: +44 (0) 845 070 3460
F: +44 (0) 845 070 3455
www.neilson.com

This company offers a selection of worldwide sporting holidays, all year round.

STA Travel
52 Grosvenor Gardens,
Victoria,
London, SW1W 0AG UK

E: victoria@statravel.co.uk
T: +44 (0) 870 1468 0649
F: +44 (0) 20 7881 1299
www.statravel.co.uk

This company has branches or agents worldwide and a Help Desk telephone service, which provides essential backup for travellers on the move.

The Year Out Group
Queensfield,
28 King's Road,
Easterton, SN10 4PX UK

E: info@yearoutgroup.org
T: +44 (0) 1380 816696
www.yearoutgroup.org

See main entry under volunteering.

the gap-year guidebook 2011

trekamerica

TrekAmerica Travel Limited, 16/17 Grange Mills, Weir Road, Balham, London SW12 0NE
T: +44 (0) 844 576 1368
E: info@trekamerica.co.uk   W: www.trekamerica.com

TrekAmerica are leaders in small group adventure travel throughout the USA, Canada, Alaska and Mexico, with over 50 action packed itineraries, from three-day mini-adventures to epic 64-day road trips. Specifically created for young, international travellers aged 18-38, TrekAmerica believes in tempting travellers away from the traditional package holiday and into the world of exciting 'off the beaten path' adventures.

With our own private transportation and a maximum group size of just 13 people, travelling with TrekAmerica is more like travelling with a group of friends than on an organised tour. You won't have to pay a single supplement either as you'll be paired with a fellow group member of the same sex – a great way to travel at an unbeatable price.

When you add up all the costs compared to other forms of travel, TrekAmerica is the "best deal on wheels". Our tours include national park fees, activities, attractions, local transportation, camping fees and equipment and the services of a professional tour leader. But most importantly, we are experts in getting you off the beaten path, exploring deep into the national, state and provincial parks, Native American Lands and wilderness areas, that are at most times difficult, if not impossible to reach on your own.

So why not challenge yourself, not your budget, on your gap-year and travel with the North American specialists and let us help you make the most of your time and money as you journey through the heart and soul of America.

Be sure to check out 'TrekAmerica Live'

TrekAmerica are excited to announce the launch of their new social networking platform, letting you find out what travelling with TrekAmerica is really like before you go on tour. Go to www.trekamericalive.com.

Travel Nation
8th Floor, Intergen House,
65-67 Western Road,
Hove, BN3 2JQ UK

E: info@travelnation.co.uk
T: 01273 320580
www.travel-nation.co.uk

Travel Nation provide expert advice and great deals on round-the-world flights and multi-stop tickets, adventure tours, accommodation, travel insurance and discounted long-haul flights.
Their staff are all well seasoned travellers who will be able to offer any destination advice needed. They have outstanding customer service levels and you'll deal with the same person for the life of your booking.

Travel Talk
Hudavendigar Cad,
No 6 Kat 2 Sirkeci,
Istanbul, Turkmenistan

E: info@traveltalktours.com
T: +44 (0) 20 7183 0910
F: +90 212 512 1553
www.traveltalkeurope.com

Turkish travel agency specializing in the Mediterranean and fun, adventure tours.

Travelbag Ltd
373-375 The Strand,
London, WC2R 0JE UK

www.travelbag.co.uk

Book flights, hotel, holidays and even find insurance on their website.

TrekAmerica Travel Limited
16/17 Grange Mills,
Weir Road, Balham,
London, SW12 0NE UK

E: info@trekamerica.co.uk
T: +44 (0) 844 576 1368
F: +44 (0) 208 675 0551
www.trekamerica.com

Offering more than 60 itineraries from one to nine weeks in TrekAmerica's fun, free, and flexible small group adventure tours are the ideal way to explore North America.

USIT
19/21 Aston Quay,
Dublin, 2 Ireland

www.usit.ie

Irish travel agents offering cheap flights from Dublin, Cork and Shannon specifically aimed at students.

Chapter 5
Working abroad

5 Working abroad

Working abroad is a great option if you desperately want to go overseas, can't really afford it and the bit you have managed to save won't cover much more than air fare.

It's one of the best ways to experience a different culture; you'll be meeting locals and experiencing what the country is really like in a way that you can't do as a traveller passing through. Most jobs give you enough spare time, in the evenings and at weekends, to enjoy yourself and make friends.

You don't have to be tied to one place for your whole **gap-**year - you can work for a bit and save up for your travels. That way you can learn more about the place and get the inside information from the locals about the best places to see before you set off.

You cover at least some of your costs, and, depending on what you do, the work experience will look good on your CV - but even if you're only doing unskilled seasonal work, prospective employers will be reassured that you at least know *something* about the basics like punctuality, fitting into an organisation and managing your time.

An internship with pay is a good way to get work experience if you already have an idea about your eventual career and will help in those early stages of the catch-22 that affects many young people - when employers want experience but won't take you on so you can get it.

Older gappers, too, may find that, despite the current global economic problems, their skills and experience are in demand, particularly in developing countries.

Despite the economic downturn, at the time of writing, the construction industry is reporting a shortage of skilled workers. Australia also has a shortage of chefs and health care professionals. The Asia Pacific region (India, China, Malaysia, Australia and the Phillipines) has also identified skills gaps in IT, particularly in support, application development and system integration.

Another option is to look at working for one of the international organisations, such as the UN, IMF or British Council. There's a useful list of contacts for these, and similar organisations, here:

www.prospects.ac.uk/cms/ShowPage/Home_page/Working_abroad/information_sources/p!eeXmbcL

Key questions to get started…

What kind of work do you want to do? There are some suggestions in this chapter but they're only a start.

- Is it to help pay your way on your **gap-**?
- Is it to get work experience/enhance your CV?

visit: www.gap-year.com

- Where do you want to work? (Don't forget to check **www.fco.gov.uk** for country info.)
- What skills and experience do you have?

It doesn't have to be work experience or education, don't forget hobbies and interests. If you can ride a horse, dance, draw, paint, or are good at a particular sport, you could use any of those skills as a basis for finding work.

Planning ahead

Choosing your destination

There are some jobs that always need to be done, whatever the state of the world, and if you're just looking at ways of funding your travel you could look for seasonal farm work.

In most cases, gappers intending to do seasonal work outside the EU need to have a job offer in order to get a visa. If you should find that, when you get there the job is no longer available, you can try elsewhere - but we would advise you to have a back-up plan before you set off on your travels (eg contacts, an emergency fund, names of companies that specialise in work overseas - see the list of websites below).

If you are a UK citizen, or hold an EU (European Union) passport, you can work in any other EU member country without a visa or work permit and there are countless jobs available to students who can speak the right languages. Not all European countries are EU members - go to the European Union website to check: www.europa.eu/index_en.htm

While even at the time of updating this guide there were beginning to be small signs that the global downturn was slowing, according to economic experts there is always a time lag between this and an upturn in job opportunities.

However, some employers of seasonal workers specifically prefer backpackers, so there will still be jobs out there.

There have also been reports of hostility among local people to so-called 'immigrant labour'. If you find yourself facing this, try not to resent it – imagine how you'd feel if it was happening to you at home.

Speaking English is always an advantage for jobs in tourism at ski resorts, beach bars and hotel receptions and if you have a TEFL (Teaching English as a Foreign Language) certificate there's always the option of teaching.

You could try using the **gap-year.com** message board to find out what other gappers have done and what it was like. If you want to be more adventurous and venture outside Europe, then check the Foreign Office website - **www.fco.gov.uk** - for the list of countries they consider are simply too dangerous to even go to.

Getting your paperwork sorted

Before you go, you should:

- Check whether you need to set up a job - you may need a confirmed work

the gap-year guidebook 2011

- offer before you can get a work permit and visa - try **www.gap-year.com** for contact lists and more advice, or refer to the internship and graduate opportunities section in the directory of this guidebook.
- Check on the work permit and visa regulations for the country you plan to work in and make sure you have the right paperwork before you leave. Remember, you don't need a work permit or visa if you're an EU citizen and planning to work in an EU country.
- Check if there's any special equipment or clothing you'll need to take, *eg* sturdy boots and trousers for manual jobs, reasonably smart clothes for office internships *etc*.
- When you're getting your insurance, remember to check that you'll be covered if you're planning on working. Working can invalidate a claim for loss or damage to your belongings on some travel policies. If in doubt, ask.
- Make sure you understand all the regulations and restrictions. You can get into serious trouble if you work without the necessary documents - you don't want to be deported during your **gap**-year! The best place to get information is the relevant embassy in London - there's a link on **www.gap-year.com** to the Foreign and Commonwealth Office website, where you will find links to all London based Embassies.

Finding a job

Finding a job may take time and effort. The more places you can send your CV to, the greater the chances of you getting a job. You can also register with international employment agencies but make sure you know what the agency fee will be if you get employment.

To find short-term jobs try:

www.transitionsabroad.com/listings/work/shortterm/index.shtml
www.pickingjobs.com/
www.seasonworkers.com/fe/
www.anyworkanywhere.com/
www.overseasjobcentre.co.uk/

If you use an agency, always insist on talking to someone who has used it before - that way you'll really find out what the deal is.

Do a search to see if there's a website for a particular area you want to go to and then send or email your CV, with a short covering note, to any interesting local companies. Don't expect to be flooded with replies. Some companies are simply too busy to respond to every enquiry, though it always helps to enclose a stamped addressed envelope. It's also true that you may get lucky and have exactly the skills or qualifications they're looking for. Some companies will also advertise vacant posts on specialist employment websites, which often have an international section. You can register with the sites too, usually for free.

Tell everyone you know, including relatives and your parents' friends that you are looking for a job abroad - someone may know someone who has a company abroad who can help you.

visit: www.gap-year.com

Check the local papers and shop window notices. Lots of jobs are advertised in the local papers, or by 'staff wanted' notices put up in windows. So if you get there, and hate the job you've got, don't put up with it, or come running home - see if you can find something better. It's always easier to find employment when you're living locally.

Over the next few pages we've listed ideas on types of employment, and any companies we know about, that offer graduate opportunities or work experience, can be found in the directory. Always ask an employment company to put you in contact with someone they have placed before - if they say no then don't use them: they may have something to hide.

Au pairing

Being an au pair is a good way to immerse yourself in a different culture, learn a new language and hopefully save some extra cash. You don't need any qualifications to be an au pair, although obviously some experience with children is a bonus. However, au pairing is a hard job and a big responsibility and you may well have to pass the equivalent of a Criminal Records Bureau (CRB) check.

In return for board, lodgings and pocket money, you'll be expected to look after the children and do light domestic chores like ironing, cooking, tidying their bedrooms and doing their washing, for up to five hours a day (six hours in France or Germany), five days a week, as well as spending two or three evenings a week babysitting. If you are asked to work more than this then technically you are not doing the work of an au pair, but of a mother's help (which pays more).

the gap-year guidebook 2011

Remember that an au pair is classified as 'non experienced', and you should never be left in sole charge of a baby. If the family gives you more responsibility than you can handle say so. If they don't stop - quit.

Finding an au pair agency

It may be safest to look for a placement through a UK-based au pair agency. It's also better for the prospective family abroad, since they will be dealing with an agency (possibly working together with an agency in the family's own country) that has met you, interviewed you and taken up references; they will want reassurance before they trust you with their children.

What you should check:

- Does the agency you use have connections with another agency in the country where you'll be working?
- Can they give you a list of other local au pairs so you have support when you're out there?
- Take time finding a suitable family. The fewer children the better, and you should expect your own room.
- What is there to do in your free time? You don't want to spend every weekend in your bedroom because you're stuck in the middle of nowhere.
- Do you get written confirmation of the hours, duties and pay agreed?
- The number and address of the local British Consulate - just in case. (See Appendix 2.)

Check that the au pair agency is a member of either the Recruitment and Employment Confederation (which has a website listing all its members and covering au pair employment in many countries -

www.rec.uk.com/regionssectors/sectors/childcare/faqs), or of the International Au Pair Association (IAPA) which has a list of its registered agencies in 38 countries around the world:

International Au Pair Association
Bredgade 25H, 1260 Copenhagen K
Denmark
Tel: +45 3317 0066
Fax: +45 3393 9676
www.iapa.org

There are, of course, perfectly good agencies that do not belong to trade associations, either because they are too small to afford the membership fees, or because they are well-established and have a good independent reputation.

You can also find information on au pair work worldwide by using the internet. Registration is usually free and your details will be matched to the families around the world, that have registered on the site and that meet your specifications (but make sure you talk to both the agents, here and abroad, and the prospective family before you make your final decision).

visit: www.gap-year.com

However, if you are considering organising an au pair placement independently, you should be aware of the risks:

- High probability of unsuitable au pair or host family candidates.
- Absence of a written contract.
- Little or no experience in the au pair industry.
- Lack of professionalism or financial stability.
- Nonexistent standards or guidelines.
- Insufficient references and/or medical certification.
- Danger of document falsification.
- No rematch policy (secondary placement) if the initial placement is unsuccessful.
- No local support during the placement.
- Limited understanding of national au pair and visa regulations.

Remember also that au pair agencies operating in the UK and sending au pairs abroad cannot, except under specified circumstances, charge for finding you a placement.

If you have a complaint against a UK agency it's best to take it up with the Department for Business, Enterprise and Regulatory Reform's (BERR) Employment Agency Standards Helpline, Tel: +44 (0) 845 955 5105. It operates Monday-Friday 9.30 am to 4.30 pm.

You can find out more about your rights on:

www.berr.gov.uk/employment/employment-agencies/index.html

Au pairing in Europe

There are EU laws governing the conditions in which au pairs can work:

- You must be 17 or over.
- You must provide a current medical certificate.
- You should have a written employment agreement signed by you and your host family; conditions of employment must be stated clearly.
- You should receive (tax exempt) pocket money.
- You should have enough free time to study.
- You should not be asked to work more than five hours a day.
- You must have one free day a week.

This is now the accepted definition for au pair jobs in the EU, but not necessarily in other countries. Some countries have different local rules.

Take a look at: www.conventions.coe.int/treaty/en/Treaties/Html/068.htm for the details of the European Agreement and any local variations.

It's important to complete all the necessary paperwork for living and working in another country. Most agencies will organise this for you, and make sure the

the gap-year guidebook 2011

legal documents are in order before you leave. You should listen to any legal advice you are given by the agency you use. Many also now require written references, police checks and other proof of suitability - which is as much a protection for you as it is for the parents of the children you might look after.

Here's an example. Most French agencies require a set of passport photos, a photocopy of your passport, two references (preferably translated into French), and your most recent academic qualifications, as well as a handwritten letter in French to your prospective family, which tells them something about you, your reasons for becoming an au pair and any future aspirations.

The agency may also ask for a medical certificate (showing you are free of deadly contagious diseases, *etc*) dated less than three months before you leave, and translated into French. Au pairs also have to have a medical examination on arrival in France.

The French Consulate advises you to check that the family you stay with obtains a 'mother's help' work contract (*Accord de placement au pair d'un stagiaire aide-familiale*). If you are a non-EU citizen you are expected to do this before you leave for France, but British au pairs do not need to.

Au pairing in North America

All au pair programmes in America are legislated and regulated by US law, and all au pairs receive pocket money in return for a maximum of 45 hours work a week (no more than ten hours per day), regardless of the agency.

The pay is linked to the US national minimum wage, which from July 2009 is $7.25 per hour, so 45 hours per week would be $326.25 (£199.56 – exchange

visit: www.gap-year.com

rate as at July 2009). This US Government website gives more details:

www.dol.gov/esa/whd/flsa/

US Government regulations stipulate that au pairs must attend education courses (because au pair work is seen primarily as a cultural exchange) of at least six hours per week. This is financed by the host family up to a limit of US$500. Au pairs are not allowed to be placed with families who have a child aged under two years, unless they can prove they have at least 200 hours of documented childcare experience, or who have a child with special needs, unless the au pair has valid experience, training and/or skills in SEN and this has been confirmed by the host family.

You need to:

- Be between 18 and 26 years.
- Hold a valid driving licence.
- Speak English to a good standard.
- Have no criminal record.
- Commit to 12 months living with an American family.
- Have not previously been an au pair in America.

Please note: the US regulations on visas and work permits are very complicated. We strongly recommend you use the help of an au pair agency or consult the US Embassy: **www.usembassy.org.uk**

The US Department of State website has all the up-to-date legislation on au pairing in the US. See:

http://exchanges.state.gov/jexchanges/programs/aupair.html

Because of strict government regulations, most agencies that organise au pairs in the USA offer very similar services. However it's worth registering with a number of agencies, if only to have a range of 'perfect match' host families to choose from.

EduCare

If you want to combine au pairing with some study, EduCare places people with families who have school-aged children and who need childcare before and after school hours. Au pairs on the EduCare scheme work no more than 30 hours per week in return for roughly two thirds of the rates paid to au pairs.

You must complete a minimum of 12 hours of academic credit or its equivalent during the programme year (financed by the host family for up to US$1000).

You can download a PDF about Educare here:

www.exchanges.state.gov/jexchanges/programs/aupair.html

Internships & paid work placements

- Are you at university?
- Are you a new graduate?

the gap-year guidebook 2011

- Are you looking for work experience to land your dream job?
- Want to spend a year in another country?

Some careers, the media for example, are extremely tough to get into, so using your **gap**-year to get relevant work experience may be a good plan. You'll have the benefit of something to put on your CV and also get an idea of what the job is actually like. Internships are not usually open to people pre-university. Many international companies offer internships but if you're thinking of the USA you should know:

1. Internships in the USA can be difficult to get without paying for the privilege, unless you have personal contacts within the organisation you hope to work for.

2. The USA has a strict job-related work permit system and won't hand out these permits for jobs that American nationals can do themselves.

3. The USA authorities also need to be convinced that the work experience offered provides an opportunity to the UK student that he or she cannot get back home.

If the companies listed in our directory can't help you try these websites:

www.cartercentre.org
www.summerjobs.com (enter internships in the search box)
www.internshipprograms.com
www.internabroad.com/search.cfm
www.soccerstreets.org/soccer_streets_internships.html
www.transitionsabroad.com/listings/work/internships/index.shtml

Before you sign up, make sure you're clear just what your placement will involve. An internship should mean you are able to do interesting paid work related to your degree studies, current or future, for at least six months, but increasingly, even on some of the internship websites listed above, the distinction between a voluntary (unpaid) placement and an internship is becoming blurred so you may have to search for a while - or be creative and try a direct approach to companies in the fields that interest you.

Sport instructors

If you're already a qualified instructor in skiing, kayaking, diving, football, or any other sport for that matter, there are many places all around the world where you can use your skills.

Here are a few websites to get you started:

Skiing:

www.ifyouski.com/jobs/job/description/instructor/
www.jobmonkey.com/ski/html/instructors.htm

Football:

www.deltapublications.co.uk/soccer.htm - soccer coaching in the USA

General Sports:

www.adventurejobs.co.uk
www.campjobs.com

Think further afield!

Skiing doesn't have to be in European resorts, don't forget there's the US and Canada, but there are also ski resorts in the foothills of the Himalayas! For diving jobs you can go pretty well anywhere there's water and water sports.

Football's popular throughout Africa and Latin America, and there are now several football academies in India looking for help to spread the message of the 'beautiful game'.

But whichever sport is your passion, you can use it as part of your **gap**-year plan.

We have much more on the opportunities available for teaching and playing sport abroad in Chapter 8.

Teaching English as a Foreign Language (TEFL)

TEFL is one of the most popular ways of earning (and volunteering) when you travel, but you need to have a recognised qualification and it does help in getting a post abroad. It also has the advantage that, if you were thinking of teaching as a career, it's a good chance to find out if you like it before you begin your teacher training.

The two best-known British qualifications are:

- TESOL (a certificate from Trinity College, London)
- CELTA (Cambridge University certificate)

the gap-year guidebook 2011

The USA has its own qualification and there are many private schools and colleges who offer their own certification. There are a great many colleges around the UK that offer TEFL courses but, ideally, you should check that the certificate you will be working for is one of these two.

It is worth doing your TEFL training within an accredited training centre, as most will help you find a placement once you qualify and face to face training can be more beneficial. One word of warning, if you were hoping to get a job with one of the many well known language schools around the world, some will insist that you undertake your TEFL training with them first. It's always worth checking this out, and deciding how you wish to use your training, before you sign up for a course.

How to find TEFL work

The availability of work for people who can teach English can vary, particularly outside the EU. In most countries it is possible to give private lessons. As stated before, if you wish to work for a language school or academy, find out what their requirements are before you begin your training.

Most professional employers will expect you to have had some teaching practice before they will employ you. You should also find out more about the country you hope to find work in before you go. The contact details of the relevant embassies in the UK can be found on the FCO website - **www.fco.gov.uk** - and you should be able to obtain up-to-date details of visas, salaries, qualifications needed and a view about the availability of work in your chosen country. Rates of pay and conditions of employment will vary greatly from country to country and will most likely depend on your own education, training, experience and expertise.

In the UK, TEFL jobs are advertised in:
The Times Educational Supplement.
The Education Guardian.
In the education section of The Independent.
The EL Gazette.

www.eslbase.com/jobs/
www.cactustefl.com/
www.eteach.com/#International
www.english-international.com/
www.esljobfeed.com/

You could also check out the various 'blacklists' that have appeared on the internet in recent years. These list schools to avoid or watch out for. These are informal sites run by people with experience of TEFL teaching. They should be a good place to find out about language schools around the world and whether or not it's worth your time pursuing a vacancy there.

The most popular destinations for TEFL teachers are China, Hong Kong, Japan, Thailand and, of course, Europe. As the EU grows, so does the demand for English teachers, and the advantage of securing a job within the EU is that the UK is a member. This will give you some protection and should involve far less paperwork than if you applied to work further afield.

visit: www.gap-year.com

In China, you are more likely to find work in a private school, rather than the public schools system, as the latter is controlled by the Department of Education in Beijing.

Hong Kong is an obvious choice as it was once a British Colony and English is a second language for nearly everyone there. The added advantage for those with no Chinese language skills is that all the road signs, public transport and government information are in English as well as Chinese and most of the shops, agencies and essential services (such as police, doctors *etc*) employ English speakers.

There is also a daily English language newspaper, *The South China Morning Post* and it may well be worth checking their online jobs section for vacancies:

www.classifiedpost.com.hk/jshome_en.html

If you want to take your skills and use them in Japan you should check out **www.jet-uk.org**. This is the Japanese Government's website for promoting their scheme to improve foreign language teaching in schools. You do have to have a Bachelor's degree to qualify though. The *Japan Times* (which is online) also lists job vacancies in English: **www.jobs.japantimes.jp/**

There is a great demand for English speakers in Thailand and so if you are taking your **gap-** in that country, and wish to earn money whilst there, TEFL could well be the answer, particularly as you will be unable to find work in a country where foreigners are forbidden from taking most unskilled occupations. The *Bangkok Post* lists job vacancies, including those for English teachers, in their online jobs section: **www.bangkokpost.net**

the gap-year guidebook 2011

Teaching English in private lessons

If you decide to supplement your income in-country by giving private lessons, you can put notices in schools, colleges, newspapers and local shops but there are some basic safety precautions you should take:

1. Be careful how you word your ad - *eg* 'Young English girl offering English lessons' is likely to draw the wrong kind of attention.

2. If you arrange one-to-one tuition, don't go to your student's home until you've checked out how safe it would be.

3. Equally, if you're living alone, don't give classes at home until you've got to know your student.

4. Arrange classes in public, well-populated locations, which will also help as teaching aids (coffee bars, restaurants, shops, markets *etc*).

5. Make sure you're both clear about your fee (per hour) and when it should be paid (preferably these should both be put in writing).

Usually, you'll be inundated by friends of friends as word gets round there's an English person willing to give private lessons.

Seasonal work in Europe

Working in Europe offers endless possibilities - from fruit picking to hospitality and tourism, leading nature trips to teaching English (for more on this see our TEFL section above). Some non-EU members need work permits so you should check the regulations in the country you want to go to.

To find short-term jobs try:

www.transitionsabroad.com/
www.pickingjobs.com/
www.seasonworkers.com/fe/

Seasonal work in North America

Probably the most popular seasonal job for gappers in the US is working on a summer camp. The US has strict regulations on visas and work permits but summer camps are a well-established way of working for a short time.

US work regulations are very complicated, and specific, and this is one time where it would help to use a placement organisation to help you through the paperwork, but make sure you check out the small print about pay, accommodation and expenses.

If you don't fancy summer camp there are lots of other possibilities, from working on a ranch to cruise ship jobs. Have a look at:

www.jobmonkey.com/main/index.html

It covers all sorts of work from fishing jobs in Alaska, to working on a ranch, to casino and gaming clubs and cruise work. But check with the US Embassy to make sure you can get a visa or a work permit for the job you fancy. See:

www.usembassy.org.uk

visit: www.gap-year.com

"Email, email, email – and start early..."

Tom Burrows went to Australia, New Zealand and Bali on his self-organised gap-year. Here he offers advice on finding work to help fund his adventures.

If I was to offer one piece of advice to potential gappers, it would be to have a clear plan mapped out before you set off. Simply boarding a plane to an exotic destination is not sufficient; without a plan or goal, your dream year could quickly become frustrating and unfulfilling.

I knew that I had to get myself plenty of seasonal work to help pay for my travels around Australia, New Zealand and Bali.

After saving up by working as a waiter in England until Christmas, I arranged a job at a boarding school in Melbourne for six months. From there, during the school vacations and over long-weekends, I was able to explore not only Australia but also New Zealand and Bali.

One great advantage of working at a school is that both food and accommodation are provided. This not only helps keep afloat that tight gap-year budget but also provides a base for travelling thereby avoiding endless and exhausting moves from one place to another.

My most memorable time in Australia was working as a sailing instructor at the school's beach camps for two months. Before going Down Under, I had never sailed before and so in the first two weeks I regularly found myself falling into the freezing shark-infested ocean. I was soon christened 'Captain Clueless' by my co-workers.

I think the key to me getting my job at the school in Australia was to send emails out to schools as early as possible. I sent many emails to schools in Sydney, Melbourne and Brisbane (about 50 in total) before I was offered something.

Ideally, emails should be written to schools about eight months before you wish to begin. A well-structured CV ought to be attached to a well-written and enthusiastic email. It is also important to note that many schools already have prior arrangements in place concerning gap-students – or do not take gap-students at all - and so there are many emails of rejection.

However, you should remain positive as eventually you should be offered a place. Indeed, there is a higher competition for gap-year jobs in Australia and so if the job search here is proving fruitless, there is always the option to look for similar jobs in New Zealand.

Finally, you should remember that a gap-year job is very poorly paid, about £60 a week, yet accommodation and food are provided for, which saves money for travelling at weekends and vacation.

Seasonal work in Australia and New Zealand

Periods of working and travelling in Australia and New Zealand are a very popular option and you can do everything from fruit picking to helping Amnesty International. However, you don't have to stick to the traditional backpacker temporary work - fruit picking, bar work or call centres. If you have a trade, IT skills or a nursing qualification they're also good for finding work.

Australia has a well worked-out system to allow you to work and travel. It's called the working holiday visa. From July 2008 the Australian Government changed the regulations so that you can qualify for any specified work and UK passport holders can apply online. Specified work is work, whether paid or unpaid, in certain specified industries or postcodes - for more details have a look at:

www.immi.gov.au/visitors/working-holiday/417/specified-work.htm

The main points are:

- You must be between 18 and 30.
- It costs around £90 (AU$195). The charge is non-refundable.

You will also be required to have a health certificate before you apply for your visa.

What you can do:

- Enter Australia within 12 months of the visa being issued.
- Stay up to 12 months.
- Leave and re-enter Australia any number of times while the visa is valid.
- Work in Australia for up to six months with each employer.
- Study or train for up to four months.

visit: www.gap-year.com

To find out more go to:
www.immi.gov.au/visitors/working-holiday/417/eligibility-first.htm

Or call the High Commission in the UK:
Australian High Commission,
Australia House, Strand, London WC2B 4LA
Tel: 020 7379 4334
www.australia.org.uk

To find seasonal work try:
www.seasonalwork.com.au/index.bsp
www.workaboutaustralia.com.au/

Australian employment author, *Barry Brebner* , who has written the book *Workabout Australia*, tells us how those wishing to travel to Australia can take advantage of the opportunities that exist.

"Seasonal and casual employment in Australia occurs right across the country creating the sense of an adventure of a lifetime waiting to happen.

"Work not only exists in the traditional fruit and vegetable growing regions, but also in numerous locations where the tourism and hospitality industries are expanding rapidly. The Australian snow season alone sees several thousand workers required with occupations ranging from ski instructors to housekeeping and hospitality staff.

"The many special events that occur in all Australian states create potential employment for many people including the travelling worker.

"When this is combined with Australia's fishing industry, grain and seed growing, cotton industry, horse studs, meat works and manufacturing sector, the opportunities are limitless.

"With over 184 locations Australia-wide and over 500,000 jobs that occur each year this gives backpackers and the travelling worker the opportunity to visit and work in places that they have never heard of. It also gives them the opportunity to meet different people, make new friends and enjoy the Australian life and culture.

"The size of the Australian continent and its great climatic diversity ensures employment opportunities occur throughout the whole year and across all Australian States.

"The Workabout Australia website (www.workaboutaustralia.com.au) will provide a host of important information as well as actual jobs that occur across the nation.

"The Workabout Australia Club is also available to help people with their travels. Each week an email bulletin is forwarded to members advising them of jobs currently available and jobs coming up in the future."

New Zealand has a similar working visa scheme for either 12 or 23 months - and also a health certificate requirement. To qualify you must:

1. Usually be permanently living in the United Kingdom - this means you can be temporarily visiting another country when you lodge your application.

2. Have a British passport that's valid for at least three months after your planned departure from NZ.

3. Be at least 18 and not more than 30 years old.

4. Not bring children with you.

5. Hold a return ticket, or sufficient funds to purchase such a ticket.

6. Have a minimum of NZ$350 per month of stay in available funds (to meet your living costs while you're there).

7. Meet NZ's health and character requirements.

8. Satisfy the authorities your main reason for going to NZ is to holiday, not work.

9. Not have been approved a visa permit under a Working Holiday Scheme before.

The regulations for British Subjects are very clearly laid out on the NZ Government website:

www.immigration.govt.nz/migrant/stream/work/workingholiday/unitedkingdomworkingholidayscheme.htm

And here are a few websites to check for seasonal work in New Zealand:

www.picknz.co.nz/
www.seasonaljobs.co.nz/
www.backpackerboard.co.nz/work_jobs/seasonal_jobs_new_zealand.php

Working Abroad

Au Pairing

Au Pair Ecosse
6 Park Place,
King's Park,
Stirling, FK7 9JR UK
E: ruth@aupairecosse.com
T: +44 (0) 1786 474573
www.aupairecosse.com

Au Pair Ecosse places au pairs with families in Scotland and sends British au pairs to families in Europe and America using established, reputable agent partners.

Au Pair in America (APIA)
37 Queen's Gate,
South Kensington,
London, SW7 5HR UK
E: info@aupairamerica.co.uk
T: +44 (0) 20 7581 7322
F: +44 (0) 20 7581 7345
www.aupairamerica.co.uk

Agency which specifically matches au pairs and nannies with families in America.

Childcare International
Trafalgar House,
Grenville Place, Mill Hill,
London, NW7 3SA UK
E: office@childint.co.uk
T: +44 (0) 20 8906 3116
F: +44 (0) 20 8906 3461
www.childint.co.uk

Childcare International, together with their partner agencies abroad, arrange au pair placements in many EU countries including France, Germany, Holland, Italy and Spain.

Delaney International
Bramble Cottage,
Thorncombe Street,
Bramley, GU5 0ND UK
E: info@delaney-nannies.com
T: +44 (0) 1483 894 300
www.delaney-nannies.com

Provides British au pair applicants with au pair positions in several EU countries including France, Germany, Italy and Spain.

Pebbles
35 rue pastorelli,
Nice, 06000 France
E: contact@pebbles.fr
F: 00 33 483 501 743 (France)
www.pebbles.fr

Pebbles recruits au pairs through universities, schools, colleges and youth centres in England and France.

Planet Au Pair
Avenida Ausias March 32, Pta. 4,
Valencia, 46006 Spain
E: info@planetaupair.com
F: +34 96 320 7832
www.planetaupair.com

Company placing au pairs throughout Europe and the USA.

the gap-year guidebook 2011

Total Nannies
37 Leamington Avenue,
Morden, SM4 4DQ UK

E: info@totalnannies.com
F: +44 (0) 8707 621387
www.totalnannies.com

This company places nannies and au pairs worldwide.

Internships

African Conservation Experience
Unit 1 Manor Farm, Churchend Lane,
Charfield,
Wotton-Under-Edge, GL12 8LJ UK

E: info@conservationafrica.net
T: +44 (0) 1454 269182
www.conservationafrica.net

African Conservation Experience offer volunteering opportunities at wildlife conservation projects in southern Africa. You can count on our full support and more than 10 years experience. See our main advert in Conservation

AgriVenture
Speedwell Farm Bungalow,
Nettle Bank,
Wisbech, PE14 0SA UK

E: uk@agriventure.com
T: +44 (0) 1945 450 999
www.agriventure.net

Spend your gap year getting fantastic work experience in South Pacific/North America/Japan/Europe. Work in agriculture or horticulture. Get paid for the work you do whilst living and working with one of our fully approved hosting enterprises.

Centro Linguistico Italiano Dante Alighieri
Piazza della Repubblica 5,
Florence, I-50123 Italy

E: internships@internship.com
F: +39 055 28 7828
www.clidante.com

Centro Linguistico Italiano Dante Alighieri (CLIDA), founded in 1965, is Italy's first private Italian language school specialising in the instruction of Italian language and culture to foreigners - both students and professionals alike.

Dragon Charm
Room 1704, Gong Xiao Commercial Building,
Wu Yi Road No 599,
Changsha, Hunan, PR China

E: mail@dragoncharm.info
T: +86 731 82765759
www.dragoncharm.info

If you are thinking about travelling to China, Dragon Charm can help you get the most from your visit through a range of Au Pair, teaching and other employment programmes.

Global Choices
Barkat House,
116-118 Finchley Road, Belsize Park,
London, NW3 5HT UK

E: info@globalchoices.co.uk
T: +44 (0) 207 433 2501
F: +44 (0) 870 330 5955
www.globalchoices.co.uk

Offers internships and working holidays in USA, Australia, Canada, UK, Ireland, Brazil, Argentina, Spain, Greece and Italy.

visit: www.gap-year.com

InterExchange
161 Sixth Avenue,
New York, NY 10013 USA

E: info@interexchange.org
F: +1 212 924 0575
www.interexchange.org

InterExchange offers J-1 & H-2B visa programs throughout the US. Options include au pair, internship, seasonal work and travel and summer camp positions.

IST Plus
Rosedale House,
Rosedale Road,
Richmond, TW9 2SZ UK

E: info@istplus.com
T: +44 (0) 208 939 9057
F: +44 (0) 208 939 9090
www.istplus.com

Internships in the USA, Australia, New Zealand. Summer work in the USA. Summer camp in the USA. Gap-year work in Australia, New Zealand. Volunteer in Thailand. Teach in Thailand, China (for graduates).

Lucasfilm
One Letterman Drive,
PO Box 29901,
San Francisco, CA 94129-0901 USA

https://jobs.lucasfilm.com/

As you can imagine, internships with Lucasfilm are few and far between. They are also quickly filled. See their website for further details.

Maasai International Challenge Africa
PO Box 14950,
Arusha, 00255 Tanzania

E: info@micatz.org
www.micatz.org

Offers low cost paid internships in Africa to students and graduates.

Mountbatten Institute
5th Floor, Michael House,
35-37 Chiswell Street, Clerkenwell,
London, EC1Y 4SE UK

E: info-uk@mountbatten.org
T: +44 (0) 845 370 3535
F: +44 (0) 845 370 3536
www.mountbatten.org

Grab a whole year's worth of paid work experience through the Mountbatten Programme and enhance your CV.

Project O
PO Box 2082, Hillcrest,
3650,
Pinetown, 3650 South Africa

E: liz@projecto.org.za
T: +27 (0) 31 700 8996
F: +27 (0) 86 550 7156
www.project-o.org

Project O are a Christian organization who support AIDS orphans in Africa. They offer a three week internship programme.

Sunrise Volunteer Programmes, 71A Church Road, Hove BN3 2BB
T: +44 (0) 1273 738 205
E: info@sunrint.com   W: en.sunrint.com

Sunrise Volunteer Programmes is the number one resource for gap-year, career break and volunteer work in China. We offer two-week to three-month volunteer opportunities abroad in **Panda conservation, English Teaching, Chinese Medical, and Journalism** in the local community in China.

Our UK offices are in London and Brighton. We've got the latest information on internship projects in China plus help and advice to get you started. The idea being that you will visit as volunteers to help us improve the service for the local community. At same time, you will have a real opportunity to get involved in Chinese people's lives and get different experiences for your life at the same time.

Our Beijing Office and local coordinators will help you settle in Beijing when you arrive. And also they can provide more information on local tours such as the region's well-known 'must-sees' and those off-the-beaten-track.

Sunrise Volunteer Programmes is providing a real insight into the China you are visiting - culture, history, landscape and natural world - and provide the opportunity for genuine interaction with the local people. Please visit our website to find more information. We require a CV and booking form for all the projects.

Sunrise Volunteer Programmes (UK Charity No. 1132373)
Hove office:71A Church Road, Hove, East Sussex. United Kingdom. BN3 2BB. Tel: +44 (0) 1273 738205
London office: Suite 40, Cameo House, Bear Street, Leicester Square, London, WC2H 7AS, United Kingdom, Tel: +44 (0) 2077 665208

visit: www.gap-year.com

The Foundation for Center for Research of Whales
1644 Plaza Way PMB 216,
Walla Walla, WA 99362 USA

E: edecuador@yahoo.com
www.researchwhales.com

Internships available in research and education.

The Institute for Public Policy Research (IPPR)
30-32 Southampton Street,
Covent Garden,
London, WC2E 7RA UK

T: +44 (0) 20 7470 6100
F: +44 (0) 20 7470 6111
www.ippr.org.uk/jobsandinternships/?id=83

The IPPR offers paid work placements throughout the year. See their website for more details.

The New England Wild Flower Society & Garden in the Woods
180 Hemenway Road,
Framingham, MA 01701 USA

E: conserve@newenglandwild.org
F: +1 508 877 3658
www.newfs.org/jobs

The oldest plant conservation organization in the USA and a leader in regional plant conservation programmes and native plant studies. They have volunteering and internship opportunities.

The Year Out Group
Queensfield,
28 King's Road,
Easterton, SN10 4PX UK

E: info@yearoutgroup.org
T: +44 (0) 1380 816696
www.yearoutgroup.org

See main entry under volunteering.

Twin Work & Volunteer
2nd Floor,
67-71 Lewisham High Street, Lewisham,
London, SE13 5JX UK

T: +44 (0)20 8297 3278
www.workandvolunteer.com

Work and volunteer programmes listed. Also offers a travel insurance package.

Work the World Ltd
The Brighton Forum,
95 Ditchling Road,
Brighton, BN1 4ST UK

E: info@worktheworld.co.uk
T: +44 (0) 1273 573 863
F: +44 (0) 1273 689 021
www.worktheworld.co.uk

Organises healthcare and community development projects that provide maximum benefit to both the participants and the overseas communities they support.

the gap-year guidebook 2011

Changing Worlds
1999 - 2011
Productive placements

NEW ZEALAND 2010

I wanted to find a programme which presented me with the opportunity of staying in a place for at least 3 months so I could really grasp its culture and traditions. I sought the security of flying out with a troupe of like minded individuals and having the guarantee of work, and a place to live upon arrival. Changing Worlds did all this and more. I feel so fortunate to have lived and worked in Queenstown. Working for the food and beverage team at the renowned Heretage Hotell and having the chance to organise and run coctail parties on the amazing rooftop terrace, work the bar at conferences and weddings, run room service and wait tables in the a la carte restaurant will look good on my CV for years to come. Earning Money meant I could truly make the most of my time in New Zealand seeing all the places and doing all the things I wanted (and some that I didn't.) I wish I was still there.

Adam Pescod Jan 2010

Stud
Hotels
Airports
Hospitality
Ski season

www.changingworlds.co.uk
ask@changingworlds.co.uk
telephone: 01883340960

Seasonal work

Acorn Venture Ltd
Acorn House,
Prospect Road,
Halesowen, B62 8DU UK

E: jobs@acornadventure.co.uk
T: +44 (0) 121 504 2042
F: +44 (0) 121 504 2052
www.jobs-acorn.co.uk

Acorn Adventure runs adventure holiday camps from April until September based in eight centres in France, Italy, and the UK – their main customers are school/youth groups and families.

Beaumont Château Ltd (UK Office)
Weardale Business Centre, Martin Street,
Stanhope,
Bishop Auckland, DL13 2UY UK

T: +44 (0) 844 8000 124
F: +44 (0) 871 2000 125
www.chateau-beaumont.co.uk

Chateau Beaumont is a small friendly language and activity centre based in the Normandy region of France.

Bellis Training Australia
Unit 7,
16-22 Miles Street,
Hawthorne, Queensland 4171 Australia

E: info@bellistraining.com
T: +61 07 3902 1782
www.bellistraining.com

Offers paid work opportunities in Australia and training.

BUNAC
(British Universities North America Club)
16 Bowling Green Lane,
Clerkenwell,
London, EC1R 0QH UK

E: enquiries@bunac.org.uk
T: +44 (0) 20 7251 3472
F: +44 (0) 20 7251 0215
www.bunac.org

Overseas work and travel programmes for people aged 18 and above. A BUNAC working holiday gives you the freedom and flexibility of spending an extended period of time living and working in another country.

Camp America
37A Queens Gate,
South Kensington,
London, SW7 5HR UK

E: brochure@campamerica.co.uk
T: +44 (0) 20 7581 7373
F: +44 (0) 20 7581 7377
www.campamerica.co.uk

Camp America sends over 7,000 people to work on summer camps in the USA every year with up to 10 weeks independent travel after camp!

Camp Leaders In America
24-26 Mount Pleasant,
Liverpool, L3 5RY UK

E: uk@campleaders.com
F: +44 (0) 151 709 6060
www.campleaders.com

Activity leaders, camp counselors and support staff needed in their summer camps. See website for further details.

the gap-year guidebook 2011

Leiths School of Food & Wine, 16-20 Wendell Road, Shepherd's Bush, London W12 9RT
T: +44 (0) 20 8749 6400
E: info@leiths.com
W: www.leiths.com

If you would like to earn money during your gap-year and maybe beyond, cooking jobs can offer a flexible short-term solution. Leiths List, Leiths School of Food and Wine's agency for cooks, can help place you in a suitable job at the right level for your ability and experience. There are jobs in the UK and abroad particularly in the summer, ranging from weekends to 6-8 week contracts, which means you could plan work around travel plans or travel as you work. Leiths School of Food and Wine has a four-week course starting in August each year which teaches the essential skills for this level of family cooking – for more information see the 'cookery courses' section of this book. Once you are qualified from any reputable cookery school (it doesn't have to be Leiths School of Food and Wine) you can contact Leiths List and register. Earning money through cooking is not necessarily restricted to your year off as we have many under and post graduates who find work through Leiths List on a regular basis during their university holidays.

"Being at university means that you have to fend for yourself. The Leiths Essential Certificate qualification has ensured that I can cook meals for not just myself but my whole house. Leiths has also taught me to cook healthy food, whilst sticking to a reasonable budget. During the holidays there are always jobs available, which is useful when cashflow as a student is difficult!" Diana Cheal, graduated from Leiths 2007

Please contact us on 01225 722 983 or email info@leithslist.com

Canvas Holidays
East Port House,
12 East Port,
Dunfermline, KY12 7JG UK

E: campingrecruitment@canvasholidays.com
T: +44 (0) 1383 629012
F: +44 (0) 1383 629071
www.canvasholidaysrecruitment.com

We have paid positions at over 100 campsites across Europe. We require a minimum of six weeks commitment between March and October.

Castaway Resorts
118 Plus City Park,
Sukhumvit Road Soi 101/1 (Soi 31), Bangchak,
10260 Bangkok, Thailand

T: +66 890 60 12 04

Castaway Resorts invite enthusiastic active young people on a gap year to join our friendly teams at one of our tropical beach resorts in Thailand.

CCUSA
Unit 6.04, 6 Morie Street,
Wandsworth Town,
London, SW18 1SL UK

E: england@ccusa.com
T: +44 (0) 20 8874 6325
F: +44 (0) 20 8871 9589
www.ccusa.com

Work in summer camps in beautiful locations in America. You don't need any experience or qualifications but you do need to be at least 18 years old. Also available, a range of worldwide programs including winter seasons in Canada.

Changing Worlds
11 Doctors Lane,
Chaldon, CR3 5AE UK

E: ask@changingworlds.co.uk
www.changingworlds.co.uk

Changing Worlds is a small, friendly organisation with charitable aims. We focus on every group of applicants we send out. This ethos has successfully sent over 1300 people on once-in-a-lifetime trips, and we are proud to say that a quarter of our applicants come from recommendations.

Go Workabout
PO Box 1865,
Fremantle,
Perth, 6959 Australia

E: info@goworkabout.com
T: +61 (0) 8 6420 5000
F: +61 (0) 862 678 184
www.goworkabout.com

Arranges work in Australia for working holiday makers before they travel.

Immigration New Zealand
Mezzanine Floor, New Zealand House,
80 Haymarket, St James's, www.immigration.govt.nz/branch/londonbranchhome
London, SW1Y 4TE UK

T: 09069 100 100 (premium rate number)
F: +44 (0) 207 973 0370

New Zealand government website offering details on working holidays for visitors to the country.

the gap-year guidebook 2011

oyster
gap year specialist

Gain first rate experience and earn a wage overseas

help finance your gap year in **Canada** and **Australia**

- Earn and ski in one of Canada's top Ski Resorts. The Rockies, Whistler or French speaking Tremblant.
- Farm training course with guaranteed job for horse riders and agricultural students in the Australian Outback.
- Paid work in Sydney in bars, restaurants and retail.

For details of our voluntary and paid placements, visit
www.oysterworldwide.com
or telephone **01892 770771** or email **emailus@oysterworldwide.com**
Oyster Worldwide, Hodore Farm, Hartfield, East Sussex TN7 4AR

Jobs In The Alps
3 Bracken Terrace,
Newquay, TR7 2LS UK

E: info@jobs-in-the-alps.co.uk
www.jobs-in-the-alps.co.uk

Jobs in the Alps provide seasonal jobs in ski resorts for students who can speak French, German or Italian.

Launchpad Australia
PO Box 2525,
Fitzroy, VIC 3065 Australia

F: +61 3 9445 9375

Launchpad Australia provide working holiday, gap-year and career break adventures in Australia and abroad!

Leiths School of Food & Wine
16-20 Wendell Road,
Shepherd's Bush,
London, W12 9RT UK

E: info@leiths.com
T: +44 (0) 20 8749 6400
www.leiths.com

Find short term cookery jobs such as chalet and holiday home work. Once qualified (see cookery section), you can earn money in your gap year or university holidays.

Mark Warner Ltd
20 Kensington Church Street,
Kensington,
London, W8 4EP UK

E: recruitment@markwarner.co.uk
T: +44 (0) 8717 033 955
F: +44 (0) 845 058 2568
www.markwarner-recruitment.co.uk

Leading independent tour operator with opportunities all year round in ski and beach resorts. Variety of hotel positions and fully inclusive benefits package on offer.

Natives.co.uk
263 Putney Bridge Road,
Putney,
London, SW15 2PU UK

E: info@natives.co.uk
T: +44 (0) 208 788 4911
www.natives.co.uk

Seasonal recruitment website for ski or summer resorts.

Oyster Worldwide Limited
Hodore Farm,
Hartfield, TN7 4AR UK

E: emailus@oysterworldwide.com
www.oysterworldwide.com

Oyster is the specialist gap-year provider offering paid work projects abroad. Whether you're a ski nut or budding jackaroo, you'll get excellent, personal support throughout.

The Year Out Group
Queensfield,
28 King's Road,
Easterton, SN10 4PX UK

E: info@yearoutgroup.org
T: +44 (0) 1380 816696
www.yearoutgroup.org

See main entry under volunteering.

the gap-year guidebook 2011

Visitoz, Springbrook Farm, 8921 Burnett Highway, Goomeri QLD 4601
T: +61 (0) 741 686 185
E: info@visitoz.org W: www.visitoz.org

Have you ever wondered what to do if you did not get your University place offered?

By now you will know - maybe even now you are considering whether to do resits, try something else or take a gap-year to discover what else there is in the world!

Australia is calling! In rural and outback Australia we have jobs a-plenty - take a working holiday for a year (maybe two) and consider your options while living in a sunny country, enjoying the real Australia and getting paid doing it!

Australian cities are much like those in Europe with lots of people and high youth unemployment - in the outback there is masses of work and this is why Visitoz (www.visitoz.org) can actually guarantee that you will have jobs, paid at the Union rate, plus food and accommodation. They are the only organisation in Australia that do this. Farm, station and rural hospitality work is all available throughout the year.

After a few months of work, when you are all 'cashed up' and have a healthy bank balance, take a trip to the cities and the coast, dive, sail, ski, snorkel and do all the rest of a myriad of things on offer in this incredible country. Cuddle a koala, catch a croc and have the time of your life on a self-financing holiday.

Enquiries to Joanna Burnet +61 741 686 185 or info@visitoz.org.

visit: www.gap-year.com

Visas Australia Ltd
Lindum House,
44 Wellington Road,
Nantwich, CW5 7BX UK

E: info@visas-australia.com
T: +44 (0) 1270 626 626
F: +44 (0) 1270 626 226
www.visas-australia.com

Visas Australia Company specialises in processing and issuing all types of visas, particularly for gappers. Their service is approved by both the Australian Tourist Board and Australian High Commission.

Visitoz
Springbrook Farm,
8921 Burnett Highway,
Goomeri, QLD 4601 Australia

E: info@visitoz.org
T: +61 (0) 741 686 185
F: +61 (0) 741 686 126
www.visitoz.org

Visitoz provides training and guarantees work for young people between the ages of 18 and 30 in agriculture, hospitality, child care and teaching all over Australia.

TEFL

Adventure Alternative
PO Box 14,
Portstewart, BT55 7WS UK

E: office@adventurealternative.com
www.adventurealternative.com

Teaching and volunteering in needy schools and orphanages in Kenya and in schools in Kathmandu (includes Himalayan trek).

CRCC Asia Ltd
106 Weston Street,
Southwark,
London, SE1 3QB UK

E: mail@crccasia.com
T: +44 (0) 207 378 6220
F: +44 (0) 207 378 6226
www.china-recruitment.co.uk

CRCC Asia Ltd organises paid internships and teaching placements in China and has both London and Beijing offices to ensure your programme goes smoothly.

Link Ethiopia
4 Orchard Mews,
Islington,
London, N1 5BS UK

E: chris@linkethiopia.org
T: +44 (0) 20 7241 3544
www.linkethiopia.org

Experience Ethiopia and teach basic English to small groups on a very inexpensive three-month placement with us. Registered Charity No. 1112390.

Saxoncourt Training & Recruitment
59 South Molton Street,
Mayfair,
London, W1K 5SN UK

E: tt@saxoncourt.com
T: +44 (0) 20 7499 8533
F: +44 (0) 20 7499 9374
www.saxoncourt.com

If you don't yet have your TEFL qualification, Saxoncourt runs full time four-week courses in London and Oxford, leading to either the Trinity TESOL diploma or the Cambridge CELTA qualification.

the gap-year guidebook 2011

Syndicat Mixte Montaigu-Rocheservière
35 avenue Villebois Mareuil,
Montaigu, 85607 France

F: +33 (0) 2 51 46 45 40
www.explomr.com/english

Receives local government funding to teach English in primary schools, offering four posts annually – and it also employs a fifth person to work as a language assistant in a local college and lycée.

Chapter 6
Volunteering abroad

6 Volunteering abroad

Voluntary work abroad can be one of the most rewarding ways to spend all, or part, of your **gap**-year. You could find yourself working with people living in unbelievable poverty, disease or hunger. It can be a humbling and hugely enriching experience and it can make you question all the things you've taken for granted in your life. It's no exaggeration to say it can be life-changing.

Some people who have done it have ended up changing their planned course of study at university or even their whole career plan. Year Out Group's members, who are all **gap-** providers, report that volunteering is the top **gap-**choice among all age groups and had risen by 20% in the last full year for which they carried out research.

Teaching and working with children are the most popular options, with requests for teaching placements going up by 10% since September 2008, according to statistics sourced from the Training & Development Agency in March 2009.

Interestingly, women gappers outnumber men, and women are also more likely to choose volunteering and expeditions rather than courses or cultural exchanges.

Why volunteer?

There's no denying that the economic situation has also added to the need for volunteers, with organisations like the UN reporting that it has affected approximately 40% more of the world's most vulnerable people.

visit: www.gap-year.com

So volunteer help is likely to be even more needed and appreciated. Voluntary work abroad can also give you wonderful memories and a new perspective on the world.

On an organised voluntary project you often live amongst the local community and tend to get closer to daily life than you do as an independent traveller. By taking part in an organised voluntary work project you can learn about a different culture, meet new people and learn to communicate with people who may not understand your way of life, let alone your language.

You will come away with an amazing sense of achievement and (hopefully) pride in what you have done. Career breakers have also found that a volunteer **gap-** has not only been a satisfying experience but given them new ideas and attitudes too. A structured volunteer placement can also give a new dimension to the skills you can highlight on your CV.

Our friends at the National Union of Students told us that they believe volunteering abroad can prove a life-changing experience for gappers.

"When considering your options for a gap year the prospect of volunteering could, and should, figure highly in your thoughts. Volunteering, whether it be at home or abroad, can provide you with valuable skills, life-changing experiences and, of course, the opportunity to make a positive difference in the world.

"In difficult economic times the jobs market for young people is incredibly competitive and volunteering, at home or internationally can help you show commitment to a cause, demonstrate your ability to see something through to the end and give you the work experience that is essential to so many employers. Even the process of raising money for a volunteering trip abroad could add valuable colour to you CV.

"Many people take a gap year to work full-time to save money for university, travelling or something else and you might end up working in a job that is less than inspiring. Planning an international volunteering trip can give you something exciting to work towards or could volunteer locally in your spare time to keep things interesting as you prepare for what comes next and gain skills and experience you might not get in your day job.

"Travelling abroad to volunteer teaching English, building a medical centre, on a conservation project or one of the myriad other projects offered around the world for many people makes their gap year as defining an experience as going away to university itself. An opportunity to experience a culture unlike anything like you've previously experienced and to survive independent of your normal support networks will inevitably make you look at yourself and the world around you in a different way.

"The two most important aspects of any volunteering project should be the value to those whom it is there to help and your own safety. Often the projects where you can be useful and therefore gain the most are not the most glamorous ones but at the end you will have a real sense of having helped and it will ultimately be more rewarding. Make sure too, that you research any organisations that you volunteer with to make sure they are legitimate, that they won't send you anywhere dangerous and that you have a ready support network if something does go wrong."

the gap-year guidebook 2011

Being realistic, voluntary work can be tough. You may be out in the middle of nowhere, with no western influence to be seen; food, language - the entire culture is likely to be totally different from what you're used to and there might not be many English speakers around: so you may have to cope with culture shock or feeling lonely, isolated and homesick at first, but if you stick with it you'll usually find those feelings will go as you get more involved in what you're doing.

Are there ethical concerns?

The debate continues about the ethics of volunteering, and covers a variety of issues:

- Is it environmentally sustainable?
- Does it really benefit the people or is it creating a dependency culture?
- What's the 'benefit balance' between volunteer satisfaction and the community being helped?

Our friends at Tourism Concern have carried out extensive research into the international volunteering sector and identified some serious problems with operating procedures by some of the businesses and agencies involved. Here's what they told us:

"Often placements are driven by demand from volunteers rather than by needs in the host communities, causing a variety of problems. In the worst cases the volunteer can actually become a burden and a resource drain to the community, whilst other cases uncovered projects that were neither planned nor monitored correctly, leaving the volunteer isolated and vulnerable. On occasion projects did not even address needs that had been identified by the local community.

"It doesn't need to be like this. Most organisations charge a significant amount of money for their ventures, so before parting with your cash it is key that you thoroughly investigate both the organisation and the projects on offer."

So before signing up with any organisation, Tourism Concern offer ten critical areas to question:

1. **Project:** Has the local community been consulted to identify the need for the project? What are its specific aims and objectives?

2. **Recruitment:** What is the selection procedure for the project? Do they check references? If they do not feel you are suitable for a specific project, will they explain why and discuss alternatives with you?

3. **Feedback:** Has the project run before, if so can you see feedback from previous volunteers AND the host community to better understand the experience and the impact of the project? Speak to a past volunteer directly if possible.

4. **Training:** What training and briefing will you receive before you depart? Will you be given guidance on the country, community and host organisation? Will you be given a specific job description?

5. **Support:** What support will you receive while you are there? Is there

visit: www.gap-year.com

telephone support during hours that suit you? Is the support appropriate to the local communication situation?

6. **Fees:** Ask for a breakdown of the fee you are paying to see how it is fully meeting all the costs to host communities and partners. Make sure you know whether you need to take additional spending money to cover local costs or whether an allowance is included. What meals, if any, are included?

7. **Risk:** Has a risk assessment been carried out for all placements, including all activities within a placement? And has that risk assessment considered the volunteer, host partner and host community?

8. **Emergencies:** Is there a 24 hour emergency procedure in place? Is it regularly rehearsed?

9. **Insurance:** Is insurance included? Is it adequate? You must read the small print!

10. **Completion:** What will happen when you get back? Will you meet up to debrief the project and your experience, and assess its impact against the stated aims and objectives?

Through asking these few questions you will discover the nature of the organisation you are dealing with, and whether it is right for you and will fulfil what you want to achieve from volunteering. These measures will help to ensure that your trip is a positive experience for both you and the local community that you become part of.

Fair Trade Volunteering (**www.fairtradevolunteering.org**) has been created and established by leading volunteer organisations and advisors in the travel industry to enable volunteers to make a choice as to which volunteer experience they would like to have, and to give organisations wishing to provide FTV projects guidelines, help and support to be able to deliver them.

The "volunteering industry" has in the past few years become just that - an industry, with different organisations giving different levels of importance to the benefit for the projects, the experience for the volunteer and the profit for the company. Just as the Fairtrade Foundation has helped the consumer to be able to make an informed decision when buying coffee, bananas and chocolate etc, Fair Trade Volunteering is looking to do the same for volunteering placements.

Here's what they told us: "Our belief is that short periods of volunteering can be positive, but only really if they are part of a longer partnership with the project, and combined with financial support above and beyond the volunteer's contribution, to ensure the work done can be continued throughout the year. Organisations which are approved by Fair Trade Volunteering not only ensure that the cost of the volunteer (and their work) is covered, but that there is also a financial premium given to the project to ensure their work can be further supported above and beyond the work done by the volunteers.

"Added to this, they must also show a long term partnership with their projects, ensuring that the work done by the volunteer and the funds being sent are part of a longer term set of objectives. This means a volunteer who is only able to commit to a short period at a project is able to see that their contribution, both financial and physical, is part of a bigger picture that is making a genuinely positive difference.

visit: www.gap-year.com

"At the end of the day, it is up to the consumer to decide. By buying non-Fairtrade coffee, you are not necessarily doing a bad thing, you are still helping to provide a living for the people who make it. If you do buy Fairtrade however, it is because you are willing to pay the premium which Fairtrade ensures for its workers. The same holds for Fair Trade Volunteering."

Rachel Heels left the UK a girl and returned a woman - and now helps others organise their own dream **gap**-years...

"It's hard to believe that I took my gap year in 2004 – six years on and it's incredible to see how it's changed my life!.

"Volunteering captured my imagination and was everything I was looking for – not only did my gap year feature a different culture, idyllic scenery and picture postcard beaches, I was also fantastically lucky to be able to become a real part of the community, teaching on a remote island in Fiji.

"I've still got a 'Fijian family' who I visit as often as I can – although I should have chosen a project a little closer to home to make visits easier.

"On my arrival back to the UK I found it difficult to settle back in - I had Fiji Sickness! Luckily, I had university to look forward to otherwise I'm sure I would have jumped on the next flight back there.

"I was humbled by my volunteering experience – not only was I able to benefit a local community, I also achieved so much personally; I went away a confused 18-year-old girl (I was even crying on my Mum's shoulder at the airport saying I'd be back in a week when I hated it!), I returned a confident woman. I knew exactly what I wanted to do and even changed my course at university to reflect this.

"I now work for Travellers Worldwide. I feel lucky to have been able to help others live their dreams and gain the confidence to travel and also that I am part of a fantastic, family run, ethical company. My advice to anyone that's not sure about taking the plunge is: choose something that they are passionate about and then go for it: it might just change your life too."

the gap-year guidebook 2011

What would you like to do?

Only you can decide what's most important to you, it depends on whether you're more into plants, animals and the environment, in which case you'd be happier on a conservation project. If you're a people person you might do something that helps disadvantaged people, whether they're children, adults, and disabled or able bodied.

Whichever you feel is right for you there's a huge range of companies and types of voluntary placements to choose from.

Even if you are straight from school or university and haven't yet had much experience of work-related skills you shouldn't underestimate the skills and qualities you may have, and take for granted, that can be far less accessible to disadvantaged people in places where such things as access to education or to communications are not universally available.

How much time do you want to spend?

This is about how committed a volunteer you want to be. Would you feel more satisfied spending two weeks on a building project providing homes for people displaced by a natural disaster? Or are you the kind of person who wants to get stuck into a long-term project, where the results you see will be more gradual?

Because voluntary work is so popular with gappers, commercial companies offering volunteering packages exist alongside the more traditional not-for-profit organisations and the idealism associated with voluntary work, though still there, has come under some commercial pressure.

Some companies offer two- to four-week holidays combined with some voluntary work, but equally there are many organisations still committed to the idealism of volunteering, offering placements from a few months to up a year or more.

However, you may not want (or be able) to offer more than a few weeks or months of your time, so the combined holiday/short volunteering option might be for you. There's no point in committing yourself to a whole year only to find that, after a few weeks, you hate it and want to go home early. The two- to four-week option may also be a good 'taster' experience to help you decide whether to commit to something more long-term.

So, it's a good idea to be honest with yourself about what you want - there's nothing wrong with wanting to travel and have a good time. But, whatever you choose, make sure you are clear about what you will be doing *before* you sign up and part with your money.

When to start applying

Applications can close early, particularly for expeditions and conservation projects needing complex funding or for those tied in with international government programmes. If you'd like to go on one of these projects, planning should start about a year ahead, usually in the autumn term of the academic year.

visit: www.gap-year.com

Others can be taken up at very short notice. In fact, some organisations can take in applications during the August period (when you are getting A level results or going through clearing), and book you on a project that starts in September. If you don't have much time before your **gap-** starts (maybe you didn't get the grades you expected, or you've made a last-minute decision to defer university for a year, or your company has offered you a sabbatical or made you redundant) it is always worth contacting a voluntary organisation about a project you're interested in. They may have had a last-minute cancellation.

Stiff competition

As more people are becoming motivated by the almost daily media reports on poverty in the developing world and on various global threats to the planet's climate, ecology and environment, to go out and do something, the competition for places can be fierce. Companies can afford to be picky - you may find you have to prove to them that you should be selected to go before they will accept your money!

They have a point. Increasingly NGOs and volunteers are trying to make sure both sides benefit from the experience, so placement organisations put a lot of effort into checking and briefing as well as getting you out there and providing in-country support. If you can't stick it, everyone loses out - including the person who could have been chosen instead of you.

What's the cost?

It varies hugely - some companies just expect you to pay for the airfare - others expect you to raise thousands of pounds for funding. It can be hard to

the gap-year guidebook 2011

combine raising money with studying for A levels or with work, but there are a lot of ways to do it.

As usual, the earlier you start, the easier it will be. The organisation that you go with should be able to give advice, but options include organising sponsored events (abseiling down a tall building), writing to companies or trusts asking for sponsorship, car boot sales, or even just getting a job and saving what you can.

If approached, many local newspapers will do a short article about your plan if it's interesting enough - but it's better to ask them during the quieter news spells, like the summer holiday months, when they'll be more likely to welcome an additional story.

The last resort is to go cap-in-hand to your parents, either for a loan or a gift, but this can be unsatisfying and they may simply not be able to afford it. If your parents or relatives do want to help, you could ask for useful items for Christmas or birthday presents - like a rucksack.

Career breakers will have different considerations. There's more on this in Chapter 3 - Career Breakers and Mature Travellers, but if you work for a large organisation it's worth asking whether they have any links to projects, or run their own charitable foundation, which might offer placements to employees.

What to expect

Placements range from a couple of weeks to a whole academic year, but most provide only free accommodation and food - a very few provide pocket money. You'll need to be resourceful, be able to teach, build, inspire confidence, communicate and share what you know. Physical and mental fitness, staying power and the ability to get on with people are essential.

This is what most placement organisers say: "We are looking for self-motivated and reliable positive thinkers. You need to be self-reliant and able to cope when you turn up at a Nepali school and find a basic room, no curtains and that the loo is a 'long-drop' down the garden."

Ruby Shorrock volunteered through the African Conservation Experience on their Shimongwe Wildlife Veterinary Experience. Here's how she described a typical day:

"Today was such an incredible day! We went to take blood samples from ten buffalo. I helped by drawing up vaccines, changing needles and making sure there were enough tubes for the blood and handing them to whoever was taking the samples. We then went back to the clinic and treated a cat who had been hit by a car before heading back out to treat a buffalo bull that had a nasty wound on his head.

"We then went and darted a lioness and injected her with a contraception stick. At the end of the day we released some black rhino into a new game reserve. We ate round the campfire looking out into the African bush. Whilst we were eating six giraffe walked past! This country is so amazing."

visit: www.gap-year.com

Some other points worth emphasizing:

Big organisation or small specialist? You might feel safer going with a big voluntary organisation because they should be able to offer help in a nasty situation. Experience is certainly important where organisations are concerned. But often a small, specialist organisation is more knowledgeable about a country, a school or other destination.

Size and status have little bearing on competence. A charity can be more efficient than a commercial company. Conversely a commercial company can show more sensitivity than a charity.

There are few general rules - talk to someone who's been with the organisation you're interested in. Organisations vary as to how much back up they offer volunteers, from virtually holding your hand throughout your stay and even after you come back, to the 'sink or swim' method.

You need to know yourself if you're going to get the most out of your volunteering **gap-**. If you feel patronised at the slightest hint of advice then you might get annoyed with too much interference from the organisation.

Though do bear in mind that they probably know more than you do about the placement, what sort of vaccinations you're going to need, what will be useful to take with you, and how to get the necessary visas and permits. Equally if you're shy or nervous it might be as well to go with an organisation that sends volunteers in pairs or groups. There's nothing wrong with either type of placement - it's about choosing what's right for you.

Talk to a few organisations before you decide which one to go with - and, probably even more useful, talk to some previous volunteers. They'll be able to tell you what it's really like; don't just ask them if they enjoyed it, get them to describe what they did, what they liked and why, what they didn't like and what they'd do differently.

Remember, wherever you're sent, you can't count on much. Regardless of the organisation, you will be going to poor countries where the infrastructure and support services can be minimal - otherwise why would they need volunteers?

Expect to be adaptable. Regardless of the reputation of the voluntary work organisation you choose, or the competence of voluntary work coordinators in a particular country, it's about your skills and human qualities and those of the people you'll be with so there's bound to be an element of chance as to whether the school you are put in, for example, really values you or whether

the gap-year guidebook 2011

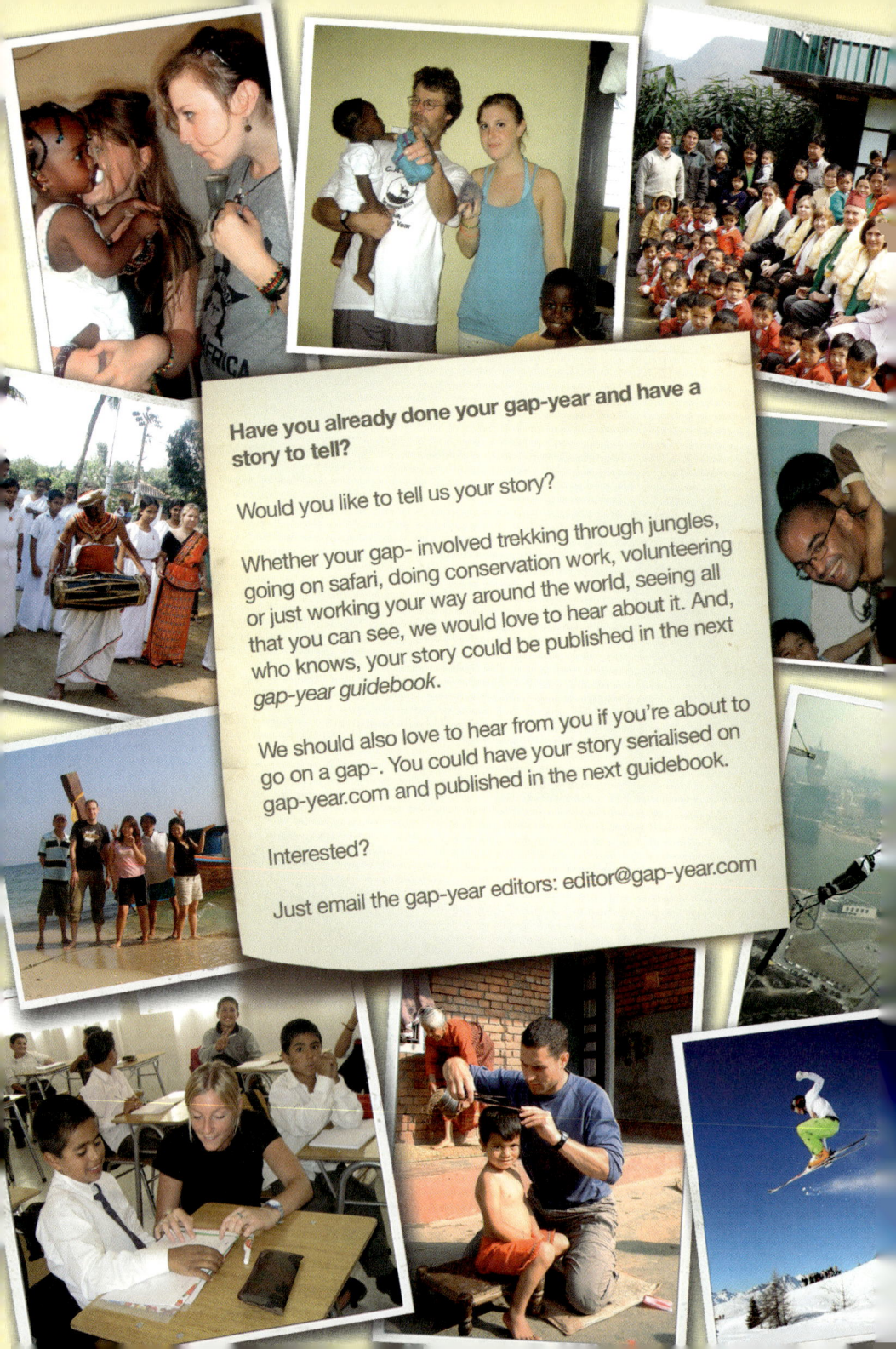

Have you already done your gap-year and have a story to tell?

Would you like to tell us your story?

Whether your gap- involved trekking through jungles, going on safari, doing conservation work, volunteering or just working your way around the world, seeing all that you can see, we would love to hear about it. And, who knows, your story could be published in the next *gap-year guidebook*.

We should also love to hear from you if you're about to go on a gap-. You could have your story serialised on gap-year.com and published in the next guidebook.

Interested?

Just email the gap-year editors: editor@gap-year.com

you get on with the family you stay with. It's worth checking first what training is given and what support there is in-country, but be aware that you may not get what you expect - you need to be adaptable and make the most of whatever situation you find yourself in.

Safety first

If you're going with a good organisation they shouldn't send you anywhere too dangerous - but situations change quickly and it's always worth finding out for yourself about where you're going.

Check out the Foreign Office's travel advice pages on: **www.fco.gov.uk** The Foreign Office site also has lots of advice on visas, insurance and other things that need to be sorted out before you go, and advice on what to do in an emergency abroad. There's much more on all this in Chapter 1 - Tips For Travellers.

Also, make sure you have proper insurance cover and that it is appropriate for where you're going, the length of time you'll be away and for any unexpected emergencies.

AFRICAN CONSERVATION EXPERIENCE

African Conservation Experience, Unit 1 Manor Farm, Churchend Lane, Charfield, Wotton-Under-Edge GL12 8LJ
T: +44 (0) 1454 269182
E: info@conservationafrica.net   W: www.conservationafrica.net

Have you ever dreamed of tracking wild leopard and cheetah through the bush, or assisting a marine biologist in whale and dolphin research? Open your eyes to a whole new world and way of looking at the natural environment. We support vital conservation projects in our heritage region of southern Africa and have over ten years experience. Whether on a gap-year, career break, retired or as a family, you can be sure you're making a vital contribution to conservation and travelling with the highest standards of environmental responsibility' Members of the Year Out Group and ATOL bonded.

Why A.C.E?
- We are a long and established organisation with over ten years experience.
- 80% of your placement cost goes directly to the project and getting you out to southern Africa.
- Our responsible travel policy ensures you travel with the highest standards of environmental responsibility.
- All our staff are qualified experts in their area of marine biology, zoology and conservation.
- Much of our effort goes into matching volunteer with a project to ensure that the experience is, as far as possible, right for you. This high level of personal care is consistent throughout your placement.
- Our flexibility means that you can chose what time of year you go and for how long. Even once you have booked on, should you wish to change anything about your placement we will do our utmost to meet your needs.
- A portion of the funds raised for your placement goes directly towards sponsoring communities and local conservation organisations in South Africa and Botswana.

visit: www.gap-year.com

Volunteering Abroad

Conservation

African Conservation Trust
PO Box 310,
Link Hills, 3652 South Africa
E: info@projectafrica.com
F: +27 86 5117 594
www.projectafrica.com

The mission of ACT is to provide a means for conservation projects to become self funding through active participation by the public.

African Gap Year
PO Box 1312,
Cresta, 2118 South Africa
E: info@africangapyear.co.za
F: +27(0)865858556
www.africangapyear.com

Various opportunities to volunteer or work a gap-year in South Africa.

All Out Africa
PO Box 153,
Lobamba, H100 Swaziland
E: info@all-out.org
F: +268 4162260
www.all-out.org

They run cutting edge wildlife conservation and social development projects in some of Africa's most amazing locations.

Amanzi Travel
4 College Road,
Westbury on Trym, BS9 3EJ UK
E: info@amanzitravel.co.uk
F: +44 (0) 117 959 4678
www.amanzitravel.co.uk

Leading Specialist in Volunteer Placements throughout Africa
Amanzi Travel is passionate about the projects offered, ATOL licensed and offers a service that is second-to-none.

Azafady
Studio 7,
1a Beethoven Street, West Kilburn,
London, W10 4LG UK
E: mark@azafady.org
T: + 44 (0) 20 8960 6629
F: +44 (0) 20 8962 0126
www.madagascar.co.uk

Pioneer Madagascar is a ten-week volunteer scheme that offers first-hand experience of frontline development and conservation work in beautiful and remote areas.

Blue Ventures
2D Aberdeen Studios, Aberdeen Centre,
22-24 Highbury Grove, Highbury,
London, N5 2EA UK
E: enquiries@blueventures.org
T: +44 (0) 20 7359 1287
F: +44 (0) 800 066 4032
www.blueventures.org

Blue Ventures runs award-winning marine research projects for conservation, education and sustainable development. Volunteers participate in diving and terrestrial activities in partnership with local communities.

Amanzi travel

Amanzi Travel, 4 College Road,
Westbury on Trym BS9 3EJ
T: +44 (0) 117 904 1924
E: info@amanzitravel.co.uk
W: www.amanzitravel.co.uk

Amanzi Travel - Leading UK Specialist in Volunteer and Adventure Travel throughout Africa

An ATOL bonded, family run company who are passionate about what we do and who offer a service that is second-to-none.

Whether you are looking for a gap-year, career break or simply a holiday with a difference - let Amanzi Travel arrange your own experience of a lifetime.

We not only offer volunteer opportunities but also exciting Overland Trips and Game Ranger Courses - why not combine your Volunteer Placement with an Overland Trip - a great way to have a real adventure and see more of this beautiful continent. We can arrange everything for you!

A few of our volunteer opportunities:

- Work up-close with a variety of endangered wildlife, including big cats, at the Namibia Wildlife Sanctuary and Noah's Ark - where animals in trouble from all over the country have found a safe home;

- Walk with and care for lion cubs on the world's leading Lion Breeding/Rehabilitation project in Zambia;

- Work alongside qualified doctors/nurses at hospitals, clinics and on community outreach programmes which bring vital medical care to people in Kenya, Namibia, Zambia and South Africa, as well as helping on HIV/AIDS education programmes;

- Assist teachers in nursery, primary and secondary schools with opportunities to specialise in sports coaching and conservation education initiatives;

- Give much needed love and care to the many children who have lost their parents – many to AIDS - and who have found homes in orphanages throughout Africa.

Contact one of the Amanzi Travel team today on: 0117 904 1924 or take a look at: www.amanzitravel.co.uk

Email: info@amanzitravel.co.uk

BSES Expeditions
at The Royal Geographical Society,
1 Kensington Gore, South Kensington,
London, SW7 2AR UK

E: info@bses.org.uk
T: +44 (0) 20 7591 3141
www.bses.org.uk

BSES Expeditions organises challenging scientific expeditions to remote, wild environments. Study climate change whilst mountaineering or kayaking in the Arctic, measure biodiversity in the Amazon or investigate human interaction with the environment in the Himalayas.

Camps International Limited
Unit 1 Kingfisher Park, Headlands Business Park,
Salisbury Road,
Ringwood, BH24 3NX UK

E: info@campsinternational.com
T: +44 (0) 844 800 1127
www.campsinternational.com

Gap-year volunteer holidays available. Spend time in community and wildlife camps and still have the time and opportunity to trek mountains and dive in the ocean.

Concordia International Volunteers
2nd Floor, 19 North Street,
Portslade,
Brighton, BN41 1DH UK

E: info@concordia-iye.org.uk
T: +44 (0) 1273 422 218
www.concordia-iye.org.uk

Concordia offers the opportunity to join international teams of volunteers working on short-term projects in 60 countries in Europe, North America, Latin-America, Africa and Asia.

Conservation Volunteers Australia
PO Box 423,
Ballarat, 3353 Australia

E: info@conservationvolunteers.com.au
F: +61 (0) 3 5330 2922
www.conservationvolunteers.com.au

Conservation Volunteers Australia offers projects across Australia, including tree planting, wildlife surveys, track building, year-round. Contribution for meals, accommodation and travel applies.

Conservation Volunteers New Zealand
Conservation Volunteers Head Office,
PO Box 423,
Ballarat, 3353 Australia

E: info@conservationvolunteers.com.au
T: +61 (0) 3 5330 2600
F: +61 (0) 3 5330 2922
www.conservationvolunteers.com.au

Conservation Volunteers New Zealand offers projects year-round, including habitat restoration, tree planting, track building. Contribution for meals, accommodation and travel applies.

blue ventures
discovery through research

Blue Ventures, 2D Aberdeen Studios, Aberdeen Centre, 22-24 Highbury Grove, Highbury, London N5 2EA
T: +44 (0) 20 7359 1287
E: enquiries@blueventures.org   W: www.blueventures.org

On Blue Ventures' award-winning, marine conservation expeditions to Madagascar, Belize and Malaysia, you will join committed volunteers from around the world to work with our field research teams, alongside local communities. You will be involved in all aspects of the expedition; from SCUBA diving, learning about the fascinating ecosystems and working with local communities and schools, to developing conservation plans.

Experience the incredible culture of the Vezo fishing peoples and the unique habitats of south west Madagascar at our remote expedition base. Dive some of the most spectacular reefs in the world and share food and festivities with the Mestizo community of northern Belize. Explore the rich marine life of Tioman Island, collect crucial data on species threatening its diversity and discover what can be found in the challenging interior rainforest.

Make the most of your gap-year, develop new skills, get some great stories and make new friends on a Blue Ventures expedition. New expeditions begin every six weeks, and you can stay between three and 52 weeks. Blue Ventures works closely with communities to ensure that the results from your work help us to propose new ideas to benefit coastal communities everywhere.

Get in touch to find out how you can help and join an expedition today!

Coral Cay Conservation
Block 1, Elizabeth House,
39 York Road, Lambeth,
London, SE1 7NQ UK

E: info@coralcay.org
T: +44 (0) 20 7620 1411
F: +44 (0) 20 7921 0469
www.coralcay.org

Volunteer with award-winning specialists in coral reef and rainforest conservation expeditions. Scuba dive or trek in tropical climes and work with local communities to aid long-term conservation efforts.

CREES The Rainforest Education and Resource Centre
5-6 Kendrick Mews,
South Kensington,
London, SW7 3HG UK

E: ukinfo@crees.expeditions.com
T: +44 (0) 20 7581 2932
www.crees-expeditions.com

Volunteering programme which combines conservation work with participation in local community projects.

Cross-Border Development
Level 20, AIA Tower,
251A - 301 Av Comercial De Macau,
Macau SAR, PR China

E: info@cbdevelopment.org
T: +853 8294 6206
F: +853 8294 2200
www.cbdevelopment.org

Offers volunteer and paid internship placements in Macau. A unique opportunity to gain work experience whilst travelling.

Discover Nepal
GPO Box: 20209,
Kathmandu, Nepal

E: stt@mos.com.np
www.discovernepal.com.np

The aim of Discover Nepal is to provide opportunities for the involvement in the development process, and to practically contribute towards the socio-economic development of the country.

Dyer Island Cruises
PO Box 78,
Gansbaai, 7720 South Africa

E: bookings@whalewatchsa.com
F: +27 (0) 28 384 1266
www.whalewatchsa.com

Offer shark cage diving, boat based whale watching and also volunteer work.

Earthwatch Institute
256 Banbury Road,
Oxford, OX2 7DE UK

E: info@earthwatch.org.uk
F: +44 (0) 1865 311 383
www.earthwatch.org.uk

Work alongside leading scientists around the world and help solve pressing environmental problems. With hundreds of expeditions on over 50 research projects to choose from, conduct hands-on conservation research in stunning locations whilst having an experience of a lifetime.

FR●NTIER.AC.UK

A NON PROFIT ORGANISATION
250 PROJECTS
OVER **50** COUNTRIES
5 CONTINENTS

ETHICAL ADVENTURES

PRICES FROM £295

BTEC Advanced Diploma in Tropical Habitat Conservation.

BTEC Advanced Certificate in: Tropical Habitat Conservation or Expedition Management.

PADI Dive Training: Advanced Open Water and Divemaster.

TEFL Certificate.

FGASA Field Guide Game Ranger Qualifications.

Find us on...

WILDLIFE CONSERVATION

TEACHING & COMMUNITIES

Earthwise Valley
Earthwise Living Foundation,
PO Box 5,
Thames, 3540 New Zealand

E: info@earthwisevalley.org
T: +64 9 355 0333
F: +64 9 355 0333
www.earthwisevalley.org

Join the Rainforest Sanctuary as a residential volunteer and experience New Zealand, while making a real difference to our natural world.

Ecoteer
23 Bearsdown Close,
Eggbuckland,
Plymouth, PL6 5TX UK

E: contact@ecoteer.com
T: +44 (0) 1752 426285
www.ecoteer.com

Community-based placements in 40 plus countries and most are free! Volunteer with us and make everlasting friends across the whole world!

Entabeni Nature Guide Training School
Entabeni Private Game Reserve,
Waterberg Escarpment, South Africa

E: sarah.g@legendlodges.co.za
F: +27 15 453 0647
www.natureguidetraining.co.za

Situated on a private game reserve three hours drive from Johannesburg, Entabeni offer a series of programmes in nature guiding, weapons handling and other tailor-made courses.

Essential Croatia
11, Plymouth Drive,
Bramhall,
Stockport, SK7 2JB UK

E: info@essentialcroatia.com
T: +44 (0)797 020 1035
www.essentialcroatia.com

Griffon Vulture and nature protection programme. Volunteer opportunities available year round on the beautiful and upspoilt island of Cres-Croatia.

Fauna Forever Tambopata
TReeS-Peru,
PO Box 28,
Puerto Maldonado, Peru

E: mail@faunaforevertambopata.org
www.faunaforevertambopata.org

Volunteer researchers needed for wildlife project in the Peruvian Amazon. Fauna Forever Tambopata is a wildlife monitoring project based in the Amazon rainforest of Tambopata in south-eastern Peru.

Friends of Conservation
Southcombe Business Centre,
11-12 Southcombe Street,
London, W14 0RA UK

E: focinfo@aol.com
T: +44 (0) 20 7348 3408
www.foc-uk.com

There are some opportunities to volunteer on overseas projects such as the Namibian based Cheetah Conservation Fund. Volunteers are also needed in the UK and at their head office in London. Registered Charity No. 328176.

the gap-year guidebook 2011

oyster
gap year specialist

Do you have a **passion** for **animals?**

Oyster offers specialist projects in **Jordan, Romania & South Africa**

- Voluntary Work Experience in Jordan for qualified Vets
- Volunteer at a Bear Sanctuary in Romania
- Volunteer with Lions, Elephants or in Marine Research in South Africa

For details of these, and other Oyster projects, please visit
www.oysterworldwide.com
or telephone **01892 770771** or email **emailus@oysterworldwide.com**
Oyster Worldwide, Hodore Farm, Hartfield, East Sussex TN7 4AR

Frontier
50-52 Rivington Street,
London, EC2A 3QP UK

E: info@frontier.ac.uk
F: +44 (0) 20 7613 2992
www.frontier.ac.uk

With 250 projects across 50 countries in Africa, Asia-Pacific, South and Central America, Frontier offers volunteers the chance to get involved in an array of activities from wildlife and marine conservation to trekking and biodiversity research, teaching and community development.

Galapagos Conservation Trust
5 Derby Street,
Mayfair,
London, W1J 7AB UK

E: gct@gct.org
T: +44 (0) 207 629 5049
F: +44 (0) 207 629 4149
www.savegalapagos.org

The Galapagos Conservation Trust has two aims: to raise funds to support the expanding conservation work and to raise awareness of the current issues the islands face. Registered Charity No. 1043470.

Gapforce
530 Fulham Road,
Fulham, SW6 5NR UK

www.gapforce.org

Gapforce has established itself as a leading provider for enjoyable gap adventures worldwide including volunteering. It is the parent company of Trekforce and Greenforce.

Global Action Nepal
Baldwins,
Eastlands Lane,
Cowfold, RH13 8AY UK

T: +44 (0) 800 587 7138
www.gannepal.org

Global Action Nepal projects are always closely in harness with grass roots level needs, focusing on community-led, participatory development. Registered Charity No. 1090773.

Global Vision International
3 High Street,
St Albans, AL3 4ED UK

E: info@gvi.co.uk
F: +44 (0) 870 609 2319
www.gvi.co.uk

With unparalled in-country support, GVI volunteers benefit from exceptional training and a Careers Abroad job placement scheme.

Global Volunteer Network
PO Box 30-968,
Lower Hutt, 5040 New Zealand

E: info@volunteer.org.nz
F: +64 4 920 1456
www.volunteer.org.nz

Volunteer through the Global Volunteer Network to support communities in need around the world. Volunteer placements include schools, refugee camps, wildlife sanctuaries and nature reserves.

the gap-year guidebook 2011

I want to see the world,
I want to save the world,
I want to be thrilled, to be fulfilled,
I want to learn, I want to teach
I want to dance, I want independence,
I want to share, I want to care,
I want to try, I want to find out why,
I want to know, I want to grow,
I want in because I want time out,
I want to soar, I want to explore,
I want to rock, I want to roll,
I want stories to tell,
I want to LOL,
I want the best year of my life,
(well, the best year yet)
creating memories I'll never forget,
I want to give, I want to take,
I need a break
for goodness sake...

what do **you** want out of **your** year?

Visit our website or call **01879 230444** to discover more about our 8 & 12 month volunteer placements in Africa, Asia and the Americas.

project TRUST — *Changing lives, year in year out...*

PT/GYGB/2010   Registered as a Charity in Scotland No. SCO25668

projecttrust.org.uk

Greenforce
530 Fulham Road,
Fulham,
London, SW6 5NR UK

E: info@greenforce.org
T: +44 (0) 20 7384 3343
www.greenforce.org

Greenforce is a not-for-profit organisation offering voluntary and paid work overseas. With ten years experience and a range of opportunities, Greenforce will have a programe to suit you.

Kwa Madwala Private Game Reserve
PO Box 192,
Hectorspruit, 1330 South Africa

E: res@kwamadwala.co.za
F: +27 (0)13 792 6735
www.kwamadwala.net/gap-year-experiences/

Kwa Madwala Private Game Reserve is located just south of Kruger National Park. They offer gap-year experiences for those interested in learning about African wildlife, conservation and eco-tourism.

Orangutan Foundation
7 Kent Terrace,
Regent's Park,
London, NW1 4RP UK

E: info@orangutan.org.uk
T: +44 (0) 20 7724 2912
F: +44 (0) 207 706 2613
www.orangutan.org.uk

Participate in hands on conservation fieldwork that really makes a difference and see orangutans in their natural habitat.

Outreach International
Bartlett's Farm,
Hayes Road,
Compton Dundon, TA11 6PF UK

E: info@outreachinternational.co.uk
T: +44 (0) 1458 274857
www.outreachinternational.co.uk

Outreach International places committed volunteers in carefully selected projects on the Pacific coast of Mexico, Sri Lanka, Cambodia, Nepal, Costa Rica, Ecuador and the Galapagos Islands.

Oyster Worldwide Limited
Hodore Farm,
Hartfield, TN7 4AR UK

E: emailus@oysterworldwide.com
www.oysterworldwide.com

Oyster is the specialist gap-year provider offering genuine opportunities with endangered or abused animals. Vets, zoologists and animal lovers all welcome. Excellent, personal support throughout.

Peace River Refuge & Ranch
PO Box 1127,
2545 Stoner Lane,
Zolfo Springs, FL 33890 USA

E: volunteer@peaceriverrefuge.org
T: +1 863 735 0804
F: +1 863 735 0805
www.peaceriverrefuge.org

Peace River Refuge & Ranch is a non-profit-making exotic animal sanctuary located in Florida. Its all-volunteer staff provides long-term care for confiscated, abused, neglected or unwanted exotic animals (from tigers to bats) to prevent them from being destroyed.

the gap-year guidebook 2011

FLEXIBILITY

VARIETY

SUPPORT

ProjectsAbroad

VOLUNTEER ABROAD

www.projects-abroad.co.uk
Tel: +44 (0) 1903 708300

Project Trust
The Hebridean Centre,
Isle of Coll, PA78 6TE UK

E: info@projecttrust.org.uk
F: +44 (0) 1879 230 357
www.projecttrust.org.uk

Project Trust (Charity No. SC025668) offers placements in over 20 countries departing in January, August or September. Projects include teaching, social work, outdoor activities instruction, journalism, conservation and medical projects.

Projects Abroad
Aldsworth Parade,
Goring, BN12 4TX UK

E: info@projects-abroad.co.uk
F: +44 (0) 1903 501026
www.projects-abroad.co.uk

8000+ placements overseas. Teach English, gain invaluable experience in Medicine, Conservation and Environment, Journalism, Business, Care and Community, Sports, IT, Law and Human Rights, Veterinary and more.

ProWorld (Real Projects...Real Experience)
Globe II Business Centre,
128 Maltravers Road,
Sheffield, S2 5AZ UK

E: info@myproworld.org
T: +44 (0) 870 750 7202
www.myproworld.org

Projects offered: conservation, health care, education, human rights, journalism, and business projects. Programmes start every month of the year.

Rainforest Nature
Lima, Peru

E: sales@perunature.com
F: +511 421 8183
www.perunature.com

Has conservation projects in countries such as Ecuador, Colombia, Chile, Brazil, Costa Rica, India, Panama, Peru and others.

Real Gap Experience
1 Meadow Road,
Tunbridge Wells, TN1 2YG UK

E: info@realgap.co.uk
F: +44 (0) 1892 523 172
www.realgap.co.uk

Real Gap offers a wide and diverse range of programmes. These include: volunteering, conservation, adventure travel and expeditions, sports, teaching English, round the world, paid working holidays and learning.

ReefDoctor Org Ltd
14 Charlwood Terrace,
Putney,
London, SW15 1NZ UK

E: volunteer@reefdoctor.org
T: +44 (0) 20 8788 6908
F: +44(0) 20 8789 2732
www.reefdoctor.org

Become a volunteer ReefDoctor and contribute to marine research, education, conservation and sustainable community development alongside our team of local and international scientists.

the gap-year guidebook 2011

Rempart
1 rue des Guillemites,
Paris, 75004 France

E: contact@rempart.com
F: +33 (0) 1 42 71 73 00
www.rempart.com

Rempart, a union of conservation associations organises short voluntary work in France. The projects are all based around restoration and maintenance of historic sites and buildings.

SA Volunteers

E: info@savolunteer.com South Africa
T: +27 28 313 0145
www.savolunteers.com

SA Volunteers is committed to voluntourism and to support and help sustain communities in all areas i.e. wildlife, disadvantaged communities and conservation volunteer work.

Shumba Experience
95 Ditchling Road,
Brighton, BN1 4ST UK

E: info@shumbaexperience.co.uk
F: +44 (0) 1273 573832
www.shumbaexperience.co.uk

Join our exciting wildlife and marine conservation projects in Africa. You'll be volunteering on game reserves to help conserve lions, elephants, leopards and rhinos.

Southern African Wildlife College
Private Bage X3015,
Hoedspruit, 1380 South Africa

E: info@sawc.org.za
F: +27 (0) 15 793 7314
www.wildlifecollege.org.za

Are you passionate about wildlife and wanting to learn more about conservation in Africa? This college is offering a unique opportunity to participate in a six month Game Ranger Course.

Starfish Ventures Ltd
PO Box 9061,
Epping, CM16 7WU UK

www.starfishvolunteers.com

Starfish has a volunteer placement for you, whatever your skills, they can be put to good use in our various projects in Thailand.

Sumatran Orangutan Society
The Old Music Hall,
106-108 Cowley Road,
Oxford, OX4 1JE UK

T: +44 (0) 1865 403 341
www.orangutans-sos.org/help/volunteer/

SOS works with local communities living alongside orangutan habitats, helping them work towards a more sustainable future for their forests.

Sunrise Volunteer Programmes
71A Church Road,
Hove, East Sussex BN3 2BB UK

E: info@sunrint.com
F: +44 (0) 1273 738 205
en.sunrint.com

Specialist for volunteer projects in China, offering volunteer opportunities of two weeks to Three months in social, environment, education, medical, journalism and community areas around China.

The Gorilla Organisation
110 Gloucester Avenue,
Camden Town,
London, NW1 8HX UK

E: info@gorillas.org
T: +44 (0) 20 7483 2681
www.gorillas.org/dtime

Formerly the Dian Fossey Gorilla Fund, the Gorilla Organisation (Registered Charity No. 1117131) list various events where you can raise money for the fund. Also lookibng for volunteers.

The Great Marine Project
Suite 6,
8 High Street,
Harpenden, AL5 2TB UK

E: turtle@w-o-x.com
T: +44 (0) 1588 469 950
www.greatmarineproject.com

Help save the turtles of the Perhentian Islands! Don't let the Green turtles follow the same fate as the Leatherbacks who are now extinct on the islands.

The Leap Overseas Ltd
121-122 High Street,
Marlborough, SN8 1LZ UK

E: info@theleap.co.uk
F: +44 (0) 1672 519944
www.theleap.co.uk

Team or solo placements in Africa, Asia or South America. Volunteer to get stuck into our unique mix of eco-tourism, community and conservation projects. Connect with local people and enjoy the satisfaction that comes from making a real impact.

The Year Out Group
Queensfield,
28 King's Road,
Easterton, SN10 4PX UK

E: info@yearoutgroup.org
T: +44 (0) 1380 816696
www.yearoutgroup.org

See main entry under volunteering.

Trekforce Worldwide
530 Fulham Road,
Fulham,
London, SW6 5NR UK

E: info@trekforce.org.uk
T: +44 (0) 207 384 3343
www.trekforce.org.uk

Trekforce offers expeditions in the jungle, mountains and desert, survival skills, teaching, trekking and conservation and community projects, new languages, work aboard programmes and expedition leadership training also available.

the gap-year guidebook 2011

Tropical Adventures
Apartado 8-7800,
Paraiso, Costa Rica

E: info@tropicaladventures.com
www.tropicaladventures.com

Provides volunteer tour packages for individuals, families and groups interested in exploring the culture, language and natural beauty of Costa Rica.

Turtle Conservation Project
No 389 Godagama,
Kosgoda, Sri Lanka

E: turtle@sltnet.lk
F: +94 91 226 4765
www.tcpsrilanka.org/volunteering.htm

Opportunities to measure turtles, undertake beach patrols and mapping, conduct education programmes, office administration, fundraising, and more.

UNA Exchange
Temple of Peace,
Cathays Park,
Cardiff, CF10 3AP UK

E: info@unaexchange.org
T: +44 (0) 29 2022 3088
F: +44 (0) 29 2022 2540
www.unaexchange.org

Arranges international volunteer projects worldwide: from Armenia to Zambia. The work is usually unskilled and you do not need qualifications or experience in most cases.

Vivisto Ltd
80 High Street,
Winchester, SO23 9AT UK

E: info@vivisto.co.uk
F: +44 (0) 870 761 7129
www.vivisto.co.uk

You can make a difference volunteering on conservation and community programmes in South Africa.

Volunteers Making a Difference - vMaD
MaD for Good!,
c/o Siem Reap Post Office,
Siem Reap, Cambodia

E: info@madforgood.org
T: +855 63 39 01 63
www.volunteer-cambodia.com

This is a non profit organization offering international volunteer work opportunities abroad in Siem Reap, Cambodia. vMaD placements are all in rural areas, so you'll get to see the real Cambodia and experience the local culture.

Voluntour South Africa
2 Riversend Court,
Riversend Road,
Capetown 7800, South Africa

E: info@voluntoursouthafrica.com
T: +27 (0) 82 416 6066
F: +27 (0) 86 547 6668
www.voluntoursouthafrica.com

Do you wish to add value to our planet? Join one of our garden projects and be an active part of community companion planting.

visit: www.gap-year.com

Voluntours
6 Visser Street,
Vorna Valley, Midrand,
Gauteng, South Africa

E: info@voluntours.co.za
T: +27 (0) 11 315-4049
F: +27 (0) 11 315-4050
www.voluntours.co.za

Volunteer in South Africa with a multiple award winning organisation in their community, wildlife and marine projects. A variety of short, medium and longer-term placements are available.

Wilderness Awareness School
PO Box 5000,
PMB 137,
Duvall, WA 98019 USA

T: +1 425 788 1301
www.wildernessawareness.org

The school, a not for profit environmental organisation, offers courses for adults in tracking, wilderness survival skills and a stewardship programme. There are also monthly nature talks in Seattle, which are often free.

Worldwide Experience
Ashley Adams Travel (UK) Ltd, Guardian House,
Borough Road,
Godalming, GU7 2AE UK

E: info@worldwideexperience.com
T: +44 (0) 1483 860 560
F: +44 (0) 1483 860 391
www.worldwideexperience.com

Worldwide Experience specialises in volunteer gap-year placements in conservation, marine and community projects throughout South Africa, Kenya, Malawi, Sri Lanka and India.

WWOOF
(World Wide Opportunities on Organic Farms)
PO Box 2154,
Winslow, MK18 3WS UK

www.wwoof.org.uk

Join WWOOF and participate in meaningful work that reconnects with nature, share the lives of people who have taken practical steps towards alternative, sustainable lifestyles.

Humanitarian

2Way Development
2Way Space,
1-4 Pope Street, Bermondsey,
London, SE1 3PR UK

E: volunteer@2waydevelopment.com
T: +44 (0) 20 7378 9600
www.2waydevelopment.com

2Way offer a support service to people looking for volunteering experiences worldwide.

African Impact

Be a traveller, a conservationist and a humanitarian
..*volunteer in Africa*

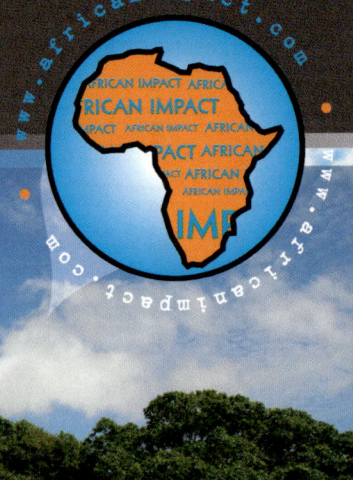

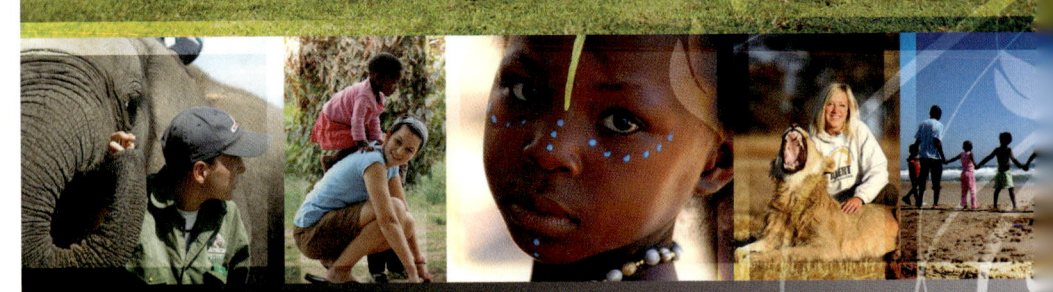

We are the African Specialists in Community and Conservation Volunteering, Internships and Adventure Travel. Based on the ground in Africa, we are proud to have been nominated as a World Travel Awards 2009 finalist.

www.africanimpact.com

Contact one of our experienced travel experts: E-mail: info@africanimpact.com
USA Toll Free: 0877 253 2899 • UK Toll Free: 0800 098 8440 • CAPE TOWN: +27 21 785 4319

Action Aid
Hamlyn House,
Macdonald Road, Upper Holloway,
London, N19 5PG UK

E: experiences@actionaid.org
T: +44 (0)20 7561 7571
F: +44 (0)20 7272 0899
www.actionaid.org.uk/experiences

Take part in ActionAid's First Hand Experience and change lives, including your own. ActionAid is offering volunteering opportunities in South Africa and Nepal, working alongside local people to build homes and centres to benefit whole communities for the better.

Action Centres UK
King's Park Conference & Sports Centre,
King's Park Road,
Northampton, NN3 6LL UK

E: enquiries@pioneercentre.org.uk
T: +44 (0) 1604 499 699
www.go-gap.com

Action Centres UK has been developing young people through gap-year and volunteer programmes since 1971 and still provides opportunities through its three UK based adventure and sports centres.

Africa & Asia Venture
10 Market Place,
Devizes, SN10 1HT UK

E: av@aventure.co.uk
F: +44 (0) 1380 720060
www.aventure.co.uk

Africa and Asia Venture enables motivated 18-24 year-olds to invest in their futures through three to five months of volunteering on teaching and sports coaching projects in Africa. Environment and community projects also take place in Kenya.

African Impact
6 Carlton Close,
Sunnydale,
Noordhoek, Western Cape South Africa

E: info@africanimpact.com
T: +27 21 785 4319
F: +27 86 618 3370
www.africanimpact.com

We are Africa's largest Voluntourism organisation, with projects throughout Southern and East Africa. Proud finalists in the 2009 British Youth Travel Awards for Green Travel.

AIDE (The Association of International Development & Exchange)
1221 South Mopac Expressway,
Suite 100,
Austin, TX 78746 USA

E: info@aideabroad.org
T: +1 (512) 457 8062
F: +1 (413) 857 1108
www.aideabroad.org

Alliance Abroad is a non-profit organisation that provides international teaching, work and volunteer placements. Our services include guaranteed placement and 24/7 personal assistance.

the gap-year guidebook 2011

Asociacion Nuevos Horizontes
3a Calle, 6-51,
Zona 2,
Quetzaltenango, Guatemala

E: nhcoordinadoras@gmail.com
T: +502 242 283 816
www.ahnh.org

Volunteers needed to help with the children in the shelter.

ATD Fourth World
48 Addington Square,
Camberwell,
London, SE5 7LB UK

E: atd@atd-uk.org
T: +44 (0) 20 7703 3231
F: +44 (0) 20 7252 4276
www.atd-uk.org

ATD Fourth World is an international voluntary organisation working in partnership with people living in poverty worldwide.

BERUDEP
PO Box 10,
Belo,
Boyo Division, 00237 Cameroon

E: admin@berudep.org
T: +237 7760 1407
www.berudep.org

BERUDEP's vision is 'to eradicate poverty and raise the living standards of the rural population of Cameroon's North West province'. They rely on volunteers to help them achieve this.

BMS World Mission
PO Box 49,
129 Broadway,
Didcot, OX14 8XA UK

E: opportunities@bmsworldmission.org
T: +44 (0) 1235 517653
www.bmsworldmission.org

BMS World Mission is a Christian organisation which sends people in teams and as individuals or families to over 35 countries worldwide.

Brathay Exploration Group
Brathay Hall,
Ambleside, LA22 0HP UK

E: admin@brathayexploration.org.uk
www.brathayexploration.org.uk

Brathay provides 'challenging experiences for young people' aged 15-25. It runs a range of expeditions from one to five weeks long which vary each year.

**Cameroon Association
for the Protection and Education
of the Child (CAPEC)**
BP 20646,
Yaounde, 00000 Cameroon

E: capecam20@yahoo.com
F: +237 22 22 33 49
www.capecam.org

Volunteer to teach children in Cameroon. See website for vacancies and details of programmes available.

visit: www.gap-year.com

Camphill Community Ballybay
Robb Farm,
Corraskea,
Ballybay, Ireland

E: ballybay@camphill.ie
T: +353 (0) 42 9748182
F: +353 (0) 42 9741 359
www.camphill.org.uk

Camphill Ballybay (registered charity CHY5861)is a caring community for adults with a variety of special needs. Check out their website for volunteering opportunities.

Camphill Community Ballytobin
Callan, Ireland

E: ballytobin@camphill.ie
F: +353 (0)56 7755213
www.camphillballytobin.eu

Camphill Communities work with people who are mentally handicapped. They are a registered charity (CHY 5861) who are always looking for volunteers in their communities.

Camphill Community Dingle
Beenbawn,
Dingle, Ireland

E: dingle@camphill.ie
F: +353 6691 2841
www.camphilldingle.org

Small rural life-sharing community with people with special needs, part of the Camphill Communities of Ireland (registered charity CHY5861).

Camphill Community Duffcarrig
Camphill Community Duffcarrig,
Gorey, 0000 Ireland

E: duffcarrig@camphill.ie
F: +353 53 9425910
www.camphill.ie

Camphill Communities work with people who are mentally handicapped. They are a registered charity (CHY 5861) who are always looking for volunteers in their communities.

Camphill Community Dunshane
Brannockstown,
Near Naas, Ireland

E: dunshane@camphill.ie
F: +353 (0) 45 483 833
www.camphill.ie

Training college, part of the Camphill Community (registered charity CHY5861), for young adults in need of special care. Check out their website for volunteering opportunities.

Camphill Community Greenacres
1A Farmhill Park,
Goatstown, 14 Ireland

E: greenacres@camphill.ie
http://homepage.eircom.net/camphillgreenacres/

Camphill Community Greenacres is part of a unique, international, charity aiming to create a sustainable, inclusive and harmonious community. The community of about 20 people provides living and working opportunities with people with special needs.

Changing Worlds
1999 - 2011
Productive placements

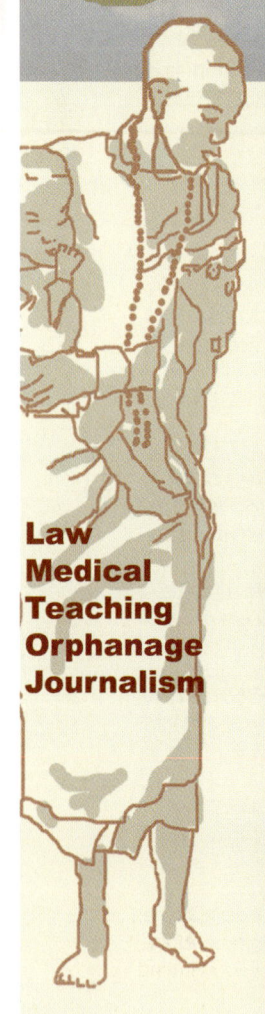

Law
Medical
Teaching
Orphanage
Journalism

If you are serious about helping others in your gap year our schools, hospitals and orphanages are looking for people who are committed, enthusiastic and dedicated who will stay for 3 to 6 months in order to provide continuity for the children and adults with whom they are working.

Living with local people and sharing their lives, the experiences you have will stand you in good stead for whatever you do in the future, be it at university or at work.

"Kenya has changed me. Those that I met there have changed me.
Christie-lee Hutt Sept 09

www.changingworlds.co.uk
ask@changingworlds.co.uk
telephone: 01883340960

Camphill Community Jerpoint
Thomastown, Ireland

E: jerpoint@camphill.ie
www.camphill.ie

Jerpoint is part of the Camphill Communities (registered charity CHY5861). It is a small community where they live together with adults with disabilities. They have an organic garden, animals and are particularly caring towards the environment.

Camphill Community Kyle
Coolagh,
Callan, Ireland

E: kyle@camphill.ie
F: +353 (0) 56 25 848
www.camphill.ie

Kyle, part of the worldwide Camphill movement, is a life sharing community of 40 people, including 12 with learning disabilities. Everyone is supported through mutual relationships and contributes in shared work of various kinds. (Registered Charity CHY5861)

Carrick-on-Suir Camphill Community
Castle Street,
Carrick-on-Suir, Ireland

E: carrick@camphill.ie
F: +353 (0) 51 64 5569
www.camphill.ie

Small residential community in county Tipperary. Part of the Camphill Community (registered charity CHY5861) their emphasis is on living a caring and meaningful life. For volunteering opportunities, check out their website.

Challenges Worldwide
54 Manor Place,
Edinburgh, EH3 7EH UK

E: kirsty@challengesworldwide.com
www.challengesworldwide.com

Volunteers with professional skills and experience needed to work on their many projects. Registered Charity SCO 28814.

Changing Worlds
11 Doctors Lane,
Chaldon, CR3 5AE UK

E: ask@changingworlds.co.uk
www.changingworlds.co.uk

Changing Worlds is a small, friendly organisation with charitable aims. We focus on every group of applicants we send out. This ethos has successfully sent over 1300 people on once-in-a-lifetime trips, and we are proud to say that a quarter of our applicants come from recommendations.
We offer paid and voluntary placements in: Argentina, Australia, China, Dubai, Ghana, Honduras, India, Kenya, Madagascar, New Zealand, Romania, Serbia, South Africa, Thailand and Uganda. So, if you like the idea of travel, meeting people and don't mind working hard, then this is for you!

Cicerones de Buenos Aires Asociación Civil
J J Biedma 883,
Buenos Aires, 1405 Argentina

E: cicerones@cicerones.org.ar
F: +54 11 5258 0909
www.cicerones.org.ar

Volunteering in Argentina: Cicerones in Buenos Aires works in a friendly atmosphere ensuring contact with local people, experiencing the city the way it should be!

Volunteer, Work and Travel Abroad
Create your Gap Year with a Difference

- Personalised advice
- Tailor-made projects
- Local NGO partnerships
- In-country support teams
- Trusted host families

GapGuru.com

Call us on 08000 32 33 50

City Year
Headquarters,
287 Columbus Avenue,
Boston, MA 02116 USA

T: +1 617 927 2500
F: +1 617 927 2510
www.cityyear.org

City Year unites young people of all backgrounds for a demanding year of community service and leadership development throughout the US. This organisation recruits from US only.

CMS (Church Mission Society)
Watlington Road,
Oxford, OX4 6BZ UK

E: info@cms-uk.org
www.cms-uk.org

Offering more of a learning experience than a giving one, the CMS runs three- to four-week Encounter programmes in Africa, Asia, the Middle East and Eastern Europe for Christians aged 18-30.

Cosmic Volunteers
3502 Scott's Lane,
Sherman Mills, Suite 3147,
Philadelphia, PA 19101 USA

E: info@cosmicvolunteers.org
T: +1 215 609 4196
F: +1 215 827 5623
www.cosmicvolunteers.org

American non-profit organisation offering volunteer and internship programmes in China, Ecuador, Ghana, Guatemala, India, Kenya, Nepal, Peru, the Philippines, and Vietnam.

Cross-Cultural Solutions
Tower Point 44,
North Road,
Brighton, BN1 1YR UK

E: infouk@crossculturalsolutions.org
T: +44 (0) 1273 666 392
F: +44 (0) 845 458 2783
www.crossculturalsolutions.org

Founded in 1995, Cross-Cultural Solutions now operates volunteer programmes in 12 countries in partnership with sustainable community initiatives. As a registered UK charity, CCS brings people together to work side-by-side with members of the local community while sharing perspectives and cultural understanding.

Cultural Canvas Thailand
1001 N. Barcelona Street,
Pensacola, FL 32501 USA

E: info@culturalcanvas.com
www.culturalcanvas.com

Cultural Canvas Thailand offers unique and meaningful volunteer experiences in Chiang Mai, Thailand. Placements are available in the following areas: hill tribe education, HIV/AIDS prevention, women's empowerment, and Burmese refugee education and assistance.

Discover Adventure Ltd.
Throope Down House, Blandford Road,
Coombe Bissett,
Salisbury, SP5 4LN UK

E: info@discoveradventure.com
T: 01722 718444
www.discoveradventure.com

Discover Adventure Fundraising Challenges are trips that are designed to be challenging, to push your limits. They are not holidays! They involve preparation in terms of fundraising and improving fitness.

Ecuador Volunteer
Yánez Pinzón,
N25-106 y Av. Colón ,
Quito, Ecuador

E: info@ecuadorvolunteer.org
T: +593 2 255 7749
F: +593 2 222 6544
www.ecuadorvolunteer.org

Ecuador Volunteer Foundation, is a non-profit organization that offers volunteer work opportunities abroad in social, environment, educational and community areas around Ecuador.

EIL (Experiment for International Living)
287 Worcester Road,
Malvern, WR14 1AB UK

E: info@eiluk.org
F: +44 (0) 168 456 2212
www.eiluk.org

Worldwide Volunteering. A typical programme lasts between two and three months. Host countries include Argentina, Brazil, India, Morocco, Nigeria and South Africa.

Federation EIL International Office
70 Landmark Hill ,
Suite 204,
Brattleboro, VT 05301 USA

E: federation@experiment.org
T: +1 802 246 1154
F: +1 802 258 3427
www.experiment.org

Volunteers required for their international partnership programme. They combine international community service projects with language training and homestay opportunities in 14 countries.

GapGuru
GapGuru, Town Hall, Market Place,
Newbury, Berkshire, RG14 5AA

E: info@gapguru.com
T: 08000 32 33 50 (UK freephone)
T: +44 (0) 1635 45556 (from overseas)
W: www.gapguru.com

GapGuru is a gap year specialist offering a wide range of exciting volunteer, travel and internship opportunities across Asia, Africa, South America & Europe.

Gap Year South Africa
PO Box 592,
Cambridge, CB1 0ES UK

E: info@gapyearsouthafrica.com
www.gapyearsouthafrica.com

Specialises in sports coaching, teaching, HIV/AIDS and health awareness, and environmental awareness projects in South Africa. Our project duration is between five weeks and three months.

visit: www.gap-year.com

Glencree Centre for Peace and Reconciliation
Glencree,
Enniskerry, Ireland

E: info@glencree.ie
F: +353 (0) 1 276 6085
www.glencree.ie

Glencree welcomes international volunteers who provide practical help in exchange for a unique experience of working with those building peace in Ireland, Britain and beyond.

Global Volunteers
375 East Little Canada Road,
St. Paul, MN 55117-1628 USA

E: email@globalvolunteers.org
F: +1 (651) 482 0915
www.globalvolunteers.org

Have opportunities worldwide. The work is hard, rewarding and diverse, from repairing old school houses in Third World countries to social work within a Native American village.

Grangemockler Camphill Community
Temple Michael,
Grangemockler,
Carrick-on-Suir, Ireland

E: grangemockler@camphill.ie
T: +353 (0) 51 647 202
F: +353 (0) 51 647 253
www.camphill.ie

Part of the Camphill Community (registered charity CHY5861), situated in County Tipperary. A community for adults which places special emphasis on integration with the local community.

Habitat for Humanity Great Britain
46 West Bar Street,
Banbury, OX16 9RZ UK

E: globalvillage@habitatforhumanity.org.uk
www.habitatforhumanity.org.uk

Working in over 90 countries, Habitat for Humanity aims to eliminate poverty housing and homelessness. Volunteer teams travel to their chosen country to spend two weeks living and working alongside future homeowners and the local community. Charity Number 1043641.

Hope For The Nations Children's Charity
23 Caldervale,
Orton Longueville,
Peterborough, PE2 7HX UK

E: info@hftn.co.uk
T: +44 (0) 1733 237 377
F: +44 (0) 1733 266 072
www.hftn.co.uk

Join our work with orphans and widows, feeding programmes and micro-enterprises in Sub-Sahara Africa.

i volunteer
D-134, 1st Floor,
East of Kailash,
New Delhi, 110065 India

E: dehli@ivolunteer.in
T: +91 11 262 174 60
www.ivolunteer.in

Volunteering opportunites are shown on their website. You could end up working in an orphanage, on a helpline, on relief effort or in a school.

the gap-year guidebook 2011

> "So many stories, memories and images, there is just so much to say about my 6 months on the other side of the world!"
> Clare, Vanuatu

LATTITUDE
GLOBAL VOLUNTEERING

Lattitude Global Volunteering is an international youth development charity.

The people who choose Lattitude Global Volunteering are choosing to change lives. On our placements volunteers are making a difference as part of a sustainable, long term programme benefiting the community they are placed in. We match every volunteer to a placement where their skills and experience are most needed. Our volunteers spend 3-12 months totally immersed in their host culture, making friends, working as part of their local community and having the type of experiences a tourist could never have.

Volunteers work hard and love it and the rewards are immense. From seeing understanding dawn on a child's face to celebrating exam results and from holding new born babies to replanting forests, our wide range of programmes offer a host of experiences that will excite, challenge and inspire you and help you to develop, to learn and to understand the world and its cultures. Our volunteers choose to make a difference.

What can you do?
Voluntary placements in the areas of:
Community Care
Teaching
Conservation
Outdoor Education
Medical

Where can you go?
Asia:
China, India, Japan, Vietnam
Africa:
Ghana, Malawi, South Africa, Tanzania
Americas:
Argentina, Brazil, Canada, Ecuador, Mexico
Oceania:
Australia, Fiji, New Zealand, Vanuatu

How long are the placements?
3 – 12 months

Do more than just travel, volunteer!

www.lattitude.org.uk | volunteer@lattitude.org.uk | 0118 959 4914

ICYE (Inter Cultural Youth Exchange) UK
Latin America House,
Kingsgate Place,
London, NW6 4TA UK

E: info@icye.co.uk
T: +44 (0) 20 7681 0983
F: +44 (0) 20 7916 1246
www.icye.co.uk

Sends people aged between 18 and 30 to work in voluntary projects overseas in including counselling centres, human rights NGOs, farms, orphanages and schools for the disabled. Registered Charity No. 1081907.

---

i-to-i
Woodside House,
261 Low Lane,
Leeds, LS18 5NY UK

E: info@i-to-i.com
T: +44 (0) 871 226 2215
F: +44 (0) 113 205 4619
www.i-to-i.com

At i-to-i, we work in partnership with locally run projects in over 30 countries offering you the chance to make a difference on your next trip in a safe, supported, and sustainable manner.

IVCS
12 Eastleigh Avenue,
South Harrow, HA2 0UF UK

E: enquiries@ivcs.org.uk
F: +44 (0) 20 8930 8338
www.ivcs.org.uk

IVCS is a small UK registered charity (No. 285872) supporting sustainable development projects in rural India, and offering opportunities to stay in one.

IVS (International Voluntary Service)
Thorn House,
5 Rose Street,
Edinburgh, EH2 2PR UK

E: scotland@ivs-gb.org.uk
T: +44 (0) 131 243 2745
F: +44 (0) 131 243 2747
http://ivsgb.org/info/

IVS exchanges volunteers with over 40 countries, mainly for international voluntary projects (living and working with a group on two to four week projects).

Josephite Community Aid
3 Nixon Avenue,
Ashfield, NSW 2131 Australia

E: help@jcaid.com
F: +61 (0) 2 9716 9950
www.jcaid.com

Australian organisation committed to helping poor and underprivileged with the aid of volunteers.

Karen Hilltribes Trust
Midgley House, Spring Lane,
Heslington,
York, YO10 5DX UK

E: enquiries@karenhilltribes.org.uk
T: +44 (0) 1904 415 124
F: +44 (0) 1904 430 580
www.karenhilltribes.org.uk

The Karen Hilltribes Trust (Registered Charity No. 1093548) sends volunteers to teach English in Thailand. You will live with a Karen Hilltribe family and your placement can be between six and ten months teaching five days a week.

the gap-year guidebook 2011

oyster
gap year specialist

Make a real difference to Children's lives

live, work and contribute for 1-6 months in
Brazil, Chile, India, Kenya, Nepal, Romania, South Africa, Tanzania & Zambia

Oyster specialises in teaching, childcare, sports coaching and medical placements in some very diverse locations.

For details of our voluntary and paid placements, visit
www.oysterworldwide.com
or telephone **01892 770771** or email **emailus@oysterworldwide.com**
Oyster Worldwide, Hodore Farm, Hartfield, East Sussex TN7 4AR

Kem Investments - Gap4Africa
PO Box 401403,
Gaborone, Botswana

E: info@gap4africa.com
F: +267 572 8598
www.gap4africa.com

Spend three months working with Botswana's rural community to build homes for people living in extreme poverty and children orphaned by HIV Aids. Produce a documentary about your experience and achievements while in Botswana.

Kings World Trust for Children
7 Deepdene,
Haslemere, GU27 1RE UK

E: kwtc@haslemere.com
F: +44 (0) 1428 653504
www.kingschildren.org

The Kings World Trust for Children is a UK-based charity (No. 1024872) which aims to provide a caring home, an education and skills training for orphaned and homeless children and young people in south India.

L'Arche
GY08,
Freepost BD 3209,
Keighley, BD20 9BR UK

E: info@larche.org.uk
T: +44 (0) 800 917 1337
F: +44 (0) 1535 656426
www.larche.org.uk

L'Arche is an international movement where people with and without learning difficulties share life together. There are Communities in 34 countries. Volunteers are involved in all aspects of community life, are trained and supported, have free board and accommodation, a modest income and other benefits.

Lattitude Global Volunteering
44 Queen's Road,
Reading, RG1 4BB UK

E: volunteer@lattitude.org.uk
F: +44 (0) 118 957 6634
www.lattitude.org.uk

Lattitude Global Volunteering is a youth development and volunteering charity that send young people to a huge range of challenging and rewarding placements worldwide.

Madventurer
Mad HQ,
The Old Smithy,
Corbridge, NE45 5QD UK

E: team@madventurer.com
T: +44 (0) 845 121 1996
F: +44 (0) 191 269 9490
www.madventurer.com

Offer group community projects in towns and villages in Ghana, Kenya, Uganda, Tanzania, South Africa, Fiji, Peru, Thailand, Vietnam and India.

Oasis UK
75 Westminster Bridge Road,
Lambeth,
London, SE1 7HS UK

T: +44 (0) 20 7921 4200
F: +44 (0) 20 7921 4201
www.oasisuk.org

A Christian charity (No. 1026487) offering volunteering opportunities in the UK and worldwide, from two weeks to two years.

Expand your horizons, invest in your future

Raleigh is a unique, revealing, and unrivalled experience that you will never forget. James Ash

raleighinternational.org
020 7183 1270
info@raleigh.org.uk

Oyster Worldwide Limited
Hodore Farm,
Hartfield, TN7 4AR UK

E: emailus@oysterworldwide.com
www.oysterworldwide.com

Oyster is the specialist gap-year provider with over 40 volunteer projects abroad. We offer a personal approach with experienced managers supporting you throughout your trip.

Pepper
Hazelpits Farm,
Ulcombe Road,
Headcorn, TN27 9LD UK

E: info@experiencepepper.co.uk
T: +44 (0) 800 030 4207
www.experiencepepper.co.uk

Pepper is a unique gap-year and adventure travel company offering tailor-made one to three month experiences, as well as custom trips, in South Africa.

Peru's Challenge
(Ultimate Tours), Urb. Ingenieros D-2-12,
Larapa, San Jeronimo,
Cuzco, Peru

E: volunteer@peruschallenge.com
T: +51 84 272 508
F: +51 84 272 508
www.peruschallenge.com

Join a volunteer and travel programme and assist the work of charity organisation, Peru's Challenge, in rural communities in Peru.

Projects Abroad
Aldsworth Parade,
Goring, BN12 4TX UK

E: info@projects-abroad.co.uk
F: +44 (0) 1903 501026
www.projects-abroad.co.uk

8000+ placements overseas. Teach English, gain invaluable experience in Medicine, Conservation and Environment, Journalism, Business, Care and Community, Sports, IT, Law and Human Rights, Veterinary and more.

Quest Overseas
15a Cambridge Grove,
Hove, BN3 3ED UK

E: info@questoverseas.com
F: +44 (0) 1273 204 928
www.questoverseas.com

Quest Overseas specializes in gap-year adventures into the very heart and soul of South America and Africa. With over ten years of experience, we offer volunteers the chance to understand life far removed from home.

Raleigh International
207 Waterloo Road,
Southwark,
London, SE1 8XD UK

E: info@raleigh.org.uk
T: +44 (0) 20 7183 1283
F: +44 (0) 20 7504 8094
www.raleighinternational.org

Develop new skills, meet people from all backgrounds and make a difference on sustainable community and environmental projects around the world.

FLEXIBILITY

VARIETY

SUPPORT

ProjectsAbroad

VOLUNTEER ABROAD

www.projects-abroad.co.uk
Tel: +44 (0) 1903 708300

Serenje Orphans School Home
SOSH, c/o Kevin Gilbert,
Ami-Argand 58,
1290 Versoix, Switzerland

E: kevingilbertau@yahoo.com.au
T: +41 798733835

Our Zambian orphanage offers a rewarding and safe experience in rural Zambia for committed volunteers.

Skillshare International UK
126 New Walk,
Leicester, LE1 7JA UK

E: info@skillshare.org
F: +44 (0) 116 254 2614
www.skillshare.org

Skillshare International recruits professionals from different sectors to share their skills, experience and knowledge with local partner organisations in Africa and Asia as volunteers.

Smile Society
Udayrajpur, Madhyamgram,
9 no railgate,
Kolkata, 700129 India

E: info@smilengo.org
T: +9 1933 973 1462
F: +9 1332 537 6621
www.smilengo.org

SMILE Society invite international volunteers and students to join us in our welfare projects, international work camps, summer camps, internship programmes and volunteer projects in India.

Spirit of Adventure Trust
PO Box 2276,
Auckland, New Zealand

E: info@spiritofadventure.org.nz
F: +64 (0) 9 379 5620
www.spiritofadventure.org.nz

Become part of the volunteer crew on one of the Trust's youth development voyages around New Zealand each year.

SPW (Students Partnership Worldwide)
7 Tufton Street,
Westminster,
London, SW1P3QB UK

E: info@spw.org
T: +44 (0)20 7976 8070
F: +44 (0)20 7233 0008
www.spw.org

SPW run Health Education and Community Resource Programmes in South Asia and Africa. Volunteers are asked to fundraise a donation to the charity.

Tanzed
80 Edleston Road,
Crewe, CW2 7HD UK

E: tanzeduk@yahoo.co.uk
www.tanzed.org.uk

Working alongside Tanzanian nursery teachers as a classroom assistant you will be living in a rural village with plenty of opportunity to contribute to the community using your energy and enthusiasm. Registered Charity No. 1064659.

TRAVELLERS WORLDWIDE

Est. 1995 - 16 Years of enriching peoples lives

MAKE A DIFFERENCE

OVER 300 VOLUNTARY PROJECTS IN 21 COUNTRIES

teaching **internships** care **drama**
language courses **work experience**
music **conservation** cultural courses

YOUR GAP YEAR STARTS HERE!

For a free brochure or more info call **01903 502595** or email **info@travellersworldwide.com**
www.travellersworldwide.com

Task Brasil Trust
PO Box 4901,
Rotherhithe,
London, SE16 3PP UK

E: info@taskbrasil.org.uk
T: +44 (0) 20 7735 5545
F: +44 (0) 20 7735 5675
www.taskbrasil.org.uk

Charity helping impoverished children in Brazil. Volunteers always needed. Registered Charity No. 1030929.

The Book Bus Foundation
c/o VentureCo Worldwide, The Ironyard,
64 -66 Market Place,
Warwick, CV34 4SD UK

E: volunteer@thebookbus.org
T: +44 (0) 1926 411 122
www.thebookbus.org

The Book Bus provides a mobile service and actively promotes literacy to underpriviledged communities in Zambia and Ecuador.

The Bridge Camphill Community
Main Street,
Kilcullen, Ireland

E: thebridge@camphill.ie
F: +353 (0) 45 481 519
www.camphill.ie

Registered charity (CHY5861) in County Kildare working with adults after they leave the sister community of Camphill Dunshane.
Check out their website for volunteering opportunities.

The Ethical Project Company
Stowford Manor Farm,
Wingfield,
Trowbridge, BA14 9LH UK

T: +44 (0) 7703 725 512

Join a team of people of various ages on a trip to Tanzania or India to do a mixture of volunteering in primary schools and fair trade travel.

The Worldwrite Volunteer Centre
Millfields Lodge,
201 Millfields Road, Lea Bridge,
London, E5 0AL UK

E: world.write@btconnect.com
T: +44 (0) 20 8985 5435
www.worldwrite.org.uk

Join WORLDwrite's campaign for young volunteers who feel strongly about global inequality, want to make an impact and use film to do it. Registered charity No. 1060869.

The Year Out Group
Queensfield,
28 King's Road,
Easterton, SN10 4PX UK

E: info@yearoutgroup.org
T: +44 (0) 1380 816696
www.yearoutgroup.org

Year Out Group is an association of the UK's leading Year Out organisations that was launched in 2000 to promote the concepts and benefits of well-structured year out programmes, to promote models of good practice and to help young people and their advisers in selecting suitable and worthwhile projects.
The Group's member organisations provide a wide range of Year Out placements in

the gap-year guidebook 2011

voluntour south africa
Travel with Soul

Voluntour South Africa, 2 Riversend Court, Riversend Road, Capetown 7800
T: +27 (0) 82 416 6066
E: info@voluntoursouthafrica.com
W: www.voluntoursouthafrica.com

Seven reasons why you should volunteer in South Africa with VSA:
- The people are fantastic.
- The climate is perfect.
- The projects are inspiring.
- The work is both meaningful and urgent.
- The country is spectacularly scenic.
- You are needed.
- You can make an impact.

Voluntour South Africa offers you a chance to visit our beautiful country and make a lasting difference to the lives of others. Our intention is to facilitate the connection between you and the communities with whom we are involved to learn from each other for the common benefit of all. We are directly linked to all the projects we support and operate through The Saville Foundation (a private foundation dedicated to meaningful change).

Fees are only charged where absolutely necessary and are monitored by VSA to ensure the integrity of your support. Some projects require specific skills such as teaching or nursing while others require your energy, warm open hearts and willingness to get involved.

Do you wish to see a deeper side to travel? Are you able to live out of your comfort zone? Are you called to more meaning in life?

If you can speak English, have a sense of adventure and feel the urge to experience new cultures and make a difference then VSA is the right place for you.

You have all the recourses you need to make a change within you as well as for others ... visit www.voluntoursouthafrica.com right now!

visit: www.gap-year.com

the UK and overseas that cover courses and cultural exchanges, expeditions, volunteering and structured work placements. All members have agreed to adhere to the Group's Code of Practice and more detailed operational guidelines for each of the four sectors mentioned above. The Group's website also contains planning advice and guidelines for students and their advisers. These include questions that potential participants should ask providing organisations as they look for the programme that best suits their needs. Year Out Group monitors information published by its members for accuracy.

Year Out Group members are expected to put potential clients and their parents in contact with those that have recently returned, and consider it important that these references are taken up at least by telephone and, where possible, by meeting face-to-face. Group members include their complaints procedure in their contracts. Year Out Group can advise on making complaints but is not itself able to deal with them, though half the members are now participating in the Independent Dispute Settlement scheme arranged by the group. Nor is Year Out Group able to 'police' the 30,000 placements provided by its members but it can take action if any member is shown to be consistently negligent.

Since Year Out Group was formed its members have worked hard and continue to do so to improve the service they offer their clients. However there will always be less-than-perfect organisations among members of a trade association and good associations that are not. There are some small specialist organisations with excellent reputations that cannot afford the membership fees. Whether or not an organisation is a member of Year Out Group, the questions in the student guidelines can be used to advantage.

Think Pacific
Old Broadcasting House,
Woodhouse Lane,
Leeds, LS2 9EN UK

E: info@thinkpacific.com
T: 0113 253 8684
www.thinkpacific.com

Think Pacific offer you the chance to make a difference to the communities and places you visit, guiding you on a meaningful adventure through the glorious islands of Fiji.

VAP (Volunteer Action for Peace)
16 Overhill Road,
East Dulwich,
London, SE22 0PH UK

E: action@vap.org.uk
T: +44 (0) 844 2090 927
www.vap.org.uk

Organises international voluntary work projects in the UK each summer and recruits volunteers to take part in affordable placements abroad that range between two weeks and 12 months.

Volunteer Latin America
London, WC1N 3XX UK

E: info@volunteerlatinamerica.com
www.volunteerlatinamerica.com

Volunteer Latin America provides a comprehensive and affordable solution to finding volunteering opportunities and Spanish language schools in Central and South America.

the gap-year guidebook 2011

Changing Worlds
1999 - 2011
Productive placements

INDIA - Medical placement Diary

Friday: We visited Jeevodaya Cancer Hospice which was pretty difficult. All of the people there were suffering from terminal cancer including a little girl who didn't even realise she was dying. We then checked out a leprosy rehabilitation centre. In the evening we sat outside under coconut palms, drinking coffee and eating toasted sandwiches.

Saturday: We started off by giving a dermatology talk to a group of 'children' they turned out to be about 40!

Sunday: Went to meet Patrick who is here to do Journalism, then went to the orphanage. We had the most insane welcome. Kids were all over us, hanging things round our necks, putting paint on our foreheads. We all felt hugely appreciated, We didn't want to leave. It's quiet, friendly and away from the buzz of the city.

Back at the hospital there was a festival going on outside. People were wheeling a massive monkey idol through the streets. These truly are crazy days.

Ros, Bryerly and Sophie on their placements

www.changingworlds.co.uk
ask@changingworlds.co.uk
telephone: 01883340960

FCO TRAVEL ADVICE - know before you go
YEAR OUT GROUP
ATOL PROTECTED 6685
InterHealth

Law
Medical
Teaching
Orphanage
Journalism

Voluntour South Africa
2 Riversend Court,
Riversend Road,
Capetown 7800, South Africa

E: info@voluntoursouthafrica.com
T: +27 (0) 82 416 6066
F: +27 (0) 86 547 6668
www.voluntoursouthafrica.com

Do you wish to add value to our planet? Join one of our garden projects and be an active part of community companion planting.

WaterAid
WaterAid, 2nd floor,
47-49 Durham Street,
Vauxhall, SE11 5JD UK

T: +44 (0) 845 6000 433
www.wateraid.org

WaterAid is an international charity enabling the world's poorest people access to safe water and sanitation. You can volunteer to help them in the UK.

Whipalong Volunteer Program
Plot 42, P O Box 63,
Kampersrus, 1371 South Africa

E: info@whipalong.co.za
F: +27 (0) 86 610 7001
www.whipalong.co.za

Volunteer programmes in South Africa.

Willing Workers in South Africa (WWISA)
P O Box 2413,
The Crags,
Plettenberg Bay, 6600 South Africa

E: volunteers@wwisa.co.za
T: +27 (0)44 534 8958
F: +27 (0)722 702 114
www.wwisa.co.za

WWISA are a volunteering organisation based in South Africa. Their core aim is to help bring desperately needed community development services to the poorly provisioned and frequently overlooked historically disadvantaged rural townships of the Bitou and Tsitsikamma regions.

WorldWide Volunteering for Young People
7 North Street Workshops,
Stoke sub Hamdon, TA14 6QR UK

E: wwv@wwv.org.uk
F: +44 (0) 1935 825775
www.wwv.org.uk

Registered charity (No. 1038253), set up to help people of all ages to find their ideal volunteering project either in the UK or in any country in the world.

Medical

A Broader View Volunteers Corp
1001 Dell Lane,
Wyncote, PA 19095 USA

E: volunteers@abroaderview.org
F: +1 215 887 0915
www.abroaderview.org

Offer volunteering opportunites worldwide in a range of projects such as HIV/AIDS awareness, medical, education, conservation, community development and child care/orphanages.

FLEXIBILITY

VARIETY

SUPPORT

ProjectsAbroad

VOLUNTEER ABROAD

→ www.projects-abroad.co.uk
Tel: +44 (0) 1903 708300

Be More - Volunteering in South Africa
Third Floor,
46 Berwick Street, Soho,
London, W1F 8SG UK

E: info@be-more.org
T: +44 (0) 203 214 6024
www.be-more.org

Be More is a UK charity that supports grassroot development and HIV/AIDS relief organizations in Africa by providing funding and international volunteers. Registered Charity No. 1116179.

Changing Worlds
11 Doctors Lane,
Chaldon, CR3 5AE UK

E: ask@changingworlds.co.uk
www.changingworlds.co.uk

Changing Worlds is a small, friendly organisation with charitable aims. We focus on every group of applicants we send out. This ethos has successfully sent over 1300 people on once-in-a-lifetime trips, and we are proud to say that a quarter of our applicants come from recommendations.
We offer paid and voluntary placements in: Argentina, Australia, China, Dubai, Ghana, Honduras, India, Kenya, Madagascar, New Zealand, Romania, Serbia, South Africa, Thailand and Uganda. So, if you like the idea of travel, meeting people and don't mind working hard, then this is for you!

Gap Guru
Town Hall,
Market Place,
Newbury, RG14 5AA UK

E: info@gapguru.com
T: +44 (0) 1635 45556
www.gapguru.com

Choose from a wide range of projects and select a programme duration from one month onwards - regular start dates every month for gap-year students or those on a career break to tailor-make their very own experience.

Gap Medics
The Brighton Forum,
95 Ditchling Road,
Brighton, BN1 4ST UK

E: info@gapmedics.com
T: +44 (0) 1273 573876
F: +44 (0) 1273 689021
www.gap-year.com

Gap Medics organise medical and nursing placements and projects in Africa and Asia.

Projects Abroad
Aldsworth Parade,
Goring, BN12 4TX UK

E: info@projects-abroad.co.uk
F: +44 (0) 1903 501026
www.projects-abroad.co.uk

8000+ placements overseas. Teach English, gain invaluable experience in Medicine, Conservation and Environment, Journalism, Business, Care and Community, Sports, IT, Law and Human Rights, Veterinary and more.

the gap-year guidebook 2011

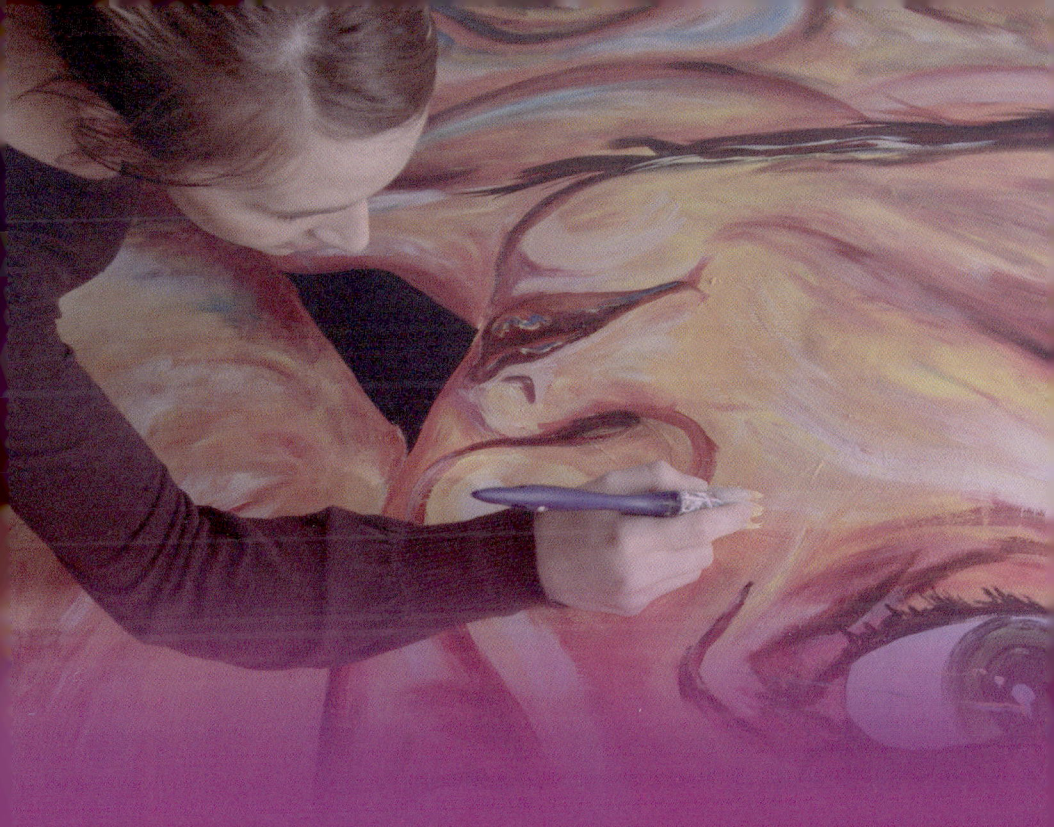

Chapter 7
Learning Abroad

Learning Abroad

While your **gap**-year will inevitably be about personal growth, because of all the new things you experience and see you, could build on this by using it as an opportunity to combine living and studying abroad.

This might not seem appealing if you've just 'escaped' from a period of intense study and exams, but consider this:

- The learning doesn't have to be goal oriented or laden with exam stress, you could learn a new skill and gain a qualification.
- You could pursue an interest, hobby or passion you haven't had time for before.
- You'll be able to explore and enrich your knowledge in your own way, rather than following a curriculum.
- You could also find you've added another dimension to your CV.
- You'll meet like-minded folk and have a lot of fun.

These are some of the things you could do:

Learn a language in-country, do a sports instructor course, music or drama summer schools, explore art, music, culture and learn about conservation. If you're not jaded with study or are at a time of life when a postgraduate qualification would be useful, and a career break possible, you could go for an academic year abroad. Another option for those of you who want to try to earn while you travel is to do a TEFL course.

Here's a good weblink for courses abroad: **www.studyabroaddirectory.com**

An academic year abroad

A good way of getting to know a place and its people in depth is to spend a whole academic year at a foreign school, either in Europe, the USA, or further afield. One possibility is an academic year before university:

- French Lycée.
- German Gymnasium.
- School in Spain.
- Spanish-speaking school in Argentina.

The most relevant EU education and training programmes are Comenius, ERASMUS, Lingua and Leonardo. For more information see:

Comenius: **www.britishcouncil.org/comenius.htm**

Erasmus: **www.britishcouncil.org/erasmus**

visit: www.gap-year.com

Lingua:

www.ec.europa.eu/education/programmes/socrates/lingua/products_en.html

Leonardo:

www.ec.europa.eu/education/lifelong-learning-programme/doc82_en.htm

A scheme called Europass provides trainees in any EU country with a 'Europewide record of achievement for periods of training undertaken outside the home member state'. So ask the school: "Is this course recognised for a Europass?"

University exchange

If you want to spend up to a year abroad at a European university as part of the European Union's ERASMUS (EuRopean community Action Scheme for the Mobility of University Students) scheme, you'll need to have some working knowledge of the relevant language - so a **gap**-year could be the time to start, either studying overseas or in Britain. Information about Erasmus courses is usually given to students in their first year at university.

To apply for ERASMUS you must be an EU citizen. When you spend your time abroad, you continue to pay tuition fees or receive loans or grants as if you were at your university back home.

There's more information on: www.britishcouncil.org/erasmus

The scheme is also open to teaching and non-teaching staff at Higher Education and HE/FE institutions, as long as your home Higher Education Institution has a formal agreement with a partner in one of the eligible countries. It must also have an Erasmus University Charter awarded by the European Commission.

Postgraduate MA/visiting fellowship/exchange

Several universities in the UK have direct links to partnership programmes with others around the world, but if you want to widen your search, the Worldwide Universities Network (WUN) is a good place to start looking for exchange, overseas study and funding for research projects. It's a partnership of 16 research-led universities from Asia, Australasia, Europe and North America.

WUN's Research Mobility Programme funds a period of study overseas, for senior postgraduates and junior faculty, to establish and cultivate research links at an institutional and individual level between the partners in Europe, North America, south-east Asia and Australia. It is also intended to encourage the personal and academic development of individuals early in their research careers.

Check out: www.wun.ac.uk/aboutus.php

Arts and culture

Art

If you want to go to art school, or have already been, no matter which art form interests you, travelling and soaking up the atmosphere is a good way to learn more and give you ideas for your own work. It's also a great opportunity to add to your portfolio.

You don't have to be an art student or graduate to enjoy the beauty of art and artefacts produced by different cultures. Most courses listed in this guidebook are open to anyone who wants to explore the arts in a bit more depth.

Culture

It's a cliché, but also true, that travel broadens the mind and you'll absorb much about the culture of the places you visit just by being there. However, if you want to develop your understanding in more depth, maybe learn a bit of the language and discover some of your chosen country's history, then you could go for the cultural component of some of the language courses listed in the directory.

Design and fashion

Every year, when the new season's collections are shown on the world's fashion catwalks, it's clear that the designers have 'discovered' the fabrics, or decoration or style, of one region or another.

So for those with a passion for fashion a **gap**-year is a great opportunity to experience the originals for themselves. Wandering the streets in other countries, and seeing how other people put their 'look' together, can be an inspiration.

Then there's the opportunity to snap up, at bargain prices, all kinds of beautiful fabrics that would cost a fortune back home.

visit: www.gap-year.com

But if you wanted to use part of your **gap-** to find out more about fashion and design you could also join a fashion summer school in one of Europe's capitals, like the ones listed on this website:

www.learn4good.com/great_schools/fashion_design_career_courses.htm

Or why not India? The country's National Institute of Fashion Technology in Delhi runs summer schools for fashion stylists - here's the link: **www.nift.ac.in/**

Film, theatre and drama

If you're thinking of a short course in performing arts, the USA is one of the most obvious places to go - most famously the New York Film Academy, which has a very useful page for international students:

www.nyfa.com/film_school/student_information/international_student.php

The Academy runs summer schools in London, Paris, Florence, Colombia, China, Japan and South Korea.

For a wider search try: **www.filmschools.com**

Or how about New Zealand? Try: **www.drama.org.nz**

If you want dance as well, the world's your oyster. You can learn salsa in Delhi (as well as in South America) and the traditional Indian Kathak dance in the USA. Here's a good place to start looking:

www.dir.yahoo.com/Arts/Performing_Arts/

And then, of course, there's Bollywood. There are courses in film direction, cinematography, sound production and editing at the Film and Television Institutes of India, in Pune (south-west of Mumbai), which runs a number of courses for overseas students: **www.ftiindia.com**

Music

Whether you're into classical or pop, world music or traditional, there are vibrant music scenes all over the world.

From the studios that have sprung up in Dakar, the West African capital of Senegal, to the club scenes of Europe, to more formal schools, check out the opportunities to combine your interest with travel and maybe learn to play an instrument, if you don't already, or another one if you do.

We've checked online for short music courses, since the UNESCO site no longer offers a directory, and although there are plenty out there, it's a case of searching by location.

Here's one for all UK summer schools, including music:
www.summer-schools.info/
Or how about helping out in a rock centre in Chennai, India?
www.unwindcenter.com

the gap-year guidebook 2011

Media and journalism

Although the print media has been suffering from the global recession there are, of course, other options.

You may want to get into media/journalism but you're not the only one, so do thousands of others and the competition is intense. The skills you'll need could include media law, shorthand, knowledge of how local and national government works and, not least, the ability to construct an attention-grabbing story!

To get a job you may need to do more than gain a media studies degree or have on-the-job training in a newsroom.

It's, therefore, always a good idea to demonstrate your commitment and a **gap-** is a good time to do this. You can try contacting your local paper for a work experience placement, though don't expect to be paid!

Plus, if you search the internet there are plenty of internships in newsrooms - many of them in India, where there's still a lot of attachment to local and national newspapers.

We Googled 'journalism placements and internships' and found possibilities around the world.

These websites may also be useful:

www.tigweb.org/resources/opps/
www.internews.org/default.shtm

Photography

Travelling offers you the chance to develop your skills as a photographer - after all almost everyone takes pictures to remember their travels. But if you've always dreamed of turning professional, it's a chance to practice.

visit: www.gap-year.com

You could be innovative by contacting a local newspaper or magazine and asking if they'll let you accompany one of their photographers on assignments. You won't be paid but you'll learn a lot and it might give you pictures to add to your portfolio.

Languages

You learn a language much more easily and quickly if you're living in the country where it's spoken, but there's more than one reason to learn a new language. There's more to a language than just words: most language courses will include local culture, history, geography, religion, customs and current affairs - as well as food and drink. A language involves more than just translating your own thoughts into someone else's words. A new language brings a whole new way of thinking with it, and therefore a much deeper understanding of the people who shaped it and use it. For example, why do some languages have no future tense - is there a different way time is conceived?

Most people will know that the Icelanders have many different words for 'snow', but did you know that they have 85 words for 'storm'? You'll find plenty of local variations on that theme wherever you are.

Think laterally about where you want to study. Spanish is spoken in many countries around the world, so you could opt for a Spanish course in South America, rather than Spain, and then go travelling around the country, or learn Portuguese in Brazil, where it's the main language, or perhaps French in Canada.

Be aware though that if you learn a language outside its original country you may learn a particular dialect that is only spoken in a specific region of the country as a whole. It may even be considered inferior by some people (or not understood) elsewhere in the country.

Finding the right place to learn

Universities often have international summer school centres or courses for foreign students, or there's the popular network of British Institutes abroad. And there are hundreds (probably thousands) of independent language colleges to choose from, either directly or through a language course organiser or agency in the UK.

The advantage in dealing with a UK-based organisation is that, if something goes wrong, it is easier to get it sorted out under UK law.

Using the internet

The following are some international language course websites that we have found from a basic internet search (but we've no idea how good they are – you need to check them out for yourselves):

www.languagecoursesabroad.co.uk
www.europa-pages.co.uk – for language courses in European countries.
www.ialc.org (International Association of Language Centres)

www.languagesabroad.co.uk
www.oise.com
www.cesalanguages.com

Living with a family

If enrolling on a language course sounds too much like school, another way of learning a language is staying with a family as an au pair or tutor (giving, say, English or music lessons to children) and going to part-time classes locally.

Language courses

Courses at language schools abroad can be divided into as many as ten different levels, ranging from tuition for the complete beginner to highly technical or specialised courses at postgraduate level. The usual classification of language classes, however, into 'beginner' or 'basic', 'intermediate' and 'advanced', works well. Within each of these levels there are usually subdivisions, especially in schools large enough to move students from one class to another with ease.

When you first phone a school from abroad or send in an application form, you should indicate how good your knowledge of the language is. You may be tested before being allocated your class, or you may be transferred from your original class to a lower or higher one, as soon as they find you are worse or better than expected.

Different schools will use different methods of teaching: if you know that you respond well to one style, check that is what your course offers. Foreign language lessons are often attended by a variety of nationalities, so they are almost always conducted in the language you are learning, forcing you to understand and respond without using English. In practice, however, most teachers can revert to English to explain a principle of grammar if a student is really stuck.

The smaller the class the better, though the quality of the teaching is most important - at more advanced levels, well-qualified graduate teachers should be available. Language schools and institutes show a mass of information, photographs and maps on their websites, so it's easy to find out if the school is near to places that interest you, whether it's in a city centre or near a coastal resort. The admissions staff should be happy to give you references from previous students.

Over the next few pages (and in the directory) we've listed some of the organisations offering language opportunities to gappers, from formal tuition to 'soaking it up' while you live with a family. We've split the organisations

visit: www.gap-year.com

according to the languages they offer: Arabic, Chinese, French, German, Greek, Indonesian, Italian, Japanese, Portuguese, Russian and Spanish.

Arabic

Arabic is the language in which the *Qur'an* is written and, although there are translations into the local languages of Muslims around the world, there's also a lot of argument about the way they're translated. This has led to differences about what Islam means.

It's all a matter of interpretation of the roots of words and what's more there are two main versions of Arabic: Fousha - Modern Standard Arabic; and Aameya - Egyptian Colloquial Arabic. We've found one organisation that runs language courses in both: **www.languagesabroad.co.uk/egypt.html**

Chinese

As Chinese enterprises become global, the language is becoming a popular choice in UK schools, with as many as 400 state schools now offering lessons.

There are two main dialects: Cantonese: the language of most Chinese people living abroad, from Singapore to Europe and the USA. Cantonese is also spoken widely in the Guangdong and Guangxi provinces of mainland China and in Hong Kong and Macau.

Mandarin: is the official language of government, international relations and much education in China is undertaken in Mandarin. It is the more formal language and most students are advised to learn it.

Both languages are tonal (the same sound said in a different tone will change the meaning of a word) and therefore can be quite difficult for English-speakers to learn. The different tonal pronunciation, vowels and consonants effectively turn Mandarin and Cantonese into two different languages, although both use the same written characters. There are many, many other Chinese dialects, including Hokkien, Hakka, Wu and Hui.

You can find course information at:
www.mandarinhouse.cn/chinesecourses.htm

It has a choice of 12 different courses in Chinese, including one for expatriates, in Beijing or Shanghai.

French

Languages have changed over time as they have been introduced to other parts of the world from their home countries and then developed in their own directions. Then there are the local dialects. French covers French as it's spoken in France, but then there's also Swiss French, Belgian French and Canadian French.

There's a busy French community in the UK, a large French Lycée in London and more than one teaching institute run by French nationals, so there are plenty of opportunities to carry on developing your French language skills when you return to the UK.

German

German has many very strong dialects (particularly in Austria, Switzerland and much of south Germany), and it is important to bear this in mind if you want to study German academically, or use it for business, in which case you may need to be learning and practising *Hochdeutsch* (standard German).

Many universities in Germany, Austria and Switzerland run summer language schools for foreign students.

Contact:

German Embassy
23 Belgrave Square
Cultural Department
London SW1X 8PZ
Tel: +44 (0) 20 7824 1300.

Their website has a section on studying in Germany: www.london.diplo.de There's also a lively German community in the UK and many courses run by the Goethe Institut (www.goethe.de/ins/gb/lon/enindex.htm). So, there are plenty of opportunities to carry on practising your German when you get back.

Greek

The thoughts of the great philosophers such as Socrates and Aristotle, upon whose ideas the foundations of western values were built, were written in ancient Greek.

Democracy, aristocracy, philosophy, pedagogy and psychology are just some of the many Greek terms that are part of our culture and language.

Modern Greek is spoken by ten million Greek citizens and by about seven million others spread around the world. The Centre for the Greek Language is a good starting point: www.greeklanguagecentre.co.uk/

Indonesian

Based on the Malay trade dialect, Bahasa Indonesia is the national language of the Republic of Indonesia. In a country of more than 230 million people, who speak over 580 different dialects, having a national language makes communication easier, in much the same way as Hindi does in India.

There's no general greeting in Indonesian; there are different words specific to the time of day. But it's said to be an easy language to learn and Indonesia is such a popular backpacker destination it's likely to be worth making the effort. Here's a web link to get you started: www.expat.or.id/info/bahasa.html

Italian

Schools vary from the very large to very small, each with its own character and range of courses in Italian, Italian culture, history, art, cooking and other subjects. As in language schools across most of Europe, the language is often taught in the morning with extracurricular activities in the afternoon. If you

visit: www.gap-year.com

want to do a course from March onwards it is advisable to get in touch with them at least two months in advance, as courses and accommodation get booked up early.

Most schools can fix you up with accommodation before your trip, either with a family, bed and breakfast, half-board, or even renting a studio or flat. If you're part of a small group, you might prefer to arrange accommodation yourself through a local property-letting agent, but this can be tricky unless you have someone on the spot to help.

Japanese

If you can get to the Japanese Embassy in London you can look up a comprehensive guide in its large library called *Japanese Language Institutes* [based in Japan]. The library also has material on learning Japanese and stocks Japanese newspapers including the English-language *Japan Times*, which runs information on jobs in Japan.

There's information about studying in Japan on the embassy website, with guidance on the type of visa you will need if you want to teach English as a foreign language or do other types of work there.

Japanese Embassy,101-104 Piccadilly, London W1J 7JT
Tel: +44 (0) 20 7465 6500
www.uk.emb-japan.go.jp/en/embassy

Portuguese

You don't have to go to Portugal to learn Portuguese - it's the main language of Brazil too, so if you're heading for Latin America on your **gap-** try:
www.linguaserviceworldwide.com/learnportuguesebrazil.htm
www.languageschoolsguide.com/Brazil.cfm

Russian

We suggest you check with the Foreign & Commonwealth Office before making any plans to travel to Russia to study.

That said, we found the following websites offering Russian language lessons in Russia:
www.abroadlanguages.com/learn/russia
www.eurolingua.com/learn_russian.htm
www.languagesabroad.com/countries/russia.html

Spanish

Spanish is the third most widespread language in the world after English and Mandarin Chinese. Over 400 million people in 23 countries are Spanish speakers - Mexico and all of Central and South America (except Brazil) designate Spanish as their official language.

Forms of Spanish can also be heard in Guinea, the Philippines and in Ceuta and Melilla in North Africa. But if you go to a language school inside or outside of Spain, you will probably be learning formal Castilian.

For information about universities and language courses, try:

Spanish Embassy, Education Department, 20 Peel Street, London W8 7PD
Tel: +44 (0) 20 7727 2462
If you want to learn it in Latin America try:
www.expanish.com
www.spanish-language.org/

Multi languages

There are companies offering courses in many different languages. When you're getting references, make sure they're not just for the company – but specifically for the country/course you're interested in.

TEFL

Recent research has revealed that, within the next ten years roughly half the world will be using English, so there's never been a better time to do a TEFL course. Like having a sports instructors' certificate, a TEFL qualification is useful if you want to earn a little money for expenses on a **gap-** and it's a passport that will get you into many countries around the world and in close contact with the people. For more information on getting a TEFL qualification go to Chapter 5 - Working Abroad.

Learning Abroad

Academic year abroad

African Leadership Academy
1050 Printech Road,
Honeydew,
Johannesburg, South Africa
T: +27 (0) 11 699 3000
F: +27 (0) 11 252 6190
www.alagapyear.org/site/

African Leadership Academy offers high school students worldwide the opportunity for an unparalleled African experience, by studying abroad or spending a gap-year with them.

Class Afloat
97 Kaulbach Street,
PO Box 10,
Lunenburg NS, B0J 2C0 Canada
E: discovery@classafloat.com
T: +1 902 634 1895
F: +1 902 634 7155
www.classafloat.com

Sail on a tall ship to exotic ports around the world and earn university credits. Also offers Duke of Edinburgh's Award Scheme.

Council on International Educational Exchange (CIEE)
300 Fore Street,
Portland, ME 04101 USA
E: contact@ciee.org
F: 1-207-553-4299
www.ciee.org

CIEE offer a wide range of international study programs such as study abroad programs for US students, gap-year abroad programs and seasonal work in the USA for international students.

Institute of International Education
1350 Edgmont Avenue, Suite 1100,
Chester, PA 19013 USA
E: info@iiepassport.org
F: +1 610 499 9205
www.iiepassport.org

Search for international education opportunities by country, language, subject and many other criteria.

Office of International Education, Iceland
Neshagi 16,
107 Reykjavík, Iceland
E: ask@hi.is
F: +354 525 5850
www.ask.hi.is/page/forsidaenglish

A service organisation for all higher education institutions in Iceland. From their website you can find information on all the higher education institutions in the country, as well as practical things to do before arriving, visas, admissions, residence permits, etc.

the gap-year guidebook 2011

JohnHallVenice

John Hall Venice, 9 Smeaton Road, London SW18 5JJ
T: +44 (0)20 88714747
E: info@johnhallvenice.com W: www.johnhallvenice.com

The **John Hall Venice Course** is a pre-university course with a difference. It is a mind, eye and ear opening experience. The course is a nine-week introduction to some of the finest and most thought-provoking achievements in the Western World, from the Classical past to today.

The course is conducted through a series of lectures and visits by a team of world-class experts and includes not only painting, sculpture and architecture but also music, world cinema, literature and global issues. There are also practical classes in studio life drawing and portraiture, as well as classes in photography, Italian language and cookery.

The course begins with a week in London and ends with a week in Florence and a week in Rome. The heart of the experience is Venice - being genuinely resident for six weeks in Venice, arguably the most beautiful city and one of the most historic in the world. The calm enjoyment of living in Venice, being able to let the many new things sink in, is a vital ingredient of the course. It is essentially a laying of cultural foundations, an inspirational experience, not a tour.

There are many privileged private visits throughout the course. There is an unforgettable night visit to St.Mark's in Venice, plus unique private visits to the Uffizi in Florence and to the Sistine Chapel in Rome.

The John Hall Venice Course gives a foretaste of a university style of living and learning. It will leave you with not only some lifelong friendships, but also a totally new awareness of what European civilization is about, and with a seriously improved CV.

visit: www.gap-year.com

Queenstown Resort College
PO Box 1566, 9348 New Zealand

F: +64 3 409 0505
www.queenstownresortcollege.com

Offers a diverse range of world class courses and programmes including diplomas, internships, a range of English language courses, leadership development programmes, and short courses for visitors.

Scuola Leonardo da Vinci
via Brunelleschi 4,
Florence, 50123 Italy

E: scuolaleonardo@scuolaleonardo.com
F: +39 055 290396
www.scuolaleonardo.com

One of Italy's largest provider of in-country Italian courses in Italy, for students who wish to experience living and studying in Italy.

The US-UK Fulbright Commission
Fulbright House,
62 Doughty Street, Bloomsbury,
London, WC1N 2JZ UK

E: programmes@fulbright.co.uk
T: +44 (0)20 7404 6880
F: +44 (0)20 7404 6834
www.fulbright.co.uk

EAS is the UK's only official source of information on the US education system, providing objective advice through in-house advising and a variety of outreach events.

Travellers Worldwide
7 Mulberry Close,
Ferring, BN12 5HY UK

E: info@travellersworldwide.com
F: +44 (0) 1903 500364
www.travellersworldwide.com

Exciting Voluntary Projects, Internships and Cultural Courses in 21 countries. Everyone welcome – all ages and nationalities. No qualifications required. Full induction and 24/7 in-country support.

Where There Be Dragons
3200 Carbon Place,
Suite #102,
Boulder, CO 80301 USA

E: info@wheretherebedragons.com
T: +1 303 413 0822
F: +1 303 413 0857
www.wheretherebedragons.com

Runs semester, gap-year and college-accredited programmes in the Andes, China, Himalayas and more.

Art

Aegean Center for the Fine Arts
Paros, 84400 Greece

E: studyart@aegeancenter.org
www.aegeancenter.org

The Aegean Center offers small group and individualized study in the visual arts, creative writing and music. Facilities are located in two stunning locations: the Aegean islands of Greece and Italy's Tuscany.

ARTIS - Art Research Tours
1709 Apache Drive,
Medford, OR 97501 USA

E: david@artis.info.
www.artis-tours.org

ARTIS (Art Research Tours and International studios) provide high quality international art and cultural study abroad programmes at affordable prices, located in beautiful art capitals throughout the world.

Atelier Montmiral
Rue Gambetta,
Castelnau de Montmiral, 81140 France

E: bmnewth@gmail.com
www.ateliermontmiral.com

Atelier Montmiral offer painting and printmaking courses in south-west France. Courses offered are six or ten days in length and can accommodate all levels of ability.

Hellenic International Studies in the Arts (HISA)
Box 11, Paroikia,
Paros, Cyclades, Greece

E: admin@hellenicinternational.org
www.hellenicinternational.org

HISA endorses the gap-year concept and encourages students to immerse themselves in the culture, historical and classical landscape of Paros, Greece.

John Hall Venice
9 Smeaton Road,
London, SW18 5JJ UK

E: info@johnhallvenice.com
www.johnhallvenice.com

A 9 Week course based in Venice, London, Florence and Rome with a sensational combination of lectures, visits and classes in art, music, world cinema, Italian, cookery and photography.

SACI Florence
Palazzo dei Cartelloni,
Via Sant'Antonino, 11,
Firenze, 50123 Italy

T: (39) 055-289948
F: (39) 055-2776408
www.saci-florence.org

A non-profit educational institution for students seeking fully accredited studio art, design, and liberal arts instruction.

SAI - Study Abroad Italy
7151 Wilton Avenue,
Suite 202,
Sebastopol, CA 95472 USA

E: mail@studyabroadflorence.com
T: (707) 824-8965
F: (707) 824-0198
www.studyabroadflorence.com

In conjunction with Florence University SAI offer the chance for international students to live in the heart of this bustling Renaissance city while experiencing modern Florentine life.

visit: www.gap-year.com

Studio Escalier
Turner Towers - Suite 9H,
135 Eastern Parkway,
Brooklyn, NY 11238 USA

E: info@studioescalier.com
T: 1-718-228-4109
F: 1-718-228-4109
www.studioescalier.com

Admission to their three month intensive courses in painting and drawing is by advance application only. Anyone is welcome to apply who has a dedicated interest in working from the human figure.

SuperBon Painting Retreat
Atelier Snow & White,
Le Château,
Saussignac, 24240 France

T: +33 (0)553243422
www.superbon.fr

SuperBon painting retreat is located in south-west France and is a one-week hands-on learning experience designed to give, the artist, more freedom of expression in their work.

The British Institute of Florence
Piazza Strozzi 2,
Florence, 50123 Italy

E: info@britishinstitute.it
F: +39 (0) 55 2677 8222
www.britishinstitute.it

Located in the historic centre of Florence within minutes of the main galleries, museums and churches, the British Institute offers courses in history of art, Italian language and life drawing.

The Marchutz School
The Institute for American Universities, 1830 Sherman Ave.,
Suite 402,
Evanston, IL 60201 USA

E: usa@iaufrance.org
T: 1 800 221-2051
F: 1 847 864-6897
www.marchutz-school.org

Offers artists a unique opportunity to live, learn and grow in the incomparable Provencal setting of Aix-en-Provence, France.

The Year Out Group
Queensfield,
28 King's Road,
Easterton, SN10 4PX UK

E: info@yearoutgroup.org
T: +44 (0) 1380 816696
www.yearoutgroup.org

See main entry under volunteering.

Culture

Alderleaf Wilderness College
18715, 299th Avenue SE,
Monroe, WA 98272 USA

E: info@wildernesscollege.com
www.wildernesscollege.com

A centre for traditional ecological knowledge offering innovative wilderness survival, animal tracking and nature courses in the Pacific Northwest of the United States.

ART HISTORY ABROAD

Art History Abroad (AHA), The Red House, 1 Lambseth Street, Eye IP23 7AG
T: +44 (0) 1379 871800
E: info@arthistoryabroad.com   W: www.arthistoryabroad.com

THE AHA GAP-YEAR COURSE

Travel through Italy with a group of new friends, studying the greatest works of art and architecture, in the most evocative and trendy cities in Europe. Discuss major themes of European history, theology & philosophy with fascinating, brilliant and dynamic tutors.

This six-week course visits Venice (11 days), Verona (five days), Florence (11 days), Siena (five days), Naples (five days) and Rome (11 days). The time spent in each location is long enough to get to know the character and haunts of each city, but not so long that the exciting energy of this course is lost and momentum is not maintained.

The tuition is world class. We select our tutors from a great deal of applicants for their passion, empathy and ability to teach. All know the cities we visit well, they have their favourite restaurants, bars and cafes which they will take you to, and all will make Italian art and history accessible and exciting. Tuition takes place on-site (no classroom or lecture halls) and is in groups no larger than 10. Maximum course size is limited to 30.

You need not have any previous experience of studying art or art history. The level is best described as pre-university, where students can shake off the shackles of exam-led school education and seriously get to grips with what is exhilarating about studying civilization.

In each city students and tutors stay in hotels that have been selected for their location and friendliness. Students share rooms in twos, threes or fours. We eat out in a huge variety of cheap and cheerful restaurants every night, and encourage students to safely sample night life in Italy.

AHA also offer shorter courses in the summer holidays.

visit: www.gap-year.com

American Institute for Foreign Study (AIFS)
River Plaza, 9 West Broad Street,
Stamford, CT 06902 USA

E: info@aifs.com
F: (203) 399 5590
www.aifs.com

One of the oldest, largest and most respected cultural exchange organizations in the world. Their programmes include college study abroad, au pair placement, camp counselors and staff.

Art History Abroad (AHA)
The Red House,
1 Lambseth Street,
Eye, IP23 7AG UK

E: info@arthistoryabroad.com
T: +44 (0) 1379 871800
www.arthistoryabroad.com

Travel through stylish Italy with a group of people just like you. Study beautiful art and architecture with brilliant tutors. Have fun and make friends for life.

Center for Purposeful Living
3983 HSA Circle,
Winston-Salem, NC 27101 USA

E: info@purposeful.org
F: +1 336 777 8828
www.purposeful.org

Provides full scholarships for a year-long service-learning experience that instils practical skills for a balanced and purposeful life.

Cultural Experiences Abroad (CEA)
2005 W. 14th Street,
Suite 113,
Tempe, AZ 85281 6977 USA

E: info@gowithcea.com
T: 480-557-7900
F: 480-557-7926
www.gowithcea.com

CEA sends thousands of students on study abroad programmes at multiple universities in 15 countries including Argentina, Australia, China, Costa Rica, Czech Republic, England, France, Germany, Ireland, Italy, Mexico, Poland, Russia, South Africa and Spain.

Eastern Institute of Technology
Private Bag 1201,
Taradale,
Napier, New Zealand

E: info@eit.ac.nz
T: +64 6 974 8000
F: +64 6 974 8910
www.eit.ac.nz

Te Manga Mâori - EIT in Hawke's Bay offers the opportunity to study the Maori language and culture from beginners through to advanced level.

El Casal
Balmes 163, 3/1,
Barcelona, 08008 Spain

E: info@elcasalbarcelona.com
F: +34 93 218 34 32
www.elcasalbarcelona.com

Based in Barcelona, El Casal offers the chance to soak in Catalan culture through a programme specifically for gappers who want to learn Spanish.

the gap-year guidebook 2011

Istituto di Lingua e Cultura Italiana Michelangelo
Via Ghibellina 88,
Florence, 50122 Italy

E: michelangelo@dada.it
F: +39 055 240 997
www.michelangelo-edu.it

The Michelangelo Institute offers cultural courses on art history, Italian language, literature, commerce and commercial correspondence, and 'L'Italia oggi'.

Knowledge Exchange Institute (KEI)
63 Sickletown Road,
West Nyack, 10994 USA

E: info@keiabroad.org
www.keiabroad.org

Study abroad and intern abroad programmes designed to meet your academic, professional and personal interests.

Lexia Study Abroad
6 The Courtyard,
Hanover, NH 03755 USA

E: info@lexiaintl.org
F: 603-643-9899
www.lexiaintl.org

Cultural study programmes that encourage students to connect with their community while pursuing academic research. Participate in the daily life and work of a community in countries worldwide.

Petersburg Studies
34 Wilkinson Street,
South Lambeth,
London, SW8 1DB UK

E: alexandra.chaldecott@gmail.com
T: +44 (0) 7762 947 656
F: +44 (0) 20 7735 5875
www.petersburgstudies.com

Offer a winter course designed to make St Petersburg accessible; its history, architecture, museums, music, literature and contemporary life are explored in the company of lecturers, guides and local contacts.

Road2Argentina
Anchorena 1676,
Capital Federal, 1425 Argentina

E: info@road2argentina.com
F: +54 11 6379 9391
www.road2argentina.com

Study abroad in Argentina and learn all about the country and its culture.

SIT Study Abroad
PO Box 676,
1 Kipling Road,
Brattleboro, VT 05302 USA

E: studyabroad@sit.edu
T: 802.258.3212
F: 802.258.3296
www.sit.edu/studyabroad/

Offers undergraduate study abroad programmes in Africa, Asia and the Pacific, Europe, Latin America and the Caribbean, and the Middle East.

Fashion & Design

Blanche Macdonald Centre
100-555 West 12th Avenue,
Vancouver BC, V5Z 3X7 Canada

E: info@blanchemacdonald.com
www.blanchemacdonald.com

Courses available in make up, nail techniques, spa therapy and fashion.

Domus Academy
Via Watt, 27,
Milan, 20143 Italy

E: info@domusacademy.it
F: +39 024 222 525
www.domusacademy.com

Offers short courses with the University of the Arts - Central Saint Martin, but they also run a five day intensive course to Chicago for advanced students of fashion.

**Florence Institute
of Design International**
Borgo Ognissanti 9,
Florence, 50123 Italy

E: registrar@florence-institute.com
F: +39 055 53 70 739
www.florence-institute.com

New school of design in Florence.

Istituto di Moda Burgo
Piazza San Babila,
5 - 20122 Milano, Italy

E: imb@imb.it
F: (+39) 02783758
www.imb.it

A fashion design school in Milan offering summer courses for basic, advanced or professional level and private tuition in drawing techniques and pattern making.

Metallo Nobile
Via Toscanella 28/r,
Florence, 50125 Italy

E: info@metallo-nobile.com
F: +39 055 280800
www.metallo-nobile.com

Summer course in jewellery design and creation, based in Florence.

**NABA - Nuova Accademia
de Belle Arti**
Via C. Darwin 20,
Milano, 20143 Italy

E: info@design-summer-courses.com
www.design-summer-courses.com

NABA summer courses are divided into two levels: introduction and intermediate. They have courses in the design, fashion, graphic design and contemporary art.

**Polimoda Institute
of Fashion Design and Marketing**
Polimoda via Pisana 77,
firenze , I-50143 Italy

E: info@polimoda.com
F: +39 055 700287
www.polimoda.com

Based in Florence, Polimoda Fashion School offers a variety of summer courses for those interested in all aspects of fashion.

the gap-year guidebook 2011

RMIT Training
PO Box 12058,
A'Beckett Street,
Melbourne, VIC 8006 Australia

E: enquiries@rmit.edu.acu
T: +61 (0) 3 9925 8111
F: +61 (0) 3 9925 8134
www.shortcourses.rmit.edu.au

Has a Career Discovery Short Course in fashion. An intensive programme which includes lectures by experienced industry professionals alongside studio workshops.

Up To Date Fashion Academy
Corso Vittorio Emanuele II,
Milano, 15-20122 Italy

E: info@fashionuptodate.com
F: +39 02 76 26 79 29
www.fashionuptodate.com/en/home.php

Learn about fashion in Milan! This academy has a variety of courses available.

Film, Theatre & Drama

Actors College of Theatre and Television
505 Pitt Street,
Sydney, NSW 2000 Australia

E: info@actt.edu.au
F: +61 (0) 2 9281 3964
www.actt.edu.au

College specialising in acting, music theatre and technical production courses.

Ariège Arts
8 cours St Jacques ,
Léran, 09600 France

www.ariegearts.com

Ariège Arts offer the chance to make documentary films in the French Pyrenees. Students learn the techniques of narrative in film and experience tuition by broadcast professionals.

EICAR - The International Film School of Paris
The International Department,
50 avenue du Président Wilson,
Bât. 136 - BP 131,
La Plaine Saint-Denis, 93214 France

E: inquiries@eicar.fr
T: (+33) 01 49 98 11 11
F: 00 33 (0)1 49 46 00 07
www.eicar-international.com

Offers short summer workshops taught in English during July and September in the following areas: filmmaking, script writing, editing, HD Video and sound.

European Film College
Carl Th Dreyers vej,
Ebeltoft, 8400 Denmark

E: info@efc.dk
F: 0045 8634 0535
www.europeanfilmcollege.com

Offering students a unique experience, an international learning environment offering young filmmakers and actors an intense eight-month course.

visit: www.gap-year.com

Flashpoint Academy
28 North Clark St.,
Chicago, IL 60602 USA

www.flashpointacademy.com

This is a two-year, direct-to-industry college focusing exclusively on the following disciplines: film/broadcast, recording arts, visual effects and animation and game development.

Full Sail University
3300 University Blvd.,
Winter Park,
Florida, 32792 USA

T: +1 407 679 6333
F: +1 407 678 0070
www.fullsail.edu

If you're after a career in music, film, video games, design, animation, entertainment business, or Internet marketing, Full Sail is the right place for you.

Hollywood Film & Acting Academy
1786 North Highland Avenue,
Hollywood, CA 90028 USA

F: +1 323 962 8555
www.hwfaa.com

The traditional film school alternative, offering shorter more intense programme in feature films, movie making and acting.

NYFA (New York Film Academy)
100 East 17th Street,
New York, USA

E: film@nyfa.edu
F: +1 212 477 1414
www.nyfa.com

The New York Film Academy runs programmes all year round in New York City and at Universal Studios in Hollywood, as well as summer workshops worldwide.

PCFE Film School
Pstrossova 19,
Prague 1, 110 00 Czech Republic

E: info@filmstudies.cz
F: +420 222 510 930
www.filmstudies.cz

Offers workshops, semester and year programmes in filmmaking including directing, screenwriting, cinematography, editing and film history and theory.

The Acting Center
5514 Hollywood Boulevard,
Hollywood, CA 90028 USA

www.theactingcenterla.com

No audition is necessary but an interview is required. Classes are available in evenings during the week and on weekends.

The Los Angeles Film School
6363 Sunset Boulevard,
Hollywood, 90028 USA

www.lafilm.com

Has degree programmes in filmmaking, game production and animation. International students must acquire a student visa before studying in the United States.

the gap-year guidebook 2011

TVI Actors Studio - Los Angeles
14429 Ventura Boulevard,
Suite 118,
Sherman Oaks, CA 91423 USA

T: +1 818 784 6500
www.tvistudios.com

Offers acting classes, workshops, and seminars for aspiring and professional actors.

Vancouver Film School
VFS Administration & Admissions Office,
198 West Hastings Street,
Vancouver BC, V6B 1H2 Canada

T: +1 604 685 5808
F: +1 604 685 5830
www.vfs.com

Centre for both training and higher learning in all areas related to media and entertainment production.

Languages

Chinese

Hong Kong Institute of Languages
6/F Wellington Plaza,
56-58 Wellington Street,
Central, PR China

E: info@hklanguages.com
T: +852 2877 6160
F: +852 2877 5970
www.hklanguages.com

Courses available in Mandarin and Cantonese. Good central location on Hong Kong Island.

Hong Kong Language Learning Centre
604, 6/F Emperor Group Centre,
288 Hennessy Road,
Wanchai, PR China

E: hkllc@netvigator.com
T: +852 2572 6488
F: +852 2385 5571
www.hkllc.com

Language school in Hong Kong which specialises in Cantonese and Mandarin conversation and Chinese reading and writing for expatriates, locals and overseas Chinese.

Talking Mandarin Language Centre
8/F, Full View Building,
140-142 Des Voeux Road,
Central, PR China

T: +852 2139 3226
F: +852 2139 3227
www.talkingmandarin.com

Language school in Central, Hong Kong, that teaches both Cantonese and Mandarin.

WorldLink Education US Office
1904 3rd Avenue, Suite 633,
Seattle, WA 98101 USA

E: info@worldlinkedu.com
F: +1 206 264 4932
www.worldlinkedu.com

WorldLink Education's Chinese language programme immerses you in Mandarin Chinese through class instruction, after-class tutoring, language exchanges with native speakers and a range of optional extra activities.

visit: www.gap-year.com

French

Accent Français
2 rue de Verdun,
Montpellier, 34000 France

E: info@accentfrancais.com
F: +33 (0) 434 221 164
www.accentfrancais.com

This school runs intensive French courses in Montpellier particularly for non-French speakers. They last between two weeks and three months.

Alliance Française de Londres
1 Dorset Square,
Marylebone,
London, NW1 6PU UK

E: courses@alliancefrancaise.org.uk
T: +44 (0) 20 7723 6439
www.alliancefrancaise.org.uk

Alliance Française is a non-profit-making organisation whose goal is to teach French and bring cultures together (group classes and bespoke tuition available).

BLS French Courses
42 rue Lafaurie de Monbadon,
Bordeaux, 33000 France

E: info@bls-frenchcourses.com
F: +33 (0) 5 56 51 76 15
www.bls-frenchcourses.com

Based in the heart of Bordeaux. You will be put up in a modest hotel or, more likely, with a host family, perhaps with another student.

CESA Languages Abroad
CESA House,
Pennance Road,
Lanner, TR16 5TQ UK

E: info@cesalanguages.com
T: +44 (0) 1209 211 800
F: +44 (0) 1209 211 830
www.cesalanguages.com

Perfect your language skills, experience the culture first-hand, get a qualification (optional) and have an amazing gap-year with CESA

CMEF, Centre Méditerranéen d'Etudes Françaises
Centre Méditerranéen, Chemin des Oliviers,
BP 38 F - 06 320,
Cap d'Ail, France

E: centremed@monte-carlo.mc
T: +33 (0)4 93 78 21 59
F: +33 (0)4 93 41 83 96
www.centremed.monte-carlo.mc

Located in the South of France between Nice and Monaco - Monte Carlo. An international language school with a long tradition on French language courses.

College Northside
CP 5158,
750 Chemin Pierre-Péladeau,
Sainte-Adèle PQ, J8B 1Z4 Canada

E: admin@college-northside.qc.ca
T: +1 450 229 9889
F: +1 450 229 1715
www.college-northside.qc.ca

Northside offers an intensive French immersion camp through the summer geared towards the 16 to 18 age range. Located in the mountains in the French-speaking village of Sainte-Adèle.

Spanish | French | Italian | German | Portuguese | Russian | Japanese | Chinese | Greek | Arabic

Travel AND learn a new language!

"Really friendly and fun!"
Katy Barnett, 16 weeks in Seville

- **Check out Gap Year** student **Photo Diaries** and first-hand Reports

- **View ALL course options**, start dates & full pricing details on our Course Finder

- **Learn French:**
  8 weeks tuition and host accommodation (self catering) in **Nice**, from: £2466.00
  2 weeks French & Surf course in **Biarritz**, French host, half-board, from: £1180.00
  23 weeks tuition and French host, self catering in **Montpellier**, from: £5454.00

- **Study Spanish:**
  24 weeks tuition and shared apartment, self catering in **Seville**, from: £4984.00
  2 weeks in **Madrid**, tuition and shared apartment, self catering from : £757.00
  8 weeks tuition and shared apartment, self catering in **Buenos Aires**, Argentina from: £2071.00

Apart from the direct pleasure of improving your language skills, a course abroad enables you to widen your horizons, gain in self confidence and experience the daily life of another culture first-hand, giving you a truly international perspective on the world.

Visit us on the web
cesalanguages.com
or call **01209 211 800**

Established 1980. CESA's language courses abroad suit anyone (from beginner to advanced linguistic ability) for as long a period as they can invest, in terms of time and budget.

simply languages abroad
cesa

En Famille Overseas
58 Abbey Close,
Peacehaven, BN10 7SD UK

E: info@enfamilleoverseas.co.uk
www.enfamilleoverseas.co.uk

En Famille Overseas arranges for you to stay with a family in France as a paying guest for a week to a year, with the board and lodging costs negotiable if you stay more than a month.

Institut ELFCA
66 avenue de Toulon,
Hyères, 83400 France

E: elfca@elfca.com
F: +33 (0) 4 94 65 81 22
www.elfca.com

Located in Hyères on the Mediterranean coast. Tutition is in small groups. Students can take the Alliance Française exams or prepare for the DELF exams.

Institut Français
14 Cromwell Place,
South Kensington,
London, SW7 2JR UK

E: language-centre@ambafrance.org.uk
T: +44 (0) 20 7581 2701 ext 1
F: +44 (0) 20 7581 0061
www.institut-francais.org.uk

The Institut Français is the official French Government centre of language and culture in London.

Institut Savoisien
d'Etudes Françaises pour Etrangers
Domaine Universitaire de Jacob,
Chambery Cedex, 73011 France

E: isefe@univ-savioe.fr
F: +33 (0) 4 79 75 84 16
www.isefe.univ-savoie.fr

An institute which specialises in teaching French as a foreign language to adults from non-Francophone countries.

Lyon Bleu International
54 Cours Lafayette,
Lyon, 69003 France

E: learnfrenchinlyon@lyon-bleu.fr
F: +33 (0) 478 607 326
www.lyon-bleu.fr

Lyon Bleu International, in Lyon, is dedicated to teaching the French language and culture.

TASIS, The American School in Switzerland
6926 Montagnola, Switzerland

E: admissions@tasis.ch
F: +41 91 994 2364
www.tasis.ch

Each year, the TASIS schools and summer programmes attract over 2400 students representing more than 40 nationalities who share in a caring, family-style international community.

Vis-à-Vis
2-4 Stoneleigh Park Road,
Epsom, KT19 0QT UK

E: visavis@donquijote.org
www.visavis.org

French courses offered in France. Various accommodation options are available, and there is the usual range of course length, level and intensity.

German

BWS Germanlingua
Hackenstr. 7, Eingang C,
Munich, 80331 Germany

E: info@bws-germanlingua.de
F: +49 (0) 89 599 892 01
www.bws-germanlingua.de

BWS Germanlingua is based in Munich and Berlin; all staff are experienced teachers, and classes have a maximum of 12 students.

CESA Languages Abroad
CESA House,
Pennance Road,
Lanner, TR16 5TQ UK

E: info@cesalanguages.com
T: +44 (0) 1209 211 800
F: +44 (0) 1209 211 830
www.cesalanguages.com

Perfect your language skills, experience the culture first-hand, get a qualification (optional) and have an amazing gap-year with CESA

German Academic Exchange Service (DAAD)
34 Belgrave Square,
Belgravia,
London, SW1X 8QB UK

T: +44 (0) 20 7235 1736
http://london.daad.de/

The German Academic Exchange Service has an inforamtion portal for those interested in learning German in Germany.

Goethe Institut
50 Princes Gate,
Exhibition Road, South Kensington,
London, SW7 2PH UK

E: info@london.goethe.org
T: +44 (0) 20 7596 4000
F: +44 (0) 20 7594 0240
www.goethe.de/enindex.htm

The Goethe Institut is probably the best-known international German language school network.

Greek

**DIKEMES - International Center
for Hellenic and Mediterranean Studies**
5 Plateia Stadiou,
Athens, GR - 116 35 Greece

E: programs@dikemes.edu.gr
F: +30 210 7561-497
www.cyathens.org

DIKEMES/College Year in Athens offers unparalleled learning opportunities for English-speaking students seeking a programme of study in Greece.

Greek Embassy Education Office
1a Holland Park,
Kensington,
London, W11 3TP UK

E: education@greekembassy.org.uk
T: +44 (0) 20 7221 0093
F: +44 (0) 20 7243 4212
www.greekembassy.org.uk

The Greek Embassy website has a link to the Greek Ministry of Education, where you can find a list of universities and schools in Athens, Thessalonika, Crete and the Greek islands among other places where modern Greek is taught.

Italian

Accademia del Giglio
Via Ghibellina 116,
Florence, 50122 Italy

E: info@adg.it
F: +39 055 23 02 467
www.adg.it

This quiet, small school takes about 30 students, taught in small classes. As well as Italian language courses, they offer classes in drawing and painting.

Accademia Italiana
Piazza Pitti 15,
Florence, 50125 Italy

E: modaita@tin.it
F: +39 055 284 486
www.accademiaitaliana.com

An international design, art and language school, the Accademia Italiana puts on summer language courses as well as full-year and longer academic and Masters courses.

Centro Machiavelli
Piazza Santo Spirito 4,
Florence, 50125 Italy

E: school@centromachiavelli.it
F: +39 (0) 55 280 800
www.centromachiavelli.it

Small language school in the Santo Spirito district of Florence. Set up to teach Italian to foreigners.

Europass
Istituto EUROPASS, Centro Studi Europeo,
Via Sant'Egidio, 12 - 50122 Italy

E: europass@europass.it
T: 0039 055 2345802
F: 0039 055 2479995
www.europass.it

Europass has offered individual and varied Italian language courses in the heart of Florence since 1992.

Il Sillabo
Via Alberti, 31,
San Giovanni Valdarno (AR), 52027 Italy

E: mail@sillabo.it
F: +39 055 942439
www.sillabo.it

Il Sillabo, a small, family-run school, in San Giovanni Valdarno. Authorised by the Italian Ministry of Education.

Instituto Donatello
via Galliano 1,
Florence, 50144 Italy

Italian language school in Florence.

Istituto Europeo
Piazza delle Pallottole n. 1 (Duomo),
Florence, 1-50122 Italy

E: info@istitutoeuropeo.it
F: +39 05528 9145
www.istitutoeuropeo.it

Istituto Europeo has three language schools: two in Italy and one in Japan. As well as running courses on Italian wine and food, they have an art and music school.

Lorenzo de' Medici
Via Faenza 43,
Florence, 50123 Italy

E: info@lorenzodemedici.it
F: +39 055 239 8920
www.lorenzodemedici.it

The Lorenzo de' Medici's offers a combination of language and cultural courses and has a large library in the adjoining San Iacopo di Corbolini church.

Japanese

Kichijoji Language School
2-3-15-701, Kichijoji Minami-cho,
Musashino-Shi,
Tokyo, 180-0003 Japan

E: info@klschool.com
T: +81 (0) 422 47 7390
F: +81 (0) 422 41 5897
www.klschool.com

Language school in Tokyo which has been teaching non-native speakers the Japanese language and about Japanese culture since 1983.

visit: www.gap-year.com

The Yamasa Institute
1-2-1 Hanehigashimachi,
Okazaki-shi, 444-0832 Japan

E: admissions@yamasa.org
F: +81 (0) 564 55 8113
www.yamasa.org

The Yamasa Institute is an independent teaching and research centre under the governance of the Hattori Foundation. It is APJLE accredited.

Multi-languages

Caledonia Languages Abroad
The Clockhouse, Bonnington Mill,
72 Newhaven Road,
Edinburgh, EH6 5QG UK

E: courses@caledonialanguages.co.uk
T: +44 (0) 131 621 7721
www.caledonialanguages.co.uk

Short courses in French, Italian, German, Russian, Spanish and Portuguese in Europe and Latin America, for all levels, start all year round, most for a minimum of two weeks.

CERAN Lingua International
Avenue des Petits Sapins ,
Spa, Belgium

E: customer@ceran.com
F: +32 (0) 87 79 11 88
www.ceran.com

CERAN runs weekly intensive residential language programmes in Dutch, French, German and Spanish.

EF International Language Schools
22 Chelsea Manor Street,
London, SW3 5RL UK

E: eflanguages@ef.com
F: + 44 (0) 207 341 8788
www.ef.com

EF International Language Schools offer you a range of programmes; perfect for perfecting an 'A' Level language, for a great Gap Year, for gaining internship experience in a foreign country.

Eurolanguages
Ido Language Travel Services Limited,
The Enterprise Centre,George's Place,
Dun Laoghaire, Ireland UK

E: help@eurolanguages.com
T: +353 1 443 4703
www.eurolanguages.com

Have a website that helps you choose a language school and book a place on a language course. Read the reviews of fellow students.

Eurolingua Institute
Eurolingua House,
61 Bollin Drive,
Altrincham, WA14 5QW UK

www.eurolingua.com

Eurolingua is a network of 70 institutes teaching nine languages in 35 countries. Group programmes give 15 hours of tuition a week, according to your level.

the gap-year guidebook 2011

Inlingua International
Belpstrasse 11,
Bern, 3007 Switzerland

E: service@inlingua.com
F: +41 31 388 7766
www.inlingua.com

Inlingua International runs language colleges throughout Europe.

Language Courses Abroad
67 Ashby Road,
Loughborough, LE11 3AA UK

E: info@languagesabroad.co.uk
www.languagesabroad.co.uk

Languages courses available in French, German, Greek, Italian, Portuguese, Russian, Spanish and others.

Learn Languages Abroad
'Sceilig', Ballymorefinn,
Glenasmole,
Dublin, County Dublin Ireland

E: info@languages.ie
T: +353 (0) 1451 1674
F: +353 (0) 1451 1636
www.languages.ie

Learn Languages Abroad will help you find the course best suited to your needs. Courses available range from two weeks to a full academic year.

Modern Language Studies Abroad (MLSA)
PO Box 548,
Frankfort, IL 60423 USA

E: info@mlsa.com
F: (815) 464-9458
www.mlsa.com

Offers language study abroad programmes in the following countries: Spain, Italy and Costa Rica.

OISE Oxford
13-15 High Street,
Oxford, OX1 4EA UK

E: oxford@oise.com
F: +44 (0)1865 723 648
www.oise.com

Have their own unique teaching philosophy which leads students to gain confidence, fluency and accuracy when speaking another language taught by a native-speaker.

The Year Out Group
Queensfield,
28 King's Road,
Easterton, SN10 4PX UK

E: info@yearoutgroup.org
T: +44 (0) 1380 816696
www.yearoutgroup.org

See main entry under volunteering.

Portuguese

CIAL Centro de Linguas
Av da Republica,
41 - 8° Esq.,
Lisbon, 1050-187 Portugal

E: portuguese@cial.pt
T: +351 217 940 448
F: +351 217 960 783
www.cial.pt

With schools in Lisbon and Faro, CIAL organises courses in Portuguese for foreigners. Accommodation is in private homes at an extra weekly cost, which includes breakfast.

Russian

Obninsk Humanities Centre
Dubravushka,
249020 Kaluga Oblast,
Obninsk, Russian Federation

E: lara.bushell@btinternt.com
T: +44 (0) 208 858 0614 (UK number)
www.dubravushka.ru

The Obninsk Humanities Centre is an independent boarding school two hours from Moscow offering intensive and reasonably priced Russian courses.

The Russian Language Centre
5a Bloomsbury Square,
Bloomsbury,
London, WC1A 2TA UK

E: info@russiancentre.co.uk
T: +44 (0) 20 7831 5330
www.russiancentre.co.uk

The Russian Language Centre in London offers a range of courses for groups and individuals: intensive, accelerated and private.

Spanish

Academia Hispánica Córdoba
C/Rodríguez Sánchez, 15,
Córdoba, 14003 Spain

E: info@academiahispanica.com
F: +34 957 488 199
www.academiahispanica.com

Small-group language tuition to suit all levels.

AIL Madrid Spanish Language School
C/Doctor Esquerdo 33, 1a2,
Madrid, 28028 Spain

F: +34 91 725 4188
www.ailmadrid.com/gap-year/home

They offer flexible gap-year programmes tailored to your needs. Learn Spanish in Madrid.

Amigos Spanish School
Zaguan de Cielo B-23,
Cusco, Peru

E: amigos@spanishcusco.com
www.spanishcusco.com

Non-profit Spanish school. With every hour of your Spanish classes, you pay for the basic care of a group of underprivileged children at their foundation.

Spanish | French | Italian | German | Portuguese | Russian | Japanese | Chinese | Greek | Arabic

Travel AND learn a new language!

"Really friendly and fun!"
Katy Barnett, 16 weeks in Seville

- **Check out Gap Year** student **Photo Diaries** and first-hand Reports

- **View ALL course options**, start dates & full pricing details on our Course Finder

- **Learn French:**
  8 weeks tuition and host accommodation (self catering) in **Nice**, from: £2466.00
  2 weeks French & Surf course in **Biarritz**, French host, half-board, from: £1180.00
  23 weeks tuition and French host, self catering in **Montpellier**, from: £5454.00

- **Study Spanish:**
  24 weeks tuition and shared apartment, self catering in **Seville**, from: £4984.00
  2 weeks in **Madrid**, tuition and shared apartment, self catering from : £757.00
  8 weeks tuition and shared apartment, self catering in **Buenos Aires**, Argentina from: £2071.00

Apart from the direct pleasure of improving your language skills, a course abroad enables you to widen your horizons, gain in self confidence and experience the daily life of another culture first-hand, giving you a truly international perspective on the world.

Visit us on the web
cesalanguages.com

or call **01209 211 800**

Established 1980. CESA's language courses abroad suit anyone (from beginner to advanced linguistic ability) for as long a period as they can invest, in terms of time and budget.

simply languages abroad
cesa

Bridge Year, Spanish Programs
Roman Diaz 297,
Providencia, Canada

E: info@bridgeyear.com
T: +44 (0) 20 7096 0369
www.bridgeyear.com

Study Spanish in Chile and Argentina! There are plenty of activities and excursions plus the homestay could be the most rewarding part of the experience.

CESA Languages Abroad
CESA House,
Pennance Road,
Lanner, TR16 5TQ UK

E: info@cesalanguages.com
T: +44 (0) 1209 211 800
F: +44 (0) 1209 211 830
www.cesalanguages.com

Perfect your language skills , experience the culture first-hand, get a qualification (optional) and have an amazing gap-year with CESA

Comunicacion Language School
Avda Las Marinas, 110,
Roquetas de Mar,
Almeria, 04740 Spain

E: info@comunicacionee.com
T: +34 950 33 34 15
F: +34 950 33 34 15
www.comunicacionee.com

Come and enjoy professional Spanish classes, a great beach and lots of outdoor and cultural activities in Almería province, Spain. Stay in an apartment, a hostel or with a Spanish host family.

Don Quijote
2/4 Stoneleigh Park Road,
Epsom, KT19 OQT UK

E: uk@donquijote.org
F: +44 (0) 20 8786 8086
www.donquijote.org

Don Quijote is a leading network of schools teaching Spanish in Spain and Latin America.

Enforex
C/Alberto Aguilera 26,
Madrid, 28015 Spain

E: info@enforex.es
F: +34 91 594 5159
www.enforex.com

Learn to speak Spanish in Spain or Latin America. Over 28 centres all in Spanish speaking countries. Summer camps also available.

Escuela Internacional
Central Office, Calle Talamanca 10,
28807 Alcala de Henares,
Madrid, Spain

E: info@escuelai.com
T: +34 91 883 1264
F: +34 91 883 1301
www.escuelai.com

Learn Spanish in Spain or Latin America. Also offers Spanish cultural and literature courses.

the gap-year guidebook 2011

Expanish
Viamonte 927, 1A,
Buenos Aries, Argentina

E: info@expanish.com
F: +54 11 4322 0011
www.expanish.com

Learn Spanish in Buenos Aires located in the city centre, home to some of the oldest historical sites in the city.

IndaPidal
C/ Granada 9,
1º Oficina 2,
Almería, 04003 Spain

E: info@indapidal.com
T: (00) (34) 950 23 33 17
F: (00) (34) 950 23 33 17
www.indapidal.com

Offer Spanish language courses in Almería, Spain.

International House Madrid
C/Zurbano, 8,
Madrid, 28010 Spain

E: spanish@ihmadrid.com
F: +34 91 308 5321
www.ihmadrid.com

Learn Spanish in Madrid.

Mente Argentina
Juncal 3184 piso 7,
Buenos Aires, C1425 Argentina

E: info@menteargentina.com
www.MenteArgentina.com

Visit Argentina and learn Spainish in a unique and different way.

Pichilemu Institute of Language Studies
138 Agustin Ross,
Pichilemu, Chile

E: chris@pichilemulanguage.com

Offers group, private, and certified courses. Students can surf and experience rural Chile.

Simón Bolivar Spanish School
Mariscal Foch E9-20 y Av. 6 de Diciembre,
Quito, Ecuador

E: info@simon-bolivar.com
F: +593 (2) 2544 558
www.simon-bolivar.com

One of the biggest Spanish schools in Ecuador. Spanish lessons are offered at the main building in Quito, the Pacific coast and the Amazon jungle.

Spanish Study Holidays
67 Ashby Road,
Loughborough, LE11 3AA UK

E: spanishstudy.holidays@btinternet.com
F: +44 (0) 1509 260 037
www.spanishstudy.co.uk

Offers Spanish courses throughout Spain and central and south America lasting from a week to nine months.

visit: www.gap-year.com

Universidad de Navarra - ILCE
Institute of Spanish Language and Culture,
Campus Universitario,
Edificio Central,
Pamplona, 31080 Spain

E: ilce@unav.es
T: +34 948 425 616 ext 2204
www.unav.es/ilce/english/

A wide range of programmes are offered for people who wish to travel to Spain to learn about the culture and the language.

Learning

Oxford International Study Centre
7 St Aldates,
Oxford, OX1 1BS UK

E: info@oxintstudycentre.com
F: 01865 201006
www.oxintstudycentre.com

Oxford International Study Centre arranges a wide range of programmes in Oxford. We can also arrange for students to work as language assistants overseas.

Music

Backbeat Tours
140 Beale Street,
Memphis, 38103 USA

E: tours@backbeattours.com
www.backbeattours.com

Offer 'rockin' rides' through Memphis music history on a vintage 1950s bus. The three hour Hound Dog Tour follows in the footsteps of the King of Rock 'n' Roll, Elvis.

Country Music Travel
PO Box 10171,
McLean, VA 22102 USA

E: mail@countrymusictravel.com
www.countrymusictravel.com

Country music-themed vacations and escorted tours, from trips to Dollywood entertainment park, to music cities tours in Nashville, Memphis and Tennessee.

Jazz Summer School
41a High Street,
Wanstead,
London, E11 2AA UK

T: +44 (0) 208 989 8129
www.jazzsummerschool.com

Jazz Summer School offering places at the French jazz summer school in the South of France or The Cuban music school in Havana.

NashCamp
PO Box 210396,
Nashville, TN 37221 USA

E: nashcamp@nashcamp.com
F: +1 615-952-4040
www.nashcamp.com

Programmes offered in acoustic music and songwriting, including bluegrass and banjo playing.

the gap-year guidebook 2011

Red Cedar Songwriter Camp
PO Box 135,
Pender Island BC, V0N 2M0 Canada

E: jill@redcedarsongwritercamp.ca
www.redcedarsongwritercamp.ca

Learn the craft of songwriting, hone your guitar skills, hike and meet new friends.

Scoil Acla - Irish Music Summer School
Achill Island,
County Mayo, Ireland

www.scoilacla.com

Summer school established to teach Irish Piping (Irish War Pipes), tin whistle, accordian, banjo, flute and harp.

Songwriter Girl Camps
PO Box 167,
Old Hickory, TN 37138 USA

E: info@songwritergirl.com
www.songwritergirl.com

They offer weekend songwriting camps for girls and women of all ages and ability!

SummerKeys
c/o Bruce Potterton,
32 North Main Street,
Boonton, NJ 07005 USA

T: 1-973-316-6220
www.summerkeys.com

Music vacations for adults in Lubec, Maine. Open to all 'musical people' regardless of ability with workshops and private tuition in a variety of instruments.

SummerSongs Inc.
PO Box 803,
Saugerties, NY 12477 USA

E: register@summersongs.com
www.summersongs.com

A not-for-profit corporation dedicated to the art and craft of songwriting.

Taller Flamenco
C/ Peral, 49,
Seville, E-41002 Spain

E: info@tallerflamenco.com
F: (+34) 954 56 40 66
www.tallerflamenco.com

Courses include flamenco dance, flamenco guitar, singing and percussion.

United DJ Mixing School
Level 10,
92-94 Elizabeth St,
Melbourne, Australia

E: admin@djsunited.com.au
T: +61 (03) 9639 9990
www.djsunited.com.au

Offer an introductory course over two weekends, which gives the basics of DJ-ing and a longer comprehensive course that runs over twelve weeks.

Welsh Jazz Society
26, The Balcony,
Castle Arcade,
Cardiff, CF10 1BY UK

E: welshjazz@btconnect.com
T: 02920 340591
F: 02920 665160
www.jazzwales.org.uk

Based in Cardiff the society promotes live jazz music of all styles and can keep you informed of gigs and jazz events going on in Wales.

World Rhythms Arts Program (WRAP)
Kalani Music,
11862 Balboa Boulevard, Suite 159,
Granada Hills, CA 91344 USA

T: +1 818 832 2028
www.drum2dance.com

Classes develop your working knowledge of instruments, rhythms, dances, songs, styles, methods and applications.

Photography

Brooks Institute
27 E. Cota Street,
Santa Barbara, CA 93101 USA

www.brooks.edu

This school offers training in filmmaking, graphic design and photojournalism. The courses are designed for anyone who aspires to a career in photography, filmmaking, visual journalism, or graphic design.

c4 Images & Safaris
Knoll Hill Cottage,
Knoll Lane,
Corfe Mullen, BH21 3RF UK

E: strat@c4images-safaris.co.za
T: +44 (0) 1202 694135
www.c4safaris.co.uk

Offers short photography workshops and wildlife safaris in South Africa with emphasis on helping you to improve your photography skills.

Joseph Van Os Photo Safaris
P.O. Box 655,
Vashon Island, WA 98070 USA

E: info@photosafaris.com
F: (206) 463-5383
www.photosafaris.com

Joseph Van Os Photo Safaris guide you to some of the world's finest wild and scenic locations with the main purpose of making great photographs.

London Photo Tours & Workshops
APT Studios, 6 Creekside,
Deptford,
London, SE8 4SA UK

T: +44 (0)7738 942 099
www.londonphototours.co.uk

Offers short courses and photography workshops. Also specialise in small group photo travel with no more than eight photo travellers in their seven-day photo holidays.

Nigel Turner Photographic Workshop
3055 Evening Wind,
Henderson, NV 89122 USA

E: npturner@cox.net
www.nigelturnerphotography.com

One- and two-week workshops on photographic technique based in Las Vegas. Your chance to capture some of the most breathtaking scenery the US has to offer, from Death Valley to Yosemite National.

Photo Holidays France
12 Middleton Grove,
Holloway, N7 9LS UK

E: aw@andrewwhittuck.co.uk
www.photoholidaysfrance.co.uk/index.html

A private photography school in the south of France offering one to one photography tuition specialising in landscape and portrait photography.

Photographers on Safari
West End Studios, 55 Stapleford Road,
Whissendine,
Oakham, LE15 7HF UK

E: info@photographersonsafari.com
T: (+44) 01664 474040
http://www.photographersonsafari.com/index.htm

Offers a variety of exciting workshops in the UK and photography Safaris overseas, ideal for the wildlife lover.

Steve Outram Crete Photo Tours & Workshops
D.Katsifarakis Street,
Galatas,
Chania, 73100 Greece

E: mail@steveoutram.com
T: +30 28210 32201
F: +30 28210 32201
www.steveoutram.com

Professional photographer Steve Outram uses his local knowledge of Zanzibar, Lesvos and western Crete to show you how to make the most of photographic opportunities and develop your skill as a photographer.

Venice School of Photography Workshops Ltd
26 York Street,
Marylebone,
London, W1U 6PZ UK

E: info@vspworkshops.com
T: +44 (0) 207 873 2136
www.vspworkshops.com

Photography workshops run throughout the year in Venice, London, Sicily, Namibia, Tuscany, Provence, New York and elsewhere.

TEFL

Cactus TEFL
Clarence House,
30-31 North Street,
Brighton, BN1 1EB UK

T: +44 (0)1273 725200
www.cactustefl.com

Cactus TEFL is an independent advice and admissions service working with over 120 TEFL course providers in 34 different countries.

The Language House
1 Bis, Rue de Verdun,
Montpellier, 34000 France

E: gb@tesolhouse.com
F: +33 467 92 44 78
www.teflanguagehouse.com

TEFL/TESOL programme available. Also courses in French, Arabic, Spanish or Italian. Small classes.

The Year Out Group
Queensfield,
28 King's Road,
Easterton, SN10 4PX UK

E: info@yearoutgroup.org
T: +44 (0) 1380 816696
www.yearoutgroup.org

See main entry under volunteering.

Chapter 8
Sport

8 Sport

Travelling abroad doesn't mean that you have to stop playing the sports that you love - sports coaching projects are also a great way to give something back to a community on a **gap**-year or career break abroad. If you are looking to join a sports volunteer project, there are many different projects and destinations available.

Lots of companies offer you the chance to live, play, train and coach many different sports all over the world. Whether your chosen sport is football, cricket, rugby, netball, tennis, sailing or even polo you can use your skills to enrich the lives of others by becoming a volunteer coach or use your time to improve your own skills for a career in your chosen sport.

And a sporting placement abroad can seriously boost your personal development - showing your commitment, teamwork and leadership skills to prospective employers.

So whether you want to use your football skills to become a coach teaching children in South Africa, join a cricket club for the season in Australia, experience the challenge of playing rugby in New Zealand or learn how to sail and dive in Thailand, there is definitely a placement out there for you.

Becoming an instructor

We spoke to experts Gap Ski & Dive, who train and examine instructors in both industries, for their thoughts on instructor courses and coaching.

"It's important to get organised. There are many options to look at but two popular and well established areas for **gap**-year students to look at are scuba diving and skiing. There are well established routes for training as a professional, and choices of courses tailored to **gap**-years.

"For example BASI ski instructor courses will qualify you to work and teach in the European Alps.

"Gaining qualifications such as these are invaluable to building your skills and CV because not only is it clear by the professional level of teaching and communication skills, but it will also make you stand out from the crowd with unique skills and qualifications (transferable skill example: structuring and delivering a presentation for a class of students).

"And above all you'll be qualified to work doing something you love.

"The next step is to get your **gap**-year organised and you can contact any of the specialist gap year training companies out there, who will take care of all organisation and train you through your national governing body sports coaching qualifications."

Once qualified as a Level 2 ski instructor, your most likely first job would be

visit: www.gap-year.com

teaching at a resort ski school. There is plenty of employment for newly qualified instructors, as long as you arrange your work visa in advance.

With a season's experience you are likely to be more in demand as an employee. Italy, Switzerland, Germany, Croatia, Spain, Andorra, USA and Japan are among the countries with established ski industries in the northern hemisphere.

Your opportunities in France are still limited, though. The French snow sports authorities have traditionally made it difficult for non-French nationals to work in the Alps.

According to Domenic Cowdell, HR manager from Altitude Ski and Snowboard School, the biggest problem for a new instructor looking for a job is the lack of experience – and so any opportunity to gain experience should be grabbed with both hands.

"Initially one of the best ways is to apply to ski schools is for part-time work during the busy holiday weeks of Christmas/New Year, half term and Easter. Do a good job, be helpful, be available whenever asked, professional at all times and it might then lead to more work. There are also several companies such as Interski in Italy who bring school groups out from the UK and often need extra instructors for a couple of weeks.

"Other things that help your CV stand out from everyone else's are: having a qualification and experience teaching in another sport, having a second language that you can teach in and knowing the resort you are applying to. Showing an interest in developing your instructor qualification further by doing some of the modules for the next level, *eg* the common theory for the BASI level 3, can also help."

In the southern hemisphere New Zealand is famous for its mountains, but don't overlook Australia which has several winter resorts too. Some schools in

the gap-year guidebook 2011

Australia and New Zealand employ new instructors from early season hiring clinics: you are expected to attend a short period of in house training and if you measure up you get a job.

The instructor lifestyle is hard work but a lot of fun, although entry-level jobs are not too highly paid. On the plus side, you work on the sea or the slopes and have plenty of time to improve your own skills and enjoy your favourite sport.

Watersports instructor courses are also amongst the most popular for those interested in learning a new sport on their **gap**-year. In addition to diving, you will also find plenty of courses to qualify you to teach windsurfing, yachting and sailing, canoeing, kite surfing, kayaking – any activity on or around water, you can teach!

Flying Fish, who provide courses to earn vocational qualifications and access to a worldwide recruitment service in yachting, watersports and winter sports, told us you can go from being a complete beginner to instructor level in as little as six weeks.

"Not only do you end up with a list of impressive qualifications from professional bodies such as the Royal Yachting Association, PADI and BASI, working as an instructor also gives you some valuable soft skills.

"There is great demand for qualified instructors, with job opportunities all over the world. Imagine spending the winter in Sydney improving your sailing skills to Yachtmaster level, then flying off to the Med to work on boats for the summer. Sounds exciting? It is.

visit: www.gap-year.com

"Working in the action sports industry is an amazing opportunity for you to be paid to teach the sport you love. Teaching windsurfing in Greece, sailing in Croatia, diving in Fiji or snowboarding in New Zealand are all achievable jobs. All you need is recognised qualifications and a 'can-do' attitude.

"You can start as a complete beginner and get qualified as a surf, windsurf or dinghy sailing instructor in just six weeks, and there are fast-track options if you already have some experience."

Getting a job

Once you have earned your qualification, the world is your oyster for potential jobs. We asked Ginger Ayres of Marine Divers, a Hong Kong and Philippines based diving school, for his advice on getting work with your instructor qualification.

"There is a lot of competition out there for jobs. So it's advisable to be as well qualified as possible. Or undertake training where jobs are available and the school may like the cut of your jib and offer positions to successful candidates. Diving centres often prefer those they have invested their time and effort in. Dive centres which are part of a group or network may offer better future career prospects than one-off centres.

"There are a lot of jobs available worldwide, maybe not in the most exotic spots, or where you would prefer, so it's advisable to apply everywhere you can. The first job will give you experience and make you more employable elsewhere.

"Dive centres may also offer diving internships. This will be a varying mix of formal training and work experience (on the job training). This may be a means of offsetting the cost of training with working for the centre for a suitable period - a barter system.

"When not instructing, diving instructors are often expected to perform other duties in the dive centre - managing dive trips, leading dives, supervising staff, looking after clients.

"When applying for any job, not just in diving, expect to be asked for a CV. Your diving CV should match the job you are applying for. When first contacting a dive centre about a job - ask them what they are looking for, so you can match your CV to these needs.

"The reason for the CV is to see what experience you have had, and if you possess not only the skills the employer is looking for, but any other useful skills which may make you more employable than other applicants.

"It's likely you will be applying for a job overseas, where an interview won't be practical, therefore you need a good covering letter - why you want to work for them, in that location; what you expect to get out of the job - sell yourself without repeating what's in your CV.

"An interview is not a one-way grilling - you can ask questions of the employer too. So in your interview, you need to ask about the things that matter to you - terms and conditions of service, accommodation, feeding arrangements, insurance and equipment requirements, days off, daily routine, annual leave, flights home *etc*. And don't forget remuneration - how do you get paid! Are there career opportunities? Is there a job description / specification available?

"You may be expected to provide a recent full-length photo. Presentation in a service industry is most important, so an employer wants to see what you look like if there is no interview.

"To be employed as a dive leader or diving instructor, you should have your own full set of equipment. They are the tools of your trade - you need to take care of them.

"Ask yourself - why do I want to become a diving instructor? If it's for the money, you will probably be disappointed - there aren't many millionaire instructors out there! If it's for a way of life, it is very rewarding and fun. The diving industry beats working in an office. Many instructors work part of the year in a 'normal' job and part of the year enjoying themselves diving."

Harry Brittain – volunteer teaching in Ghana

In some ways Ghana is similar to Narnia, it messes with time. I left England as a child, apparently just six months later, I returned, but not as a child.

The experiences I had in Ghana are not and cannot be paralleled with the UK, I didn't know what I was going to do, who would be there, where I would go, what I should do, I really didn't know much. Only an idea, a very brief outline of my excuse for being there, for me that was both teaching and a local orphanage. But as I walked away from my family at the airport I knew it was massively exciting.

I arrived in Ghana after a six hour sleepless flight, I boarded a coach for a further six hours of sleepless travelling to get to Kumasi, the city I would be living and working in. I had to wait for a couple of days after I arrived before I could begin teaching but finally the day came. It wasn't a brilliant day; I had barely been in the school for thirty minutes before I was thrown in front of thirty kids and asked to begin teaching.

After a week of teaching it was easy for me to forget how afraid I was and the lessons quickly became really enjoyable. I am even pretty confident that the kids were learning. Brilliant!

There was one class I didn't enjoy so much, ICT to thirteen to sixteen year olds (JHS 3). It was difficult to teach with no computers, textbooks or even exercise books, also I don't really know much about ICT. It was therefore very strange when I was appointed head of ICT for a term.

I preferred teaching to working in the orphanage; therefore I only went for a couple of afternoons a week, my problem with the orphanage was that I didn't think I was really making a lasting difference, it was just short term help, filling a gap. Also in a very selfish way I didn't enjoy it as much as the teaching. I didn't like the way that you could spend an entire day there

visit: www.gap-year.com

working really hard, go home and then come back the next day to find nothing's changed. With the teaching it was easy to see progress is being made, allot of progress in most cases.

What I enjoyed most of all however was coaching cricket, even though I'm certainly no expert at the game. A fellow volunteer and I created a women's cricket in the Kumasi area. It was amazing, before we had really noticed what was happening we were coaching part (if not the majority) of the national team. This was fantastic; all of a sudden I was meeting government ministers and all sorts of bosses regarding sponsorship, including Vodafone. I was asked to do and interview for BBC radio Gloucestershire, I featured in a couple of newspapers, I even had contact with a famous film star (who wishes to remain anonymous) regarding equipment donations.

Unfortunately just as I had really got going my time was up, the fastest and the slowest six months of my life.

Coaching sport as a volunteer programme

There are hundreds of sports-based volunteer programmes available, from coaching cricket to underprivileged children in India to coaching football in inner cities in the UK.

Gap-years can be spent doing practically every sport you can think of, from hockey to netball and from basketball to football. There's also a range of countries you can do them in.

As a sports-coaching volunteer, you will have the opportunity to help build communities through sport. For example, in working with a local football

the gap-year guidebook 2011

academy in Ghana, you will be able to establish relationships with young players who often have a fantastic talent and profound love of the game – but have been unable to progress because of a lack of physical training, emotional guidance and financial support. Giving them the opportunity to develop both their skills and their character can be a life-changing experience. Even without formal coaching qualifications, you can offer them constructive advice and new ideas on tactics, skills and their mental approach to training and competition, simply by arriving with enthusiasm, imagination and a general understanding of the game.

Development may not simply be about coaching. It may also involve education to understand how and why their ideas count, perhaps even some time as an English language teacher. On the best placements, you'll find yourself contributing to community development, in sport and beyond.

The attributes you need depend on the activity you go for. If it involves teaching kids, you'll obviously need to have empathy with children, and if it involves a lot of hardcore activity, you'll need to be reasonably fit and resilient.

Even if the sport has nothing to do with your future career path, it will boost your CV. Better still, if in an interview you can make an energetic case for why you did it, it will make you stand out above others who have sat around on their bums in the summer. It can only impress a future employer.

In the developing world, sport is often more than just competition or idle pastime. Often sport can have a real impact at the heart of communities, and play a pivotal role in the health and prosperity of the people.

Playing sport

More and more people are looking to take a sports gap year with a purpose, so they are using their time out to play a season of sport abroad: for example cricket in Australia, or rugby in New Zealand or South Africa.

Placements on these 'academy programmes' will usually mean you are matched with a club abroad at a suitable level for your standard, for whom you play at the weekends whilst perfecting your game throughout the week with coaching, fitness training and sports psychology from local coaches.

Kayleigh Higson played a season of netball in Sydney, arranged through Sport Lived. "Playing netball in Sydney is an experience not to be missed. The standard of the coaching and training was second to none. I was made to feel like part of the team from day one and thoroughly enjoyed my five months playing for my club."

You may be set a specific training regime to stick to, which might include things like:

- Gym fitness work and flexibility training
- Sport-specific fitness training
- One-on-one sessions to develop specific skills
- Video analysis

visit: www.gap-year.com

- Group training sessions with other academy players
- Club practice sessions
- Sessions with players of a higher standard, perhaps even professionals

Of course, you don't have to be looking at improving your skills to a semi-professional standard. You can also use your **gap**-year to take up a completely new sport. Perhaps you are interested in learning jiu-jitsu in Brazil, or polo in Argentina – you can certainly find placements to cover most sports in a huge range of countries.

Sport Abroad

Air

Fly Gap
Chalet Anguillita,
Chemin de la Côte,
Le Chable, 1934 Switzerland

E: stu@flygap.com
T: +41 (0) 79 313 5677
F: +41 (0) 27 776 1134
www.flygap.com

Paragliding school whose flying courses are specifically designed for British gap-year students.

Great Lake Skydive Centre
Taupo Airport,
Taupo, New Zealand

E: skydive@freefall.net.nz
F: +64 7 377 4851
www.freefall.net.nz

Freefall skydiving over Lake Taupo.

Mokai Gravity Canyon
P.O. Box 84,
Taihape, New Zealand

E: info@gravitycanyon.co.nz
F: +64 6 388 9106
www.gravitycanyon.co.nz

Mokai Gravity Canyon boasts three world-class adventure activities: our extreme flying fox; our mighty 80-metre bungy; or feel the thrill of a 50-metre freefall on our bridge swing.

New Zealand Skydiving School
PO Box 21,
Methven, 7345 New Zealand

E: info@skydivingnz.com
F: +64 (03) 302 9140
www.skydivingnz.com

Jump start your career with a diploma in commercial skydiving. This comprehensive course includes 200 skydives. Graduates have proven to be highly employable in skydiving with employment rates exceeding 95%.

Nimbus Paragliding
25b Lower Sumnervale Drive,
PO Box 17712,
Sumner, New Zealand

E: nimbus.pg@xtra.co.nz
T: 64 03 326 7373
www.nimbusparagliding.co.nz

Paragliding courses, tandem paragliding flights and paragliding equipment sales in Christchurch, New Zealand. For those of you who wish to jump, no training is necessary and there are almost no age or size limits for tandem paragliding.

Nzone
PO Box 554,
35 Shotover Street,
Queenstown, New Zealand

E: skydive@nzone.biz
T: +64 3 442 5867
www.nzone.biz

Experience the ultimate adrenaline rush of tandem parachuting while on vacation in New Zealand. Or train to be a Sport Skydiver yourself with an Accelerated Freefall Course, no prior training needed.

Paul's Xtreme Skydiving
51 Sheridan St,
Cairns, Australia

F: +61 (0) 7 4051 2626
www.australiaskydive.com.au

Challenge yourself to the thrill of a lifetime with an Xtreme Skydive with Paul's, the original North Queensland crew.

Skydive Arizona
4900 N Taylor Rd.,
Eloy, 85231 USA

E: jump@skydiveaz.com
skydiveaz.com

Located halfway between Phoenix and Tucson is the largest skydiving resort in the world! The clear desert weather allows over 340 flying days a year.

Skydive Cairns
82 Grafton Street,
Cairns, 4870 Australia

E: reservations@skydivecairns.com.au
www.skydivecairns.com.au

Based in Cairns, North Queensland, this company specializes in tandem skydiving for both the novice and the professional skydiver.

Skydive Las Vegas
1401 Airport Road,
Boulder City, NV 89005 USA

E: jump@skydivelasvegas.com
www.skydivelasvegas.com

Skydive over the quiet and peaceful views of Hoover Dam, Lake Mead, the Colorado River, the Las Vegas Strip and the entire Las Vegas Valley. Tandem skydiving is the easiest, fastest, cheapest and safest way to make your first skydive.

Skydive Switzerland GmbH
PO Box 412,
Interlaken, 3800 Switzerland

E: info@skydiveswitzerland.com
F: +41 (0) 33 821 6414
www.skydiveswitzerland.com

Learn how to skydive in Switzerland. Tandem jumps, fun and glacier jumps also available.

Skydive Taupo
Lot 26, Anzac Memorial Drive,
PO Box 1525,
Taupo, New Zealand

E: info@skydivetaupo.co.nz
T: +64 7 377 8300
www.skydivetaupo.co.nz

Skydiving over the central plateau of New Zealand and Lake Taupo could be one of the most breathtaking experiences you'll ever have!

Taupo Bungy
PO Box 919,
Taupo, New Zealand

E: jump@taupobungy.co.nz
www.taupobungy.co.nz

Located in the Waikato River Valley, Taupo Bungy is considered one of the world's most spectacular bungy sites. Featuring the world's first cantilever platform and New Zealand's first 'splash cam'.

Earth

Action Professionals Ltd
9 Edwy Parade,
Kingsholm,
Gloucester, GL1 2QH UK

E: info@actionprofessionals.co.uk
T: +44 (0) 1452 312 724
www.actionprofessionals.co.uk

Get an internationally recognised qualification in Argentina or South Africa. The 12-week course in personal fitness training will give you the opportunity to enjoy a fully-inclusive gap-year experience.

Adventure Bound
2392 H Road,
Grand Junction, CO 81505 USA

E: info@adventureboundusa.com
F: +1 970 241 5633
www.adventureboundusa.com

Whitewater rafting in Colorado and Utah. Also kayaking on the Colorado and Green Rivers.

Bucks and Spurs
HC 71 Box 163,
Ava, USA

E: csonny@getgoin.net
www.bucksandspurs.com

Horseback riding vacations in Missouri. Round up cattle, see a horse whisperer use his natural horsemanship, and enjoy the ride at this Missouri Dude Ranch.

Cape Trib Horse Rides
MS 2041,
Cape Tribulation, Australia

www.capetribbeach.com.au

Experience where the rainforest meets the reef whilst on horseback! Ride through the rainforest and canter up the beach. We cater for beginners, intermediate and experienced rides.

Dvorak Expeditions
17921 US Highway 285,
Nathrop, CO 81236 USA

E: info@dvorakexpeditions.com
F: +1 719 539 3378
www.dvorakexpeditions.com

White water rafting, kayaking and fly fishing trips offered in Colorado, Utah, New Mexico, Idaho and Texas.

Gravity Assisted Mountain Biking
Av 16 de Julio #1490, Edificio Avenida,
Planta Baja, Oficina #10,
La Paz, Bolivia

E: info@gravitybolivia.com
T: +591 2 231 3849
F: +591 2 231 0023
www.gravitybolivia.com

Downhill mountain biking in Bolivia, also cross-country.

Hike Japan
Hike Japan Ltd., Registered office,
89 Fleet Street,
London, EC4Y 1DH UK

E: info@hikejapan.com
T: (+44) (0)207 353 2363
www.hikejapan.com

This company offers guided walking holidays and tailor-made tours for individuals and small groups, from the island of Yakushima south of Kyushu, to the Kii and Hida mountain ranges in Central Japan, and the island of Hokkaido.

Jagged Globe
The Foundry Studios,
45 Mowbray Street,
Sheffield, S3 8EN UK

T: +44 (0) 845 345 8848
F: +44 (0) 114 2755 740
www.jagged-globe.co.uk

Jagged Globe provides mountaineering expeditions and treks. They also offer courses which are based in Wales, Scotland and the Alps for both the beginner and those wishing to improve their skills.

Megalong Australian Heritage Centre
Megalong Road,
Megalong Valley,
Blue Mountains, Australia

E: admin@megalongcc.com
T: +61 (02) 4787 8188
F: +61 (02) 4787 9116
www.megalongcc.com.au

Horse riding in the Blue Mountains of New South Wales. Jackaroo and Jillaroo courses available. Also courses in how to work with horses.

Mountaineering Council of Ireland
Sport HQ, 13 Joyce Way,
Park West Business Park,
Dublin, 12 Ireland

E: info@mountaineering.ie
T: +353 1 625 1115
F: +353 1 625 1116
www.mountaineering.ie

They have lists of mountaineering clubs in Ireland, useful information and can give advice on insurance.

PoloSkool Ltd
Sportskool,
37-39 Southgate Street,
Winchester, SO23 9EH UK

E: team@poloskool.co.uk
T: +44 (0) 1962 855 138
www.poloskool.co.uk

PoloSkool offers intensive polo tuition programmes in Argentina. Fully residential courses of two, four and ten weeks are available for players of all abilities.

Qufu Shaolin Kung Fu School China
Jubao Shanzhuang,
Bei Wai Huan Rd,
Qufu, 273100 PR China

E: shaolinskungfu@gmail.com
T: 0086 537 491 1022
F: 0086 537 491 1021
www.shaolinskungfu.com

Shaolin Temple in Shandong, China, where you can learn Kung Fu and Mandarin Chinese.

Rock'n Ropes
Karetoto Road,
Wairakei, 3330 New Zealand

E: info@rocknropes.co.nz
www.rocknropes.co.nz

A Rock'n Ropes course is 'as exciting as skydiving or bungee jumping'. Check out their website for full details.

Rua Reidh Lighthouse
Melvaig,
Gairloch, IV21 2EA UK

E: ruareidh@tiscali.co.uk
www.ruareidh.co.uk

Courses in basic rock climbing available - one or two days also one to one teaching. Their one day course has a class limit of four people.

Shoestring Polo Ltd
2 Street Cottages, Wheatsheaf Lane,
Oaksey,
Malmesbury, SN16 9SZ UK

E: info@shoestringpolo.com
T: +44 (0) 7780 822 452
www.shoestringpolo.com

Playing polo in Argentina, the home of polo, is a fantastic opportunity for individuals regardless of previous experience.

Sporting Opportunities
The Clock House,
Station Approach,
Marlow, Buckinghamshire SL7 1NT UK

E: info@sportingopportunities.com
T: +44 (0)208 123 8702
www.sportingopportunities.com

Sporting Opportunities takes sporty people to Africa, Asia and South America to coach sport, play sport and volunteer in sports. Perfect for sports gap years, career breaks and volunteer sports travel.

Altitude Futures - Gap Course Verbier, Case Postale 55, Verbier 1936
T: +41 (0) 79 5305 224
E: info@altitude-futures.com   W: www.altitude-futures.com

Altitude Futures Ski and Snowboard Instructor Courses
Altitude Futures run official BASI and CSIA ski and snowboard instructor courses in Verbier, Whistler and Tignes.
Our winter and summer gap instructor training courses offer an intensive nine or ten weeks of training geared towards developing your personal skiing or snowboarding skills and also training you to become a fully qualified ski or snowboard instructor.
When you book a course with Altitude you benefit from an experienced and established training program run by instructors for instructors.
The Altitude Futures Gap Year Programme is famous for:
· 100% satisfied gap students
· Highest pass rates in the Alps
· Up to 40% off skis, boots and boards
· High quality accommodation
· Over 200 hours of on snow coaching
· Video debriefs and lectures
· Work experience with local ski schools
· Gain your BASI/CSIA level 1 and 2 licence

Altitude Futures Coaching Team
Altitude Ski and Snowboard School employs top qualified coaches and trainers from Britain, Switzerland, Canada and Sweden. This depth on knowledge and experience makes Altitude the premier provider of instructor training in the Alps.
'The Altitude Futures gap students are the most successful and strongest group I have ever been within 16 years of being a BASI trainer.'
Andy Lockerbie - BASI Trainer & previous CEO of BASI

visit: www.gap-year.com

White Peak Expeditions
Agents for Atlantic & Pacific Travel,
49 Conduit Street, Mayfair,
London, W1B UK

E: mail@whitepeakexpeditions.co.uk
T: +44 (0)1909 564466
www.whitepeakexpeditions.co.uk

Specialists in trekking and climbing for small groups in Nepal, Tibet, Kazakhstan/Kyrgyzstan, Ecuador and Peru. Climbs are suitable for the less experienced climber and are generally combined with trekking expeditions.

Snow

Alltracks Limited
The Lawns,
Longstock Road,
Goodworth Clatford, SP11 7RE UK

E: info@alltracksacademy.com
T: +44 (0) 1794 388034
www.alltracksacademy.com

This company runs high performance ski and snowboard instructor courses at Whistler, Revelstoke and Banff in Canada. Ideal for a constructive and fun gap-year.

Altitude Futures - Gap Course Verbier
Case Postale 55,
Verbier, 1936 Switzerland

E: info@altitude-futures.com
www.altitude-futures.com

Altitude Futures run official BASI and CSIA ski and snowboard instructor courses in Verbier, Whistler and Tignes.
See www.altitude-futures.com for more details.

BASI
(British Association of Snowsport Instructors)
British Association Of Snowsports Instructors,
Morlich House,
17 The Square,
Grantown-on-Spey, PH26 3HG UK

E: basi@basi.org.uk
T: +44 (0)1479 861 717
F: +44 (0)1479 873 657
www.basi.org.uk

The UK authority for training, examining and grading snowsport instructors and its qualifications are recognised worldwide.

Cardrona Alpine Resort
PO Box 117,
18 Dunmore Street,
Wanaka, 9343 New Zealand

E: info@cardrona.com
T: +64 3 443 7341
F: +64 3 443 8818
www.cardrona.com

Ski resort in New Zealand with ski school attached.

Deutsch-Institut Tirol
A-6370 Kitzbuehel,
Am Sandhügel 2, Austria

E: office@deutschinstitut.com
F: +43 53 56 72363
www.deutschinstitut.com

Our gap-year course, set in the famous Austrian ski resort of Kitzbuehel, provides intensive German lessons followed by skiing or snowboarding tuition, sufficient to

the gap-year guidebook 2011

Deutsch-Institut Tirol

Deutsch-Institut Tirol, A-6370 Kitzbuehel, Am Sandhügel 2
T: +43 53 56 71274
E: office@deutschinstitut.com   W: www.deutschinstitut.com

Founded in 1981, the Deutsch-Institut is celebrating its 30th birthday in 2011. We've been teaching German for over a quarter of a century from the beautiful alpine ski resort of Kitzbühel. The combination of German and skiing is so successful, we've survived in a difficult market when bigger schools have closed.

In 2002 we launched our first ever gap-year course and have continued to refine it ever since. We were the one of the first schools to offer a gap-year course which enabled students to qualify as ski instructors at the beginning of the ski season instead of at the end. Every year we get a motivated and energetic group of students who are determined to get the best out of the 12-week course. They graduate with excellent language skills and a new qualification as a ski or snowboard instructor. They can then stay on in Kitzbühel or any other ski resort and work the whole season as an instructor. This is not your average gap-year!

The course is full and demanding; you learn German in the mornings from Monday to Thursday in Kitzbühel then travel to Kaprun to ski for three days on the glacier. You also get a great break in the middle of the course with a week's tour of Eastern Europe, visiting Vienna, Prague and Budapest.

The language element is original, motivating and fun. School was never like this! Everyone needs a language on their CVs these days, and there's no better way to get it than this! The Deutsch-Institut method ensures you get a comprehensive grounding in the basics with heavy emphasis on spoken command of the language.

You get outstanding training in preparation for the Austrian ski instructors' exams from instructors who have passed it themselves and who every year encourage and guide our Gappers towards the exam. Yes, it's rigorous, and yes you have to put a lot into it, but you really come out of it a changed person. Exhilaration, excitement, the energy-charge of the alpine air, the adrenaline rush of conquering the most difficult slopes, if this sounds like the gap-year you're looking for, then contact us without delay.

visit: www.gap-year.com

enable you to take the Austrian ski or snowboard instructors' exam, leaving you free to work as a ski/snowboard instructor for the whole winter season.

Harris Mountains Heli-Ski
The Station, Cnr Shotover and Camp Sts,
PO Box 634,
Queenstown, 9348 New Zealand
E: hmh@heliski.co.nz
T: +64 3 442 6722
F: +64 3 441 2983
www.heliski.co.nz

If you are a strong intermediate skier or ski-boarder, then try this for that extra thrill!

ICE Snowsports Ltd
3 - 4 Bath Place,
Aberdovey, LL35 0LN UK
E: info@icesi.org
www.icesi.org

Ski instructor courses from eight to ten weeks in Argentina or Val d'Isere.

Non-Stop Ski
3B, Plough Brewery,
516 Wandsworth Road,
London, SW8 3JX UK
E: info@nonstopski.com
T: +44 (0)207 720 6500
www.nonstopski.com

Offering a variety of ski instructor courses in Fernie, Banff, Whistler, Red Mountain and New Zealand. An ideal gap-year, career break or chance to fast track into the ski industry.

OnTheMountain
Pro Snowsports Instructor Training
in Switzerland
Neige Aventure Ski & Snowboard School,
CH-1997 Haute-Nendaz, Switzerland
F: +41 (0)27 288 3133
www.onthemountainpro.co.uk

Provides exceptional training and loads of fun, after training stay and enjoy the slopes until the end of the season at no extra cost.

Outdoor Interlaken AG
Haupstrasse 15,
PO Box 451,
Interlaken-Matten, CH 3800 Switzerland
E: mail@outdoor-interlaken.ch
T: +41 (0) 33 826 77 19
F: +41 (0) 33 826 77 18
www.outdoor-interlaken.ch

Ski/Snowboard school for complete beginners and for those who wish to brush up their skills. Have local guides who know the best trails, snow and shortest lift lines.

Ski le Gap
220 Chemin Wheeler,
Mont-Tremblant PQ, J8E 1V3 Canada
E: info@skilegap.com
F: +1 819 425 7074
www.skilegap.com

Offers ski and snowboard instructor training courses based in the popular Canadian resort of Tremblant.

Ski-Exp-Air
913 rue Senneterre,
Québec PQ, G1X 3Y2 Canada

E: info@ski-exp-air.com
www.ski-exp-air.com

Ski-exp-air is a Canadian ski and snowboard school offering quality, professional instruction in a fun atmosphere.

SnowSkool
SportSkool,
37-39 Southgate Street,
Winchester, SO23 9EH UK

E: team@snowskool.co.uk
T: +44 (0) 1962 855 138
F: +44 (0) 1962 855 138
www.snowskool.co.uk

Ski and Snowboard instructor courses in Canada and New Zealand. SnowSkool offers four, five, nine and eleven week programmes earning internationally recognised qualifications.

Snowsport Consultancy
Aandammergouw 13,
1153 PA Zuiderwoude, Netherlands

E: info@snowsportconsultancy.com

www.snowsportconsultancy.com/english/index.html

Skiing lessons leading to ski instructor exams. Lessons are taught in German and so you will need a good working knowledge of the language.

Whistler Summer Snowboard Camps
106-4368 Main Street,
Suite 981,
Whistler BC, V0N 1B4 Canada

E: info@whistlersnowboardcamps.com
T: +1 604 932 3238
F: +1 604 932 0565
www.whistlersnowboardcamps.com

Summer camp for snowboarders who want to improve their skills.

Sport Instructors

Britannia Sailing East Coast
Victory House,
Shotley Marina,
Ipswich, IP9 1QJ UK

E: enquiry@britanniasailingschool.co.uk
T: +44 (0) 1473 787019
F: +44 (0) 1473 787018
www.britanniasailingschool.co.uk

Based at Shotley Marina near Ipswich, Britannia Sailing is a well-established company with first-class facilities offering all aspects of sailing instruction and yacht charter.

Crewseekers Limited
Hawthorn House, Hawthorn Lane,
Sarisbury Green,
Southampton, SO31 7BD UK

E: info@crewseekers.co.uk
T: +44 (0) 1489 578319
F: +44 (0) 1489 578319
www.crewseekers.net

Work available as yachting crew cruising, racing, yacht delivering around the world. Beginners welcome.

Flying Fish UK Ltd
25 Union Road,
Cowes, PO31 7TW UK

E: mail@flyingfishonline.com
www.flyingfishonline.com

Flying Fish trains and recruits over 1000 people each year to work worldwide as yacht skippers and as sailing, diving, surfing, windsurfing, ski and snowboard instructors.

Goal-Line Soccer Clinics
PO Box 1642,
Corvallis, OR 97339 USA

E: info@goal-line.com
F: +1 541 753 0811
www.goal-line.com

Offers paid soccer coaching vacations for qualified applicants. Their programme operates in a number of communities in the Pacific Northwest of the USA.

International Academy
Sophia House,
28 Cathedral Road,
Cardiff, CF11 9LJ UK

E: info@international-academy.com
T: +44 (0) 29 2066 0200
www.international-academy.com

Become a ski or snowboard Instructor on a five to 12 week gap-year or career break course. Experience world class resorts and gain recognised CSIA, CASI, NZSIA or SBINZ instructor qualifications.

PJ Scuba
Mermaids Dive Center S-2694,
PADI 5 Star Career Development Center,
Jomtien Beach Road, 75/124 Moo 12,
Nongprue, 20260 Thailand

E: pjscuba@gmail.com
T: +66 (0) 382 322 19
F: +66 (0) 382 322 21
www.pjscuba.com

Offers the chance to study scuba diving to instructor level (PADI) and then teach in Thailand, Vietnam or Cambodia.

Play Soccer
24 St Martins Drive,
Unit 10,
Marlborough, MA 01752 USA

T: +1 508 460 6570
F: +1 508 460 6580
www.playsoccer.com

Play Soccer is New England's leader in soccer education, currently working with over 30,000 children each year.

Ski Academy Switzerland
6 Lane Side,
Kirkburton,
Huddersfield, HD8 0TN UK

E: info@skiacademyswitzerland.com
T: +44 (0) 141 416 0146
www.skiacademyswitzerland.com

Provider of quality ski instructor programmes with work opportunities for gap-year students and for those on a career break or just fancy a challenge!

The Instructor Training Co
PO Box 791,
Queenstown, 9348 New Zealand

E: info@skiinstructortraining.co.nz
F: +64 (0) 3 442 5460
www.skiinstructortraining.co.nz

The Instructor Training Co offers you the opportunity to train for your ski instructor qualification in New Zealand. Six, eight and eleven week courses available.

The Year Out Group
Queensfield,
28 King's Road,
Easterton, SN10 4PX UK

E: info@yearoutgroup.org
T: +44 (0) 1380 816696
www.yearoutgroup.org

See main entry under volunteering.

Xtreme-gap.com
9 Victoria Terrace,
Manchester, M13 0HY UK

E: info@xtreme-gap.com
www.xtreme-gap.com

Gap company offering extreme sporting adventures.

Various

Adventure Ireland
Donegal Adventure Centre & Sports Training College,
Bayview Avenue,
Bundoran, Ireland

E: info@adventure-ireland.com
T: +353 7198 424 18
F: +353 7198 424 29
www.adventure-ireland.com

Live and work in Ireland. Learn to surf, climb, kayak. Classes on Irish culture, history, language and literature.

Avon Ski & Action Centre
Lyncombe Drive,
Churchill, BS25 5PQ UK

E: mail@avonski.co.uk
www.highaction.co.uk

Centre is on the edge of the Mendip hills, where you can ski, snowboard, mountain board, as well as pursue archery, rifle shooting, power kiting, 4x4 driving, quad biking, rock climbing, abseiling and many more exciting outdoor pursuits.

Base Camp Group
Unit 30, Baseline Business Studios,
Whitchurch Road, Notting Hill,
London, W11 4AT UK

E: contact@basecampgroup.com
T: +44 (0) 20 7243 6222
www.basecampgroup.com

Become a ski or snowboard instructor, take your surfing to the next level, or gain worldwide scubadiving certifications. Whether on a gap year or a career break, Base Camp Group offer a range of courses around the world.

Bear Creek Outdoor Centre
45 Barnet Boulevard,
Renfrew ON, K7V 2M5 Canada

E: info@bearcreekoutdoor.com
www.bearcreekoutdoor.com

Offers courses in canoeing skills also swiftwater and rescue courses and wilderness first aid.

Camp Challenge Pte Ltd
1 Gunner Lane,
Sentosa,
Singapore, 099562 Singapore

E: enquiries@camp-challenge.com
T: +65 6278 9823
F: +65 6278 9693
www.camp-challenge.com

At CAMP-CHALLENGE, we believe that every youth is a CELL of this global community. We provide the platform for this growth through our programmes.

Canyon Voyages Adventure Co
211 North Main,
Moab, UT 84532 USA

E: info@canyonvoyages.com
www.canyonvoyages.com

River rafting, kayaking, canoeing, hiking, horseback, mountain bike and 4x4 trips available in the canyons of Utah.

Class VI River Runners
PO Box 88,
Lansing, USA

E: info@rafttoday.com
www.class-vi.com

Organised sporting trips for students and also family and corporate groups.

Peak Leaders
Mansfield,
Strathmiglo, KY14 7QE UK

E: info@peakleaders.com
F: +44 (0) 1338 868 176
www.peakleaders.com

Make the most of your once in a lifetime experience in some of the world's leading resorts whilst gaining internationally recognised instructor qualifications, plus plenty of CV enhancing extras.

Plas Menai
The National Watersports Centre,
Caernarfon, LL55 1UE UK

E: info@plasmenai.co.uk
F: +44 (0) 1248 673939
www.plasmenai.co.uk

Plas Menai offers a range of courses training people to work as watersports, yachting and adventure instructors abroad and in the UK.

Raging Thunder
PO Box 1109,
Cairns, QLD 4870 Australia

E: res@ragingthunder.com.au
F: +61 (0) 7 4030 7911
www.ragingthunder.com.au

Selection of day tours, once in a lifetime experiences available, such as Great Barrier Reef excursions, sea kayaking, ballooning and white water rafting.

the gap-year guidebook 2011

Rapid Sensations Rafting
PO Box 1725,
Taupo, New Zealand

E: info@rapids.co.nz
F: +64 7 378 7904
www.rapids.co.nz/whitewaterrafting.htm

White water rafting, kayaking and mountain biking on offer. They also have a kayaking school.

River Deep Mountain High
Clocktower Buildings,
Low Wood,
Haverthwaite, LA12 8LY UK

T: +44 (0) 15395 31116
www.riverdeepmountainhigh.co.uk

Outdoor activities and activity Holidays in the Lake District. Where you can try canoeing, kayaking, gorge walks, abseiling, climbing, sailing, walking, trail-cycling or mountain biking.

River Rats Rafting
PO Box 7208,
Te Ngae,
Rotorua, 3402 New Zealand

E: rafting@riverrats.co.nz
T: +64 7 345 6543
F: +64 7 345 6321
www.riverrats.co.nz

River Rats are located in Rototua, New Zealand and are specialists in rafting. They also offer a gondola ride up Mount Ngongotaha and Formula 1500 Sprint Car racing.

Rogue Wilderness Adventures
PO Box 1110,
325 Galice Road,
Merlin, OR 97532 USA

E: webmaster@wildrogue.com
T: +1 (800) 336-1647
F: +1 (541) 476-8051
www.wildrogue.com

Hiking, fishing and rafting trips are designed to give you a thrilling, relaxing and fun experience. Based in Rogue River Canyon.

Sport Lived Ltd
40 Broadgate ,
Beeston,
Nottingham, NG9 2FW UK

E: info@sportlived.co.uk
T: +44 (0) 870 950 3837
www.sportlived.co.uk

Sporting gap-year company which arranges for young people to play sport overseas.

Surfaris
353 Loftus Road,
Crescent Head, NSW 2440 Australia

E: surf@surfaris.com
F: +61 266 00 96
www.surfaris.com

Company offering camping in remote areas and surfing off Byron Bay in New South Wales.

The Year Out Group
Queensfield,
28 King's Road,
Easterton, SN10 4PX UK

E: info@yearoutgroup.org
T: +44 (0) 1380 816696
www.yearoutgroup.org

See main entry under volunteering.

Torquay Wind & Surf Centre
Shop and Booking Office, 55 Victoria Rd,
Ellacombe,
Torquay, UK

E: info@kitesurfingtorquay.co.uk
T: +44 (0)1803 212411
www.kitesurfingtorquay.co.uk

Courses available in kitesurfing, kitebuggying, powerkiting and stand up paddle surfing.

Wilderness Aware Rafting
PO Box 1550 WS,
Buena Vista, CO 81211 USA

E: rapids@inaraft.com
F: +1 719 395 6716
www.inaraft.com

Extreme tours, also downhill mountain biking, horseback riding, 4X4 tours and lost mine tours in Arkansas and Colorado.

Wilderness Escapes
PO Box 271,
Taupo, 2730 New Zealand

E: info@wildernessescapes.co.nz
F: +64 7 378 3493
www.wildernessescapes.co.nz

Kayaking, guided walks, abseiling, rock climbing and caving in Taupo.

Water

All Outdoors California Whitewater Rafting
1250 Pine Street,
Suite 103,
Walnut Creek, CA 94596 USA

E: rivers@aorafting.com
T: +1 925 932 8993
F: +1 925 932 3436
www.aorafting.com

California River Rafting trips for the beginner, intermediate and experienced rafter.

Allaboard Sailing Academy
7 The Square,
Marina Bay, Spain

E: info@sailing.gi
www.asa.gi

Tailor-made sailing courses available in Gibraltar.

Alpin Raft
Hauptstrasse 7,
Interlaken, CH-3800 Switzerland

E: info@alpinraft.com
F: +41 (0) 33 823 41 01
www.alpinraft.com

Located in Interlaken in the Swiss Alps, Alpin Raft offers fantastic fun and adventures - join us for some thrilling and scenic rafting, canyoning or bungy-jumping!

the gap-year guidebook 2011

CDC CAIRNS DIVE CENTRE

Cairns Dive Centre, 121 Abbott Street, Cairns 4870
T: +61 7 40 510 294
E: info@cairnsdive.com.au
W: www.cairnsdive.com.au

Cairns Dive Centre is one of the largest certifying agencies in the world and one of Australia's leading dive and snorkel tours showcasing the Great Barrier Reef. We have been operating in Cairns for over 25 years, maintaining outstanding customer service. Cairns Dive Centre offers day cruises and live aboard trips for the snorkeller and diver, as well as great value learn-to-dive courses through all levels from Open Water to Instructors.

Learn-to-dive courses commence daily in our training facility, which includes air-conditioned classroom and heated, four-metre deep pool. Study materials and exams are available in various foreign languages.

Day cruises operate daily onboard the M.V. Sun-Kist. She carries a maximum of 25 passengers for our day trip and visits two different snorkel/dive sites. All snorkel/dive equipment is included, as well as buffet lunch, tea/coffee. Introductory Scuba dives are available on request.

Live aboard trip transfers to the M.V. Kangaroo Explorer commence daily. She is a modern, 25-metre catamaran, each of our 16 cabins (twin, double and four-berth) is fully air-conditioned, carpeted, has its own en-suite facilities and window. Our twin and double rooms do not cost any extra. They are booked on a first come first serve basis.

Our chef freshly prepares food, with most dietary requirements catered for.

Our dive sites have been selected for their diversity and abundance of Marine Life, with their magnificent array of coral formation, giant clams, walls, drop offs, swim throughs and brilliantly coloured fish. Our great number of dive locations allows us to pick the right dive spot for any particular day, making it as enjoyable as possible for our passengers.

visit: www.gap-year.com

AO Nang Divers
208/2-3 Moo 2,
Ao Nang, 81000 Thailand

E: aonang@aonang-divers.com
F: +66 (0) 75 637 246
www.aonang-divers.com

Learning to dive in Thailand at the Ao Nang diving school.

Appalachian Wildwaters
PO Box 100,
Rowlesburg, WV 26425 USA

E: aw@awrafts.com
F: +1 304 454 2472
www.awrafts.com

White water rafting on the New River and Gauley River in West Virginia.

Aquatic Explorers
40 The Kingsway,
Cronulla Beach 2230,
Sydney, Australia

E: info@aquaticexplorers.com.au
T: +61 2 9523 1518
F: +61 2 9523 1030
www.aquaticexplorers.com.au

Aquatic Explorers is an SSI (Scuba Schools International) Platinum Facility offering new divers, as well as local and international scuba divers the best scuba diving training in Australia.

Barque Picton Castle
PO Box 1076,
132 Montague Street,
Lunenburg NS, B0J 2C0 Canada

E: info@picton-castle.com
T: +1 (902) 634 9984
F: +1 (902) 634 9985
www.picton-castle.com

Explore Europe, Africa and the Caribbean as crew on a square rigger. No experience needed. Join Barque Picton Castle. Come aboard, come alive!

Bermuda Sub Aqua Club
PO Box HM 3155,
Hamilton, HM NX Bermuda

E: timothy.r.molineux@marsh.com

http://sites.google.com/a/bsac.bm/bermuda-sub-aqua-club/

The Bermuda Sub Aqua Club is a branch of the British Sub Aqua Club and offers members a varied programme of club-organised dives; a safe, structured, proven training programme.

Catalina Ocean Rafting
PO Box 2075,
Avalon, CA 90704-2075 USA

E: oceanraft@gmail.com
www.catalinaoceanrafting.com

Half day and full day excursions around Catalina. Snorkelling trips also available.

Cave Diving Florida
PO Box 519,
High Springs, FL 32655 USA

E: richard@superiordivetraining.com
www.superiordivetraining.com

Full training offered in diving including cave diving. Guided dives available, for those who are already cavern or cave certified. Website also offers details of several other Florida caves.

the gap-year guidebook 2011

flying fish

Flying Fish UK Ltd, 25 Union Road, Cowes PO31 7TW
T: +44 (0) 871 250 2500
E: mail@flyingfishonline.com   W: www.flyingfishonline.com

A gap-year with Flying Fish is a unique opportunity for you to learn new skills, meet new people and travel the world.

We train and recruit over 1000 people each year to work as yacht skippers and as sailing, diving, surfing and windsurfing instructors, ski and snowboard instructors. Watersports courses are run in the UK, Australia and Greece while snow sports instructor training takes place in Canada at Whistler.

A great way of combining education with travel and adventure, the Flying Fish "Three Year Plan" enables you to train, work and travel in your gap-year and to pick up interesting jobs throughout your degree during those long summer vacations. Teaching skiing in Canada, sailing in Sydney or windsurfing in Greece are all regular jobs for our gappers once qualified.

If you intend to start working, we offer free membership to our worldwide job placement service. Of course not everyone wants to work during their gap-year. If you intend to travel, you will find a new bunch of friends on the course with similar plans.

Courses range from one to 18 weeks and are available for complete beginners and for those who already have some experience. Our programmes in Australia and the UK run throughout the year, with training in Greece from May to September and in Canada from November to April. Our courses lead to professional qualifications and with over 17 years experience in the business and a great team of highly qualified instructors, you will be in very good hands. So join us in some of the best training locations in the world.

visit: www.gap-year.com

Challenge Rafting
Queenstown Information Centre,
PO Box 634,
Queenstown, New Zealand

E: challenge@raft.co.nz
T: +64 3 442 7318
F: +64 3 441 2983
www.raft.co.nz

Challenge Rafting offers exciting half-day whitewater rafting trips on the Shotover and Kawarau Rivers.

Dart River Safaris
27 Shotover Street,
PO Box 76,
Queenstown, New Zealand

E: info@dartriverjetsafaris.co.nz
T: +64 3 442 9992
www.dartriver.co.nz

Jet boat up the Dart River and kayak back or take the bus back. In between explore the ancient forest. The Dart River Valley featured in the Lord of the Rings films.

Deep Sea Divers Den
319 Draper Street,
Cairns, 4870 Australia

E: info@diversden.com.au
F: +61-7-4031 1210
www.diversden.com.au

Your guide to the finest Great Barrier Reef scuba diving and snorkelling off Cairns Tropical Queensland, Australia.

Dive Kaikoura
Yarmouth Street,
Kaikoura, 7300 New Zealand

E: divekaikoura @xtra.co.nz
F: +64 3 3196868
www.divekaikoura.co.nz

Professional instructors and small groups make Dive Kaikoura the ideal place to start your diving journey or advance your diving qualification.

Diversity
Local 125, Centro Comercial Puerto Colon,
Playa de las Americas,
Tenerife, Spain

E: info@diver-sity.com
T: +34 9227 171 29
F: +34 9227 171 29
www.divingtenerife.net

A Gold Palm 5 Star resort based in Tenerife who offer the full range of PADI courses, including the PADI Open Water and PADI Dive Master.

Elite Sailing
Chatham Maritime Marina,
Leviathan Way,
Chatham, ME4 4LP UK

E: sue@elitesailing.co.uk
T: 01634 890512
www.elitesailing.co.uk

Sailing school and RYA Training Centre based at Chatham, Kent. Suitable for absolute beginner to professional skippers and crew.

the gap-year guidebook 2011

Have fun during your Career Break!

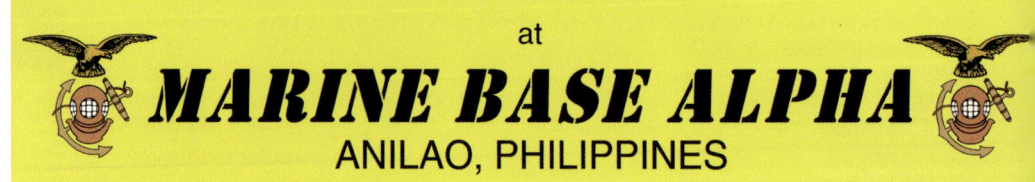

at

MARINE BASE ALPHA
ANILAO, PHILIPPINES

with

MARINE DIVERS

* Spend your time and money wisely, gain qualifications and skills *

* Courses from Beginner to Instructor *

* Boat-handling and Seamanship courses *

* British ex-military Instructors *

* Just training or training followed by short / long term internships *

* Job opportunities with Marine Divers for suitable candidates *

* We train you to fill BSAC Centre's job vacancies *

* Job placement with BSAC Centres all over the world *

Based at a Luxury Resort only 2.5 hrs from Manila:
80 rooms, 4 bars, 3 freshwater & 1 saltwater pools,
International & Local cuisine, 5 private beaches

www.marinedivers.com   info@marinedivers.com

MARINE DIVERS - Training and Diving in Hong Kong and Philippines
MD is a non-smoking, eco-friendly organization - Save The Planet

Gap Year Diver Ltd
Tyte Court,
Farbury End,
Great Rollright, OX7 5RS UK

T: +44 (0) 845 257 3292
F: +44 (0) 1608 730 574
www.gapyeardiver.com

Diver training and a wide range of activities and excursions included which make the entire experience more exciting and enjoyable.

Hawaii Ocean Rafting
PO Box 381,
Lahaina,
Maui, HI 96767 USA

E: info@islandstarexcursions.com
T: +1 808 661 7238
F: +1 808 878 3574
www.hawaiioceanrafting.com

Whale watching, rafting, sailing and speed boating all off the coast of Hawaii. Small groups only.

Island Divers
Chao Koh Service Ltd Part,
157 Moo 7 T. Aonang, Muang,
Phi Phi, Krabi 81000 Thailand

E: info@islanddiverspp.com
T: +66 (0)898732205
F: +66 (0)75601082
www.islanddiverspp.com

Looking for a new adventure? Then join our friendly and highly qualified staff for dive courses and dive trips for all levels, from beginner to professional.

Kiwi River Safaris
PO Box 434,
Taupo, New Zealand

E: rafting@krs.co.nz
F: +64 7 377 6572
www.krs.co.nz

White water rafting, scenic rafting and kayaking trips in Taupo.

Marine Divers Ltd
3E, Block 18, Dynasty View,
11 Ma Wo Road, Tai Po, New Territory,
Hong Kong, SAR, PR China

E: info@marinedivers.com
T: +852 2656 9399
F: +852 2656 9399
www.marinedivers.com

Marine Divers (Hong Kong and Philippines): British Sub-Aqua Club (BSAC) Premier Centres 388, 822 and 833. Training, Diving, Internships, Jobs. info@marinedivers.com. www.marinedivers.com.

Neptune's Dive College
PADI 5 Star Instructor Developement Center,
59 Calle Las Palmas,
Manzanillo, 28860 Mexico

E: training@neptunesdiving.com
T: +52 314 334 3001
www.neptunesdiving.com

Neptune's Dive College offers college or university credit eligible scuba instructor training and internships.

Ocean Rafting
PO Box 106,
Canonvale, Australia

E: oceanrafting@airlie.net.au
www.oceanrafting.com

Ocean rafting around the coast of Queensland and the Whitsunday Islands which includes exploring Whitehaven Beach. They also offer snorkelling trips along pristine reefs and tropical island guided walks.

OzSail
PO Box 582,
Airlie Beach, Australia

E: bookings@ozsail.com.au
T: +61 7 4946 5434
F: +61 7 4948 2096
ozsail.com.au

OzSail presents an extensive range of sailing and diving holidays from which to choose.

Penrith Whitewater Stadium
PO Box 1120,
Penrith Post Business Centre,
Penrith, NSW 2751 Australia

E: bookings@penrithwhitewater.com.au
T: +61 2 4730 4333
F: +61 2 4730 4300
www.penrithwhitewater.com.au

Introduction packages and courses in whitewater rafting offered and whitewater kayaking.

Pocono Whitewater Rafting
1519 State Route 903,
Jim Thorpe, PA 18229 USA

E: info@poconowhitewater.com
F: +1 570 325 4097
www.whitewaterrafting.com

Trail biking, paintball skirmish, kayaking and whitewater rafting available in the LeHigh River Gorge.

River Expeditions
900 Broadway Avenue,
Oak Hill, WV 25901 USA

www.raftinginfo.com

Rafting in West Virginia on the New and Gauley Rivers.

Sabah Divers
G27 Wisma Sabah,
Jln Haji Saman,
Kota Kinab Alu, 88000 Malaysia

E: sabahdivers2u@yahoo.com
T: +6088256483
F: +6088255482
www.sabahdivers.com

Sabah Divers offer both PADI and SSI scuba diving courses in Sabah, Malaysian Bourneo.

Saracen Sailing Mallorca
Apartado 162,
Pollensa, E-07460 Spain

E: office@saracensailing.com
www.saracensailing.com

A RYA approved sea school whioh offers a broad range of practical tidal sailing courses aboard their yachts based in North East Mallorca all year round.

visit: www.gap-year.com

Scuba Junkie
PO Box 458, Block B Lot 36,
Semporna, Semporna Seafront,
Sabah, 91308 Malaysia

E: info@scuba-junkie.com
T: +60 89 785372
F: +60 89 785372
www.scuba-junkie.com

Scuba Junkie is a fully licensed and insured PADI operation offering courses for beginners to advanced in the Celebes Sea.

Straits Sailing
10 The Square,
Marina Bay, Gibraltar

E: info@straits-sail.com
F: +350 51373
www.straits-sail.com

Expert tuition with the full range of RYA courses.

Sunsail
The Port House,
Port Solent,
Portsmouth, PO6 4TH UK

E: yachting@sunsail.com
T: +44 (0) 23 9222 2894
www.sunsail.com

Sunsail offers the full range of RYA yacht courses as well as their own teaching programmes. Their instructors are RYA qualified.

Surfing Queensland
PO Box 233,
Burleigh Heads, Australia

E: info@surfingqueensland.com.au
F: +61 07 557 624 33
www.surfingqueensland.com.au

Surfing Queensland has a surf school system with 16 licensed surf schools operating on beaches from Coolangatta to Yeppoon.

Ticket To Ride
263 Putney Bridge Road,
London, SW15 2PU UK

E: info@ttride.co.uk
www.ttride.co.uk

Ticket to Ride develop all of our worldwide surfing adventures around the combination of doing something for yourself, something for others, travelling the world and having something to show for it all at the end.

Wavehunters UK
Animal Surf Academy, Wavehunters UK Ltd,
6 Fore Street,
Port Isaac, PL29 3RB UK

E: mail@wavehunters.co.uk
T: 0870 242 2856
www.wavehunters.co.uk

Wavehunters UK offer a complete package with selected lodges and surf academies.

the gap-year guidebook 2011

Chapter 9
Working in the UK

9 Working in the UK

Why work on a year out?

If you're not working to raise money for **gap-** travel and you've just finished school or university, you might want a break from study and take a deep breath or two for a while. But even though work doesn't seem too appealing, just try going through the complex claiming procedure for jobseekers' allowance and then living on it for a few weeks, and you'll soon see that working has its advantages.

But there are plenty of much better reasons to use a **gap-** for work:

- Saving money for university

Going to university is an expensive thing to do. Today, the vast majority of graduates are heavily in debt and this burden will be with them for many years to come.

This extract is from an article in the online version of the *Birmingham Post* and illustrates the point: "In 2004 the average graduate came out of university £12,000 worth in debt. The predicted amount of debt for a graduate leaving in 2009 is between £30,000-£40,000. It's an astonishing amount of money to pay back."

So earning just a little bit now could really help your bank balance in the future.

- Showing commitment

If you're attracted to a career in popular professions like media, medicine and law, which are incredibly competitive and hard to get into, it could well prove necessary to grab any experience you can; paid or unpaid. It might make all the difference down the line when you have to prove to a potential employer that you really are committed.

- Work experience

Another consideration is the frequency with which people applying for jobs report being rejected at interview 'because of a lack of work experience'. A **gap-** is a great time to build up an initial experience of work culture as well as getting a foot in the door and getting recognised; in fact many students go back to the same firms after graduation.

- Not sure what you want to do?

If your degree left you with several possible options and you couldn't face the university final year/graduate 'milk round' or you're undecided what career direction you want to head in, then a **gap-** could be a great time to try out different jobs and to get a feel for what you might want to do in the future.

Whatever your reasons for working during a **gap-** you should start looking early to avoid disappointment.

visit: www.gap-year.com

Writing a CV

Fashions change in laying out a CV and in what order you arrange the various sections.

The advice is that a CV should be no more than two A4 pages and also that it should be tailored to the sector you're applying for.

The thing to remember is that employers are busy people, so they won't have time to read many pages, especially if they're trying to create a shortlist of maybe six interviewees from more than 100 applications for just one job.

If you're at the start of your working life, there's a limit to how much tailoring you can do. A good tip is to put a short summary of your skills, and experience to date, at the top so the recruiter knows what you can do. It can either be a bullet point list or a short paragraph, but remember that it's essentially your sales pitch explaining why you're useful to the company. It should only be a short summary of what's contained in the sections that follow.

There are a number of online CV-writing advice sites and templates that can help you, but do check for any fees before you start.

Here's a selection:
www.careersadvice.direct.gov.uk/helpwithyourcareer/writecv/
www.cv-service.org/
www.alec.co.uk/cvtips/
www.soon.org.uk/cvpage.htm

Here's a list of headings for the details your CV should include:

- Personal details: name, address, phone and email. You do not have to include gender, age, date of birth, marital details or nationality nor send a photograph, in fact some employers actively discourage photos for fear of being accused of bias in selecting people for interview.

- Short skills paragraph or key skills bullet points (see above).

- Work experience and skills: in order with most recent first. You can include part time working that you've combined with education, as well as any voluntary work you've done, but if neither is directly within the job sector you're applying for, you need to focus on the transferable skills you got from it *eg*: familiarity with office routines, record keeping, filing, if you've been in an office, or people skills if you worked in a shop.

- Achievements: have you been on any committees? (student council?), organised any events or fundraisers? Again, concentrate on what you learned from it, such as organisational skills, persuading companies to

donate prizes for a raffle, planning catering and refreshments.
- Other skills: such as the Duke of Edinburgh's Award Scheme, workshops you've attended, hobbies *etc*.
- Education: again most recent first, with subjects studied and grades.
- References: you usually need two, one of them a recent employer, the other from school or university, though on a CV you only need to say 'references can be supplied'.

Getting the job

How do you get that first job with no prior experience? What can you possibly offer?

The key is creativity. Show the company you're applying to that you can offer them something that nobody else can and do this by giving them an example. Be creative: If you're applying to an advertising firm, for instance, then mock up some adverts to show them.

Want to go into journalism? Write some specimen articles and send them to local newspapers. Write to the editor and ask whether you could volunteer to help out in the newsroom to get a feel for the environment and the skills you'll need - a kind of extended work experience to add to what you should have had via school.

You could try this with companies in other fields you're interested in. Be proactive and persevering. It will show you have initiative and commitment and whatever your eventual career it will also help you to learn the basics of acting professionally in a professional environment.

Do the research: Whatever your chosen field, find out about the company and show your knowledge about the industry.

If you are going for an industry, such as medicine or law, then showing that you are more than competent and willing is all that you can really do. Saying this, you have to make sure that you stick out from other applicants.

Contacts

In the directory of this guidebook we list some companies that specifically employ **gap**-year students or offer graduate opportunities. But take this as a starting point - the tip of the iceberg - there are hundreds of other companies out there waiting to be impressed by you.

Research is crucial. Tailor your approach towards that specific company and never just expect to get a job; you have to work at it. The general rule is that nobody will call you back - be the one who gets in contact with them.

Job surfing

Most major job agencies, and many smaller ones, now have websites. You don't get the personal touch from a website that you do by going into a local branch and getting advice, or registering face-to-face, but recruitment

visit: www.gap-year.com

websites are really useful if you know what you want to do and you have a 'skills profile' that one of their customers is looking for. Some of them are aimed at graduates and students, others at a general audience, others at specific areas of work (IT, for example).

Here are a few to start with:

Student summer jobs:

www.activate.co.uk

(This one contains **gap**-jobs, summer jobs, internships and jobs for new graduates.)

Graduate careers:

www.milkround.com

www.jobs.guardian.co.uk

General vacancies:

www.reed.co.uk
www.search.co.uk/jobs/
www.monster.com

(Good for jobs in UK, but also Europe and across the world.)

www.fish4jobs.co.uk
www.gumtree.com

the gap-year guidebook 2011

Technology specialists:

www.agencycentral.co.uk/jobsites/IT.htm

(This site has a list of IT specialist recruiters.)

Finance - FT jobs site:

www.ft.com/jobsclassified

On spec

If you can't find what you're looking for by using contacts, advertisements, agencies or the internet there is always DIY job hunting. You can walk into shops and restaurants to ask about casual work or use a phone directory (*eg Yellow Pages*) to phone businesses (art galleries, department stores, zoos...) and ask what is available.

Ring up, ask to speak to the personnel or HR manager and ask if and when they might have jobs available and how you should apply. If they ask you to write in, you can do so after the call. If you go in, make sure you look smart.

Remember, opportunities in the big professional firms are not always well publicised.

Temporary jobs (except agency-filled ones) are often filled by personal contact. If you have a burning desire to work for an architects' or lawyers' firm, for example, and you find nothing advertised, you could try making a list and phoning to ask if work is available.

Think about people you might already know in different work environments and ask around for what's available.

Banking: approach your local branches for work experience. You can also try: www.hays.com/banking/

Education: most educational work experience is tied in with travelling abroad, to places like Africa or Asia, mostly to teach English. However, there are ways of gaining experience back home in England.

A very popular way is to see if the school that you have just left would like classroom helpers, or perhaps they need help in teaching a younger sports team. The key to this is to ask around and see what might be available.

But remember, for any work with children you will have to have a CRB (Criminal Records Bureau) check.

For more information, see: www.crb.gov.uk

As well as straight teaching, any experience with children can be very useful, so try looking at camps and sports teams that may need help - there are a few contacts for camps within the Seasonal Work section.

Legal and medical: it's well known that studying for these two professions is lengthy and rigorous, so any amount of work experience could prove very useful. There's plenty available, but lots of competition for the places so you need to start looking early.

visit: www.gap-year.com

Nearly all NHS hospitals look for volunteer staff. So, if you can't find a worthwhile paid job, just contact the HR Manager at your local hospital.

Try also:
www.jobs.nhs.uk/

(for all NHS jobs)
www.lawgazettejobs.co.uk/content_static/home.asp

(for law jobs, including trainee positions)

Media, publishing and advertising: working on television or the radio is a favourite and it is no surprise that, because of this, the media is one of the hardest industries to break into.

Work experience is highly recommended. Many companies are very willing to try out **gap**-year students as trainees, as raw talent is such a limited commodity they want to nurture it as much as possible - plus it's cheap.

There are many websites dedicated to media jobs, but a good place to look for publishing vacancies is: **www.thebookseller.com**

Theatre: many theatres provide work experience for **gap**-year students, so it's definitely worthwhile contacting your nearby production company. This industry recognises creativity and application probably more than any other, so starting out early and fiercely is the only way to do it.

Try also: **www.thestage.co.uk/recruitment/**

Internships

Graduates cannot rely on the safety net of the traditional internship or graduate job this year: we are facing the highest level of graduate unemployment in over a decade. Applicants for jobs are expected to have more skills, better grades and some form of industry experience as a minimum. In such turbulent times it is essential to make your CV stand out and rise above the competition of the near 400,000 graduates leaving the UK's 168 universities every year.

Rajeep Dey, founder of Enternships, a company which connects students with entrepreneurial work experience and full time roles, told us: "Remember that the workplace is becoming increasingly competitive. Gaining work experience from an early age is essential and you're never too young to start.

"One of the most important pieces of advice I was given while being an intern was: "Do not just follow directions. Think about why you are doing what you are doing". This is such an important point: the education system doesn't always prepare us to think for ourselves. So entering the world of university where you are given far less direction in how to manage yourself and your time (and not to mention your money!) taking initiative and being entrepreneurial in your outlook can be a culture shock for some. Nevertheless it is essential.

"One of the most important benefits of an 'enternship' is that enterns are given the opportunity to build this skill and also their own self-confidence. This means that not only is an enternship before university an impressive addition to your CV for when you leave university, it will also equip **gap**-year students with skills they will need while at university, and help them to get the most out of time that will seem to fly by.

"You should take every opportunity to develop new skills and gain experience; do not think that the only time to get work experience will be the summer holidays of your penultimate year at university. Times have changed – you need to get more proactive about the world of work; take every opportunity you have to do short term work placements."

Check out **www.enternships.com** for ideas about some of the opportunities which are out there.

Interviews

Once your persistence has got you an interview, you need to impress your potential employers.

Attitude - confidence and knowledge are probably top of the list for employers, so that is what you must portray, even if you're a bag of nerves and haven't got a clue. They want to know you're committed.

Dress - make sure you are dressed appropriately (cover tattoos, remove nose piercings *etc*, don't show too much flesh, have clean and brushed hair - all the stuff that your teachers/parents tell you and really annoys you). If you're going for a creative job (advertising, art, *etc*) then you can probably be a little more casual - when you phone the secretary to confirm your interview time and venue, you can ask whether you'll be expected to dress formally. Alternatively, you could go to the company's offices around lunchtime (usually 1pm) and have a look at how people coming out are dressed.

Manner - stand straight; keep eye contact with the interviewer and smile. Be positive about yourself - don't lie, but focus on your good points rather than your bad ones.

visit: www.gap-year.com

Be well prepared to answer the question: "So, why do you want this job?" - remember they'll want to know you're keen, interested in what they do and what benefit you think you can bring to their company.

Gap-year specialists

If you would like to get a work placement from a **gap**-year specialist, the contacts listed in the directory sections in this guidebook are a good starting point for organisations to approach.

Another option is The Year Out Group, the voluntary association of **gap**-specialists formed to promote the concept and benefits of well-structured year out programmes and to help people select suitable and worthwhile projects. The group's member organisations are listed on their website and provide a wide range of year out placements in the UK and overseas, including structured work placements.

Year Out Group members are expected to put potential clients and their parents in contact with those who have recently returned. They consider it important that these references are taken up at least by telephone and, where possible, by meeting face-to-face.

The Year Out Group
Queensfield
28 Kings Road
Easterton
Wiltshire SN10 4PX
Tel: +44 (0) 1380 816696
www.yearoutgroup.org

Gap-year employers

In the directory we've listed companies that either have specific **gap**-year employment policies or ones that we think are worth contacting. We've split them into three groups: festivals, seasonal work and graduate opportunities and work experience.

This isn't a comprehensive list, so it's still worth checking the internet and your local companies (in the *Yellow Pages*, for example).

Festivals

Whether musical, literary or dramatic, there are all kinds of festivals taking place up and down the country every year. You need to apply as early as possible, as there aren't that many placements. Satellite organisations spring up around core festivals; so if you are unsuccessful at first, try to betransferred to another department. The work can be paid or on a voluntary basis. Short-term work, including catering and stewarding, is available mainly during the summer. Recruitment often starts on a local level, so check the local papers and recruitment agencies.

the gap-year guidebook 2011

Seasonal and temporary work

A great way to make some quick cash, either to save up for travelling or to spend at home, is seasonal work. There are always extra short-term jobs going at Christmas: in the Post Office sorting office or in local shops. In the summer there's fruit or vegetable picking for example. There's a website which links farms in the UK and worldwide with students looking for holiday work: **www.pickingjobs.com**

Another option, if you have reasonable IT skills, is to temp in an office. July and August are good months for this too, when permanent staff are on holiday. You can register with local job agencies, which will almost certainly want to do a simple test of your skills. Temping is also a great idea if you're not at all sure what sector you want to work in - it's a good chance to find out about different types of work.

Pay, tax and National Insurance

You can expect to be paid in cash for casual labour, by cheque (weekly or monthly) in a small company and by bank transfer in a large one. Always keep the payslip that goes with your pay, along with your own records of what you earn (including payments for casual labour) during the tax year: from 6 April one year to 5 April the next. You need to ask your employer for a P46 form when you start your first job and a P45 form when you leave (which you take to your next employer). If you are out of education for a year you are not treated as a normal taxpayer.

Personal allowances - that is the amount you can earn before paying tax – are reviewed in the budget each year in April. To find out the current tax-free personal allowance rate call the Inland Revenue helpline or go to: **www.hmrc.gov.uk/nic/**

Minimum wages, maximum hours

In the UK, workers aged 16 and 17 should get a 'development rate' of £3.57 an hour; 18- to 21-year-old workers should receive £4.83 an hour; and workers aged 22 and over should get £5.80 per hour.

To check on how the National Minimum Wage applies to you, go to the Department for Business, Enterprise and Regulatory Reform (formerly called the DTI) website:
www.berr.gov.uk/employment/pay/national-minimum-wage/index.html

or phone the National Minimum Wage Helpline on 0845 6000 678.

If you think you are not being paid the national minimum wage you can call this helpline number: 0800 917 2368

All complaints about underpayment of the National Minimum Wage are treated in the strictest confidence.

The UK also has a law on working hours to comply with European Union legislation. This says that (with some exemptions for specific professions) no employee should be expected to work more than 48 hours a week. Good employers do give you time off in lieu if you occasionally have to work more than

visit: www.gap-year.com

this. Others take no notice, piling a 60-hour-a-week workload on you. This is against the law and, unless you like working a 12-hour day, they must stop.

Working in the UK

Festivals

Aldeburgh Music
Snape Maltings Concert Hall,
Snape,
Saxmundham, IP17 1SP UK

E: enquiries@aldeburgh.co.uk
T: +44 (0) 1728 687 100
F: +44 (0) 1728 687 120
www.aldeburgh.co.uk

Internships and work experience available in arts administration. Registered charity No. 261383.

Brighton Festival
12a Pavillion Buildings,
Castle Square,
Brighton, BN1 1EE UK

E: info@brightonfestival.org
T: +44 (0) 1273 700747
www.brightonfestival.org

A handful of volunteer posts are open during the festival in May, working in the education and press office departments.

Cheltenham Festivals
Town Hall,
Imperial Square,
Cheltenham, GL50 1QA UK

www.cheltenhamfestivals.com

This company runs festivals throughout the year, including jazz, science, music, folk, fringe and literary events. There are usually a number of placements available, although they tend to be unpaid.

Edinburgh Festival Fringe
180 High Street,
Edinburgh, EH1 1QS UK

E: eventsadmin@edfringe.com
www.edfringe.com

Big and long-established late summer festival that has managed to stay cutting-edge.

Harrogate International Festival
Raglan House,
Raglan Street,
Harrogate, HG1 1LE UK

E: info@harrogate-festival.org.uk
T: +44 (0) 1423 562 303
F: +44 (0) 1423 521 264
www.harrogate-festival.org.uk

Harrogate International Festival hosts a number of arts festivals, and offers 6 month internships and short-term work experience placements for 3-4 weeks during festivals.

Hay Festival
The Drill Hall,
25 Lion Street,
Hay-on-Wye, HR3 5AD UK

E: admin@hayfestival.com
T: +44 (0) 870 787 2848
F: +44 (0) 1497 821066
www.hayfestival.com/wales/jobs.aspx

One of the most famous literary festivals in the UK. Most departments take on extra workers for festival fortnight, including stewards, extra staff for the box-office and the bookshop and three interns.

Holloway Arts Festival
c/o The Rowan Arts Project,
83 Sussex Way, Holloway,
London, N7 6RU UK

E: info@therowanartsproject.com
T: +44 (0) 20 7561 1381
www.therowanartsproject.com

Volunteering opportunities include being a steward for a day. Check out their website for further details.

Ilkley Literature Festival
Manor House,
2 Castle Hill,
Ilkley, LS29 9DT UK

T: +44 (0) 1943 601 210
F: +44 (0) 1943 817 079
www.ilkleyliteraturefestival.org.uk/user/Volunteer.php

If you want to become a volunteer at the Ilkley Literature Festival fill in their online form. Jobs include stewarding and helping with mailouts.

Lichfield Festival
Festival Office,
7 The Close,
Lichfield, WS13 7LD UK

E: info@lichfieldfestival.org
T: +44 (0) 1543 306 270
www.lichfieldfestival.org

Volunteers required backstage, to assist with stage management and to help with the education programmes. Contact Richard Bateman, volunteer coordinator, for more details.

Mananan International Festival of Music and the Arts
The Erin Arts Centre,
Victoria Square,
Port Erin, IM9 6LD UK

E: information@erinartscentre.com
T: +44 (0) 1624 835 858
F: +44 (0) 1624 836 658
www.erinartscentre.com/get_involved/volunteer.html

Volunteers needed for stewarding duties, programme selling, transportation of artists, administration, catering, bar duties, technical support and manning galleries and shops.

visit: www.gap-year.com

Manchester International Festival
Festival Office, 3rd Floor,
81 King Street,
Manchester, M2 4AH UK

E: volunteering@mif.co.uk
T: +44 (0) 161 834 6695
F: +44 (0) 161 832 7047
www.mif.co.uk/work-with-us-volunteering/

Your chance to volunteer to be a part of the world's first international festival of original, new work. Particularly good for those people interested in the arts or the cultural sector.

Norfolk and Norwich Festival Ltd
Festival Office, First Floor, Augustine Steward House,
14 Tombland,
Norwich, NR3 1HF UK

E: info@nnfestival.org.uk
T: +44 (0) 1603 877 750
F: +44 (0) 1603 877766
www.nnfestival.org.uk/volunteers.aspx

Volunteers needed from January to May to help out with administration, marketing and even event production.

Portsmouth Festivities
Pippa Cleary, Administrator,
10 High Street,
Portsmouth, PO1 2LN UK

E: festivities@pgs.org.uk
T: +44 (0) 23 9268 1390
www.portsmouthfestivities.co.uk

Volunteers required to help out with the many varied festivities in Portsmouth.

Salisbury International Arts Festival
87 Crane Street,
Salisbury, SP1 2PU UK

E: info@salisburyfestival.co.uk
www.salisburyfestival.co.uk

Volunteering opportunities include stage manager, helping out with crowd management and leaflet distribution. Registered charity No. 276940.

Winchester Hat Fair
5a Jewry Street,
Winchester, SO23 8RZ UK

www.hatfair.co.uk

This vibrant and entertaining festival takes over the centre of Winchester each year during the first weekend in July. Volunteers are needed to help out before and during the festival.

Youth Music Theatre
40 Parkgate Road,
Battersea,
London, SW11 4JH UK

T: +44 (0) 844 415 4858
www.youth-music-theatre.org.uk/volunteers.html

Internships are available in their London office for recent arts graduates or for professionals looking to change career direction. Also need UK-wide volunteers for one to two days per week.

the gap-year guidebook 2011

Graduate opportunities & work experience

3M United Kingdom Plc
3M Centre,
Cain Road,
Bracknell, RG12 8HT UK

T: +44 (0) 8705 360 036
www.3m.com

Industrial placement opportunities available, also graduate opportunities. See their website for more details.

Accenture
60 Queen Victoria Street,
London, EC4N 4TW UK

E: ukgraduates@accenture.com
www.accenture.com/ukschemes

Apply for graduate placements with Accenture, a global management consulting, technology services and outsourcing company.

Alliance & Leicester plc
Carlton Park,
Narborough, LE19 0AL UK

F: +44 (0) 116 200 4040
www.alliance-leicester-group.co.uk

A&L can't guarantee work but it will keep your CV on file in case a project comes up that needs extra staff, usually at the Narborough customer services centre.

Arcadia Group plc
Colegrave House,
70 Berners Street, Soho,
London, W1T 3NL UK

T: +44 (0) 20 7636 8040
www.arcadiagroup.co.uk

They have placement postions in their finance and HR departments, suitable for those undertaking a year's placement as part of their degree. See their website for more details.

BBC Recruitment
PO Box 48305,
Shepherd's Bush,
London, W12 6YE UK

E: careers@bbchrdirect.co.uk
www.bbc.co.uk/jobs

Work experience placements available across the UK in all areas. These are unpaid placements that can last up to four weeks. Competition is fierce so you need to apply at least a year in advance.

Cadbury Schweppes plc
Head Office, Cadbury House,
Uxbridge Business Park,
Uxbridge, UB8 1DH UK

T: +44 (0) 1895 615000
F: +44 (0) 1895 615001
www.cadbury.com

Cadbury Schweppes places people on work experience in response to specific business needs. Contact the business units direct.

visit: www.gap-year.com

Cancer Research UK
PO Box 123,
Lincoln's Inn Fields,
London, WC2A 3PX UK

T: +44 (0) 20 7242 0200
F: +44 (0) 20 7121 6700
http://supportus.cancerresearchuk.org/

Internships of 12 week duration for people who wish to gain valuable work experience in fundraising, as well as marketing, campaigning and communications. Registered Charity No. 1089464.

Civil Service Recruitment
HMGCC, Hanslope Park,
Hanslope,
Milton Keynes, MK19 7BH UK

E: recruitment@hmgcc.gov.uk
T: +44 (0) 1908 510 052
www.careers.civil-service.gov.uk

The Civil Service website has no central contact office for recruitment. This address is for just one of the many different departments with vacancies for undergraduates and graduates. Check each department for details.

Colgate-Palmolive (UK) Ltd
Human Resources, Guildford Business Park,
Middleton Road,
Guildford, GU2 8JZ UK

www.colgate.co.uk

Twelve month placements offered to exceptional students wishing to acquire work experience. Send in your CV to Human Resources for consideration.

Deloitte
Stonecutter Court,
1 Stonecutter Street,
London, EC4A 4TR UK

E: aroe@deloitte.co.uk
T: +44 (0)118 322 2054
http://scholars.deloitte.co.uk

This company runs a 'Scholars Scheme' which provides successful candidates the opportunity to combine travel during a gap year with paid business experience.

EMI Group plc
27 Wrights Lane,
South Kensington,
London, W8 5SW UK

T: +44 (0) 20 7795 7000
www.emimusic.co.uk/careers.html

See website for details about a career or work experience with one of the largest record companies in the world.

Foreign & Commonwealth Office
King Charles Street,
St James's,
London, SW1A 2AH UK

T: +44 (0) 20 7008 1500
www.fco.gov.uk

See their website for more about careers and opportunities in the Diplomatic Service.

the gap-year guidebook 2011

Future Publishing Plc
Beauford Court,
30 Monmouth Street,
Bath, BA1 2BW UK

T: +44 (0) 1225 442 244
www.futureplc.com/future/

Work experience placements offered in their Bath and London offices. One week duration in all areas of publishing. See website for current opportunities.

GlaxoSmithKline UK
GSK House,
980 Great West Road,
Brentford, TW8 9GS UK

T: +44 (0) 20 8047 5000
www.gsk.com/careers/uk-students-graduates.htm

Industrial placements placement available.

HSBC Holdings plc
8 Canada Square,
Canary Wharf,
London, E14 5HQ UK

T: +44 (0) 20 7991 8888
www.hsbc.com/1/2/student-careers

HSBC has a worldwide graduate and internship programme. See their website for further details.

IBM
UK Head Office, North Harbour,
Cosham,
Portsmouth, PO6 3XJ UK

E: student_pgms@uk.ibm.com
T: +44 (0) 870 542 6426
www-05.ibm.com/employment/uk/

IBM run a number of Student Schemes for 'very talented individuals' in all aspects of their business.

IMI plc
Lakeside, Solihull Parkway,
Birmingham Business Park,
Birmingham, B37 7XZ UK

E: info@imiplc.com
T: +44 (0) 121 717 3700
www.thesearch-imiplc.com/vac.asp

IMI operates a global graduate development programme and offers vacation work from June to September to penultimate year engineering (mechanical, electrical or manufacturing) students leading to possible sponsorship through the final year at university.

L'Oréal (UK) Ltd
255 Hammersmith Road,
Hammersmith,
London, W6 8AZ UK

E: talent@uk.loreal.com
T: +44 (0) 20 8762 4000
F: +44 (0) 20 8762 4001
www.loreal.co.uk

L'Oréal have over 2000 internships worldwide. Apply online.

Majestic Wine Warehouse
Majestic House,
Otterspool Way,
Watford, WD25 8WW UK

E: careers@majestic.co.uk
www.majestic.co.uk/careers

Majestic have a graduate recruitment programme and placement schemes for students needing work experience.

Marks & Spencer Plc
PO Box 288,
Warrington, WA5 7WZ UK
http://corporate.marksandspencer.com/mscareers/opportunities/graduates
M&S have a Student Support Scheme where they will give you a yearly grant providing you commit to 200 hours paid work in store and your parents have not gone to university.

Penguin Group UK
80 Strand,
Strand,
London, WC2R 0RL UK

E: jobs@penguin.co.uk
www.penguin.co.uk

Has a variety of areas where you could gain valuable work experience. Placements are of two week durations and take place throughout the year. Apply online. You must be 18.

RAF
Walters Ash,
High Wycombe, HP14 4UE UK

www.raf.mod.uk/careers/

Work experience places are available in RAF bases all over the UK. As each base runs its own work experience programme you need to check the RAF website to find one near you.

S & N Genealogy
West Wing, Manor Farm,
Chilmark,
Salisbury, SP3 5AF UK

T: +44 (0) 1722 716121
www.sandn.net/vacancies.htm

Gap-year students required to do office work such as document scanning.

Snatch Recruitment
Overdale ,
Northend Common,
Nr Henley – on – Thames , RG9 6LJ UK

E: enquiries@snatchrecruitment.com
T: 07747 603 629
F: 0871 900 4879
www.snatchrecruitment.com

Looking to earn some money to pay for your gap-year? Snatch is a hospitality recruitment company that supply temporary staff to events and hospitality industry.

The National Magazine Company Ltd
National Magazine House,
72 Broadwick Street, Soho,
London, W1F 9EP UK

E: hr.recruitment@natmags.co.uk
T: +44 (0) 20 7439 5000
F: +44 (0) 20 7439 6886
www.natmags.co.uk

Publishers of many of the UK's leading magazines, including Esquire, Cosmo and Good Housekeeping. To apply for work experience positions you need to email the editor of the magazine you are interested in.

The Random House Group Ltd
20 Vauxhall Bridge Road,
Westminster,
London, SW1V 2SA UK

E: workexperience@randomhouse.co.uk
www.careersatrandom.co.uk/rhc_workexperience.asp

Work experience opportunities are available in editorial, publicity and marketing. Complete their online form to apply.

UNHCR
Strand Bridge House,
138-142 Strand,
London, WC2R 1HH UK

E: gbrloea@unhcr.org
T: +44 (0) 20 7759 8090
F: +44 (0) 20 7759 8119
www.unhcr.org.uk/interns/index.html

The UNHCR have six month internships which give the participant the opportunity to gain valuable experience working with refugees.

Virgin Radio
Gareth & Hannah, Work Experience,
1 Golden Square, Soho,
London, W1F 9DJ UK

www.absoluteradio.co.uk/about_us/workex.html

They have work experience places for over 18-year-olds currently studying media related courses. Send CV and covering letter.

Seasonal

Brightsparks Recruitment
Parsons Green House,
27 Parsons Green Lane, Parsons Green,
London, SW6 4HH UK

E: info@brightsparksUK.com
T: +44 (0)560 310 7967
F: +44 20 7751 3401
www.brightsparksuk.com

Immediate vacancies in bar, waiting and hospitality work in the UK.

Facilities Management Catering
Church Road,
Wimbledon,
London, SW19 5AE UK

E: resourcing.fmc@aeltc.com
T: +44 (0) 20 8971 2465
F: +44 (0) 20 8944 6362
www.fmccatering.co.uk

If you would like to work at the most prestigious sporting event of the year then log onto our website now and click on the work opportunities page to apply online.

visit: www.gap-year.com

Hot Recruit
Beaumont House, Kensington Village,
Avonmore Road, Earl's Court,
London, W14 8TS UK

E: sales@hotrecruit.com
T: +44 0845 468 0568
www.hotrecruit.com

Search for temporary work, paid or unpaid, charity and fundraising jobs and seasonal holiday jobs abroad.

Kingswood Learning & Leisure Group
Kingswood House,
Alkmaar Way,
Norwich, NR6 6BF UK

E: jobs@kingswood.co.uk
T: +44 (0) 1603 309350
www.kingswoodjobs.co.uk

Kingswood offer an 'earn while you learn' development programme.

PGL Recruitment Team
PGL Travel Ltd, Alton Court,
Penyard Lane,
Ross-on-Wye, HR9 5GL UK

E: recruitment@pgl.co.uk
T: +44 (0) 870 401 4411
F: +44 (0) 870 401 4444
www.pgl.co.uk/recruitment

PGL runs activity holidays and courses for children. Each year the company employs over 2000 young people to work as instructors, group leader, catering and support staff at its centre in the UK, France and Spain.

Chapter 10
Volunteering in the UK

10 Volunteering in the UK

Volunteering doesn't have to be done in a developing country, amongst the poorest on the planet, to bring a sense of satisfaction. There are many deserving cases right on your doorstep. You might also find that, if you do voluntary work close to home, it will make you more involved in your own community.

What's more, the global recession that began towards the end of 2008 has prompted a greater need for volunteers, as charities have had to cut back on paid staff in the wake of reduced donations.

Equally some, like the British Red Cross, have also reported a huge increase in the numbers of potential volunteers - in some cases up to four times as many per month as they'd normally expect. Arguably this reflects the numbers of graduates coming out of university unable to find work as well as high numbers of reported redundancies.

A Red Cross spokeswoman said: "In response to the huge increase in applications from volunteers during 2009, we have increased the number of internships we offer, and have widened our volunteering roles to use the skills that people are offering us. We're seeing people coming from all sorts of occupations - banking, marketing, estate agents. These people have valuable skills to offer.

"Volunteer roles with the British Red Cross include first aiders, supporting emergency services, drivers, sales assistants, school and youth workers, refugee support, helpers for people recently discharged from hospital, fundraisers and office staff."

The charity offers training for qualifications and says volunteering could help people get back into work. Some companies have also offered staff long holidays or sabbaticals in order to cut back on their salary bills during the downturn, in the hope of being able to take them back once the worst is over.

Benefits of UK volunteering

You can:

- Do some things you couldn't do abroad. Good examples are counselling, befriending and fundraising, all of which need at least some local knowledge.
- Have more flexibility: you can do a variety of things rather than opting for one programme or project.
- Combine volunteering with a study course or part time job.
- Get to know more about your own community.
- Get experience before committing to a project abroad.

visit: www.gap-year.com

- Develop career options - a now well-accepted route into radio for example is to do a volunteer stint on hospital radio.

It is sometimes argued that it's a little presumptuous to go off somewhere exotic, and help sort out the problems of the local disadvantaged people when things are plainly not all well in one's own backyard. While there may occasionally be some truth in this charge of 'cultural imperialism', it depends on what particular problems we're talking about and on the attitudes and knowledge of those seeking to help tackle them.

Equally there's no denying there are environmental issues, endangered species and disadvantaged people all over the world, and the skills of people willing to volunteer are desperately needed. So one element of deciding where to volunteer is likely to depend on your interests and skills.

If you choose to spend at least some of your **gap-** doing something for the benefit of others here in the UK, you'll get the same satisfying sense of achievement as volunteers who have been on programmes elsewhere.

To get the most out of volunteering during you gap year, you must consider what you would like to achieve. Try asking yourself about your interests, skills and experience to define what type of volunteering role you are looking for.

Volunteering England (**www.volunteering.org.uk**) is a volunteer development agency committed to supporting, enabling and celebrating volunteering in all its diversity. Their work links research, policy innovation, good practice and grant making in the involvement of volunteers.

Here's what they told us: "There are literally thousands of exiting gap year projects going on in exotic locations all around the globe; but if you are serious about building skills and improving your employability, a job specific placement in the UK may be more useful.

"If you would like a career in the media, three months at a local hospital radio station may not sound as exciting as counting bottle-nosed dolphins in Costa Rica but it is a lot more relevant to prospective employers.

"If you are considering a competitive career such as law or media, bear in mind internships can be difficult to get, but even a day's work shadowing or working more hours at your part-time job can help demonstrate those all-important employability skills such as team working and motivation. If you are interested in law, see if you can help out at your local citizen's advice bureau. If you would like to be a doctor, see if you can help out at your local hospital. They often need volunteers to run the hospital shop and to befriend patients and it will also give you a good idea of what working in a hospital will be like.

"Volunteering in the UK has other benefits too: it is usually cheaper and it can provide a tangible benefit to your local community. For example student volunteers contribute over £42 million to the economy each year through their activities (*National Student Volunteering Survey 2003*) and many people go on to find jobs as a direct result of their volunteering.

"Research has also proved that those who do voluntary work or are helped by volunteers, adopt healthier lifestyles, can cope better with their own ill-health, have greater confidence and self-esteem, have an improved diet and even have a higher level of physical activity."

To find out more about volunteering you can visit Volunteering England's website **www.volunteering.org.uk** to find your nearest Volunteer Centre.

www.do-it.org or **http://vinspired.com/opportunities/marketplace** also list volunteering opportunities online.

Wherever you are, volunteering is an opportunity to learn about other people and about yourself.

If you're just starting out on a career path and are unsure what you want to do, volunteering can be an opportunity to gain relevant work experience. If you know, for example, that you want a career in retail, a stint with Oxfam will teach you a surprising amount. Many charity shops recognise this and offer training. Careers in the charity sector are also extremely popular and can be quite hard to get into, so a period of voluntary work will demonstrate your commitment and willingness to learn.

Volunteering for a while can also be useful for those who are maybe thinking of a career change or development. For example you could use your skills to develop a charity's website, or perhaps you have experience of marketing or campaigning.

While you're volunteering your services you can also use the time to find out more about the organisation's work, whom to talk to about training or qualifications and about work opportunities within the organisation.

What can you do?

Before contacting organisations it is a good idea to think about what you would like to do in terms of the activity and type of organisation you would like to work for. There's good advice on this at:
www.volunteering.org.uk/IWantToVolunteer

The UK has its share of threatened environments and species, homeless people and the economically disadvantaged, and those with physical disabilities or mental health problems. In some ways, therefore, the choices for projects to join are no different in the UK from the ones you'd be making if you were planning to join a project abroad.

Cash strapped hospitals are always in need of volunteers - Great Ormond Street Children's Hospital in London is a good example. They look after seriously ill children and need volunteers to play with the children and make their stay less frightening. It also runs a hospital radio station - Radio Lollipop - in the evenings and on Sundays, for which it needs volunteers.

Or you could help with a youth

visit: www.gap-year.com

sports team, get involved in a street art project, or with a holiday camp for deprived inner city youngsters - there are many options and there are any number of inner-city organisations working to improve relations between, and provide/identify opportunities for, people from different ethnic groups, faiths and cultures.

Remember, though, that any volunteer work you do that puts you directly in contact with young people and other vulnerable groups, such as people with mental health problems, or care of the elderly, is likely to mean you'll need a CRB (Criminal Records Bureau) check for both their protection and yours. In some cases, you'll have to pay for this yourself.

Where to start?

Your own hometown will have its share of charity shops on the high street, and they're always in need of volunteers. But you could also try local churches or sports groups. Check your local paper for stories on campaigns, special conservation days and other stories about good causes close to home that you might be able to support.

Community Service Volunteers is one of the UK's leading volunteering and training charity. Every year, CSV involves over 150,000 volunteers in high quality opportunities that enrich lives and tackle real need, helping transform the lives of over one million people across the UK.

A **gap**-year with CSV lasts between four months and a year and does not cost a penny. Volunteers live away from home and are provided with free accommodation, food and travel expenses, plus a weekly living allowance.

Dominica Cole, 19, from Luton was planning on starting her degree in Medicine straight after her A Levels, however was forced to take a break after missing her offer. "I was placed at Huddersfield University to provide support, along with two other volunteers, for a student with Cerebral Palsy. The university offered us free training in youth issues, skills for work and management which I was really pleased with.

"People have commented on how impressive and diverse my CV is for my age, and I'm really proud of that. I've found employers to be very encouraged by my volunteering experience. I was offered a job I was quite under qualified for because I was able to demonstrate my maturity and confidence at interview and had experience in the workplace.

"I would recommend volunteering to all A Level students. People notice I volunteer and then remember me; it really makes my applications stand out from others. There are few opportunities to take time out of formal work and education and my Gap Year has given me skills and experience to prepare me for my next step.

"I feel much more confident, mature and ready for my degree course. I've lived away from home, made new friends and really thrived this past year and can now look forward to concentrating on my degree."

Volunteers can start their CSV placement at any time during the year. Full-time volunteers are aged 16-35 years. Volunteers are given the opportunity to work

the gap-year guidebook 2011

on exciting projects supporting homeless people, socially excluded people, disabled people and the elderly.

For volunteer information and an application pack about **gap**-year volunteering for people aged 16 plus call 0800 374 991 or visit the website **www.csv.org.uk/gapyear** to apply online.

What qualities does a good volunteer need?

The Samaritans is one organisation that's reported an upsurge in calls to its confidential helpline as a result of the recession - and if you've been in the position of losing your job, and are maybe thinking of volunteering to help others, it would be a good idea to think hard about whether you're able to offer what's needed.

Here's what the Samaritans have to say:

"Samaritans volunteers need to be able to listen. They are not professional counsellors. They can also:

- question gently, tactfully - without intruding;
- encourage people to tell their own story in their own time and space;
- refrain from offering advice and instead offer confidential emotional support; and
- always try to see the other point of view, regardless of their own religious or political beliefs."

From the Samaritans website:
www.samaritans.org/support_samaritans/volunteer.aspx

You can find out more here on the training and support you will be given before you are taken on.

ChildLine too has good advice for volunteers on its website and sees them as the essential basis of ChildLine's service. They need volunteers to speak to children and young people on their helpline, to work with them in schools, and to support fundraising, administration and management.

The charity provides full training and support, and has centres in London,

visit: www.gap-year.com

Nottingham, Glasgow, Aberdeen, Manchester, Swansea, Rhyl, Leeds, Belfast, Exeter and Birmingham.
www.nspcc.org.uk/getinvolved/volunteer/childline/childlinevolunteering_wda56391.html

There's a need for volunteers to help with disadvantaged people of all ages and if you're older, and considering volunteering, your work skills could come in handy. Many charities may need professional advice from time to time. If you have expertise in accountancy, administration, construction and maintenance, the law, psychiatry or treasury you might be able to help.

Helping refugees

The International Red Cross has a long history of helping traumatised and displaced people around the world, from being the first port of call in an emergency to monitoring the treatment of political prisoners, it is often trusted as the only impartial authority allowed access to detainees.

The British Red Cross has a specific scheme dedicated to helping refugees adjust to life in the UK. Trained volunteers provide much needed support to thousands of people every year, helping them to access local services and adjust to life in a new country. The Red Cross' services provide practical/emotional help to vulnerable asylum seekers and refugees. This includes offering orientation services to help refugees adapt to life in the UK, providing emergency support

for large-scale arrivals, providing emergency provisions for those in crisis and offering peer-befriending support to young refugees.

You can volunteer to help out in charity shops or with fundraising. There are also internships but the Red Cross doesn't send its volunteers overseas.

Here's what they say:

"The Red Cross Movement is made up of 179 National Societies, the British Red Cross being one of these. As each National Society has the capacity to draw upon its own body of volunteers, we don't send volunteers overseas. Not only does the Movement save time and money, but local volunteers have the advantage of speaking the language, knowing the region, and understanding the culture."

To find out more about volunteering with the Red Cross go to:
www.redcross.org.uk/TLC.asp?id=75777

Conservation

Perhaps you're more interested in conservation work. The British Trust for Conservation Volunteers is a good place to start. It offers short (and longer) training courses which are informal and designed to be fun – including practical skills such as building a dry stone wall, creating a pond or a wildlife garden. It also has a number of options for volunteer schemes you can join:
www2.btcv.org.uk/display/volunteer

Animals

Volunteer jobs with animal welfare organisations can vary from helping with kennel duties, assisting with fundraising events, carrying out wildlife surveys, to working on specific projects.

Animal Jobs Direct has information on paid work with animals but it also has a section for volunteers.

The web address below gives direct links to animal welfare and rescue charities that offer a variety of different and interesting volunteering opportunities - there are an amazing range of voluntary jobs available. Remember, many animal charities exist on limited funds and therefore voluntary workers are much needed and appreciated.

To find out more, visit:
www.animal-job.co.uk/animal-volunteer-work-uk.html

Volunteering - with pay?

Although the definition for voluntary work is, strictly-speaking, work that you're not paid for, voluntary schemes (especially the government-inspired ones) will often pay you some pocket money and may also give you free meals and accommodation.

Each scheme varies in what it provides - there are no rules. The point is that these are not 'jobs'; what you will be doing is altruistic: helping someone or a specific cause, usually a charity, whether you're working on a nature reserve or doing the office filing.

For example, Shelter, the charity for the homeless, details the expenses it pays to its volunteers on its website:
www.england.shelter.org.uk/what_you_can_do/volunteer/expenses_for_our_volunteers

In the directory we list the contact details of a number of charities and organisations that are grateful for volunteers. If you can't find anything that interests you there, then there are a number of organisations that place people with other charities or thta have a wide national network of their own – an internet search should give you a good list.

The following websites provide useful links and information about volunteering:
www.do-it.org.uk
www.ncvo-vol.org.uk
www.timebank.org.uk
www.vois.org.uk (specifically working with young people)

Volunteering in the UK

Fundraising

Marie Curie Cancer Care (Head Office)　　　T: +44 (0) 800 716 146
89 Albert Embankment,
Vauxhall,
London, SE1 7TP UK
　　　www.mariecurie.org.uk/supportus/helpingmariecuriecancercare/volunteer/
Volunteer. Help in their shops, hospices and/or offices, or get involved in fundraising for Marie Curie (Registered Charity No. 207994).

Scope　　　E: events@scope.org.uk
6 Market Road,　　　T: +44 (0) 207 6197100
Holloway,　　　www.scope.org.uk/adventures
London, N7 9PW UK

Cerebral palsy charity (No. 208231) which needs your help in raising funds.

SOS Rhino　　　E: info@sosrhino.org
Lot 15, Block B, 2nd Floor,　　　T: +60 88 388 405
Visa Light Industrial Centre,　　　www.sosrhino.org
Mile 5-1/2 Tuaran Road, 88856 Inanam Malaysia

SOS Rhino needs donations to help them in their work to save the Sumatran rhinoceros. Why not choose them as your charity fundraising beneficiary?

War on Want　　　E: mailroom@waronwant.org
FAO David Rudkin, Development House,　　　T: +44 (0) 20 7549 0555
56-64 Leonard Street, St Luke's,　　　F: +44 (0) 20 7549 0556
London, EC2A 4LT UK　　　www.waronwant.org

Fundraise for War on Want. Registered Charity No. 208724.

Wesser and Partner　　　E: wesser@wesser.info
St John Ambulance County HQ, The White House,　　　T: +44 (0) 845 20 937 737
Argyle Way,　　　F: +44 (0) 1438 356 444
Stevenage, SG1 2AD UK　　　www.wesser.co.uk

Wesser offers you the chance to fundraise for St John Ambulance, work outside, socializing and living with like-minded individuals and earning an uncapped sum of money.

the gap-year guidebook 2011

Volunteering

Amnesty International
The Human Rights Action Centre,
17-25 New Inn Yard, Shoreditch,
London, EC2A 3EA UK

E: sct@amnesty.org.uk
T: +44 (0) 20 7033 1500
F: +44 (0) 20 7033 1503
www.amnesty.org.uk/volunteer.asp

Amnesty International (registered charity No: 1051681) have a selection of volunteering vacancies throughout their UK offices. Volunteer roles are advertised on their website. Speculative applications are not accepted.

Ashbourne Arts Ltd
St John's Community Hall,
King Street,
Ashbourne, DE6 1EA UK

E: info@ashbournefestival.org
T: +44 (0) 1335 348 707
www.ashbournefestival.org

Ashbourne Arts is a not-for-profit company who rely entirely on volunteers.

Beamish, The North of England Open Air Museum
The Friends' Office,
Beamish, DH9 0RG UK

E: info@friendsofbeamish.co.uk
http://friendsofbeamish.co.uk/volunteers.html

Beamish Museum is a unique place. A registered charity (No. 517147) they rely on volunteers to help them in their work: from taking visitor surveys to working on their many restoration projects.

Born Free Foundation
3 Grove House,
Foundry Lane,
Horsham, RH13 5PL UK

E: info@bornfree.org.uk
T: +44 (0)1403 240 170
www.bornfree.org.uk

The Born Free Foundation has grown into a global force for wildlife. Volunteer with their major international projects devoted to animal welfare, conservation and education. They also list other possible overseas volunteering vacancies.

British Red Cross
44 Moorfields,
Barbican,
London, EC2Y 9AL UK

E: information@redcross.org.uk
T: +44 (0) 844 871 1111
F: +44 (0) 207 7562 2000
www.redcross.org.uk

'Volunteers are the lifeblood of the British Red Cross.'
As well as volunteering, the British Red Cross (Charity No. 220949) offered internships and work experience opportunities for those still at school.

visit: www.gap-year.com

BTCV
Sedum House, Mallard Way,
Potteric Carr,
Doncaster, DN4 8DB UK

E: information@btcv.org.uk
T: +44 (0) 1302 388 888
F: +44 (0) 1302 311 531
www.btcv.org.uk

BTCV runs working conservation holidays in the UK and in more than 25 countries abroad working in partnership with other organisations.

Camphill Communities in the UK
Co-worker Development Office,
55 Cainscross Road,
Stroud, GL5 4EX UK

E: coworker@camphill.org.uk
T: +44 (0) 1453 753142
www.camphill.org.uk

Camphill is a worldwide network of communities dedicated to work and life with children, adolescents or adults with developmental and other disabilities. See website for volunteering opportunities.

Careforce
35 Elm Road,
New Malden, KT3 3HB UK

E: enquiry@careforce.co.uk
F: +44 (0) 20 8942 3331
www.careforce.co.uk

Each year Careforce recruits Christians aged 17 to 30 and places them at churches and community projects across the UK.

Cats Protection League
National Cat Centre,
Chelwood Gate,
Haywards Heath, RH17 7TT UK

E: helpline@cats.org.uk
T: +44 (0) 8707 708 649
www.cats.org.uk/supportus/volunteering.asp

Volunteering opportunities available in a wide variety of roles, please see our website for more details. Registered charity No. 203644.

Central Scotland Forest Trust
Hillhouseridge,
Shottskirk Road,
Shotts, ML7 4JS UK

F: +44 (0) 1501 823 919
www.csft.co.uk

CSCT organises volunteers to help with ecological improvements in Central Scotland. Work includes fence repairing and path building. Reg Charity SC015341

Centre for Alternative Technology
Llwyngwern Quarry,
Pantperthog,
Machynlleth, SY20 9AZ UK

E: barbara.wallace@cat.org.uk
T: +44 (0) 1654 705 955
F: +44 (0) 1654 702 782
www.cat.org.uk

CAT has volunteer placements from one week to six months in length. Reg Charity 265239

Children with Leukaemia
51 Great Ormond Street,
Bloomsbury,
London, WC1N 3JQ UK

E: info@leukaemia.org
T: +44 (0) 20 7404 0808
F: +44 (0) 20 7404 3666
www.leukaemia.org

Britain's leading charity (Registered No. 298405) dedicated to the conquest of childhood leukaemia through pioneering research, new treatment and support of leukaemic children and their families.

Children's Country Holidays Fund
Stafford House,
91 Keymer Road,
Hassock, BN6 8QJ UK

E: info@childrensholidays.org.uk
T: +44 (0) 1273 847 772
F: +44 (0)1273 841 993
www.childrensholidays.org.uk

CCHF (registered charity number 206958) Volunteers required to help out on week long or weekend activity breaks for severely disadvantaged children. Meals and accommodation provided, subject to interview, CRB check and references.

Christian Aid Gap Year
2a Deans Court Lane,
Wimborne, BH21 1EE UK
http://www.christianaid.org.uk/getinvolved/volunteer/gapyear/gap_year.aspx

E: gapyear@christian-aid.org

Have placements between September and June each year for volunteers in their offices around the UK.

Churchtown - A Vitalise Centre
Volunteering Team, Shap Road Industrial Estate,
Shap Road,
Kendal, LA9 6NZ UK

E: volunteer@vitalise.org.uk
T: +44 (0) 1539 814 682
www.vitalise.org.uk

Vitalise provide essential services for the disabled and visually impaired people. They always need volunteers. Registered Charity No.295072.

Conservation Volunteers Northern Ireland
Beech House,
159 Ravenhill Road,
Belfast, BT6 0BP UK

E: cvni@btcv.org.uk
T: +44 (0) 28 9064 5169
F: +44 (0) 28 9064 4409
www.cvni.org

Conservation Volunteers, part of BTCV, provides all-year-round volunteering opportunities on a broad range of practical environmental projects across Northern Ireland.

CSV (Community Service Volunteers)
237 Pentonville Road,
Islington,
London, N1 9NJ UK

E: volunteer@csv.org.uk
T: +44 (0) 800 374 991
www.csv.org.uk/gapyear

CSV is the largest volunteering organisation in the UK. Has full-time volunteering programme provides hundreds of free gap-year placements at social care projects throughout the UK.

visit: www.gap-year.com

Dartington International Summer School
The Barn,
Dartington Hall,
Totnes, TQ9 6DE UK

E: summerschool@dartington.org
T: +44 (0) 1803 847 080
F: +44 (0) 1803 847 087
www.dartington.org/summer-school

Volunteer as a Steward or a Trog. The work is physically demanding and involves long hours but you do get free accommodation, food and the opportunity to gain experience in arts administration. Reg Charity No. 279756.

Dogs Trust
Personnel Officer,
17 Wakley Street, Pentonville,
London, EC1V 7RQ UK

E: jobs@dogstrust.org.uk
www.dogstrust.org.uk/howtohelp/

Volunteers needed to help out in the following areas: fundraising, dog walking, dog socialising and pre-adoption home visiting. Registered Charity No. 227523.

Elizabeth Finn Care
1 Derry Street,
South Kensington,
London, W8 5HY UK

E: info@elizabethfinn.org.
T: +44 (0) 20 7396 6700
F: +44 (0) 20 7396 6739
www.elizabethfinncare.org.uk

Charity (No. 207812) that aims to help by giving financial support where needed to those with limited resources who live in their own homes, or by providing accommodation for older people in their own care homes. Volunteers always needed. See their website for more details.

Emmaus UK
48 Kingston Street,
Cambridge, CB1 2NU UK

E: contact@emmaus.org.uk
F: +44 (0) 1223 576 203
www.emmaus.org.uk

Emmaus Communities (Registered Charity No. 1064470) offer homeless people a home and full time work refurbishing and selling furniture and other donated goods. They list various volunteer opportunities on their website.

English Heritage
Education Volunteers Manager,
PO Box 569,
Swindon, SN2 2YP UK

E: kate.davies@english-heritage.org.uk
T: +44 (0) 1793 414 438
www.english-heritage.org.uk/server/show/nav.10543

English Heritage are looking for people who are aged 18 and over to assist with workshops, tours and other activities associated with learning and school visits.

Friends of The Earth
26-28 Underwood Street,
Hoxton,
London, N1 7JQ UK

T: +44 (0) 20 7490 1555
F: +44 (0) 20 7490 0881
www.foe.co.uk

Friends of The Earth welcomes volunteers at their head office in London, or at any of their regional offices. Registered Charity No. 281681

Global Adventure Challenges Ltd
Red Hill House, Hope Street,
Saltney,
Chester, CH4 8BU UK

E: start@globaladventurechallenges.com
T: +44 (0) 1244 676 454
F: +44 (0) 1244 683 962
www.globaladventurechallenges.com

Raise money for your chosen charity whilst having the adventure of a lifetime. Many adventures to choose from are listed on their website.

Greenpeace
Human Resources Department,
Canonbury Villas, Islington,
London, N1 2PN UK

E: info@uk.greenpeace.org
T: +44 (0) 20 7865 8100
F: +44 (0) 20 7865 8200
www.greenpeace.org.uk

Greenpeace need volunteers either as an active supporter or in their London office to help out with their administration.

Groundwork Oldham & Rochdale
Environment Centre, Shaw Road,
Higginshaw,
Oldham, OL1 4AW UK

T: +44 (0) 161 624 1444
F: +44 (0) 161 624 1555
http://oldham.groundworknw.org.uk/

Volunteering opportunities for people aged 16-25. Registered Charity No. 514726

Hearing Dogs for Deaf People
The Grange, Wycombe Road,
Saunderton,
Princes Risborough, HP27 9NS UK

E: info@hearingdogs.org.uk
T: +44 (0) 1844 348 100
F: +44 (0) 1844 348 101
www.hearingdogs.org.uk

Become a volunteer with Hearing Dogs for Deaf People (Registered charity No.293358). Contribute to the life changing work of this Charity by visiting their website and clicking on "Work with us".

ILA (Independent Living Alternatives)
Trafalgar House,
Grenville Place, Mill Hill,
London, NW7 3SA UK

E: paservices@ilanet.co.uk
T: +44 (0) 20 8906 9265
F: +44 (0) 20 8959 1910
www.ilanet.co.uk

Aims to enable people who need personal assistance, to be able to live independently in the community and take full control of their lives.

Latin Link
Latin Link,
87 London Street,
Reading, RG1 4QA UK

E: info@latinlink.org
T: +44 (0) 118 957 7100
www.stepteams.org

Latin Link sends teams and individuals to work in mission with Latin American and Spanish Christians for between four weeks and two years. Registered Charity No. 1020826.

visit: www.gap-year.com

London 2012
One Churchill Place,
Canary Wharf,
London, E14 5LN UK

T: +44 (0) 203 2012 000
www.london2012.com/get-involved/index.php

Recruitment of volunteers begins in 2010 and they advise early registration of your interest. Selection of successful candidates will not be on a first come, first served, basis but on volunteering experience and appropriate skills.

Macmillan Cancer Support
(UK Office - Volunteering)
89 Albert Embankment,
Vauxhall,
London, SE1 7UQ UK

E: vcoordinators@macmillan.org.uk
T: +44 (0) 20 7840 7840
F: +44 (0) 20 7840 7841
www.macmillan.org.uk/Get_Involved/GetInvolved.aspx

Share your skills to improve the lives of people affected by cancer. Assist our fundraising activities or support us in our offices and gain new experience whilst having fun. Registered Charity No. 261017.

Mind
15-19 Broadway,
Stratford,
London, E15 4BQ UK

E: contact@mind.org.uk
T: +44 (0) 20 8519 2122
F: +44 (0) 20 8522 1725
www.mind.org.uk

Mind (Registered Charity No. 424348) would like to hear from you if you would like to take part in a fundraising event, or have an idea for fundraising for the charity.

Museum of London
150 London Wall,
Barbican,
London, EC2Y 5HN UK

E: recruitment@museumoflondon.org,uk
T: +44 (0) 20 7814 5792
www.molg.org.uk/English/Jobs/Work/VolunteerInfo.htm

Volunteer at the Museum of London. See their website for further details.

NSPCC
Weston House,
42 Curtain Road, Shoreditch,
London, EC2A 3NH UK

T: +44 (0) 20 7825 2500
F: +44 (0) 20 7825 2525

www.nspcc.org.uk/getinvolved/volunteer/volunteerhub_wda40426.html
Volunteers needed to help with fundraising, office work, manning the switchboard at Childline or even helping on a specific project. (Reg. Charity No. 216401)

PDSA
Whitechapel Way,
Priorslee,
Telford, TF2 9PQ UK

T: +44 (0)1952 290999
F: +44 (0)1952 291035
www.pdsa.org.uk

A wide range of volunteering opportunities offered. Use the contact form on their website to find out about opportunities in the UK and Ireland. Registered Charity No. 208217.

the gap-year guidebook 2011

Plan UK
5-6 Underhill Street,
Camden Town,
London, NW1 7HS UK
E: mail@plan-international.org.uk
T: +44 (0) 20 7482 9777
F: +44 (0) 20 7482 9778
www.plan-uk.org/involved/volunteering/

Plan UK works with children and their communities in the world's poorest countries aiming to vastly improve their quality of life. Volunteer opportunities and internships available.

Rainforest Concern
8 Clanricarde Gardens,
Notting Hill,
London, W2 4NA UK
E: info@rainforestconcern.org
T: +44 (0) 20 7229 2093
F: +44 (0) 20 7221 4094
www.rainforestconcern.org

Sends volunteers to Ecuador, Costa Rica and Panama to work with important conservation programmes in the Amazon and the Andes, as well as the Leatherback Turtle project.

RNLI
HR Core Services,
West Quay Road,
Poole, BH15 1HZ UK
T: +44 (0) 845 122 6999
www.rnli.org.uk/jobs

Volunteer lifeguards required. Registered Charity No. 209603.

Rock UK
Carroty Wood,
Higham Lane,
Tonbridge, TN11 9QX UK
E: carroty.wood@rockuk.org
T: +44 (0) 1732 361361
F: +44 (0) 1732 366767
www.rockuk.org

Opportunities are available to assist in the practical running of the Barnabas Trust centres. (Registered Charity No. 1107724)

Royal Botanic Gardens
Volunteer Co-ordinator, Museum Number 1,
Kew,
Richmond, TW9 3AB UK
E: info@kew.org
T: +44 (0) 20 8332 5000
F: +44 (0) 20 8332 5197
www.kew.org/aboutus/volunteers

Volunteers can help out at the Royal Botanic Gardens in five different areas: School explainers, horticultural, friends of Kew, volunteer guides and in the climbers and crepers play zone.

RSPB (Royal Society for the Protection of Birds)
The Lodge,
Potton Road,
Sandy, SG19 2DL UK
E: volunteers@rspb.org.uk
T: +44 (0) 1767 680 551
F: +44 (0) 1767 685 417
www.rspb.org.uk/volunteering/residential

Want a career in conservation? Check out the volunteering pages on the RSPBs website for advice, volunteering opportunities and case studies (Registered Charity No. 207076)

visit: www.gap-year.com

RSPCA
Wilberforce Way,
Southwater,
Horsham, RH13 9RS UK

T: 0300 1234 555
F: 0303 123 0284
www.rspca.org.uk/volunteer

The RSPCA (registered charity no. 219099) are always looking for volunteers. Check out their website for vacancies in a home near you.

Samaritans
The Upper Mill,
Kingston Road,
Ewell, KT17 2AF UK

T: +44 (0) 8705 62 72 82
www.samaritans.org.uk/support_samaritans/volunteer.aspx

The Samaritans (Registered Charity No. 219432) depend entirely on volunteers. They are there 24/7 for anyone who needs help. Can you spare the time to help them?

Sense
Head Office,
101 Pentonville Road, Pentonville,
London, N1 9LG UK

E: info@sense.org.uk
T: +44 (0) 845 127 0060
F: +44 (0) 845 127 0061
www.sense.org.uk

Volunteers always required by Sense (Registered Charity No. 289868) in a variety of areas. See their website for further details of how you can help.

SHAD
5 Bedford Hill,
Balham,
London, SW12 9ET UK

E: info@shad.org.uk
T: +44 (0) 20 8675 6095
F: +44 (0) 20 8673 2118
www.shad.org.uk

Are you aged over 18 years, with four months (or more) to spare? Personal Assistants are needed to enable physically disabled adults to live independently in their own homes.

Shelter
88 Old Street,
St Luke's,
London, EC1V 9HU UK

E: info@shelter.org.uk
T: +44 (0) 844 515 2000
F: +44 (0) 844 515 2956
www.shelter.org.uk

Volunteering opportunities available throughout the UK. Registered Charity No. 263710.

The Blue Cross
Shilton Road,
Burford, OX18 4PF UK

E: info@bluecross.org.uk
www.bluecross.org.uk

The Blue Cross is Britain's pet charity (No. 224392), providing practical support, information and advice for pet and horse owners. For information on volunteering visit their website.

The Children's Trust
Tadworth Court,
Tadworth, KT20 5RU UK

www.thechildrenstrust.org.uk

The Children's Trust (Registered Charity No. 288018) run a residential centre for about 80 severely disabled children, and is always looking for people to get involved.

The Monkey Sanctuary Trust
St Martins,
Looe, PL13 1NZ UK

E: volunteer@monkeysanctuary.org
www.monkeysanctuary.org

Monkey Sanctuary Trust (Registered Charity No. 1102532) needs volunteer help all year round, making monkey food, cleaning enclosures, helping serve the public in the summer and maintenance and other projects in the winter. Volunteers do not work directly with the monkeys.

The National Trust
National Trust Central Volunteering Team, Heelis,
Kemble Drive,
Swindon, SN2 2NA UK

E: volunteers@nationaltrust.org.uk
T: +44 (0) 1793 817632
F: +44 (0) 1793 817401

www.nationaltrust.org.uk/main/w-trust/w-volunteering.htm

Learn new skills whilst helping to conserve the UK's heritage. Volunteering opportunities can be found on their website. Registered Charity No. 205846.

The National Trust for Scotland
Volunteering Office, Wemyss House,
28 Charlotte Square,
Edinburgh, EH2 4ET UK

T: +44 (0) 844 493 2407
F: +44 (0) 131 243 9301
www.nts.org.uk/Volunteering/

The National Trust for Scotland is a conservation charity (No. SC 007410) that protects and promotes Scotland's natural and cultural heritage for present and future generations to enjoy. Contact them to find out about volunteering opportunities.

The Prince's Trust
Head Office,
18 Park Square East, Regent's Park,
London, NW1 4LH UK

E: webinfops@princes-trust.org.uk
T: +44 (0) 20 7543 1234
F: +44 (0) 20 7543 1200
www.princes-trust.org.uk

Volunteer with the Prince's Trust (Registered Charity No. 1079675) and help young people achieve something with their lives. Opportunities in fundraising, personal mentoring, volunteer co-ordinator and training. See website for vacancies in your area.

The Simon Community
129 Malden Road,
Camden,
London, NW5 4HS UK

E: info@simoncommunity.org.uk
T: +44 (0) 20 7485 6639
www.simoncommunity.org.uk

The Simon Community is a partnership of homeless people and volunteers living and working with London's homeless. They need full-time residential volunteers all year round. Registered Charity No. 283938.

The Wildlife Trusts
The Kiln, Waterside,
Mather Road,
Newark, NG24 1WT UK

E: enquiry@wildlifetrusts.org
T: +44 (0) 1636 6777 11
F: +44 (0) 1636 670 001
www.wildlifetrusts.org

The Wildlife Trusts (Registered Charity No. 207238) always need volunteers. Check out their website or contact your local office for information about vacancies in your area.

UNICEF (United Nations Childrens Fund)
Africa House,
64-78 Kingsway, Holborn,
London, WC2B 6NB UK

T: +44 (0) 844 801 2414
www.unicef.org.uk

UNICEF normally has two or three volunteers working in its main office at any one time, and local offices will always need help: apply to them direct. Registered Charity No. 1072612.

Vinspired
5th Floor, Dean Bradley House,
52 Horseferry Road, Westminster,
London, SW1P 2AF UK

E: info@vinspired.com
T: +44 (0) 800 089 9000
www.vinspired.com

Formerly the Millennium Volunteer Programme, Vinspired is a volunteering site for those aged between 16 and 25. Registered Charity No. 1113255.

Vitalise
Volunteer Team, Shap Road Industrial Estate,
Shap Road,
Kendal, LA9 6NZ UK

E: volunteer@vitalise.org.uk
T: +44 (0) 845 330 0148
F: +44 (0) 1539 735 567
www.vitalise.org.uk

Vitalise runs centres providing holiday and respite opportunities for people with disabilities and their carers. Volunteers are welcomed and needed, and will receive accommodation and board.

Volunteer Reading Help
Charity House, 14-15 Perseverance Works,
38 Kingsland Road, Hackney,
London, E2 8DD UK

E: info@vrh.org.uk
T: +44 (0) 20 7729 4087
F: +44 (0) 20 7729 7643
www.vrh.org.uk

National charity (No. 296454) that helps primary school children who find reading a struggle. Training takes six hours and volunteers work with the same children every week, giving at least an hour of their time.

Whizz-Kidz
Elliott House,
10-12 Allington Street, Westminster,
London, SWIE 5EH UK

E: info@whizz-kidz.org.uk
T: +44 (0) 20 7233 6600
F: +44 (0) 20 7233 6611
www.whizz-kidz.org.uk

Whizz-Kidz aims to improve the lives of disabled under-18s by providing wheelchairs, trikes, walking aids and so on. Contact them direct to find out about overseas challenge events such as climbing Kilimanjaro or walking the Great Wall of China.

the gap-year guidebook 2011

Youth Hostel Association
Trevelyan House,
Dimple Road,
Matlock, DE4 3YH UK

E: volunteers@yha.org.uk
T: +44 (0) 1629 592 600
F: +44 (0) 1629 592 702
www.yha.org.uk

The YHA has Youth Hostels around the country and needs volunteers to help with running them and maintaining the local environment and paths, as well as fundraising.

Chapter 11
Learning in the UK

Learning in the UK

You don't have to spend your **gap**-year travelling the globe if that doesn't appeal to you. The point about taking a **gap-** is to try out new experiences that leave you feeling refreshed and stimulated, to learn something new and possibly come up with some new ideas about where you want your life to head next.

So if you're frustrated that hardly anything you were taught at school seems relevant to your life, why not use your **gap**-year to learn new skills that you choose yourself? You can make them as useful as you want.

There are plenty of evening classes available at local colleges, though usually only in term time, and, if you're thinking of training that doesn't involve university or are looking for ways to expand your skill set as part of a change of career direction, check out the Learning and Skills Council, which exists to promote lifelong learning, with the aim of young people and adults having skills to match the best in the world by the year 2010. There's lots of information on what's available, including financial help, on:
www.lsc.gov.uk/

A **gap-** is also a good opportunity to explore interests that may, up to now, have been hobbies; here are some suggestions:

Archaeology

Do relics from the past fascinate you? Would you love to find one? You could get yourself on an actual archaeological dig. One good place to start is with your local county council's Archaeology Department, which may know of local digs you could join. Nowadays, whenever a major building development is going through the planning application process, permission to build often includes a condition allowing for archaeological surveys to be done before any work can begin; so another source of information could be the planning departments of local district councils.

Art

If you're seriously interested in painting, sculpting or other artistic subjects, but don't know if you want to carry it through to a full degree, there is the useful option of a one-year art foundation course. These are available from a wide variety of art colleges.

A foundation course at Art College doesn't count towards an art degree, in the sense that you can then skip the first year of your three-year degree course, but it can help you find out whether you are interested in becoming a

visit: www.gap-year.com

practising artist, maybe an illustrator, an animator, a graphic designer, or are more interested in things like art history, or perhaps working in a gallery or a museum or in a field like interior design.

If you do want to go onto the three-year art school degree, competition for undergraduate places is based on the volume and standard of work in a candidate's entry portfolio. Having a portfolio from your foundation course puts you at a natural advantage. Course providers also advise against specialising in one discipline, say sculpture, before covering the more wide-ranging syllabus of a foundation course.

Cookery

Can you cook? There are really two types of cookery courses for gappers: basic skills and how to earn money.

The basic skills courses are for those who want to be able to feed themselves more than baked beans or packet soup. These courses can take you from boiling water through to quite a reasonable level - you may not be able to cook for a dinner party of 12, but you should finish the course with enough skills to be able to cook a variety of tasty meals without poisoning anyone.

Cheap and cheerful cookery courses (standard, ethnic, exotic) can be found at day or evening classes at local colleges of further education. Usually the fees are low but you have to pay for, or provide your own, ingredients.

The second type of course is aimed at teaching you the skills needed to work as a cook during your **gap**-year. Working as a cook in ski resorts, on yachts in

the gap-year guidebook 2011

the Caribbean or in villas in Tuscany or the south of France not only allows you to see the world, but also pays you while you see it.

Cookery schools tell us that the majority of those who want to work after doing a cookery course do find cooking work.

What's involved in being a chalet cook depends on what a ski company or employer wants. Usually the day starts with a cooked breakfast for the ski party, then possibly a packed lunch, tea and cake when hungry skiers get back, possibly canapés later, and a three- or four-course supper. The food does need more than the usual amount of carbohydrate.

Ski companies expect high standards and may ask for sample menus when you apply for chalet cooking jobs. Sometimes the menus are decided in advance and the shopping done locally by someone else; sometimes the cook has to do the shopping.

Perhaps surprisingly, ski companies and agencies rarely ask about language skills - the cooks seem to manage without.

Drama

There are plenty of amateur dramatic and operatic societies in small towns across the UK. If you've always had a hankering to tread the boards, they're a great way to find out more about all the elements of putting on a production. You may be able to volunteer at your local theatre and gain valuable experience that way. Ring them up or check out their website to see if they have a volunteers bank.

Then there are short courses and summer schools. This site lists a wide range of programmes available over the summer holidays:

www.summer-schools.info

Driving

There may be a lot of pressure to minimise car use in an effort to reduce carbon emissions and tackle global warming, but there are still plenty of good reasons for learning to drive.

First, unless you're intending to live in an inner city indefinitely, you may need a driver's licence to get a job; secondly, it will give you independence and you won't have to rely on everyone else to give you lifts everywhere. Even though you might not be able to afford the insurance right now, let alone an actual car, your **gap**-year is an ideal time to take driving lessons.

The test comes in two parts, theory and practical: and you need to pass the theory test before you apply for the practical one. However, you can start learning practical driving before you take the theory part, but to do that you need a provisional driving licence. You need to complete a driving licence application form and a photocard application form D1- available from most post offices. Send the forms, the fee and original documentation confirming your identity such as your passport or birth certificate (make sure you keep a photocopy) and a passport-sized colour photograph to the DVLA.

visit: www.gap-year.com

You also need to check that you are insured for damage to yourself, other cars or other people, and if you are practising in the family car, your parents will have to add cover for you on their insurance.

The DSA (Driving Standards Authority) is responsible for driving tests. However, to avoid duplication all information on learning to drive, including fees, advice on preparing for the test and booking one has been moved to the Direct Gov website:

www.direct.gov.uk/en/Motoring/LearnerAndNewDrivers/LearningToDriveOrRide/index.htm

Theory

The theory test is in two parts: a multiple-choice part and a hazard perception section. You have to pass both. If you pass one and fail the other, you have to do both again.

The multiple-choice is a touch-screen test where you have to get at least 43 out of 50 questions right. You don't have to answer the questions in turn and the computer shows how much time you have left. You can have 15 minutes practice before you start the test properly. If you have special needs you can get extra time for the test - ask for this when you book it.

In the hazard test, you are shown 14 video clips filmed from a car, each containing one or more developing hazards. You have to indicate as soon as you see a hazard developing, which may necessitate the driver taking some action, such as changing speed or direction. The sooner a response is made the higher the score. Test results and feedback information are given within half an hour of finishing. The fee for the standard theory test is currently £31.00.

Your driving school, instructor or local test centre should have an application form, although you can book your test over the phone (0300 200 1122) or online at:
www.direct.gov.uk/en/Motoring/LearnerAndNewDrivers/TheoryTest/DG_4022537

Practical test

You have two years to pass the practical test once you have passed the theory part. The practical test for a car will cost £62.00, unless you choose to take it in the evening or on Saturday, in which case the cost will increase to £75. It's more expensive for a motorbike and the test is now in two modules - module 1 is £10 for both evenings and weekends, module 2 is £70.00 for weekday and £82 for weekend and evening tests. You can book the practical test in the same way as the theory test. The bad news is that the tests are tough and it's quite common to fail twice or more before a pass. The practical test requires candidates to drive on faster roads than before - you'll need to negotiate a dual carriageway as well as a suburban road. You'll fail if you commit more than 15 driving faults. Once you pass your practical test, you can exchange your provisional licence for a full licence.

the gap-year guidebook 2011

Instructors

Of course some unqualified instructors (including parents) are experienced and competent, as are many small driving schools - but some checking out is a good idea if a driving school is not a well-known name. You can make sure that it is registered with the Driving Standards Agency and that the instructor is qualified. AA and BSM charges can be used as a benchmark if you're trying other schools. There's information about choosing an instructor and what qualifications they must have if they're charging you here:
www.direct.gov.uk/en/Motoring/LearnerAndNewDrivers/LearningToDriveOrRide/DG_4022528

Language courses

Even if the job you are applying for doesn't require them, employers are often impressed by language skills. With the growth of global business, most companies like to think of themselves as having international potential at the very least.

If you didn't enjoy language classes at school, that shouldn't necessarily put you off. College courses and evening classes are totally different - or at least they should be. If in doubt, ask to speak to the tutor, or to someone who has already been on the course, before you sign up.

And even if you don't aspire to learn enough to be able to use your linguistic skills in a job, you could still take conversation classes so you can speak a bit of the language when you go abroad on your holidays. It is amazing what a sense of achievement and self confidence you can get when you manage to communicate the simplest things to a local in their own language: such as ordering a meal or buying stamps for your postcards home.

visit: www.gap-year.com

The best way to improve your language skills is to practice speaking; preferably to a native speaker in their own country. But if you don't have the time or the money to go abroad yet, don't worry. There are plenty of places in the UK to learn a wide variety of languages, from Spanish to Somali. We've listed some language institutions in the directory, but also find out what language courses your local college offers, and what evening classes there are locally.

Online learning

There are plenty of online language learning courses for those who are welded semi-permanently to their computers.

You can now get very comprehensive language courses on CD-ROM, which include booklets or pages that can be printed off. The better ones use voice recognition as well, so you can practise your pronunciation. These can also be found in bookstores.

The internet itself is also a good source of language material. There are many courses, some with free access, some that need a very healthy credit card. If all you want is a basic start, then take a look at:

www.bbc.co.uk/languages/

This site offers you the choice of beginner's French, German, Italian, Mandarin, Portuguese, Greek, Spanish, Japanese, Urdu and some other languages, complete with vocabulary lists to download, all for free.

As well as courses, there are translation services, vocabulary lists and topical forums - just do a web search and see how many sites come up. Many are free but some are extremely expensive so check before you sign up.

Practice makes perfect

When you need to practise, find out if there are any native speakers living in your town - you could arrange your own language and cultural evenings.

Terrestrial TV stations run some language learning programmes, usually late at night. If you have satellite or cable TV you can also watch foreign shows though this can be a bit frustrating if you're a beginner. It's best to record the programmes so you can replay any bits that you didn't understand the first time round.

Once you get a bit more advanced then you can try tuning your radio into foreign speech-based shows from the relevant countries. This is also a good way to keep up-to-date with current affairs in your chosen country, as well as keeping up your listening and understanding skills. Subjects are wide-ranging, and there's something to interest everyone.

Most self-teach language tapes have been well received by teachers and reviewers, but can be a bit expensive for the average **gap**-year student. So, you might be glad to hear that, if you have iTunes, you can download language podcasts from the store. Most of these are free and you have the option of subscribing so that new podcasts are automatically downloaded next time you log on.

the gap-year guidebook 2011

Music

Perhaps you always wanted to learn the saxophone, but never quite got round to it? Now would be an ideal time to start. If you're interested, your best bet is to find a good private tutor. Word of mouth is the best recommendation, but some teachers advertise in local papers, and you could also try an online search engine like Musicians' Friend: **www.musiciansfriend.co.uk**

If you already play an instrument, you could broaden your experience by going on a residential course or summer school. These are available for many different ability levels, although they tend to be quite pricey. There's no central info source on the net, as there is for drama courses, but we searched the internet for residential summer music schools and found loads of individual schools offering courses, so there are bound to be some near you. See the directory for more information.

Photography

There are lots of photography courses available, from landscape photography to studio work. Don't kid yourself that a photography course is going to get you a job and earn you pots of money, but there's nothing to stop you enjoying photography as a hobby or sideline.

If you do want to find out more about professional photography you could try contacting local studios and asking about the possibility of spending some time with them as a studio assistant. Another option is to contact your local paper and ask if you can shadow a photographer, so you can get a feel for how they work and perhaps start building a portfolio of your own.

Sport

After all that studying maybe all you want to do is get out there and do something. The same applies if you've been stuck in an office at a computer for most of your working life. If you're the energetic type and hate the thought of spending your **gap**-year stuck behind a desk, why not get active and do some sport? There are sports courses for all types at all levels, from scuba diving for beginners to advanced ski instructor qualification courses. Of course if you manage to get an instructor's qualification you may be able to use it to get a job (see Chapter 8 - Sports).

TEFL

Teaching English as a Foreign Language qualifications are always useful for earning money wherever you travel abroad. The important thing to check is that the qualification you will be gaining is recognised by employers. Most courses should also lead on to help with finding employment. There's more on TEFL courses in Chapter 5 - Working Abroad.

X-rated

If you hated sport at school, try giving it another chance during your **gap**-year - you may be surprised how much you like it. There are plenty of unusual sports to try.

For a real adrenalin rush, go for one of the extreme sports like sky boarding, basically a combination of skydiving and snowboarding - you throw yourself out of a plane wearing a parachute and perform acrobatic stunts on a board.

Or, if you like company when you're battling against the elements, then you could get involved in adventure racing: teams race each other across rugged terrain without using anything with a motor, *eg* skiing, hiking, sea kayaking. Team members have to stay together throughout the race. Raid Gauloises (five person teams, two weeks, five stages, half the teams don't finish!) and Eco-Challenge (ten days, 600km, several stages and an environmental project) are the two most well known adventure race events.

the gap-year guidebook 2011

The annual X Games feature a wide range of extreme sports and take place during one week in summer (including aggressive in-line skating) and another week in winter (including mountain bike racing on snow). Check out their website (**www.expn.go.com**) for the full details.

If you want to get wet, then try diving, kayaking, sailing, surfing, water polo, windsurfing, or white-water rafting.

And if those don't appeal then there's always abseiling, badminton, baseball, basketball, bungee jumping, cave diving, cricket, fencing, football, golf, gymnastics, hang gliding, hockey, horse riding, ice hockey, ice skating, jet skiing, motor racing, mountain biking, mountain boarding, netball, parachuting, polo, rock climbing, rowing, rugby, running, skateboarding, skating, ski jumping, skiing, skydiving, sky surfing, snooker, snow mobiling, snowboarding, squash, stock car racing, tennis or trampolining! If the sport you are interested in isn't listed in our directory then try contacting the relevant national association (eg the LTA for tennis) and asking them for a list of course providers.

Have a look at what's on offer here:
www.extremesportscafe.com/
http://library.thinkquest.org/13857/–

Learning in the UK

Archaeology

Archaeology Abroad
Institute of Archaeology, University College,
31-34 Gordon Square, Bloomsbury,
London, WC1H OPY UK

E: arch.abroad@ucl.ac.uk
T: +44 (0) 20 8537 0849
F: +44 (0) 20 8537 0849
www.britarch.ac.uk/archabroad

For info on digs abroad try the Archaeology Abroad bulletin and web pages.

Council for British Archaeology
St Mary's House,
66 Bootham,
York, YO30 7BZ UK

E: info@britarch.ac.uk
T: +44 (0) 1904 671 417
F: +44 (0) 1904 671 384
www.britarch.ac.uk

CBA's magazine, British Archaeology, contains information about events and courses as well as digs. Reg Charity 287815.

School of Archaeology & Ancient History
University of Leicester,
University Road,
Leicester, LE1 7RH UK

E: arch-anchist@le.ac.uk
T: +44 (0) 116 252 2611
F: +44 (0) 116 252 5005
www.le.ac.uk/archaeology/dl/dl_intro.html

Offers a series of modules in archaeology which can be studied purely for interest, or as part of a programme towards a Certificate in Archaeology.

**University College London -
Institute of Archaeology**
31-34 Gordon Square,
St Pancras,
London, WC1H 0PY UK

E: ioa-ugadmissions@ucl.ac.uk
T: +44 (0) 207 679 7495
F: +44 (0) 20 7383 2572
www.ucl.ac.uk/archaeology/

UCL offers a range of short courses in archaeology many of which are open to members of the public.

**University of Bristol -
Department of Archaeology & Anthropology**
Short Courses, 43 Woodland Road,
Clifton,
Bristol, BS8 1UU UK

E: arch-lifelong@bristol.ac.uk
T: +44 (0) 117 954 6070
F: +44 (0) 117 954 6067
www.bristol.ac.uk/archanth/continuing/shortcourses

A variety of short courses offered, including: anthropology, archaeology, egyptology, history, Latin, Minoan, Roman and techniques. They also have a new one week intensive 'get started in archaeology' course.

the gap-year guidebook 2011

Art

Burton Manor
The Village,
Burton,
Neston, CH64 5SJ UK

T: +44 (0) 151 336 5172
F: +44 (0) 151 336 6586
www.burtonmanor.com

Various residential courses available in art and other subjects.

Camberwell College of Arts
Peckham Road,
Camberwell,
London, SE5 8UF UK

E: enquiries@camberwell.arts.ac.uk
T: +44 (0) 20 7514 6302
F: +44 (0) 20 7514 6310
www.camberwell.arts.ac.uk

Offers various short courses in art and art related subjects.

Heatherley School of Art
75 Lots Road,
Chelsea,
London, SW10 0RN UK

E: info@heatherleys.org
T: +44 (0) 20 7351 4190
F: +44 (0) 20 7351 6945
www.heatherleys.org

Offers various summer courses in art as well as part-time and full-time courses.

The Prince's Drawing School
19-22 Charlotte Road,
Broadgate,
London, EC2A 3SG UK

E: admin@princesdrawingschool.org
T: +44 (0) 20 7613 8568
F: +44 (0) 20 7613 8599
www.princesdrawingschool.org

The Prince's Drawing School is an educational charity (No. 1101538) dedicated to teaching drawing from observation. Daytime, evening and summer school courses are run for artists and the general public.

University College London -
Slade School of Fine Art
Slade Studios,
Woburn Square, Bloomsbury,
London, WC1H 0AB UK

E: slade.enquiries@ucl.ac.uk
T: +44 (0) 20 7679 2313
www.ucl.ac.uk/slade

The Slade Summer School for Fine Art runs each summer.

University of the Arts -
Central Saint Martins College of Art and Design
Southampton Row,
Holborn,
London, WC1B 4AP UK

E: info@csm.arts.ac.uk
T: +44 (0)20 7514 7022
F: +44 (0)20 7514 7254
www.csm.arts.ac.uk

Short courses available in fashion, photography, graphic design, textiles and more.

visit: www.gap-year.com

University of the Arts -
Wimbledon College of Art
Main Building,
Merton Hall Road, Wimbledon,
London, SW19 3QA UK

E: info@wimbledon.arts.ac.uk
T: +44 (0) 20 7514 9641
F: +44 (0) 20 7514 9642
www.wimbledon.arts.ac.uk

They have a series of short courses in fashion, etching, filmmaking, sewing and more.

University of the Arts London -
Chelsea College of Art and Design
16 John Islip Street,
Westminster,
London, SW1P 4JU UK

E: shortcourses@chelsea.arts.ac.uk
T: +44 (0) 20 7514 7751
F: +44 (0) 20 7514 7777
www.chelsea.arts.ac.uk

Short courses available in interior design, drawing, painting and life drawing.

University of Wales Institute -
Cardiff School of Art and Design
Howard Gardens,
Cardiff, CF24 0SP UK

E: csad@uwic.ac.uk
F: +44 (0) 29 2041 6944
www.csad.uwic.ac.uk

They run a ten week summer school programme designed to introduce you to the variety of art and design.

Cookery

Ashburton Cookery School
Hare's Lane Cottage,
76 East Street,
Ashburton, TQ13 7AX UK

E: info@ashburtoncookeryschool.co.uk
T: +44 (0) 1364 652784
F: +44 (0) 1364 653825
www.ashburtoncookeryschool.co.uk

Cookery courses available from one to five days.

Belle Isle School of Cookery
Lisbellaw,
Enniskillen, BT94 5HG UK

www.irishcookeryschool.com

Essential Cooking is an intensive four week course designed for people who are interested in learning the key skills for a gap-year job in cooking

CookAbility
Sherlands,
54 Stonegallows,
Taunton, TA1 5JS UK

E: cookability@hotmail.com
T: +44 (0) 1823 461374
F: +44 (0) 1884 432419
www.residentialcookery.com

CookAbilty caters for all types of gap-year students. Whether you have set your sights on a chalet cooking season, self-catering at university or a new life skill, then this is the place to become inspired in the culinary arts.

the gap-year guidebook 2011

TANTE MARIE
50 YEARS TRAINING THE WORLD'S TOP CHEFS

Gordon Ramsay's Tante Marie School of Cookery, Woodham House, Carlton Road, Woking GU21 4HF
T: +44 (0) 1483 726957
E: info@tantemarie.co.uk
W: www.tantemarie.co.uk

Tante Marie School of Cookery, now under the ownership of Gordon Ramsay, is the UK's oldest independent cookery school and is now the only school in the world able to award both the internationally acclaimed Cordon Bleu Diploma, and the CTH Level 4 Diploma in Professional Culinary Arts – one of the world's highest rated practical cookery qualifications, worth 96 points on the Qualifications Credit Framework. This means that students attending the Diploma course during their gap-year, may earn valuable credit towards future training.

In addition to our Diploma course, we run a four-week Essential Skills course and an 11-week Cordon Bleu Certificate course. Both of these courses are popular with gap-year students and offer excellent employment prospects with skiing and yachting agencies and other gap-year employers.

At Tante Marie, we don't just teach you how to cook a week's worth of menu's to get you through your ski season, or to give you a selection of recipes you can follow. We teach much more than that! We focus on teaching you the skills and knowledge so that you can create your own dishes and menus, run your own kitchen in a profitable and organised manner, and fully understand the complex and intricate art of cooking. With courses designed by Gordon Ramsay and taught by our chef instructors, Tante Marie graduates are in demand all over the world, and many of our graduates go on to run their own businesses, from restaurants, events design companies and pubs, to food journalism, photography and PR. The options are endless! Come and take up the challenge!

Cookery at The Grange
The Grange,
Whatley,
Frome, BA11 3JU UK

E: info@cookeryatthegrange.co.uk
T: +44 (0) 1373 836 579
www.cookeryatthegrange.co.uk

Cookery at the Grange in Somerset offers immensely popular four week residential cookery courses. The course leads on to cooking for family and friends or to working professionally - in chalets, on boats or outside catering - ideal for generating a little cash.

Cookery School at Little Portland Street
15B Little Portland Street,
London, W1W 8BW UK

E: info@cookeryschool.co.uk
www.cookeryschool.co.uk

Cookery School at Little Portland Street has something to offer all food lovers: check out the huge array of classes on offer on our website.

Cutting Edge Food & Wine School
Hackwood Farm,
Robertsbridge, TN32 5ER UK

Based in a 16th century farmhouse you will be taught in small groups by Cutting Edge London Chef, who has an excellent reputation.

Edinburgh School of Food and Wine
The Coach House,
Newliston,
Edinburgh, EH29 9EB UK

E: info@esfw.com
T: +44 (0) 131 333 5001
www.esfw.com

Courses of interest to gappers are the four week Intensive Certificate Course which is geared towards chalet work, and the one week Survival Course which is ideally suited to those leaving home for the first time.

Food of Course
Middle Farm House,
Sutton,
Shepton Mallet, BA4 6QF UK

E: info@foodofcourse.co.uk
T: +44 (0) 1749 860116
F: +44 (0) 1749 860441
www.foodofcourse.co.uk

A four-week residential course providing all essential skills to cook in a ski chalet, on a yacht or in holiday homes worldwide.

Gordon Ramsay's Tante Marie School of Cookery
Woodham House,
Carlton Road,
Woking, Surrey GU21 4HF UK

E: info@tantemarie.co.uk
T: +44 (0) 1483 726957
F: +44 (0) 1483 724173
www.tantemarie.co.uk

Tante Marie, accredited by the BAC and under the ownership of Gordon Ramsay, offers gap-year courses ranging from one to 11 weeks.

Leiths School of Food & Wine, 16-20 Wendell Road, Shepherd's Bush, London W12 9RT
T: +44 (0) 20 8749 6400
E: info@leiths.com W: www.leiths.com

Leiths School of Food and Wine is a leading London cookery school for professional and amateur cooks. Learning to cook in your gap year is the perfect time to acquire an essential life skill. Whether cooking for family and friends or using your new skills to earn money at home or abroad, knowing how to cook will always be an advantage. Leiths runs a 4 week course starting in August each year which teaches essential cookery skills and a 10 week course starting at the end of September each year which will build your cookery skills and confidence. Both courses are exam based certificate courses which include health and safety and food hygiene certificates as well as offering budgeting, healthy eating and menu planning. Leiths List our agency for cooks, can help place you in a suitable job once qualified - further information can be found under 'working in the UK' in this book. Alternatively, Leiths run 1 week cookery classes throughout the year which are ideal for university survival and teach you to cook delicious simple food. There are also a number of one- day classes, from knife skills to chocolate workshops for interested enthusiasts. Whether you are an aspiring professional or enthusiastic amateur, you will leave Leiths with the essential skills and confidence necessary to be a culinary success. Contact Leiths for a prospectus now on +44 (0) 20 8749 6400 or view all our courses at www.leiths.com alternatively for any other questions please email us info@leiths.com

Le Cordon Bleu
114 Marylebone Lane,
Mayfair,
London, W1U 2HH UK

E: london@cordonbleu.edu
T: +44 (0) 20 7935 3503
F: +44 (0) 20 7935 7621
www.lcblondon.com

Le Cordon Bleu has courses ranging from their famous diplomas in 'Cuisine and Pâtisserie' to shorter courses in techniques, seasonal cooking, essentials and healthy eating.

Leiths School of Food & Wine
16-20 Wendell Road,
Shepherd's Bush,
London, W12 9RT UK

E: info@leiths.com
T: +44 (0) 20 8749 6400
www.leiths.com

Learn how to cook and earn money from it on your gap year. Leiths certificate cookery courses will give you the confidence and skill to achieve this.

Murray School of Cookery
Glenbervie House,
Holt Pound,
Farnham, GU10 4LE UK

E: info@cookeryschool.net
T: +44 (0) 1420 23049
F: +44 (0) 1420 23049
www.cookeryschool.net

The Murray School of Cookery offers two non-residential courses for gappers, including a one week Chalet Chef Course which teaches students how to be a successful chalet host.

Orchards Cookery
The Orchards,
Salford Priors,
Nr Evesham, WR11 8UU UK

T: +44 (0) 1789 490 259

Specialises in training and recruiting chalet cooks. Courses are one or two weeks long, residential and great fun with 24 students trained in three separate kitchens.

The Avenue Cookery School
74 Chartfield Avenue,
Putney,
London, SW15 6HQ UK

E: info@theavenuecookeryschool.com
T: +44 (0) 208 788 3025
F: +44 (0) 208 788 3025
www.theavenuecookeryschool.com

Offer courses aimed specifically at gap-year students, chalet assistants and undergraduates.

The Bertinet Kitchen
12 St Andrew's Terrace,
Bath, BA1 2QR UK

E: info@thebertinetkitchen.com
www.thebertinetkitchen.com

They run a beginners' course for those who have no clue what a kitchen is actually for.

The Cordon Vert
Parkdale,
Dunham Road,
Altrincham, WA14 4QG UK

E: jane@cordonvert.co.uk
T: +44 (0) 161 925 2014
www.cordonvert.co.uk

Cookery school run by the Vegetarian Society (Charity No. 259358). One and two day courses available.

The Gables School of Cookery
Pipers Lodge,
Bristol Road,
Falfield, GL12 8DF UK

E: info@thegablesschoolofcookery.co.uk
T: +44 (0) 1454 260 444
www.thegablesschoolofcookery.co.uk

Achieve your dreams through a professional four week cookery course where you can learn the skills required to work your gap-year in a ski resort or on a yacht.

Webbe's Cookery School
17 Tower Street,
Rye, East Sussex TN31 7AT UK

www.webbesrestaurants.co.uk

Respected five-day, complete, hands-on, intensive, cutting edge foundation cooking certificate course for healthy eating and cooking for friends on a budget at university and beyond.

Driving

AA (Automobile Association)
Contact Centre, Lambert House,
Stockport Road,
Cheadle, SK8 2DY UK

T: +44 (0) 161 495 8945
F: +44 (0) 161 488 7544
www.theaa.co.uk

The AA website has lots of useful information on driving in the UK and abroad, including stuff about breakdown, insurance and travel planning. You can find hotels, good places to stop whilst driving and you're even able to find out about up-to-date traffic news.

Driving Standards Agency
The Axis Building,
112 Upper Parliament Street,
Nottingham, NG1 6LP UK

E: central.operations@dsa.gsi.gov.uk
T: +44 (0) 115 936 6449
F: +44 (0) 115 936 6881
www.dsa.gov.uk

Information on theory and practical driving tests, fees and other relevant information.

DVLA (Driver and Vehicle Licencing Agency)
Swansea, SA6 7JL UK

www.dvla.gov.uk

UK government agency responsible for driving licences and vehicle registration.

visit: www.gap-year.com

RAC Motoring Services   www.rac.co.uk
8 Surrey Street,
Norwich, NR1 3NG UK

The RAC website has lots of useful information on driving in the UK and abroad, with breakdown, insurance and other services.

Fashion & Design

Leicester College - St Margaret's   E: info@leicestercollege.ac.uk
St Margaret's Campus,   T: +44 (0) 116 224 2240
St John Street,   www.leicestercollege.ac.uk
Leicester, LE1 3WL UK

Has part-time courses in footwear, fabrics and pattern cutting.

Newcastle College   E: enquiries@ncl-coll.ac.uk
Rye Hill Campus,   T: +44 (0) 191 200 4000
Scotswood Road,   www.ncl-coll.ac.uk
Newcastle upon Tyne, NE4 7SA UK

Short courses available in fashion illustration, bridalwear design, textile dyeing and printing, pattern cutting and embroidery.

The Fashion Retail Academy   E: info@fashionretailacademy.ac.uk
15 Gresse Street,   T: +44 (0) 20 7307 2345
Soho,   www.fashionretailacademy.ac.uk
London, W1T 1QL UK

Short courses available in visual merchandising, styling, PR, buying and range planning there are also tailor-made courses for those wishing to run their own retail business.

University of the Arts -   E: shortcourses@fashion.arts.ac.uk
London College of Fashion   T: +44 (0) 20 7514 7566
20 John Princes Street,   www.fashion.arts.ac.uk
Mayfair,
London, W1G 0BJ UK

Short courses available in pattern cutting, principles of styling techniques, film and TV make up, childrenswear and maternitywear, retro fashion design and how to recycle your second hand clothes.

University of the Arts - London Milan Courses   T: +44 (0) 20 7514 7015
Short Course Office, Central Saint Martins,   F: +44 (0)20 7514 7016
10 Back Hill, Clerkenwell,   www.london-milan-courses.com
London, EC1R 5EN UK

Short courses in London and Milan in fashion design, fashion styling, graphic design, interior and product design.

the gap-year guidebook 2011

University of Westminster -
School of Media, Arts & Design
Watford Road,
Northwick Park,
Harrow, HA1 3TP UK

E: mad@wmin.ac.uk
T: +44 (0) 20 7911 5944
F: +44 (0) 20 7911 5943
www.wmin.ac.uk

Westminster offers a range of short courses in fashion, including fashion design, textile printing, and pattern cutting.

Film, Theatre & Drama

DramaScene
Kemp House,
152-160 City Road, St Luke's,
London, EC1V 2DW UK

E: info@dramascene.com
T: +44 (0) 20 7193 6693
www.dramascene.com

Weekend and evening courses in drama

Metropolitan Film School
Ealing Studios,
Ealing Green,
London, W5 5EP UK

E: info@metfilmschool.co.uk
T: +44 (0) 20 8280 9119
F: +44 (0) 20 8280 9111
www.metfilmschool.co.uk

Practical courses for aspiring filmmakers. Short courses and one year intensive course available.

RADA (Royal Academy of Dramatic Art)
62-64 Gower Street,
Bloomsbury,
London, WC1E 6ED UK

E: enquiries@rada.ac.uk
T: +44 (0) 20 7636 7076
F: +44 (0) 20 7323 3865
www.rada.org

This legendary drama college runs a variety of summer school courses.

The Central School of Speech and Drama
Embassy Theatre,
Eton Avenue, Belsize Park,
London, NW3 3HY UK

E: enquiries@cssd.ac.uk
T: +44 (0) 20 7722 8183
F: +44 (0) 20 7722 4132
www.cssd.ac.uk

Central offers short courses in acting, singing, stand-up comedy, puppetry, cabaret and burlesque, and directing.

The Oxford School of Drama
Sansomes Farm Studios,
Woodstock,
Oxford, OX20 1ER UK

E: info@oxforddrama.ac.uk
T: +44 (0) 1993 812883
F: +44 (0) 1993 811220
www.oxforddrama.ac.uk

The Oxford School of Drama runs a six-month Foundation Course, including acting, voice, movement, music and stage fighting. Registered Charity No. 1072770.

visit: www.gap-year.com

The Year Out Group
Queensfield,
28 King's Road,
Easterton, SN10 4PX UK

E: info@yearoutgroup.org
T: +44 (0) 1380 816696
www.yearoutgroup.org

See main entry under volunteering.

Year Out Drama
Stratford upon Avon
Further Education College,
The Willows North,
Alcester Road,
Stratford upon Avon, CV37 9QR UK

E: yearoutdrama@stratford.ac.uk
T: +44 (0) 1789 266 245
www.yearoutdrama.co.uk

Full-time practical drama course with a unique Company feel; work with theatre professionals to develop a wide range of skills; perform in a variety of productions; write and direct your own work; benefit from close contact with the RSC.

Land studies

Berkshire College of Agriculture
Hall Place,
Burchetts Green,
Maidenhead, SL6 6QR UK

E: enquiries@bca.ac.uk
T: +44 (0) 1628 824 444
www.bca.ac.uk
F: +44 (0) 1628 824 695

Short courses in wildlife care, animal behaviour, lambing management, poultry breeding, BHS stages 1 & 2, BHS teaching test, pasture management, horticulture, garden design, hedge laying, wildlife gardening, hurdle making, machinery management, tractor management and more ...

Bishop Burton College
York Road,
Bishop Burton, HU17 8QG UK

F: +44 (0) 1964 553 101
www.bishopb-college.ac.uk

Short courses available in tractor driving, pest control, tree felling, sheep shearing, animal husbandry and more...

Capel Manor College
Bullsmoor Lane,
Enfield, EN1 4RQ UK

E: enquiries@capel.ac.uk
F: +44 (0)1992 717544
www.capel.ac.uk

They have short courses in lorinery, flower arranging, CAD in garden design, practical gardening, aboriculture, botanical illustration, leathercraft and more ...

Chichester College
Westgate Fields,
Chichester, PO19 1SB UK

F: +44 (0) 1243 539 481
www.chichester.ac.uk

Short courses available in animal care, farming, bushcraft, coppicing, hedgerow planting and managment, watercourse management, moorland management and more ...

the gap-year guidebook 2011

Plumpton College
Ditchling Road,
Lewes, BN7 3AE UK

F: +44 (0) 1273 890 071
www.plumpton.ac.uk

Courses available in animal care, welding, tractor driving, machinery, wine trade, aboriculture, chainsaw, bushcraft, pond management, wildlife, woodcraft and more...

Rodbaston College
Penkridge, ST19 5PH UK

E: rodenquiries@rodbaston.ac.uk
F: +44 (0) 1785 715701
www.southstaffs.ac.uk

Short courses available in keeping chickens, tractor driving, animal care, hurdle fencing, machinery, pest control and chainsaws.

Royal Agricultural College
Cirencester, GL7 6JS UK

F: +44 (0) 1285 650 219
www.rac.ac.uk

Have a two day residential taster course in April which gives an insight into the career options in land-based industries.

Sparsholt College
Westley Lane,
Sparsholt,
Winchester, SO21 2NF UK

E: enquiry@sparsholt.ac.uk
T: +44 (0) 1962 776441
www.sparsholt.ac.uk

Have part-time courses in forklift operation, tractor driving, health & safety, horticulture, floristy, landscaping and more.

The Open College of Equine Studies
Boxted,
Bury St Edmunds, IP29 4JT UK

E: info@equinestudies.co.uk
F: +44 (0) 1787 280 278
www.equinestudies.co.uk

Have a series of short courses available in horse training, estate management, business etc.

Warwickshire College - Moreton Morrell
Moreton Morrell Campus,
Warwick, CV35 9BL UK

F: +44 (0) 1926 318 300
www.warkscol.ac.uk

Have taster days in land-based studies. Also have an Equine Centre and the first purpose built School of Farriery in the UK.

Languages

Berlitz - London
Lincoln House,
296-302 High Holborn, Holborn,
London, WC1V 7JH UK

T: +44 (0) 20 7611 9640
F: +44 (0) 20 7611 9656
www.berlitz.co.uk

International language school. Intense courses in Chinese French, German, Italian, Japanese, Portuguese, Russian and Spanish available. Other schools in the UK can be found in Birmingham, Brighton, Bristol, Edinburgh, Manchester and Oxford.

Canning House
2 Belgrave Square,
Belgravia,
London, SW1X 8PJ UK

E: culture@canninghouse.com
T: +44 (0) 20 7235 2303
F: +44 (0) 20 7838 9258
www.canninghouse.com

Canning House runs evening courses in Brazilian Portuguese, as well as a wide range of events on Latin America, Spain and Portugal

International House London
Unity Wharf,
13 Mill Street, Bermondsey,
London, SE1 2BH UK

E: affiliates@ihworld.co.uk
T: +44 (0) 207 394 6580
F: +44 (0) 207 394 2149
www.ihworld.com

Worldwide network of language schools offering courses in Arabic, Chinese, French, German, Italian, Japanese and Spanish.

Italian Cultural Institute in London
39 Belgrave Square,
Belgravia,
London, SW1X 8NX UK

E: icilondon@esteri.it
T: +44 (0) 20 7235 1461
F: +44 (0) 20 7235 4618
www.icilondon.esteri.it/IIC_Londra

The Italian Cultural Institute has a wide programme of Italian language courses as well as a mass of information about Italy and its culture.

Languages @ Lunchtime
Modern Foreign Languages Section,
Hetherington Building,
Bute Gardens,
Glasgow, G12 8RS UK

E: mfl@gla.ac.uk
T: +44 (0) 141 330 6521
F: +44 (0) 141 330 4114

www.gla.ac.uk/services/languagecentre/modernforeignlanguages/

Small informal classes run at Glasgow University for two hours per week over 18 weeks.

OISC

Oxford International Study Centre, 7 St Aldates, Oxford OX1 1BS
T: 01865 201009
E: info@oxintstudycentre.com W: www.oxintstudycentre.com

Studying abroad is a valuable opportunity for students to explore their interests and widen their experience. It is also an opportunity to think about study and career choices for the future.

Oxford International Study Centre is able to arrange tailor-made programmes in Oxford, itself an inspiring and culturally fascinating city, with some of the best teachers in the world. We also work with overseas partner schools worldwide and can arrange for students to be placed in schools as language assistants and/or to take part in a customised travel itinerary.

Programmes in Oxford include:
- Languages...all European languages and also Chinese and Japanese;
- English Literature, History and Culture;
- Classical Languages (Latin, Greek) and Classical Civilisation;
- Art and Art History;
- Theatre Studies and Creative Writing;
- Business and Marketing.

A social and cultural programme runs throughout the year, and daily in July and August. This is an opportunity for gap-year students to meet students from all over the world who are taking programmes at OISC.

It is also possible for students to (re)take exams as part of their gap-year, *eg* A Levels, GCSE, IB, Oxford and Cambridge University preparation, and the gap-year courses or projects.

We can also help students find paid or voluntary work in Oxford alongside their programme.

Since the gap-year programmes are designed individually for each student fees vary enormously. If you would like an estimate please email us with further information about your plans.

visit: www.gap-year.com

Oxford International Study Centre
7 St Aldates,
Oxford, OX1 1BS UK

E: info@oxintstudycentre.com
F: 01865 201006
www.oxintstudycentre.com

Oxford International Study Centre arranges a wide range of programmes in Oxford. We can also arrange for students to work as language assistants overseas.

The Japan Foundation - London Language Centre
6th Floor, Russell Square House,
10-12 Russell Square, Bloomsbury,
London, WC1B 5EH UK

E: info.language@jpf.org.uk
T: +44 (0) 20 7436 6698
F: +44 (0) 20 7323 4888
www.jpf.org.uk/language

The Japan Foundation London Language Centre provides courses in Japanese. Also has regular newsletter and resource library.

University of London - School of Oriental and African Studies
Thornhaugh Street,
Russell Square, Bloomsbury,
London, WC1H 0XG UK

E: languages@soas.ac.uk
T: +44 (0) 20 7898 4888
F: +44 (0) 20 7898 4889
www.soas.ac.uk

The SOAS (part of the University of London) runs courses for numerous African and Asian languages. Small classes of not more than 12.

Music

BIMM - Brighton Institute of Modern Music
7 Rock Place,
Brighton, BN2 1PF UK

E: info@bimm.co.uk
www.bimm.co.uk

Various part-time courses available, also summer schools, for bass, drums, guitar, vocals, songwriting and live sound/tour management.

Dartington International Summer School
The Barn,
Dartington Hall,
Totnes, TQ9 6DE UK

E: summerschool@dartington.org
T: +44 (0) 1803 847 080
F: +44 (0) 1803 847 087
www.dartington.org/summer-school

Dartington International Summer School (Registered Charity No. 279756) is both a festival and a music school. Teaching and performing takes place all day, every day.

Lake District Summer Music
Stricklandgate House,
92 Stricklandgate,
Kendal, LA9 4PU UK

E: info@ldsm.org.uk
T: +44 (0) 845 6 44 21 44
F: +44 (0) 8456 442506
www.ldsm.org.uk

The Lake District Summer Music School is an ensemble-based course for string players and pianists intending to pursue careers as professional musicians. Registered Charity no 516350.

London Music School
9-13 Osborn Street,
Whitechapel,
London, E1 6TD UK

E: music@londonmusicschool.com
T: +44 (0) 20 8986 7885
www.tlms.co.uk

The London Music School offers a Diploma in Music Technology, open to anyone with musical ability aged 17 or over. The course explores professional recording and you get to use a 24-track studio.

London School of Sound
35 Britannia Row,
Islington,
London, N1 8QH UK

E: info@londonschoolofsound.co.uk
T: +44 (0) 20 7354 7337
www.londonschoolofsound.co.uk

Based in the recording studio previously owned by Pink Floyd, we offer part and full-time courses of between five weeks and two years in music production, sound engineering and DJ skills.

Music Worldwide Drum Camp
Music Worldwide Ltd, 4 Dencora Apartments,
Chapel Field East,
Norwich, NR2 1SF UK

E: gary@musicworldwide.org
T: +44 (0) 1603 626003
www.musicworldwide.org

Drum Camp is an annual worldwide percussion event in Norfolk specialising in world rhythms and drum and dance programs. Offers an amazing variety of classes over four days, in music, singing and dance.

NLMS Music Summer School
5 Thame Road,
Sydenham,
Chinnor, OX39 4LA UK

E: brochure@nlmsmusic-summerschool.co.uk
T: +44 (0) 1844 354 083
F: +44 (0) 1844 354 083
www.nlmsmusic-summerschool.co.uk

Each year over 100 enthusiastic adult amateur musicians get together for a week of enjoyment.

North London Piano School
78 Warwick Avenue,
Edgware, HA8 8UJ UK

F: +44 (0) 20 8366 9665
www.learn-music.com/nlps/index.htm

The North London Piano School offers a residential Summer Course.

The British Kodály Academy
c/o 13 Midmoor Road,
Wimbledon,
London, SW19 4JD UK

E: enquiries@britishkodalyacademy.org
T: +44 (0) 208 971 2062
F: +44 (0) 208 946 6561
www.britishkodalyacademy.org

A registered charity (No. 326552) working towards the improvement of music education in the UK. They run various music courses for teachers and young children but also have courses for those wishing to improve their skills.

visit: www.gap-year.com

The DJ Academy Organisation
1 Damaskfield,
Worcester, WR4 0HY UK

E: office@djacademy.org.uk
www.djacademy.org.uk

Offer an eight-week part time DJ course (in various cities in the UK), private tuition, one day superskills course, the ultimate mobile DJ course and the superclub experience.

The Recording Workshop
Unit 10, Buspace Studios,
Conlan Street, Kensal Town,
London, W10 5AP UK

E: recordingworks@btconnect.com
T: +44 (0) 20 896 88 222
F: +44 (0) 20 7460 3164
www.recordwk.dircon.co.uk

The Recording Workshop offer part time and full time courses on all aspects of music production, sound engineering and music technology.

UK Songwriting Festival
Bath Spa University,
Newton Park,
Bath, BA2 9BN UK

T: +44 (0) 1225 876 133
www.uksongwritingfestival.com

This festival is a five-day event held at Bath Spa University every August. The Songwriting Workshop includes daily lectures on the craft of songwriting, small group sessions, live band sessions and an acoustic live recording on CD. Includes studio sessions with a producer.

Photography

Brook School of Photography
113 Penn Hill Avenue,
Poole, BH14 9L9 UK

E: brookstudio@btinternet.com
www.brookschoolofphotography.co.uk

Offer portrait and wedding photography courses and workshop diploma.

Digitalmasterclass
105 Barton Road,
Dover, CT16 2LX UK

E: brian@digitalmasterclass.co.uk
www.digitalmasterclass.co.uk

Small group classes in digital photography for beginners and those wishing to improve their basic skills.

Experience Seminars
Unit 1-4, Hill Farm,
Wennington,
Huntingdon, PE28 2LU UK

E: info@experience-seminars.co.uk
T: +44 (0) 1487 772804
F: +44 (0) 1487 772809
www.experience-seminars.co.uk

Experience Seminars hosts a range of workshops throughout the UK, which are designed to provide a fast track way of learning photography and digital imaging techniques.

London School of Photography
Coaching & Training,
77 Oxford Street, Soho,
London, W1D 2ES UK

E: lsptraining@yahoo.com
T: +44 (0) 20 7659 2085
www.lsptraining.com

Short courses available in digital photography, photojournalism, as well as travel, adventure and street photography. Small classes of up to eight people. One to one training also available.

Photo Opportunity Ltd
Unit 8, Cedar Way,
Camley Street, Camden Town,
London, NW1 0PD UK

E: chris@chrisbellphoto.demon.co.uk
T: +44 (0) 20 7388 4500
F: +44 (0) 20 7388 4119
www.photoopportunity.co.uk

Courses offered lasting from one to five days in length. Tailored to suit your own particular needs and classes are small.

Photofusion
17a Electric Lane,
Brixton, SW9 8LA UK

E: info@photofusion.org
www.photofusion.org

This independent photography resource centre, situated in Brixton, offers digital photography courses.

Picture Weddings -
Digital wedding photography workshops
2 Farriers Mews, Bourton Grange,
Bourton,
Swindon, SN6 8HZ UK

E: info@pictureweddings.co.uk
T: (+44) 01793 780501
www.pictureweddings.co.uk

Fast-track workshops in digital wedding photography.

Shoot Experience Ltd
32b Kingsland Rd,
Hackney, E2 8DA UK

E: hello@shootexperience.com
www.shootexperience.com

Offer fun photography workshops and courses in London

Simon Watkinson Photo Training
The Spout Farmhouse Studio,
Reapsmoor,
Longnor near Buxton, SK17 0LL UK

E: info@swphototraining.co.uk
T: +44 (0) 1298 687477
www.swphototraining.co.uk

Offer a range of courses for beginners upwards, including landscape, portraits, weddings, and courses in the Dales and the Lake district

The Photography School
Oakview House, 1 Newlands Avenue,
Caversham,
Reading, RG4 8NS UK

E: info@thephotographyschool.co.uk
T: +44 (0) 118 901 7272
www.thephotographyschool.co.uk

Offers intensive photography courses for beginners and professionals.

The Royal Photographic Society
Fenton House,
122 Wells Road,
Bath, BA2 3AH UK

E: reception@rps.org
T: +44 (0) 1225 325 733
www.rps.org/workshops

Holds photography courses, from landscape photography to studio work, throughout the year.

The Trained Eye
The Studios, Luckings Estate,
Magpie Lane,
Coleshill, HP7 0LS UK

E: info@thetrainedeye.co.uk
T: +44 (0)1494 353637
www.thetrainedeye.co.uk

Offer creative courses in wedding and portrait photography, for amateurs or advanced photographers to improve their skills.

Sport

BASP UK Ltd
20 Lorn Drive,
Glencoe, PH49 4HR UK

E: skipatrol@basp.org.uk
www.basp.org.uk

BASP offers First Aid and Safety Training courses designed specifically for the outdoor user, suitable for all NGB Awards.

Big Squid Scuba Diving Training and Travel
Unit 2F, Clapham North Arts Centre,
26-32 Voltaire Road, Clapham,
London, SW4 6DH UK

E: info@bigsquid.co.uk
T: +44 (0) 20 7627 0700
www.bigsquid.co.uk

Big Squid offers a variety of dive courses using the PADI and TDI systems of diver education.

British Hang Gliding & Paragliding Association Ltd
The Old Schoolroom,
Loughborough Road,
Leicester, LE4 5PJ UK

E: office@bhpa.co.uk
T: +44 (0) 116 261 1322
F: +44 (0) 116 261 1323
www.bhpa.co.uk

The BHPA oversees the standards of instructor training and runs coaching course for pilots. They also list all approved schools in the field of paragliding, hang gliding and parascending.

British Mountaineering Council
The Old Church, 177-179 Burton Road,
West Didsbury,
Manchester, M20 2BB UK

E: office@thebmc.co.uk
T: +44 (0) 161 445 6111
F: +44 (0) 161 445 4500
www.thebmc.co.uk

BMC travel insurance covers a range of activities and is designed by experts to be free from unreasonable exclusions or restrictions, for peace of mind wherever you travel.

British Offshore Sailing School - BOSS
Hamble Point Marina, School Lane,
Hamble,
Southampton, SO31 4NB UK

T: +44 (0) 23 8045 7733
F: +44 (0) 23 8045 6744
www.boss-sail.co.uk

BOSS offers complete RYA shore-based and practical training courses, also women only courses, from Hamble Point Marina.

British Sub Aqua Club
Telford's Quay,
South Pier Road,
Ellesmere Port, CH65 4FL UK

E: postmaster@bsac.com
T: +44 (0) 151 350 6200
F: +44 (0) 151 350 6215
www.bsac.com

Why not discover scuba diving or snorkelling during your gap-year?

CricketCoachMaster Academy
2 Bolsover Close,
Long Hanborough,
Witney, OX29 8RA UK

E: garypalmer123@btinternet.com
T: +44 (0) 1993 880 471
www.ccmacademy.co.uk

The CCM Academy has a coaching programme to further develop players with the recognised potential to play at county and international level.

Curling in Kent
Fenton's Rink, Dundale Farm,
Dundale Road,
Tunbridge Wells, TN3 9AQ UK

E: info@fentonsrink.co.uk
T: +44 (0) 1892 826 004
F: +44 (0) 1892 823 121
www.fentonsrink.co.uk

Come to Fenton's Rink and try your hand at this exciting Olympic sport. New season begins 1st October.

Earth Events
Franks Yard, Baileys Hard,
Beaulieu,
Brockenhurst, SO42 7YF UK

E: info@earth-events.co.uk
T: +44 (0) 1590 612 377
www.newforestactivities.co.uk

Organises group activities such as canoeing, rope work, cycling and climbing. Also offer environmental courses in the New Forest.

Explorers Tours
8 Minster Court,
Tuscam Way,
Camberley, GU15 3YY UK

E: dive@explorers.co.uk
T: +44 (0) 845 644 7090
F: +44 (0) 1276 406 854
www.explorers.co.uk

Learn to dive. Destinations include Thailand, the Red Sea, Maldives and the Galapagos Islands.

Flybubble Paragliding
1 Manor Close,
Ringmer,
Lewes, BN8 5PA UK

T: +44 (0) 1273 812 442
www.flybubble.co.uk

A paragliding school registered with the British Hang Gliding and Paragliding Association (BHPA).

Glasgow Ski & Snowboard Centre
Bellahouston Park,
16 Drumbreck Road,
Glasgow, G41 5BW UK

E: info@ski-glasgow.org
T: +44 (0) 141 427 4991
F: +44 (0) 141 427 3679
www.ski-glasgow.org

Learn to ski, improve your existing skills or learn to snowboard. Fully qualified instructors waiting to teach you.

Green Dragons
Warren Barn Farm,
Slines Oak Road,
Woldingham, CR3 7HN UK

E: fly@greendragons.co.uk
T: 01883 652 666
F: 01883 652 600
www.greendragons.co.uk

Paragliding and hang gliding centre. You do not need any experience or knowledge, just the desire to fly and follow your instructor's guidance on positions for take off, time spent in the air and landing.

Jubilee Sailing Trust
Hazel Road,
Woolston,
Southampton, SO19 7GB UK

E: info@jst.org.uk
T: +44 (0) 23 8044 9108
F: +44 (0) 23 8044 9145
www.jst.org.uk

Tall Ships Sailing Trust. Join their JST Youth Leadership@Sea Scheme, no sailing experience needed. Registered Charity No. 277810.

London Fencing Club
Finsbury Leisure Centre,
Norman Street, St Luke's,
London, EC1V 3QN UK

T: +44 (0)7951 414409
www.londonfencingclub.co.uk

Fencing tuition available in various centres in London - beginners to advanced training available.

the gap-year guidebook 2011

London Scuba Diving School
Raby's Barn,
Newchapel Road,
Lingfield, RH7 6LE UK

E: ianp@londonscuba.com
T: +44 (0) 1342 837 837
F: +44 (0) 1342 837 722
www.londonscuba.com

The London Scuba Diving School teaches beginners in swimming pools in Battersea and Bayswater. They also offer advanced courses for the experienced diver.

Mendip Outdoor Pursuits
The Warehouse,
Silver Street,
Congresbury, BS49 5EY UK

E: info@mendipoutdoorpursuits.co.uk
T: +44 (0) 1934 834 877
F: +44 (0) 1934 834 888
www.mendipoutdoorpursuits.co.uk

Lessons in abseiling, archery, bridge building, caving, climbing, bush craft, kayaking, navigation, orienteering and more available.

National Mountaineering Centre
Plas y Brenin,
Capel Curig,
Conwy, LL24 0ET UK

E: info@pyb.co.uk
T: +44 (0) 1690 720 214
F: +44 (0) 1690 720 394
www.pyb.co.uk

For those hoping to reach dizzy heights, the National Mountaineering Centre offers a vast range of activities and courses.

North London Parachute Centre Ltd
Block Fen Drove,
Wimblington,
March, PE15 0FB UK

E: office@ukskydiving.com
T: +44 (0) 871 664 0113
F: +44 (0) 871 664 0114
www.ukskydiving.com

They have different sky diving and parachuting experiences and various courses for the complete beginner.

Pod Zorbing
393 Selsdon Road,
Croydon, CR2 7AW UK

E: info@zorbing.co.uk
www.zorbing.co.uk

Harness zorbing in London - two person ball. Also do aqua zorbing.

Poole Harbour Watersports
284 Sandbanks Road,
Lilliput,
Poole, BH14 8HU UK

E: info@pooleharbour.co.uk
T: +44 (0) 1202 700503
F: +44 (0) 1202 701518
www.pooleharbour.co.uk

Learn to windsurf and kitesurf at Poole in Dorset. Courses available for both beginners and improvers.

ProAdventure Limited
23 Castle Street,
Llangollen, LL20 8NY UK

E: sales@proadventure.co.uk
www.proadventure.co.uk

Based in Wales, ProAdventure offers different activity courses around the UK, including canoeing, kayaking, rock climbing and mountain biking.

Province of London Curling Club
c/o James Hustler, Secretary,
524 Galleywood Road,
Chelmsford, CM2 8BU UK

E: secretary@londoncurling.org.uk
T: +44 (0) 1245 358 615
www.londoncurling.org.uk

New curlers always welcome. Free coaching and equipment available. New season starts 1st October.

Skydive Brid
East Leys Farm,
Grindale,
Bridlington, YO16 4YB UK

E: info@skydivebrid.co.uk
T: +44 (0) 1262 677 367
www.skydivebrid.co.uk

Skydiving courses for complete beginners. Free skydiving in aid of charity and jumps organised for more experienced people.

South Cambridgeshire Equestrian Centre
Barrington Park Farm,
Foxton Road,
Barrington, CB22 7RN UK

T: +44 (0) 1763 263 213
www.scec.co.uk

This riding school is set in 260 acres of Cambridgeshire countryside. They offer riding tuition to the beginner and also more advanced teaching for experienced riders.

Sportscotland
National Centre Cumbrae
Isle of Cumbrae,
Ayrshire, KA28 0HQ UK

E: cumbraecentre@sportscotland.org.uk
F: +44 (0) 1475 530013
www.nationalcentrecumbrae.org.uk

Sportscotland national watersport centre offer a range of courses from a fully residential three weeks Powerboat Instructor or 18 weeks Professional Yachtmaster Training, to a one day introduction to Windsurfing.

Suffolk Ski Centre
Bourne Hill,
Wherstead,
Ipswich, IP2 8NQ UK

E: info@suffolkskicentre.co.uk
T: +44 (0) 1473 602347
F: +44 (0) 1473 603756
www.suffolkskicentre.co.uk

Learn to ski or snowboard in Suffolk. Courses also available for those wishing to improve their existing skills.

the gap-year guidebook 2011

Sussex Hang Gliding & Paragliding
Tollgate,
Lewes, BN8 6JZ UK

E: info@sussexhgpg.co.uk
F: +44 (0) 1273 858 177
www.sussexhgpg.co.uk

Learn to paraglide or hang glide over the beautiful Sussex countryside.

Sussex Polo Club
Landfall House,
Sandhill Lane,
Crawley Down, RH10 4LE UK

E: info@sussexpolo.co.uk
T: +44 (0) 1342 714 920
F: +44 (0) 871 661 5948
www.sussexpolo.co.uk

Learn something new - learn to play polo.

The Lawn Tennis Association
The National Tennis Centre,
100 Priory Lane, Roehampton,
London, SW15 5JQ UK

E: Info@LTA.org.uk
T: +44 (0) 20 8487 7000
F: +44 (0) 20 8487 7301
www.lta.org.uk/PlayAndCompete/StartToPlay/

You're never too young or too old to learn to play tennis and the LTA will help you.

The Talland School of Equitation
Dairy Farm,
Ampney Knowle,
Cirencester, GL7 5ED UK

E: secretary@talland.net
T: +44 (0) 1285 740155
F: +44 (0) 1285 740153
www.talland.net

World renowned BHS and ABRS approved equestrian centre offering top class training for professional qualifications. Variety of courses including competition training on quality horses.

Tollymore Mountain Centre
Bryansford,
Newcastle, BT33 0PT UK

E: admin@tollymore.com
F: +44 (0) 28 4372 6155
www.tollymore.com

Tollymore have a range of courses designed to suit your own skills and experience. Their courses include rambling, mountaineering, climbing, canoeing and first aid.

UK Parachuting
Old Buckenham Airfield,
Attleborough, NR17 1PU UK

E: jump@ukparachuting.co.uk
F: +44 (0) 1953 861031
www.ukparachuting.co.uk

AFF courses available. Also tandem skydiving and Accelerated Free Fall tuition slots available every day.

UK Skydiving Ltd
Globe House,
Love Lane,
Cirencester, GL7 1YG UK

T: +44 (0) 845 330 1676
www.ukskydiving.co.uk

UK Skydiving is a company run by British Parachute Association (BPA) Instructors. They have courses for the absolute beginner, which are tailored to suit the individual.

UKSA (United Kingdom Sailing Academy)
The Martime Academy,
Artic Road,
West Cowes, PO31 7PQ UK

E: info@uksa.org
T: +44 (0) 1983 203038
www.uksa.org

UKSA have a wealth of options for a thrilling gap-year to suit all budgets, from extreme watersports instructor programmes to the six-week crew training course, designed to provide the yachting skills and experience for a career on luxury yachts and superyachts!

Wellington Riding
Heckfield,
Hook, RG27 OLJ UK

E: info@wellington-riding.co.uk
www.wellington-riding.co.uk

Riding lessons available for any level - children and adults.

X-isle Sports
Unit 6a,
Embankment Road,
Bembridge, PO25 5NR UK

E: lucy@xisle.co.uk
T: +44 (0) 1983 761 678
F: +44 (0) 1983 760 245
www.x-is.co.uk

Centre on the Isle of Wight offering courses in waterskiing, kitesurfing, windsurfing, surfing, sailing and wakeboarding.

TEFL

CILC - Cheltenham International Language Centre
University of Gloucestershire, Cornerways,
The Park,
Cheltenham, GL50 2RH UK   www.glos.ac.uk/international/Pages/default.aspx

E: cilc@glos.ac.uk
T: +44 (0) 1242 714 092
F: +44 (0) 1242 714 425

Gloucestershire University offer intensive courses in TEFL leading to the Cambridge ESOL CELTA award.

ETC - The English Training Centre
53 Greenhill Road,
Moseley,
Birmingham, B13 9SU UK

E: info@englishtc.co.uk
T: +44 (0) 121 449 2221
www.englishtc.co.uk

Professionally-designed TESOL courses offered accredited by ACTDEC. Experienced tutors provide comprehensive feedback and helpful support. Free grammar guide and teaching resource book.

Golders Green Teacher Training Centre
11 Golders Green Road,
Golders Green,
London, NW11 8DY UK

T: +44 (0) 208 731 0963
F: +44 (0) 208 455 6528
www.englishlanguagecollege.co.uk

Full-time and part-time TEFL/TESOL courses available.

the gap-year guidebook 2011

ITC - Intensive TEFL Courses
26 Cockerton Green,
Darlington, DL3 9EU UK

E: info@tefl.co.uk
F: +44 (0) 1325 366167
www.tefl.co.uk

Intensive TEFL Courses (ITC) have been running weekend TEFL (Teach English as a Foreign Language) courses throughout the UK since 1993.

LTTC - London Teacher Training College
Dalton House,
60 Windsor Avenue, Wimbledon,
London, SW19 2RR UK

E: lttc@teachenglish.co.uk
T: +44 (0) 208 133 2027
F: +44 (0) 208 242 6927
www.teachenglish.co.uk

Over the years the college has trained a vast number of teachers from around the world, and prides itself on the quality of its courses and the individual attention it provides every student who enrols.

OxfordTEFL
6-7 Southampton Place,
Bloomsbury,
London, WC1A 2DB UK

E: tesol@oxfordtefl.com
T: +34 934 580 111
F: +34 934 586 638
www.oxfordtefl.com

OxfordTEFL offer a four week training course, accredited by Trinity College London, at the end of which you should get a Certificate in TEFL.

TEFL Training LLP
Friends Close,
Stonesfield,
Witney, OX29 8PH UK

E: info@tefltraining.co.uk
T: +44 (0) 1993 891 121
F: +44 (0) 1993 891 996
www.tefltraining.co.uk

Teaching English UK or Abroad? Prepare yourself while still working or studying. Our weekend course will give you a very practical introduction to Teaching English as a Foreign Language.

Windsor TEFL
21 Osborne Road,
Windsor, SL4 3EG UK

E: info@windsorschools.co.uk
F: +44 (0) 1753 831 726
www.windsorschools.co.uk

Offer their TEFL course in their centres in London and Windsor as well as in Europe. Also offer the CELTA TEFL course in various places worldwide.

visit: www.gap-year.com

Appendices

Choosing a tutorial college

Standards vary and it's best to check out two or three colleges before you make your final choice. Here are some things to check before you decide:

- Does the college get results? For the last few years the *Daily Telegraph* has regularly published a table in early September giving the average A level retake grade improvements at tutorial colleges.
- Does the college have a good reputation? Get references from former students - the college should be happy to supply you with contact names.
- Has the college been inspected by the Department for Children, Schools and Families (DCSF) or an independent body such as BAC (the British Accreditation Council for Independent Further and Higher Education) or CIFE (the Council for Independent Further Education)?
- Does the college teach the right subjects?
- Does the college teach the same syllabus (*eg* OCR/French) that you studied at school?
- What time of year are the courses run? This affects what you can do during the rest of your year out.
- Who will be teaching you? Check their qualifications and how familiar they are with the syllabus.
- Is the place up-to-date? Near transport? Does it have quiet study rooms and good facilities?
- What does it cost? What are the hourly rates?
- What do get for your money? How many hours of group teaching each week and how many one-to-one tutorials?

Retakes

Please note: The information contained in these appendices is for guidance only. We would strongly advise you to talk to your school or college examination officer, chosen university or exam board for up-to-the-minute advice and information.

Retakes

There are several reasons why you might find yourself considering retakes: maybe because your grades are too low to meet a conditional offer (and the university won't negotiate with you to admit you on lower grades), or because illness interfered with exams.

But beware, getting better grades second time round doesn't guarantee you a university place - often universities will demand even higher grades if it's taken you two bites at the cherry (unless of course you've got a really good excuse, like illness).

Grade appeals

The now almost habitual media comment about the devaluation of A level marks has left many people wondering just how much we can trust exam results. If you really think you've been done down by a tired exam marker, a misleading or misprinted question or some other factor, you can appeal against your result.

You appeal first to the examination board that set the exam, and if you don't think the adjudication is just, you can go on to appeal to the Examination Appeals Board (EAB). But be warned: this process takes a long time and there's no guarantee the appeal will go your way.

Retake timing

Now that modular A levels are firmly entrenched, you may be able to retake the modules you did badly while you are still at school, instead of having to retake them in your year out.

However, you need to check with both your exam board and chosen university before you make any plans.

Every exam board has its own timetable for retakes (see below for contact details) and universities also vary considerably in their regulations on retakes.

You need to make sure your chosen university course doesn't set higher entry grades for exams taken at a second sitting.

In some cases you may find that when you retake a certain exam you have to change exam board - this can be a problem in some subjects (*eg* languages

the gap-year guidebook 2011

with set texts) and you may therefore have to resit your A levels a whole year after the original exams, which can seriously disrupt your **gap-**year. Check with your exam board as early as you can.

Tutorial colleges like to keep students working on A levels for a full year. That keeps the college full and tutors paid. But many agree that the best thing is to get resits over before you forget the work you've already done. So the best timing, if you are academically confident and want to enjoy your **gap-**year, is to go to a tutorial college in September and resit the whole exam or the relevant modules in January - if sittings are available then.

Languages

If you have only language AS levels, A2 levels or A levels to retake, there are several options:

- Take an extra course or stay in the country of the relevant language and return to revise for a summer resit, choosing the same exam board (courses abroad, however, are not usually geared to A level texts).
- Check with tutorial colleges how much of your syllabus module or modules (the chosen literature texts are crucial) overlap with those of other exam boards. This may give you the chance to switch exam boards and do a quick retake in January.
- Cram for as long as necessary at a specialist language college. Some British tutorial colleges and language course organisers have links with teaching centres in other countries so it's worth checking this out before signing on.

Retake results

Those who sit A level retakes in January, and get the grades needed for a chosen place, will not have to wait until August for that place to be confirmed.

Examining boards will feed the result directly into UCAS so you will know your place has been clinched. A technicality, but comforting for **gap-**year students who want to travel.

And don't forget that if you have a firm choice conditional offer and you make the grades asked for, the university can't back out. It has an obligation to admit you.

A level examining boards

There are five A level examining boards: AQA (Assessment and Qualifications Alliance), Edexcel, OCR (Oxford, Cambridge & RSA), Northern Ireland (CCEA) and Wales (WJEC). There's also the IB, which has its own curriculum and syllabus, geared towards the IB Diploma. All these boards now provide their exam timetables on the internet about nine months in advance: we've provided their contact details below, along with those of other exam-related organisations.

visit: www.gap-year.com

AQA (Assessment and Qualifications Alliance)
Stag Hill House,
Guildford, Surrey GU2 7XJ
www.aqa.org.uk
Tel: +44 (0) 1483 506506
Email: mailbox@aqa.org.uk

CCEA (Northern Ireland Council for the Curriculum, Examinations and Assessment)
29 Clarendon Road, Clarendon Dock
Belfast, County Antrim BT1 3BG
www.ccea.org.uk
Tel: +44 (0) 28 9026 1200
Fax: +44 (0) 28 9026 1234
Email: info@ccea.org.uk

EAB (Examination Appeals Board)
83 Piccadilly,
London W1J 8QA
www.theeab.org.uk
Tel: +44 (0) 20 7509 5995

This is the final court of appeal for exam grades. Centres and private candidates only go to the EAB if an appeal to the relevant examination board has failed. The EAB website has a notice board showing when appeals are going to be heard.

EDEXCEL
190 High Holborn,
London WC1V 7BH
www.edexcel.org.uk
Tel: see website for contact numbres

IB (International Baccalaureate)
Peterson House, Malthouse Avenue
Cardiff Gate
Cardiff CF23 8GL
www.ibo.org
Tel: +44 (0) 29 2054 7777
Fax: +44 (0) 29 2054 7778
Email: ibca@ibo.org

Currrently the UK office and central body for the development, administration and assessment of the International Baccalaureate Diploma Programme.

OCR (Oxford Cambridge & RSA Examinations)
1 Hills Road,
Cambridge,
Cambridgeshire CB1 2EU
www.ocr.org.uk
Tel: +44 (0) 1223 553 998
Fax: +44 (0) 1223 552 627
Email: general.qualifications@ocr.org.uk

QCA (Qualifications and Curriculum Authority)
83 Piccadilly,
London W1J 8QA
www.qca.org.uk
Tel: +44 (0) 20 7509 5555
Fax: +44 (0) 20 7509 6666
Email: info@qca.org.uk

The QCA is the body that (along with the Qualifications, Curriculum and Assessment Authority for Wales: ACCAC) approves all syllabuses and monitors exams (grading standards, for example).

SQA (Scottish Qualifications Authority)
The Optima Building, 58 Robertson Street,
Glasgow, Lanarkshire G2 8DQ
www.sqa.org.uk
Tel: +44 (0) 845 279 1000
Fax: +44 (0) 845 213 5000
Email: customer@sqa.org.uk

Central body for the development, administration and assessment of Scottish qualifications, including Standard Grade, Highers, Advanced Highers, HNCs, HNDs and SVQs.

WJEC
245 Western Avenue,
Cardiff, Glamorgan CF5 2YX

www.wjec.co.uk
Tel: +44 (0) 29 2026 5000
Email: info@wjec.co.uk

WJEC's qualifications include Entry Level, GCSE and AS/A level, as well as Key Skills. They also handle the Welsh Baccalaureate and provide examinations, assessment, educational resources and support for adults who wish to learn Welsh.

Colleges accredited by BAC and CIFE

The following independent sixth form and tutorial colleges offering A level tuition (one-year, two-year, complete retakes, modular retakes or intensive coaching) are recognised by the British Accreditation Council (BAC, Tel: 020 7447 2584, www.the-bac.org) and/or the Council for Independent Further Education (CIFE, Tel: 020 8767 8266, www.cife.org.uk). Of course a college can have a good reputation and achieve excellent results without accreditation.

College	Accreditation	Telephone
Abacus College (Oxford)	BAC	Tel:+44 (0) 1865 240 111
Abbey College Birmingham	BAC	Tel:+44 (0) 121 236 7474
Abbey College Cambridge	BAC	Tel:+44 (0) 1223 578 280
Abbey College London (SW1)	BAC	Tel:+44 (0) 20 7824 7300
Abbey College Manchester	BAC	Tel:+44 (0) 161 817 2700
Acorn Independent College (Southall)	BAC	Tel:+44 (0) 20 8571 9900
Ashbourne Independent Sixth Form College, (London W8)	BAC/CIFE	Tel:+44 (0) 20 7937 3858
Bales College (London W10)	BAC/CIFE	Tel:+44 (0) 20 8960 5899
Basil Paterson Tutorial College (Edinburgh)	BAC	Tel:+44 (0) 131 225 3802
Bath Academy (Bath)	BAC/CIFE	Tel:+44 (0) 1225 334 577
Bellerbys College – Brighton	BAC	Tel:+44 (0) 1273 339 200
Bellerbys College – Cambridge	BAC	Tel:+44 (0) 1223 517 037
Bellerbys College – London	BAC	Tel:+44 (0) 20 8694 7000
Bosworth Independent College (Northampton)	CIFE	Tel:+44 (0) 1604 239 995
Brampton College (London NW4)	BAC	Tel:+44 (0) 20 8203 5025

visit: www.gap-year.com

Brooke House College (Market Harborough)	BAC/CIFE	Tel:+44 (0) 1858 462 452
CATS (Cambridge)	BAC	Tel:+44 (0) 1223 314 431
CATS (Canterbury)	BAC	Tel:+44 (0) 1227 866 540
Cambridge Centre for Sixth Form Studies	CIFE	Tel:+44 (0) 1223 716 890
Cambridge Seminars	BAC	Tel:+44 (0) 1223 313 464
Cambridge Tutors College	CIFE	Tel:+44 (0) 20 8688 5284
Chelsea Independent College	BAC/CIFE	Tel:+44 (0) 20 7610 1114
Cherwell College (Oxford)	BAC	Tel:+44 (0) 1865 242 670
College of International Education (Oxford)	BAC	Tel:+44 (0) 1865 202238
Collingham (London SW5)	BAC/CIFE	Tel:+44 (0) 20 7244 7414
Commonwealth Law College	BAC	Tel:+44 (0) 20 7247 8082
David Game College (London W11)	BAC	Tel:+44 (0) 20 7221 6665
Davies, Laing & Dick (London, W1)	BAC/CIFE	Tel:+44 (0) 20 7935 8411
Duff Miller College (London SW7)	BAC/CIFE	Tel:+44 (0) 20 7225 0577
Ealing Independent College (London, W5)	BAC	Tel:+44 (0) 20 8579 6668
EF Brittin College – Torquay	BAC	Tel:+44 (0) 1803 202 932
Exeter Tutorial College (Exeter)	BAC/CIFE	Tel:+44 (0) 1392 278 101
Harrogate Tutorial College	BAC/CIFE	Tel:+44 (0) 1423 501 041
Holborn College	BAC	Tel:+44 (0) 20 8317 6000
International College Britain	BAC	Tel:+44 (0) 131 313 1988
King's School, Oxford	BAC	Tel:+44 (0) 1865 711 829
Lansdowne College (London W2)	CIFE	Tel:+44 (0) 20 7616 4400
London College Wimbledon	BAC	Tel:+44 (0) 20 8944 1134

College	Accreditation	Telephone
London School of Science & Technology	BAC	Tel:+44 (0) 208 795 3863
Mander Portman Woodward (Birmingham)	BAC	Tel:+44 (0) 121 454 9637
Mander Portman Woodward (London SW7)	BAC/CIFE	Tel:+44 (0) 20 7835 1355
Mander Portman Woodward (Cambridge)	BAC	Tel:+44 (0) 1223 350 158
Middlesex College of Law	BAC	Tel:+44 (0) 20 8424 2442
Midlands Academy of Business & Technology (MABT)	BAC	Tel:+44 (0) 116 261 9426
Oxford Business College (Oxford)	BAC	Tel:+44 (0) 1865 791 908
Oxford Tutorial College (Oxford)	BAC/CIFE	Tel:+44 (0) 1865 793 333
Pinnacle International College (Formerly CRTS International College)	BAC	Tel:+44 (0) 20 8885 5577
Rayat London College	BAC	Tel:+44 (0) 20 8754 3330
Reach Cambridge	BAC	Tel:+44 (0) 870 8031 732
Regent College (Harrow)	BAC	Tel:+44 (0) 20 8966 9900
San Michael College	BAC	Tel:+44 (0) 121 454 7949
St Andrew's (Cambridge)	BAC	Tel:+44 (0) 1223 358 073
The Abbey College (Malvern)	BAC	Tel:+44 (0) 1684 892300
Tudor College London	BAC	Tel:+44 (0) 20 7837 8382

Applying to university

At the time of writing, UCAS was reporting that the number of students taking up university and college places has again risen this year (up 13.8% on 2009 figures as of 31 May 2010). The previous record was set in autumn 2009 which recorded the highest ever uptake, according to annual figures released by UCAS. The total number of applicants rose in 2009 to 639,860 from 588,689 in 2008. The number of full-time students accepted on to undergraduate courses starting in 2009 rose by 5.5%. 25,227 more students were accepted in 2009, taking the total from 413,430 in 2008 to 456,627.

For some, the decision to take a year off is made well in advance. Often students make the decision to defer their entry into higher education with specific projects in mind. Some choose not to apply at all until after their A level results. Others find themselves taking a **gap**-year at much shorter notice once they receive their grades. If UCAS applicants have not met the conditions of the offers they are holding then a **gap**-year can allow them to reassess their plans. Equally, one option for those who have done better than expected can use the time to aim for something they had originally considered beyond them.

Application process

UCAS (the Universities and Colleges Admissions Service) handles applications to all UK universities (except the Open University) as well as to most other institutions that offer full-time undergraduate higher education courses. This includes applications for Oxford, Cambridge and for degrees in medicine, dentistry and veterinary science/medicine, although they have to be in earlier than for other universities and colleges and for other subjects.

UCAS
PO Box 28,
Cheltenham GL52 3LZ

www.ucas.com
Tel: +44 (0) 871 468 0468
Email: enquiries@ucas.co.uk

Sending an email to this address will get you an automated response with general information and guidance on UCAS procedures.

If you have hearing difficulties, you can call the Text Relay service on 18001 0871 468 0 468 from within the UK or on 0044 151 494 1260 (text phone) from outside the UK. You will need to ask the operator to disal 0871 468 0468. There is no extra charge for this service. Calls are charged at normal rates.

UCAS offers a distribution service to companies who wish to send promotional material to students. UCAS handles the distribution itself and does not pass on your personal details, which remain confidential. If you prefer not to receive this kind of material however, you can opt out when completing your UCAS application.

You can apply for five different courses at any UCAS institutions, except for medicine courses A100, A101, A102, A103, A104, A105, A106, dentistry courses: A200, A201, A202, A203, A204, A205, A206, A300, A400 and veterinary science/medicine courses: D100, D101, and D102 for each of which you can make just four choices. Note that some art and design courses use the deadline of 24 March for entries while others use 15 January - be sure to check on Course Search which deadline applies to each of your chosen courses. You can hold on to no more than two of the offers you get: one 'firm (first choice) offer and one 'insurance (second choice) offer'. So you may have to be cautious about the courses you pitch for.

Online application

UCAS has a secure, web-based application system called Apply. Each school, college, careers agency or British Council Office that has registered with UCAS to use Apply appoints a coordinator who manages the way it is used. For students, registering to the new system takes a few minutes and costs nothing. Once a student has registered, you are given a username and are asked to choose a password that they will need to use each time they want to access their application. Applicants can use this system anywhere that has access to the web. The service works in tandem with the online Course Search service. Check out the UCAS website for more information at: **www.ucas.com**

Students who are not at a school or college also make their applications using the online Apply system. Independent applicants can either cut and paste in a reference which has been sent to them, or contact their old school or college and ask whether they will supply a reference online. In either case they send the completed application together with payment to UCAS themselves.

Please remember you do not have to apply for all your choices at the same time. You can add further choices as long as you have not used up all your choices and have not yet replied to any offers and places are still available.

A level results

A level results come out in mid-August. Depending on your grades one of the following will happen:

- Firm (first) choice university confirms offer of a place. (If your grades meet and exceed your offer you may research alternatives for up to five days while retaining your firm offer, a process known as Adjustment.)
- Insurance (second choice) university confirms offer of a place.
- Clearing.
- Retakes.

Before you make any decisions make sure you know all the angles. Retakes may be the only way for you to get to university, but most universities will demand even higher results the second time around. An expectation confirmed by Glasgow University: "We expect slightly higher requirements if you don't get good enough grades in one A level attempt."

visit: www.gap-year.com

The UCAS Tariff

The UCAS Tariff was first used for those applying to enter higher education (HE) in 2002. Since its introduction it has expanded to cover additional qualifications. It is a points-based system that establishes agreed equivalences between different types of qualifications. It provides admissions tutors with a way of comparing applicants with different types and volumes of achievement.

UCAS is keen to encourage all universities and colleges to use the Tariff to make the application system more uniform across the country. Over three quarters of universities and colleges now use the Tariff, but some admissions tutors still choose to make offers in terms of grades.

More information and a copy of the latest Tariff is available at: **www.ucas.com/students/ucas_tariff/**

Newly tariffed qualifications include the Cambridge ESOL Examinations, CISI Introduction to Securities and Investments, OCR Level 3 Certificate in Maths for Engineering, Principal Learning Wales. New for 2012: Hong Kong Diploma of Secondary Education.

Key dates

This is what will happen if you apply for a university course starting in autumn 2011 or for deferred entry in 2012, so if you are thinking of taking a **gap**-year you'll need to know that:

- The main deadline for applications for all universities (except Oxford, Cambridge, medicine, dentistry, veterinary medicine or veterinary science courses and certain art and design programmes) is 15 January. See list of dates below.

- There is a 'commitment to clear, transparent admissions policies'. More than 85% of courses on Course Search universities include 'Entry Profiles' to tell students about entry requirements, including skills, personal qualities, or experience not necessarily connected with academic qualifications. These are often included on universities' own websites as well.

- Extra has been designed for applicants who have used all five of their choices, but who do not have a place. Extra allows them to make additional choices through UCAS, one at a time. The service runs from February 25th to July 6th, so you won't have to wait until Clearing to find a place. If you are eligible for Extra, UCAS will tell you how to refer your application to a university or college with vacancies, using the Track service on its website.

- 'Invisibility of choices' means that universities and colleges cannot see which other universities or colleges a student has applied to until that applicant has replied to an offer or has no live choices.

The autumn term is when Year 13 students usually begin to apply for university and college places through the UCAS system (though some super-organised schools and students start preparations in the summer of Year 12).

The information you need for applying to university or college is online at **www.ucas.com** where an up-to-date list of courses is always available.

The Gap-Year Guidebook 2011

Here are some key dates:

- University open days organised from spring each year.
- UCAS has three main application deadlines. The first is 15 October for all applications to Oxford and Cambridge universities and applications for medicine, dentistry and veterinary medicine/science as listed above. The deadline for all other courses except some art and design courses is 15 January. The third deadline is 24 March which applies to all art and design courses not using the 15 January deadline.
- Universities and colleges do not guarantee to consider applications they receive after 15 January, and some popular courses may not have vacancies after that date. Please check with individual universities and colleges if you are not sure. You are advised to apply as early as possible.
- Not all courses start in September or October - some start between January and May. Check the start dates for the courses you are interested in on the 'Course information' screen in Course Search. For courses that start between January and May, you may need to apply before the three application deadlines above, as the universities and colleges will need time to consider your application. Contact the university or college direct for advice about when they need your application. Although some will be happy to receive applications right up to the start of the course, be prepared to send your application early.
- Applications for 2011 entry which include any Oxford or Cambridge choices or any medicine courses: A100, A101, A102, A103, A104, A105, A106, dentistry courses: A200, A201, A202, A203, A204, A205, A206, A300, A400 or veterinary science/medicine courses: D100, D101 and D102 must be at UCAS by 15 October 2010.
- When your application is processed UCAS sends you a welcome letter stating your choices and your Personal ID. If there seems to be a mistake, call UCAS immediately, quoting your Personal ID.

Universities and colleges start to notify UCAS of their decisions for 2011 entry from October 2009. Applicants receive decisions via UCAS (unconditional offer, conditional offer or unsuccessful application). If the university or college want you to attend an interview, or submit a portfolio or other additional material, they will contact you directly or send you an invitation letter via UCAS.

You should reply to offers by the deadline given when you receive all your university decisions from UCAS. Remember:

- A level results will be published on 18 August 2011.
- UCAS Track automatically notifies all eligible applicants about Clearing – all those who have: missed their grades and have been turned down, not received offers earlier in the year, declined all offers made to them, applied after the final closing date (see above), or not found a place using Extra.
- A list of vacancies for degrees, HNDs and other undergraduate courses is published on the UCAS website at **www.ucas.com** as soon as results have been processed by UCAS. This online vacancy service is updated several

visit: www.gap-year.com

times a day. Vacancy listings are also published by *The Independent* and *The Belfast Telegraph*.

- Clearing closes on 20 September.

Track

The Track facility on the UCAS website enables those who have applied not only to check the progress of your application, but also to reply to offers online, to cancel choices from which they no longer wish to hear and even to change their address for correspondence. It is an invaluable tool for managing an application, but particularly useful to those who apply during a **gap**-year and are overseas when important decisions are being made.

Deferred entry, rescheduled entry, or post A level application?

There are three ways to handle university entrance if you want to take a **gap**-year. The safest is usually to apply for deferred entry, but not all courses accept deferred entry candidates.

Our advice is to talk to the admissions office before making a decision about taking a **gap**-year.

1. Deferred entry

- Check first with the appropriate department of the university you want to go to that they are happy to take students after a **gap**-year. If it's a popular course, preference may go to the current year applications.

- On your UCAS application there is a 'Start date' field in the 'Choices' section. For each choice click on the 'see list' button to the right of the 'Start date' field and choose a deferred entry start date or current entry start date. Talk to your teachers first and follow instructions in the Apply online help text.

- If you are planning to take a **gap**-year, you will need to explain why in your Personal Statement on the UCAS application. You need to convince the university that a year off will make you a better applicant, so give an outline of what you plan to do and why.

- Send your completed application to UCAS, like any other student applying for entry without taking a **gap**-year. Those who do so well before the appropriate deadline, however, may be among the first to start receiving replies (via UCAS). You will get a call for selection interview(s) (directly from the university or college or through UCAS), an unsuccessful decision, an offer which is conditional on getting specific exam grades or Tariff points score, or an unconditional offer.

- Up until 30 June, UCAS will continue to forward applications to universities 'for consideration at their discretion'. Applications received after 30 June go straight into Clearing.

NOTE: Some academics are not happy with deferred entry because it means it might be nearly two years before you start your higher education. During that time a course may have changed, or you may have changed. So your application may be looked on unfavourably without your knowing why. Most departments at many universities are in favour of a **gap-**year but they are not all in favour of deferred entry. If they interview you in November 2010 for a place in October 2012 it will be 23 months before they see you again. Check it out with the university department first.

2. Deferring entry after you have applied

If you apply for a place in the coming university year and, after A level results decide to defer, you can negotiate direct with the university or college at which you are holding a place. If they agree to defer your place they will inform UCAS, who will confirm this to you in writing.

NOTE: Some admissions tutors say that to give up a place on a popular course is risky, because the university will not be happy after you have messed them about. Others say that if a course has over-recruited, your deferral will be welcome. Tread carefully.

3. Post A level applications

If you take A levels in June 2011, you can still apply through UCAS after the results come out in August. You will go straight into Clearing. If you do not send in a UCAS application before the end of the 2011 entry cycle, (20 September 2011) you should apply - between early September 2011 and the appropriate deadlines for your universities or courses - for entry in the following year. Universities and colleges will not accept those who do not apply through UCAS.

Faculty check: all subjects

If you want to take a **gap-**year, remember (before you apply) to contact the appropriate department or faculty at the university you would like to go to, and find out if they approve of a **gap-**year or not. Prepare a good case for it before you phone. It is advisable to do this even if you are an absolutely outstanding candidate, because on some courses a year off is considered a definite disadvantage. This is usually the case where a degree course is very long or requires a large amount of remembered technical knowledge at the start.

Art and design

Applying through UCAS to your chosen college of art and design might involve applying to courses using either of two deadline dates, 15 January or 24 March. Check the date for each of the courses you are interested in on Course Search.

Medicine, dentistry and veterinary science/medicine

If you hope to pursue a career in medicine, dentistry or veterinary science/medicine, you can use no more than four (of your possible five) choices in any one of those three subject areas. The courses involved are:

visit: www.gap-year.com

- Medical courses: A100, A101, A102, A103, A104, A105, A106.
- Dentistry courses: A200, A201, A202, A203, A204, A205, A206, A300, A400.
- Veterinary science/medicine courses: D100, D101 and D102.

Don't forget that UCAS must receive ALL applications for these courses by 15 October.

Foundation degrees

Foundation degrees are the equivalent of the first two years of an Honours degree, may be studied full- or part-time, and consist of academic study integrated with relevant work-based learning undertaken with an employer. It may be studied as a stand-alone qualification or upon completion you may progress to the final year of an Honours degree.

Financing your studies

How you obtain finance for your study depends on where you live (your family home), because there are significant differences between the systems in England, Scotland, Wales and Northern Ireland. The government-funded student finance systems are studentfinanceengland, the Student Awards Agency for Scotland (SAAS), studentfinancewales and studentfinancenorthernireland.

Over 90% of all UK students are domiciled in England, so the following advice is aimed at them, with a recommendation that those applying from elsewhere visit the website that serves their part of the UK.

Those applying for their first student loan for the academic year beginning in September 2010 will apply direct to studentfinanceengland. Over the following three years, ALL English applicants will apply to studentfinanceengland, rather than to a local authority. Use this link to find out more:

www.direct.gov.uk/en/EducationAndLearning/UniversityAndHigherEducation/StudentFinance/index.htm

For English students, there is a varied package of available finance (and there are equivalents elsewhere in the UK). Everyone on an eligible course is automatically entitled to 72% of the maximum maintenance loan (determined by whether you are living at home or away from home during the academic year, and whether you are studying in London, where the amount is higher). The remaining 28% is means-tested against an applicant's family income. There are now very generous grants available, on a sliding scale, for applicants whose family income is less than £50,788, the maximum amount (£2,906) being available to all those with a family income of less than £25,000. Universities now have to sign an access agreement with the Office for Fair Access to be allowed to charge the full permitted tuition fee, in return for which they MUST provide bursaries of a minimum of £319 for all students who qualify for grant funding. In addition, ALL students based in England are entitled to tuition fee loans. These are not means-tested and everyone may borrow up to the full tuition fee amount (capped at £3,225). Only the maintenance loan and the tuition fee loan need to be repaid - all other financing is given free.

The Gap-Year Guidebook 2011

Loans don't have to be paid back until your income reaches £15,000 a year before tax and what you repay will always be 9% of your earnings above £15K, collected automatically by Her Majesty's Revenue & Customs from your employer. If you earn less, you don't pay.

To keep up-to-date with progress on this:

www.direct.gov.uk/en/EducationAndLearning/UniversityAndHigherEducation/StudentFinance/FinanceForNewStudents/DG_070693

Scholarships and sponsorship

Every university is an independent institution with its own rules and most have their own special bursaries and scholarships for academic excellence which they award on their own criteria.

In addition, there are still many organisations that offer sponsorship to students to study for a degree. This is sometimes on condition that they join the sponsoring company or institution for a period when they graduate. The Army is one example from the public sector, information is available on:

www.armyjobs.mod.uk/education/grants/Pages/default.aspx

If you're looking for sponsorship, The Year in Industry improves your chances and removes the need to write endless letters. Go to: **www.yini.org.uk**

1C Universities in the UK

University of Aberdeen	www.abdn.ac.uk Tel: +44 (0) 1224 272 000
University of Abertay Dundee	www.abertay.ac.uk Tel: +44 (0) 1382 308 000
Aberystwyth University	www.aber.ac.uk Tel: +44 (0) 1970 623 111
Anglia Ruskin University	www.anglia.ac.uk Tel: +44 (0) 845 271 3333
Arts University College at Bournemouth	www.aib.ac.uk Tel: +44 (0) 1202 533 011
Aston University	www.aston.ac.uk Tel: +44 (0) 121 204 3000
Bangor University	www.bangor.ac.uk Tel: +44 (0) 1248 351 151
University of Bath	www.bath.ac.uk Tel: +44 (0) 1225 388 388
Bath Spa University	www.bathspa.ac.uk Tel: +44 (0) 1225 875 875
University of Bedfordshire	www.beds.ac.uk Tel: +44 (0) 1234 400 400
University of Birmingham	www.bham.ac.uk Tel: +44 (0) 121 414 3344
Bishop Grosseteste University College, Lincoln	www.bishopg.ac.uk Tel: +44 (0) 1522 527347
University of Bolton	www.bolton.ac.uk Tel: +44 (0) 1204 900 600
Bournemouth University	www.bournemouth.ac.uk Tel: +44 (0) 1202 524 111

The Gap-Year Guidebook 2011

University of Bradford	www.bradford.ac.uk Tel: +44 (0) 1274 232 323
University of Brighton	www.brighton.ac.uk Tel: +44 (0) 1273 600 900
University of Bristol	www.bristol.ac.uk Tel: +44 (0) 117 928 9000
Brunel University, West London	www.brunel.ac.uk Tel: +44 (0) 1895 274 000
University of Buckingham	www.buckingham.ac.uk Tel: +44 (0) 1280 814 080
Bucks New University	http://bucks.ac.uk Tel: +44 (0) 1494 522 141
University of Cambridge	www.cam.ac.uk Tel: +44 (0) 1223 337 733
Cardiff University	www.cardiff.ac.uk Tel: +44 (0) 29 2087 4000
Canterbury Christ Church University	www.canterbury.ac.uk Tel: +44 (0) 1227 767 700
Birmingham City University	www.bcu.ac.uk Tel: +44 (0) 121 331 5000
University of Central Lancashire	www.uclan.ac.uk Tel: +44 (0) 1772 201 201
University of Chester	www.chester.ac.uk Tel: +44 (0) 1244 511000
University of Chichester	www.chi.ac.uk Tel: +44 (0) 1243 816000
City University, London	www.city.ac.uk Tel: +44 (0) 20 7040 5060
Coventry University	www.coventry.ac.uk Tel: +44 (0) 2476 88 76 88
Cranfield University	www.cranfield.ac.uk Tel: +44 (0) 1234 750 111

visit: www.gap-year.com

University	Website	Telephone
University of Cumbria	www.cumbria.ac.uk	Tel: +44 (0) 1524 384 384
De Montfort University	www.dmu.ac.uk	Tel: +44 (0) 116 255 1551
University of Derby	www.derby.ac.uk	Tel: +44 (0) 1332 590 500
University of Dundee	www.dundee.ac.uk	Tel: +44 (0) 1382 383 000
Durham University	www.dur.ac.uk	Tel: +44 (0) 191 334 2000
University of East Anglia	www.uea.ac.uk	Tel: +44 (0) 1603 456 161
University of East London	www.uel.ac.uk	Tel: +44 (0) 20 8223 3000
Edge Hill University	www.edgehill.ac.uk	Tel: +44 (0) 1695 575 171
The University of Edinburgh	www.ed.ac.uk	Tel: +44 (0) 131 650 1000
University of Essex	www.essex.ac.uk	Tel: +44 (0) 1206 873 333
• Writtle College	www.writtle.ac.uk	+44 (0) 1245 424 200
University of Exeter	www.exeter.ac.uk	Tel: +44 (0) 1392 661 000
University College Falmouth	www.falmouth.ac.uk	Tel: +44 (0) 1326 211077
University of Glamorgan	www.glam.ac.uk	Tel: +44 (0) 1443 480 480
University of Glasgow	www.gla.ac.uk	Tel: +44 (0) 141 330 2000
Glasgow Caledonian University	www.caledonian.ac.uk	Tel: +44 (0) 141 331 3000

University	Contact
University of Gloucestershire	www.glos.ac.uk Tel: +44 (0) 844 801 0001
University of Greenwich	www.gre.ac.uk Tel: +44 (0) 20 8331 8000
Harper Adams University College	www.harper-adams.ac.uk Tel: +44 (0) 1952 820280
Heriot-Watt University	www.hw.ac.uk Tel: +44 (0) 131 449 5111
University of Hertfordshire	www.herts.ac.uk Tel: +44 (0) 1707 284 000
University of Huddersfield	www.hud.ac.uk Tel: +44 (0) 1484 422 288
The University of Hull	www.hull.ac.uk Tel: +44 (0) 1482 346 311
Institute for System Level Integration	www.sli-institute.ac.uk Tel: +44 (0) 1506 469 300
Keele University	www.keele.ac.uk Tel: +44 (0) 1782 732 000
University of Kent	www.kent.ac.uk Tel: +44 (0) 1227 764 000
Kingston University	www.kingston.ac.uk Tel: +44 (0) 20 8417 9000
Lancaster University	www.lancs.ac.uk Tel: +44 (0) 1524 65201
Leeds College of Music	www.lcm.ac.uk Tel: +44 (0) 113 222 3400
Leeds Metropolitan University	www.leedsmet.ac.uk Tel: +44 (0) 113 812 0000
Leeds Trinity & All Saints	www.leedstrinity.ac.uk Tel: +44 (0) 113 283 7100
University of Leeds	www.leeds.ac.uk Tel: +44 (0) 113 243 1751

visit: www.gap-year.com

University of Leicester	www.le.ac.uk Tel: +44 (0) 116 252 2522
University of Lincoln	www.lincoln.ac.uk Tel: +44 (0) 1522 882 000
University of Liverpool	www.liv.ac.uk Tel: +44 (0) 151 794 2000
Liverpool Hope University	www.hope.ac.uk Tel: +44 (0) 151 291 3000
Liverpool John Moores University	www.ljmu.ac.uk Tel: +44 (0) 151 231 2121
University of London (contact colleges directly)	www.london.ac.uk Tel: +44 (0) 20 7862 8360
• Barts and The London School of Medicine and Dentistry	www.smd.qmul.ac.uk Tel: +44 (0) 20 7882 2239
• Birkbeck College	www.bbk.ac.uk Tel: +44 (0) 20 7631 6000
• Courtauld Institute of Art	www.courtauld.ac.uk Tel: +44 (0) 20 7872 0220
• Goldsmith's College	www.gold.ac.uk Tel: +44 (0) 20 7919 7171
• Heythrop College	www.heythrop.ac.uk Tel: +44 (0) 20 7795 6600
• Imperial College	www.imperial.ac.uk Tel: +44 (0) 20 7589 5111
• Institute of Advanced Legal Studies	www.ials.sas.ac.uk Tel: +44 (0) 20 7862 5800
• Institute of Education	www.ioe.ac.uk Tel: +44 (0) 20 7612 6000
• Institute in Paris	www.bip.lon.ac.uk Tel: +33 (0) 1 44 11 73 76
• King's College London	www.kcl.ac.uk Tel: +44 (0) 20 7836 5454

- London School of Economics
  and Political Science
  www.lse.ac.uk
  Tel: +44 (0) 20 7405 7686

- London School of Hygiene
  and Tropical Medicine
  www.lshtm.ac.uk
  Tel: +44 (0) 20 7636 8636

- Queen Mary
  www.qmul.ac.uk
  Tel: +44 (0) 20 7882 5555

- Royal Academy of Music
  www.ram.ac.uk
  Tel: +44 (0) 20 7873 7373

- Royal Free
  and University College Medical School
  www.ucl.ac.uk/medicalschool
  Tel: +44 (0) 20 7679 2000

- Royal Holloway
  www.rhul.ac.uk
  Tel: +44 (0) 1784 434 455

- School of Advanced Study
  www.sas.ac.uk
  Tel: +44 (0) 20 7862 8659

- School of Oriental
  and African Studies
  www.soas.ac.uk
  Tel: +44 (0) 20 7637 2388

- School of Slavonic
  and East European Studies
  www.ssees.ac.uk
  Tel: +44 (0) 20 7679 8700

- St George's
  www.sgul.ac.uk
  Tel: +44 (0) 20 8672 9944

- The Royal Veterinary College
  www.rvc.ac.uk
  Tel: +44 (0) 20 7468 5000

- The School of Pharmacy
  www.pharmacy.ac.uk
  Tel: +44 (0) 20 7753 5800

- University College London
  www.ucl.ac.uk
  Tel: +44 (0) 20 7679 2000

London Metropolitan University
www.londonmet.ac.uk
Tel: +44 (0) 20 7423 0000

London South Bank University
www.lsbu.ac.uk
Tel: +44 (0) 20 7815 7815

Loughborough University
www.lboro.ac.uk
Tel: +44 (0) 1509 263 171

visit: www.gap-year.com

The University of Manchester	www.manchester.ac.uk
	Tel: +44 (0) 161 306 6000
• Manchester Business School	www.mbs.ac.uk
	Tel: +44 (0) 161 3061 320
Manchester Metropolitan University	www.mmu.ac.uk
	Tel: +44 (0) 161 247 2000
Middlesex University	www.mdx.ac.uk
	Tel: +44 (0) 20 8411 5000
Napier University	www.napier.ac.uk
	Tel: +44 (0) 8452 606 040
Newcastle University	www.ncl.ac.uk
	Tel: +44 (0) 191 222 6000
Newman College of Higher Education	www.newman.ac.uk
	Tel: +44 (0) 121 476 1181
The University of Northampton	www.northampton.ac.uk
	Tel: +44 (0) 1604 735500
Northumbria University	www.northumbria.ac.uk
	Tel: +44 (0) 191 232 6002
The University of Nottingham	www.nottingham.ac.uk
	Tel: +44 (0) 115 951 5151
Nottingham Trent University	www.ntu.ac.uk
	Tel: +44 (0) 115 941 8418
The Open University	www.open.ac.uk
	Tel: +44 (0) 845 300 6090
University of Oxford	www.ox.ac.uk
	Tel: +44 (0) 1865 270 000
Oxford Brookes University	www.brookes.ac.uk
	Tel: +44 (0) 1865 741 111
University of Plymouth	www.plymouth.ac.uk
	Tel: +44 (0) 1752 600 600
University of Portsmouth	www.port.ac.uk
	Tel: +44 (0) 2392 84 84 84

Queen Margaret University	www.qmu.ac.uk Tel: +44 (0) 131 474 0000
Queen's University Belfast	www.qub.ac.uk Tel: +44 (0) 28 9024 5133
• Stranmillis University College	www.stran.ac.uk Tel: +44 (0) 28 9038 1271
University of Reading	www.reading.ac.uk Tel: +44 (0) 1189 875 123
Roehampton University	www.roehampton.ac.uk Tel: +44 (0) 20 8392 3000
Royal College of Art	www.rca.ac.uk Tel: +44 (0) 20 7590 4444
Royal College of Music	www.rcm.ac.uk Tel: +44 (0) 20 7589 3643
University of Salford	www.salford.ac.uk Tel: +44 (0) 161 295 5000
The University of Sheffield	www.sheffield.ac.uk Tel: +44 (0) 114 222 2000
Sheffield Hallam University	www.shu.ac.uk Tel: +44 (0) 114 225 5555
University of Southampton	www.soton.ac.uk Tel: +44 (0) 23 8059 5000
Southampton Solent University	www.solent.ac.uk Tel: +44 (0) 23 8031 9000
Staffordshire University	www.staffs.ac.uk Tel: +44 (0) 1782 294 000
St Mary's University, Belfast	www.smucb.ac.uk Tel: +44 (0) 28 9032 7678
University of Strathclyde	www.strath.ac.uk Tel: +44 (0) 141 552 4400
University of St Andrews	www.st-andrews.ac.uk Tel: +44 (0) 1334 476 161

visit: www.gap-year.com

University of Stirling	www.stir.ac.uk Tel: +44 (0) 1786 473 171
University of Sunderland	www.sunderland.ac.uk Tel: +44 (0) 191 515 2000
University of Surrey	www.surrey.ac.uk Tel: +44 (0) 1483 300 800
University of Sussex	www.sussex.ac.uk Tel: +44 (0) 1273 606 755
Swansea University	www.swansea.ac.uk Tel: +44 (0) 1792 205 678
University of Teesside	www.tees.ac.uk Tel: +44 (0) 1642 218 121
Thames Valley University	www.tvu.ac.uk Tel: +44 (0) 208 579 5000
The Liverpool Institute for Performing Arts	www.lipa.ac.uk Tel: +44 (0) 151 330 3000
The Robert Gordon University	www.rgu.ac.uk Tel: +44 (0) 1224 262 000
Trinity College of Music	www.tcm.ac.uk Tel: +44 (0) 20 8305 4444
University of Ulster	www.ulster.ac.uk Tel: +44 (0) 8 700 400 700
University College for the Creative Arts	www.ucreative.ac.uk
• Canterbury	Tel: +44 (0) 1227 817302
• Epsom	Tel: +44 (0) 1372 728811
• Farnham	Tel: +44 (0) 1252 722441
• Maidstone	Tel: +44 (0) 1622 620000
• Rochester	Tel: +44 (0) 1634 888702
University Marine Biological Station Millport	www.gla.ac.uk/marinestation Tel: +44 (0) 1475 530 581

University of Wales
(contact institutions directly)
www.wales.ac.uk
Tel: +44 (0) 29 2037 6999

- University of Wales – Glyndwr University
www.glyndwr.ac.uk
Tel: +44 (0) 1978 290 666

- University of Wales – Royal Welsh College of Music and Drama
www.rwcmd.ac.uk
Tel: +44 (0) 29 2034 2854

- University of Wales – Swansea Metropolitan University
www.sihe.ac.uk
Tel: +44 (0) 1792 481 000

- University of Wales – Trinity University College, Carmarthen
www.trinity-cm.ac.uk
Tel: +44 (0) 1267 676 767

- University of Wales, Newport
www.newport.ac.uk
Tel: +44 (0) 1633 430 088

- University of Wales Institute, Cardiff
www.uwic.ac.uk
Tel: +44 (0) 29 2041 6070

- University of Wales, Lampeter
www.lamp.ac.uk
Tel: +44 (0) 1570 422 351

- University of Wales, Coleg Harlech WEA
www.harlech.ac.uk
Tel: +44 (0) 1766 781 900

- University of Wales, Llandrillo College
www.llandrillo.ac.uk
Tel: +44 (0) 1492 546 666

University of Warwick
www.warwick.ac.uk
Tel: +44 (0) 2476 523 523

University of Westminster
www.wmin.ac.uk
Tel: +44 (0) 20 7911 5000

University of The Arts
www.arts.ac.uk
Tel: +44 (0) 20 7514 6000

University of the West of England, Bristol
www.uwe.ac.uk
Tel: +44 (0) 117 965 6261

University of the West of Scotland
www.paisley.ac.uk
Tel: +44 (0) 141 848 3000

The University of Winchester
www.winchester.ac.uk
Tel: +44 (0) 1962 841515

visit: www.gap-year.com

University of Wolverhampton	www.wlv.ac.uk
	Tel: +44 (0) 1902 321 000
University of Worcester	www.worcester.ac.uk
	Tel: +44 (0) 1905 855 000
University of York	www.york.ac.uk
	Tel: +44 (0) 1904 430 000
York St John University	www.yorksj.ac.uk
	Tel: +44 (0) 1904 624 624

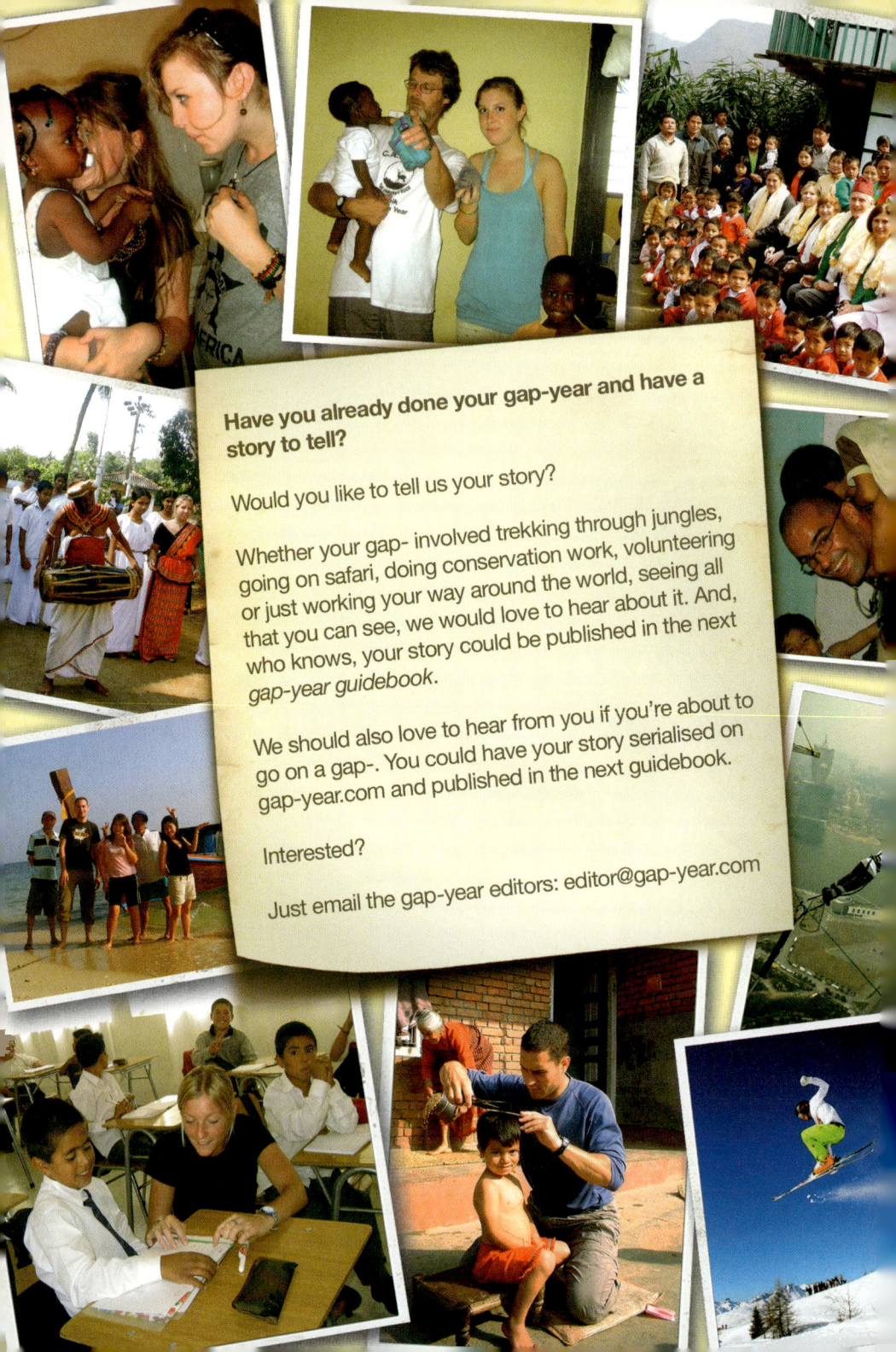

Have you already done your gap-year and have a story to tell?

Would you like to tell us your story?

Whether your gap- involved trekking through jungles, going on safari, doing conservation work, volunteering or just working your way around the world, seeing all that you can see, we would love to hear about it. And, who knows, your story could be published in the next *gap-year guidebook*.

We should also love to hear from you if you're about to go on a gap-. You could have your story serialised on gap-year.com and published in the next guidebook.

Interested?

Just email the gap-year editors: editor@gap-year.com

2 Country info

Once you have chosen where you want to go, whether one country or a dozen, do some research. It would be a shame to travel to the other side of the world and then miss what it has to offer. There are loads of websites giving interesting and useful factual advice (weather, geographical, political, economic) as well as those that are more touristy.

Foreign Office warnings

It's worth bearing in mind that economic and political situations can change rapidly in countries, so check with the Foreign and Commonwealth Office that the country is still safe to travel to before you go. There's a link to their website on: **www.gap-year.com**

It's important to look at the lists of specific areas which travellers should avoid. It's also worth noting the phone numbers of all British embassies and consulates in areas where you may be travelling, in case you need to contact them for help.

Telephone or email home regularly to save your family a lot of worry and British embassies a lot of wasted time. The following pages contain data for individual countries: make sure you check with the FCO for up-to-date information.

Afghanistan, The Islamic Republic of
- Population: estimated to be 28.7 million (UN)
- Location: South Asia
- Capital: Kabul
- Currency: Afghani (AFN)
- Religion: mainly Sunni Muslim
- Languages: Farsi (Dari), Pashtu (Pashto or Pukhto)
- British Embassy, Kabul: +93 (0) 700 102 000

Albania, The Republic of
- Population: estimated to be 3.6 million
- Location: South-east Europe
- Capital: Tirana
- Currency: Lek (ALL)
- Religion: Sunni Muslim, Albanian Orthodox, Roman Catholic
- Languages: Albanian (Tosk is the official dialect), Greek, Vlach, Romani, Slavic dialects
- British Embassy, Tirana: +355 4 223 4973/4/5

the gap-year guidebook 2011

Algeria, The People's Democratic Republic of
- Population: 32 million
- Location: North Africa
- Capital: Algiers
- Currency: Algerian Dinar (DZD)
- Religion: Sunni Muslim, Christian, Jewish
- Language: Arabic (official language), French and Amazigh
- British Embassy, Algiers: +213 21 23 00 68

Andorra, The Principality of
- Population: 76,875
- Location: Southern Europe
- Capital: Andorra la Vella
- Currency: Euro (EUR)
- Religion: Roman Catholic
- Language: Catalan (official), French, Spanish
- British Consulate-General, Barcelona: +34 933 666 200

Angola, The Republic of
- Population: 16.4 million (2006 estimate)
- Location: Southern Africa
- Capital: Luanda
- Currency: Kwanza (AOA)
- Religion: Indigenous beliefs, Roman Catholic, Christian, Muslim
- Language: Portuguese (official), local African languages
- British Embassy, Luanda: +244 (222) 334582

Anguilla (British Overseas Territory)
- Population: 13,600 (2005 estimate)
- Location: Caribbean
- Capital: The Valley
- Currency: Eastern Caribbean Dollar (XCD); US dollars accepted (USD)
- Religion: Christian
- Language: English
- Government House, Anguilla: +1 (264) 497 2621/2

visit: www.gap-year.com

Antigua and Barbuda
- Population: 85,700 (EIU 2007 estimate)
- Location: Caribbean
- Capital: Saint John's City
- Currency: East Caribbean dollar (XCD)
- Religion: Anglican, Moravian, Methodist and Roman Catholic
- Language: English
- British High Commission, Barbados: +1 246 430 7800

Argentina (The Argentine Republic)
- Population: 36.2 million
- Location: Southern South America
- Capital: Buenos Aires
- Currency: Peso (ARS)
- Religion: Roman Catholic, Protestant, Jewish and Muslim
- Language: Spanish
- British Embassy, Buenos Aires: +54 (11) 4808 2200

Armenia, The Republic of
- Population: 3.2 million
- Location: Europe
- Capital: Yerevan
- Currency: Dram (AMD)
- Religion: Armenian Orthodox, Christian, Yezidi
- Language: Armenian, Russian, Yezidi
- British Embassy, Yerevan: +374 (0) 10 264 301

Ascension Island (British Overseas Territory)
- Population: 1000
- Location: Atlantic Ocean
- Capital: Georgetown
- Currency: St Helena/Ascension Pound (SHP)
- Religion: Christian
- Language: English
- Government House, Georgetown: +00 247 7000

the gap-year guidebook 2011

Australia, The Commonwealth of
- Population: 20.7 million
- Location: Australasia
- Capital: Canberra
- Currency: Australian dollar (AUD)
- Religion: Christian, Buddhist, Jewish, Muslim
- Language: English, Aboriginal
- British High Commission, Canberra: +61 (0) 2 6270 6666

Austria, The Republic of
- Population: 8.3 million
- Location: Central Europe
- Capital: Vienna
- Currency: Euro (EUR)
- Religion: Roman Catholic, Muslim and Protestant
- Language: German
- British Embassy, Vienna Tel: +43 (1) 716 130

Azerbaijan, The Republic of
- Population: 8.5 million
- Location: South-west Asia
- Capital: Baku
- Currency: Manat (AZN)
- Religion: Muslim, Russian Orthodox, Armenian Orthodox,
- Language: Azeri, Russian, Armenian
- British Embassy, Baku: +994 (12) 497 5188/89/90

Bahamas, The Commonwealth of The
- Population: 333,800
- Location: Caribbean
- Capital: Nassau
- Currency: Bahamian Dollar (BSD)
- Religion: Baptist, Anglican, Roman Catholic, Methodist, Church of God, Evangelical Protestants
- Language: English, Creole (among Haitian immigrants)
- refer to British High Commission, Kingston, Jamaica: +1 (876) 510 0700

visit: www.gap-year.com

Bahrain, The Kingdom of
- Population: 698,585 (including expatriate residents)
- Location: Middle East
- Capital: Manama (Al Manamah)
- Currency: Bahraini Dinar (BHD)
- Religion: Muslim
- Language: Arabic, English
- British Embassy, Manama: +973 1757 4100; +973 1757 4167 (Information)

Bangladesh, The People's Republic of
- Population: 135 million (2003 estimate)
- Location: South Asia
- Capital: Dhaka
- Currency: Taka (BDT)
- Religion: Muslim, Hindu, Buddhist, Christian
- Language: Bangla, English, some tribal languages
- British High Commission, Dhaka: +880 (2) 882 2705/6/7/8/9

Barbados
- Population: 274,000 (June 2006)
- Location: Caribbean
- Capital: Bridgetown
- Currency: Barbadian Dollar (BBD)
- Religion: Protestant, Roman Catholic, Jewish, Muslim
- Language: English
- British High Commission, Bridgetown: +1 (246) 430 7800

Belarus, The Republic of
- Population: 9.7 million (2007 estimate)
- Location: Eastern Europe
- Capital: Minsk
- Currency: Belarusian Ruble (BYR)
- Religion: Eastern Orthodox Christian, Roman Catholic, Protestant, Jewish, Muslim
- Language: Belarusian, Russian
- British Embassy, Minsk: +375 (17) 210 5920/1

the gap-year guidebook 2011

Belgium
- Population: 10.25 million
- Location: Central Europe
- Capital: Brussels
- Currency: Euro (EUR)
- Religion: Roman Catholic, Protestant
- Language: Dutch, French, German
- British Embassy, Brussels: +32 (2) 287 6211

Belize
- Population: 291,600 (June 2005)
- Location: Central America
- Capital: Belmopan
- Currency: Belizean Dollar (BZD)
- Religion: Roman Catholic, Protestant, Muslim, Buddhist, Hindu, Bahá'í
- Language: English, Creole, Spanish, indigenous languages
- British High Commission, Belmopan: +501 822 2981/2717

Benin, The Republic of
- Population: 8.4 million (UN Estimate 2005)
- Location: West Africa
- Capital: Porto-Novo
- Currency: CFA Franc BCEAO (XOF)
- Religion: Indigenous beliefs, Christian, Muslim
- Language: French, Fon, Yoruba, other African languages
- Community Liaison Officer, Contonou: +229 21 30 32 65

Bermuda (British Overseas Territory)
- Population: 64,000 (2007)
- Location: Atlantic Ocean
- Capital: Hamilton
- Currency: Bermuda Dollar (BMD)
- Religion: Christian, African Methodist Episcopalian
- Language: English, Portuguese
- Government House, Hamilton: +1 (441) 292 3600

visit: www.gap-year.com

Bhutan, The Kingdom of
- Population: 658,888 (2007)
- Location: South Asia
- Capital: Thimphu
- Currency: Ngultrum (BTN), Indian Rupee (INR)
- Religion: Buddhist, Hindu
- Language: Dzongkha, various Tibetan and Nepalese dialects, English widely spoken
- UK has no diplomatic representative in Bhutan. Contact British Deputy High Commission, Kolkata (Calcutta), India: +91 33 2288 5173-76

Bolivia, The Republic of
- Population: 9.7 million (2008)
- Location: Central South America
- Capital: La Paz
- Currency: Boliviano (BOB)
- Religion: Roman Catholic, Evangelical Methodist
- Language: Spanish, Quechua, Aymara and Indigenous dialects
- British Embassy, La Paz: +591 (2) 243 3424

Bosnia and Herzegovina
- Population: 4 million (estimated 2005)
- Location: South-east Europe
- Capital: Sarajevo
- Currency: Convertible Mark (BAM)
- Religion: Roman Catholic, Orthodox, Muslim
- Language: Bosnian, Serbian, Croatian
- British Embassy, Sarajevo: +387 33 282 200 (main); +387 33 20 4780 (Consular/Visa)

Botswana, The Republic of
- Population: 1.8 million (2007)
- Location: Southern Africa
- Capital: Gaborone
- Currency: Pula (BWP)
- Religion: Christian, indigenous beliefs
- Language: English, Setswana
- British High Commission, Gaborone: +267 395 2841

the gap-year guidebook 2011

Brazil, The Federative Republic of
- Population: 189.6 million (2008 estimate)
- Location: Eastern South America
- Capital: Brasilia
- Currency: Real (BRL)
- Religion: Roman Catholic, Pentecostal, Animist
- Language: Portuguese
- British Embassy, Brasilia: +55 61 3329 2300

British Antartic Territory
- Population: no indigenous population; scientific stations only
- Location: South Pole
- Currency: Sterling
- Language: English
- refer to Foreign & Commonwealth Office, London: +44 (0) 20 7008 1500

British Virgin Islands
- Population: 27,000 (2005 estimate)
- Location: Caribbean
- Capital: Road Town, Tortola
- Currency: US Dollar (USD)
- Religion: Christian
- Language: English
- Government House, Tortola: +1 284 494 2345/2370

Brunei (Darussalam)
- Population: 390,000 (2007 estimate)
- Location: South-east Asia
- Capital: Bandar Seri Begawan
- Currency: Brunei Dollar (BND)
- Religion: Muslim
- Language: Malay, English, Cantonese, Mandarin, Hokkein, Hakka
- British High Commission, Bandar Seri Begawan: +673 (2) 222 231; +673 (2) 226 001 (Consular/Visa)

visit: www.gap-year.com

Bulgaria, The Republic of
- Population: 7.6 million (UN 2007)
- Location: South-east Europe
- Capital: Sofia
- Currency: Lev (BGN)
- Religion: Bulgarian Orthodox, Muslim, Roman Catholic, Jewish
- Language: Bulgarian
- British Embassy, Sofia: +359 (2) 933 9222

Burkina Faso
- Population: 15.02 million (2008 UN estimate)
- Location: West Africa
- Capital: Ouagadougou
- Currency: CFA Franc BCEAO (XOF)
- Religion: Animist, Muslim, Christian
- Language: French, indigenous languages
- British Honorary Consul, Ouagadougou: +226 (50) 30 88 60

Burma (The Union of Myanmar)
- Population: 52 million
- Location: South-east Asia
- Capital: Rangoon
- Currency: Kyat (MMK)
- Religion: Buddhist, Christian, Muslim, Animist
- Language: Burmese, ethnic minority languages
- British Embassy, Rangoon: +95 (1) 370 863

Burundi, The Republic of
- Population: 8.3 million
- Location: Central Africa
- Capital: Bujumbura
- Currency: Burundi Franc (BIF)
- Religion: Muslim, Roman Catholic, Animist
- Language: Kirundi, French, Swahili
- British Embassy, Liaison Office, Bujumbura: +257 22 246 478

Cambodia, The Kingdom of
- Population: 13.995 million (2007 estimate)
- Location: South-east Asia
- Capital: Phnom Penh
- Currency: Riel (KHR), and US Dollar (USD)
- Religion: Buddhist, Muslim, Christian
- Language: Khmer, Cambodian
- British Embassy, Phnom Penh: +855 23 427124/48153

Cameroon, The Republic of
- Population: 16.3 million (2005 UN estimate)
- Location: West Africa
- Capital: Yaounde
- Currency: CFA Franc BEAC (XAF)
- Religion: Christian, Muslim, indigenous beliefs
- Language: French, English, Pidgin, numerous African dialects
- British High Commission, Yaounde: +237 2222 05 45

Canada
- Population: 33.4 million (2008)
- Location: North America
- Capital: Ottawa
- Currency: Canadian Dollar (CAD)
- Religion: Roman Catholic, Protestant, Muslim
- Language: English, French
- British High Commission, Ottawa: +1 (613) 237 1530

Cape Verde, The Republic of
- Population: 426,800 (2008 estimate)
- Location: West Africa
- Capital: Praia
- Currency: Escudo (CVE)
- Religion: Roman Catholic
- Language: Portuguese, Crioulo
- British Honorary Consulate, Sao Vincente: +238 232 3512

visit: www.gap-year.com

Cayman Islands (British Overseas Territory)
- Population: 53,252 (2006 estimate)
- Location: Caribbean
- Capital: George Town (Grand Cayman)
- Currency: Caymanian Dollar (KYD)
- Religion: Christian
- Language: English
- Government House, George Town, Grand Cayman: +1 345 244 2401

Central African Republic, The
- Population: 4.3 million (2007 estimate)
- Location: Central Africa
- Capital: Bangui
- Currency: CFA Franc BEAC (XAF)
- Religion: Christian, Muslim, indigenous beliefs
- Language: French, Sangho
- refer to British High Commission, Yaoundé, Cameroon: +237 2222 05 45

Chad, The Republic of
- Population: 9.8 million (2006 estimate)
- Location: Central Africa
- Capital: N'Djamena
- Currency: CFA Franc BEAC (XAF)
- Religion: Muslim, Christian, indigenous beliefs
- Language: French, Arabic, local languages
- refer to British High Commission, Yaoundé, Cameroon: +237 2222 05 45

Chile, The Republic of
- Population: 15.1 million
- Location: Southern South America
- Capital: Santiago de Chile
- Currency: Peso (CLP)
- Religion: Roman Catholic, Evangelical, Jewish, Muslim
- Language: Spanish, Mapuche, Aymara, Quechua
- British Embassy, Santiago: +56 (2) 370 4100

the gap-year guidebook 2011

China, The People's Republic of
- Population: 1.29 billion
- Location: East Asia
- Capital: Beijing
- Currency: Yuan Renminbi (CNY)
- Religion: Officially atheist. Daoist, Buddhist, Muslim, Roman Catholic, Protestant (the 5 state-registered religions)
- Language: Putonghua (Mandarin), many local Chinese dialects
- British Embassy, Beijing: +86 (10) 5192 4000

Colombia, The Republic of
- Population: 42 million
- Location: Northern South America
- Capital: Bogotá
- Currency: Peso (COP)
- Religion: Roman Catholic, Evangelical
- Language: Spanish, indigenous languages
- British Embassy, Bogotá: +57 (1) 326 8300

Comoros, The Union of The
- Population: 711,417 (2007 estimate)
- Location: Southern Africa, group of islands in the Mozambique Channel
- Capital: Moroni (Ngazidja)
- Currency: Comoros Franc (KMF)
- Religion: Muslim, Roman Catholic
- Language: Comoran, French, Arabic
- refer to British High Commission, Port Louis, Mauritius: +230 202 9400

Congo, The Republic of The
- Population: 4 million (2005)
- Location: West Africa
- Capital: Brazzaville
- Currency: CFA Franc BEAC (XAF)
- Religion: Roman Catholic, Christian, Muslim, traditional beliefs
- Language: French (official), Lingala, Kikongo, Munukutuba
- refer to British Embassy, Kinshasa, Democratic Republic of Congo: +243 81 715 0761

visit: www.gap-year.com

Congo, The Democratic Republic of the
- Population: 58.7 million
- Location: Central Africa
- Capital: Kinshasa
- Currency: Congolese Franc (CDF)
- Religion: Roman Catholic, Protestant, Kimbanguist, Muslim, indigenous beliefs
- Language: French (official), Lingala (trade language), Swahili, Kikongo, Tshiluba
- British Embassy, Kinshasa: +243 81 715 0761

Costa Rica, The Republic of
- Population: 4.2 million
- Location: Central America
- Capital: San José
- Currency: Colon (CRC)
- Religion: Roman Catholic, Evangelical Protestant
- Language: Spanish
- British Embassy, San José: +506 2258 2025

Côte d'Ivoire, The Republic of (Ivory Coast)
- Population: 20 million (2008 UN estimate)
- Location: West Africa
- Capital Yamoussoukro
- Currency: CFA Franc BCEAO (XOF)
- Religion: Muslim, Christian, indigenous beliefs
- Language: French (official), Dioula, Baoule and other local native dialects
- refer to British High Commission, Accra, Ghana: +233 (21) 221 665

Croatia, The Republic of
- Population: 4.5 million (2004 estimate)
- Location: South-east Europe
- Capital: Zagreb
- Currency: Kuna (HRK)
- Religion: Roman Catholic, Orthodox, Muslim
- Language: Croatian
- British Embassy, Zagreb: +385 (1) 6009 100

the gap-year guidebook 2011

Cuba, The Republic of
- Population: 11.2 million
- Location: Caribbean
- Capital: Havana
- Currency: Convertible Peso (CUC) or Peso (CUP)
- Religion: Roman Catholic, Santeria, Protestant
- Language: Spanish
- British Embassy, Havana: +53 (7) 214 2200

Cyprus, The Republic of
- Population: 754,064
- Location: Mediterranean
- Capital: Nicosia
- Currency: Euro (EUR), Turkish Lira (in the north) (TRY)
- Religion: Greek Orthodox, Muslim, Maronite, Armenian Apostolic
- Language: Greek, Turkish, English
- British High Commission, Nicosia: +357 22 861100

Czech Republic, The
- Population: 10.47 million
- Location: Central Europe
- Capital: Prague
- Currency: Czech Koruna (Crown) (CZK)
- Religion: Roman Catholic, Protestant, Orthodox, Atheist
- Language: Czech
- British Embassy, Prague: +420 257 402 111

Denmark, The Kingdom of
- Population: 5.4 million
- Location: Northern Europe
- Capital: Copenhagen
- Currency: Danish Krone (DKK)
- Religion: Evangelical Lutheran, Christian, Muslim
- Language: Danish, Faroese, Greenlandic (an Inuit dialect), English is the predominant second language
- British Embassy, Copenhagen: +45 35 44 52 00

visit: www.gap-year.com

Djibouti, The Republic of
- Population: 852,844 (2008 estimate)
- Location: East Africa
- Capital: Djibouti
- Currency: Djiboutian Franc (DJF)
- Religion: Muslim, Christian
- Language: French (official), Arabic (official), Somali, Afar
- British Honorary Consul, Djibouti: +253 (3) 85007

Dominica, The Commonwealth of
- Population: 72,000
- Location: Caribbean
- Capital: Roseau
- Currency: East Caribbean Dollar (XCD)
- Religion: Roman Catholic, Protestant
- Language: English (official), French patois (Creole)
- British High Commission, Roseau: +767 255 3116 / 275 4000

Dominican Republic, the
- Population 8.9 million (2005 UN estimate)
- Location: Caribbean
- Capital: Santo Domingo
- Currency: Dominican Peso (DOP)
- Religion: Roman Catholic
- Language: Spanish
- British Embassy, Santo Domingo: +1 809 472 7111

East Timor - see Timor-Leste

Ecuador, The Republic of
- Population: 13.2 million (WHO 2005)
- Location: South America
- Capital: Quito
- Currency: US Dollar (USD)
- Religion: Roman Catholic
- Language: Spanish (official), Amerindian languages (especially Quechua)
- British Embassy, Quito: +593 (2) 2970 800/1

Egypt, The Arab Republic of
- Population: 76.5 million (2006)
- Location: North Africa
- Capital: Cairo
- Currency: Egyptian Pound (EGP)
- Religion: Muslim (mostly Sunni), Coptic Christian
- Language: Arabic (official), English and French
- British Embassy, Cairo: +20 (2) 2791 6000

El Salvador, The Republic of
- Population: 6.9 million
- Location: Central America
- Capital: San Salvador
- Currency: US Dollar (USD), Colon (SVC)
- Religion: Roman Catholic
- Language: Spanish
- British Honorary Consulate, El Salvador: +503 281 5555

Equatorial Guinea, The Republic of
- Population: 523,051 (2004)
- Location: West Africa
- Capital: Malabo
- Currency: CFA Franc BEAC (XAF)
- Religion: Christian (predominantly Roman Catholic), indigenous religions
- Language: Spanish (official), French (official), Fang, Bubi, Ibo
- Refer to British High Commission, Abuja, Nigeria: +234 (9) 413 2010

Eritrea
- Population: 4.9 million (2007 estimate)
- Location: East Africa
- Capital: Asmara
- Currency: Nafka (ERN)
- Religion: Christian, Muslim
- Language: Tigrinya, Tigre, Arabic, English
- British Embassy, Asmara: +291 1 12 01 45

visit: www.gap-year.com

Estonia, The Republic of
- Population: 1.34 million
- Location: East Europe
- Capital: Tallinn
- Currency: Kroon (EEK)
- Religion: Lutheran, Orthodox Christian
- Language: Estonian (official), Russian
- British Embassy, Tallinn: +372 667 4700

Ethiopia, The Federal Democratic Republic of
- Population: 76-78 million (2005 estimate)
- Location: East Africa
- Capital: Addis Ababa
- Currency: Ethiopian Birr (ETB)
- Religion: Orthodox Christian, Muslim, Animist, Protestant
- Language: Amharic, Tigrinya, Oromigna, Guaragigna, Sidaminga, Somali, Arabic, other local dialects, English (major foreign language taught in schools)
- British Embassy, Addis Ababa: +251 (11) 661 2354

Falkland Islands (British Overseas Territory)
- Population: 2955 (2006 census)
- Location: South Atlantic Ocean
- Capital: Stanley
- Currency: Falkland Island Pound (FKP)
- Religion: Christian, Roman Catholic, United Reformed Church, Anglican
- Language: English
- Government House, Stanley: +500 282 00

Fiji (The Republic of the Fiji Islands)
- Population: 837,271 (2007 Fiji national census)
- Location: Pacific Ocean
- Capital: Suva
- Currency: Fijian Dollar (FJD)
- Religion: Christian, Hindu, Muslim
- Language: English (official), Hindustani, Gujarati, numerous Fijian dialects
- British High Commission, Suva: +679 3229 100

the gap-year guidebook 2011

Finland, The Republic of
- Population: 5.3 million
- Location: Northern Europe
- Capital: Helsinki
- Currency: Euro (EUR)
- Religion: Lutheran, Orthodox
- Language: Finnish (official), Swedish (official), growing Russian speaking minority and small Sami speaking community
- British Embassy, Helsinki: +358 (0) 9 2286 5100/5210/5216

France (The French Republic)
- Population: 63.4 million
- Location: West Europe
- Capital: Paris
- Currency: Euro (EUR)
- Religion: Roman Catholic, Protestant, Jewish, Muslim
- Language: French
- British Embassy, Paris: +33 1 44 51 31 00

Gabon (The Gabonese Republic)
- Population: 1.45 million (estimate 2007)
- Location: West Africa
- Capital: Libreville
- Currency: CFA Franc BEAC (XAF)
- Religion: Christian, Muslim, indigenous beliefs
- Language: French (official), Fang, Myene, Bateke, Bapounou/Eschira, Badjabi
- British Honorary Consulate, Libreville: +241 762 200

Gambia, The Republic of
- Population: 1.5 million
- Location: West Africa
- Capital: Banjul
- Currency: Dalasi (GMD)
- Religion: Muslim, Christian, indigenous beliefs
- Language: English (official), Mandinka, Wolof, Fula, indigenous languages
- British High Commission, Banjul: +220 449 5133

visit: www.gap-year.com

Georgia
- Population: 4.4 million
- Location: South-west Asia
- Capital: Tbilisi
- Currency: Lari (GEL)
- Religion: Georgian Orthodox, Muslim, Russian Orthodox, Armenian Apostolic
- Language: Georgian (official), Russian, Armenian, Azeri, Abkhaz
- British Embassy, Tbilisi: +995 32 274 747

Germany, The Federal Republic of
- Population: 82.5 million
- Location: Central Europe
- Capital: Berlin
- Currency: Euro (EUR)
- Religion: Protestant, Roman Catholic, Muslim
- Language: German
- British Embassy, Berlin: +49 (30) 20457-0

Ghana, The Republic of
- Population: 23.3 million (2008 estimate)
- Location: West Africa
- Capital: Accra
- Currency: Cedi (GHS)
- Religion: Muslim, Christian, indigenous beliefs
- Language: English (official), African languages (including Akan, Mossi, Ewe, and Hausa), Fante, Ga-Adangme, 75 spoken languages
- British High Commission, Accra: +233 (21) 221 665

Gibraltar (British Overseas Territory)
- Population: 29,257 (2007)
- Location: Atlantic Ocean
- Capital: Gibraltar
- Currency: Gibraltar Pound (GIP)
- Religion: Roman Catholic, Protestantism, Muslim, Hindu, Jewish
- Language: English
- Governor's Office, Main Street: +350 200 45 440

the gap-year guidebook 2011

Greece (The Hellenic Republic)
- Population: 10.94 million (2001 census estimate)
- Location: South-east Europe
- Capital: Athens
- Currency: Euro (EUR)
- Religion: Greek Orthodox, Muslim
- Language: Greek
- British Embassy, Athens: +30 210 727 2600

Grenada
- Population: 89,703 (July 2006 estimate)
- Location: Caribbean
- Capital: St George's
- Currency: East Caribbean Dollar (XCD)
- Religion: Roman Catholic, Anglican, Protestant
- Language: English (official), French patois
- British High Commission, Bridge Town: +1 246 430 7800/7860 (resides in Barbados)

Guatemala
- Population: 12.7 million (2007 estimate)
- Location: Central America
- Capital: Guatemala City
- Currency: Quetzal (GTQ)
- Religion: Roman Catholic, Protestant, Judasim, Muslim, indigenous Mayan beliefs
- Language: Spanish, there are 23 officially recognized Amerindian languages
- British Embassy, Guatemala City: +502 2380 7300

Guinea, The Republic of
- Population: 9.2 million (2008 UN estimate)
- Location: West Africa
- Capital: Conakry
- Currency: Guinean Franc (GNF)
- Religion: Muslim, Christian, traditional beliefs
- Language: French (official), eight local languages taught in schools (Basari, Pular, Kissi, Koniagi, Kpelle, Loma, Malinke and Susu)
- British Embassy, Conakry: +224 63 35 53 29

visit: www.gap-year.com

Guinea-Bissau, The Republic of
- Population: 1.5 million (2008 UN estimate)
- Location: West Africa
- Capital: Bissau
- Currency: CFA Franc BCEAO (XOF)
- Religion: Muslim, Christian, indigenous beliefs
- Language: Portuguese (official), Crioulo, indigenous African languages
- Honorary British Consulate: +245 320 1224/1216

Guyana, The Co-operative Republic of
- Population: 751,000
- Location: South America
- Capital: Georgetown
- Currency: Guyanese Dollar (GYD)
- Religion: Christian, Hindu, Muslim
- Language: English, Amerindian dialects, Creole
- British High Commission, Georgetown: +592 226 58 81

Haiti, The Republic of
- Population: 8.5 million (2007 estimate)
- Location: Caribbean
- Capital: Port-au-Prince
- Currency: The Gourde (HTG)
- Religion: Roman Catholic, Protestant, Baptist, Pentecostal, Adventist, also Voodoo
- Language: French (official), Creole (official)
- British Consulate, Port-au-Prince: +509 257 3969

Holy See, Rome (Vatican City State)
- Population: 890
- Location: Italy
- Capital: Vatican City
- Currency: Euro (EUR)
- Religion: Roman Catholic
- Language: Latin, Italian, English and French
- British Embassy, Rome: +39 06 4220 4000

Honduras, The Republic of
- Population: 7.2 million (UN 2005)
- Location: Central America
- Capital: Tegucigalpa
- Currency: Lempira (HNL)
- Religion: Roman Catholic, Protestant
- Language: Spanish, English (business), Amerindian dialects
- British Embassy, Tegucigalpa: +504 237 6577/6459

Hong Kong (The Hong Kong Special Administration of China)
- Population: 6.8 million (2004)
- Location: East Asia
- Currency: Hong Kong Dollar (HKD)
- Religion: Buddhist, Taoist, Christian, Muslim, Hindu, Sikhist, Jewish
- Language: Chinese (Cantonese), English
- British Consulate General, Hong Kong: +852 2901 3281

Hungary, The Republic of
- Population: 10.1 million (2005)
- Location: Central Europe
- Capital: Budapest
- Currency: Forint (HUF)
- Religion: Roman Catholic, Calvinist, Lutheran, Jewish, Atheist
- Language: Hungarian
- British Embassy, Budapest: +36 (1) 266 2888

Iceland, The Republic of
- Population: 309,000 (April 2007)
- Location: North Europe
- Capital: Reykjavik
- Currency: Icelandic Krona (ISK)
- Religion: Evangelical Lutheran, Protestant, Roman Catholic
- Language: Icelandic
- British Embassy, Reykjavik: +354 550 5100

visit: www.gap-year.com

India, The Republic of
- Population: 1.13 billion (2007 estimate)
- Location: South Asia
- Capital: New Delhi
- Currency: Rupee (INR)
- Religion: Hindu, Muslim, Christian, Sikhist
- Language: Hindi (official), 18 main and regional official state languages, plus 24 further languages, 720 dialects and 23 tribal languages, English (officially an associate language, is used particularly for political, and commercial communication)
- British High Commission, New Delhi: +91 (11) 2687 2161

Indonesia, The Republic of
- Population: 234.7 million (2007)
- Location: South-east Asia
- Capital: Jakarta
- Currency: Rupiah (IDR)
- Religion: Muslim, Protestant, Roman Catholic, Hindu, Buddhist
- Language: Bahasa Indonesia (official), over 583 languages and dialects
- British Embassy, Jakarta: +62 (21) 2356 5200

Iran, The Islamic Republic of
- Population: 70 million (2000 UN estimate)
- Location: Middle East
- Capital: Tehran
- Currency: Rial (IRR)
- Religion: Shi'a Muslim, Sunni Muslim, Zoroastrian, Jewish, Christian, Bahá'i
- Language: Persian (Farsi), Azeri, Kurdish, Arabic, Luri, Baluchi
- British Embassy, Tehran: +98 (21) 6405 2000

Iraq, Republic of
- Population: 24.6 million (2003 estimate)
- Location: Middle East
- Capital: Baghdad
- Currency: New Iraqi Dinar (IQD)
- Religion: Muslim, Christian
- Language: Arabic, Kurdish, Assyrian, Armenian, Turkoman
- British Embassy, Bagdad: +964 7901 911 684

Ireland, Republic of
- Population: 4.2 million (preliminary 2006 census)
- Location: West Europe
- Capital: Dublin
- Currency: Euro (EUR)
- Religion: Roman Catholic, Church of Ireland
- Language: Irish, English
- British Embassy, Dublin: +353 (1) 205 3700

Israel, The State of
- Population: 7 million
- Location: Middle East
- Capital: Tel Aviv
- Currency: New Israeli Shekel (ILS)
- Religion: Jewish, Muslim, Christian
- Language: Hebrew, Arabic, English, Russian
- British Embassy, Tel Aviv: +972 (3) 5100 166

Italy
- Population: 59.1 million
- Location: South Europe
- Capital: Rome
- Currency: Euro (EUR)
- Religion: Roman Catholic, Jewish, Protestant, Muslim
- Language: Italian (official), German, French, Slovene
- British Embassy, Rome: +39 06 4220 0001

Ivory Coast - see Côte d'Ivoire

Jamaica
- Population: 2.7 million (2007 estimate)
- Location: Caribbean
- Capital: Kingston
- Currency: Jamaican Dollar (JMD)
- Religion: Anglican, Baptist and other Protestant, Roman Catholic, Rastafarian, Jewish, Seventh-Day Adventist
- Language: English, Patois
- British High Commission, Kingston: +1 (876) 510 0700

visit: www.gap-year.com

Japan
- Population: 127.7 million
- Location: East Asia
- Capital: Tokyo
- Currency: Yen (JPY)
- Religion: Shinto, Buddhist, Christian
- Language: Japanese
- British Embassy, Tokyo: +81 (3) 5211 1100

Jordan, The Hashemite Kingdom of
- Population: 5.3 million
- Location: Middle East
- Capital: Amman
- Currency: Jordanian Dinar (JOD)
- Religion: Sunni Muslim, Christian
- Language: Arabic (official), English
- British Embassy, Amman: +962 6 590 9200

Kazakhstan, The Republic of
- Population: 15.2 million
- Location: Central Asia
- Capital: Astana
- Currency: Kazakh Tenge (KZT)
- Religion: Muslim, Russian Orthodox, Protestant
- Language: Kazakh, Russian
- British Embassy, Almaty: +7 573 150 2200

Kenya, The Republic of
- Population: 38.6 million (2008 estimate)
- Location: East Africa
- Capital: Nairobi
- Currency: Kenyan Shilling (KES)
- Religion: Protestant (including Evangelical), Roman Catholic, indigenous beliefs, Muslim
- Language: English (official), Kiswahili, numerous indigenous languages
- British High Commission, Nairobi: +254 (20) 284 4000

the gap-year guidebook 2011

Kiribati, The Republic of
- Population: 99,000 (2007 UN)
- Location: Pacific Ocean
- Capital: Tarawa
- Currency: Australian Dollar (AUD)
- Religion: Roman Catholic, Protestant (Congregational), Seventh-Day Adventist, Bahá'í, Latter-day Saints, Church of God
- Language: English (official), I-Kiribati
- refer to British High Commission, Suva, Fiji: +679 3229 100

Korea, The Democratic People's Republic of (North Korea)
- Population: 22.66 million (2003 UN estimate)
- Location: East Asia
- Capital: Pyongyang
- Currency: North Korean Won (KPW); foreigners are required to use Euros
- Religion: Buddhist, Christian, Chondo
- Language: Korean
- British Embassy, Pyongyang: +850 2 381 7980 (International); 02 382 7980 (Local dialling)

Korea, The Republic of (South Korea)
- Population: 48.49 million (2007 estimate)
- Location: East Asia
- Capital: Seoul
- Currency: South Korean Won (KRW)
- Religion: Shamanist, Buddhist, Confuciant, Chondogyo, Roman Catholic, Protestant
- Language: Korean
- British Embassy, Seoul: +82 (2) 3210 5500

Kosovo
- Population: 2 million (estimate)
- Location: Southern Europe
- Capital: Pristina
- Currency: Euro (EUR)
- Religion: Muslim, Serbian Orthodox, Roman Catholic
- Language: Albanian, Serbian, Bosniak, Turkish
- refer to British Embassy, Belgrade, Serbia: +381 (11) 2645 055

visit: www.gap-year.com

Kuwait, The State of
- Population: 2.6 million (estimate)
- Location: Middle East
- Capital: Kuwait City
- Currency: Kuwaiti Dinar (KWD)
- Religion: Muslim, Christian, other religions restricted
- Language: Arabic (official), English (second official language)
- British Embassy, Dasman: +965 2259 4320

Kyrgyzstan (The Kyrgyz Republic)
- Population: 5 million
- Location: Central Asia
- Capital: Bishkek
- Currency: Som (KGS)
- Religion: Muslim, Russian Orthodox, Christian minorities
- Language: Kyrgyz, Russian
- British Honorary Consul, Bishkek: +996 312 584 245

Laos (The Lao People's Democratic Republic)
- Population: 6.5 million (2007)
- Location: South-east Asia
- Capital: Vientiane
- Currency: Kip (LAK)
- Religion: Buddhist, Animist, Christian, Muslim
- Language: Lao
- British Embassy (resident at Bangkok): +66 (0) 2 305 8333

Latvia, The Republic of
- Population: 2.27 million
- Location: East Europe
- Capital: Riga
- Currency: Lat (LVL)
- Religion: Lutheran, Roman Catholic, Russian Orthodox
- Language: Latvian, Russian
- British Embassy, Riga: +371 6777 4700

Lebanon (The Lebanese Republic)
- Population: 4 million
- Location: Middle East
- Capital: Beirut
- Currency: Lebanese Pound (LBP)
- Religion: 18 registered sects including Druze, Maronite Christian, Shi'a and Sunni Muslim
- Language: Arabic (official), English, French, Armenian
- British Embassy, Beirut: +961 (1) 9608 00 (24 hours)

Lesotho, The Kingdom of
- Population: 2.1 million (2007 estimate)
- Location: Southern Africa
- Capital: Maseru
- Currency: Loti (LSL)
- Religion: Christian, indigenous beliefs
- Language: Sesotho, English
- British Honorary Consulate, Maseru: +266 2231 3929

Liberia, The Republic of
- Population: 3.35 million (2008 estimate)
- Location: West Africa
- Capital: Monrovia
- Currency: Liberian Dollar (LRD), US Dollar (USD)
- Religion: Christian, Muslim, indigenous beliefs
- Language: English (official), indigenous languages
- British Honorary Consulate, Monrovia: +231 226 056

Libya (The Great Socialist People's Libyan Arab Jamahiriya)
- Population: 5.41 million
- Location: North Africa
- Capital: Tripoli
- Currency: Dinar (LYD)
- Religion: Sunni Muslim
- Language: Arabic, Italian and English understood in major cities
- British Embassy, Tripoli: +218 (21) 340 3644/5

visit: www.gap-year.com

Liechtenstein, The Principality of
- Population: 35,000 (2006)
- Location: Central Europe
- Capital: Vaduz
- Currency: Swiss Franc (CHF)
- Religion: Roman Catholic, Protestant
- Language: German (official), Alemannic dialect
- refer to British Embassy, Berne, Switzerland: +41 (31) 359 7700

Lithuania, The Republic of
- Population: 3.4 million (2005)
- Location: East Europe
- Capital: Vilnius
- Currency: Litas (LTL)
- Religion: Roman Catholic
- Language: Lithuanian (official), Russian, English
- British Embassy, Vilnius: +370 5 246 29 00

Luxembourg, The Grand Duchy of
- Population: 451,000
- Location: Central Europe
- Capital: Luxembourg
- Currency: Euro (EUR)
- Religion: Roman Catholic, Protestant, Jewish, Muslim
- Language: Luxembourgish, German, French
- British Embassy, Luxembourg: + 352 22 98 64

Macao (The Macao Special Administrative Region of the People's Republic of China)
- Population: 488,100 (2005)
- Location: East Asia
- Currency: Pataca (MOP)
- Religion: Buddhist, Christian, Taoist
- Language: Cantonese, Portuguese, English
- British Honorary Consulate, Macao: +853 685 0886

the gap-year guidebook 2011

Macedonia, republic of
- Population: 2 million (2004 estimate)
- Location: East Europe
- Capital: Skopje
- Currency: Macedonian Denar (MKD)
- Religion: Orthodox, Muslim
- Language: Macedonian, Albanian, Turkish, Serbian, Vlach, Roma
- British Embassy, Skopje: +389 (2) 3299 299

Madagascar, The Republic of
- Population: 20 million (2008 estimate)
- Location: Southern Africa
- Capital: Antananarivo
- Currency: Ariary (MGA)
- Religion: Christian, indigenous beliefs, Muslim
- Language: Malagasy, French
- British Consulate, Toamasina: +261 (20) 53 325 48/325 69

Malawi, The Republic of
- Population: 13.6 million (2006 estimate)
- Location: Southern Africa
- Capital: Lilongwe
- Currency: Kwacha (MWK)
- Religion: Protestant, Roman Catholic, Muslim, Hindu, indigenous beliefs
- Language: English (official), Chichewa (national)
- British High Commission, Liongwe: +265 (1) 772 400

Malaysia, The Federation of
- Population: 27.5 million (2008)
- Location: South-east Asia
- Capital: Kuala Lumpur
- Currency: Ringgit (MYR)
- Religion: Muslim, Buddhist, Taoist, Christian, Hindu, Animist
- Language: Bahasa Malay (national language), Iban, English widespread, Chinese, Tamil
- British High Commission, Kuala Lumpur: +60 (3) 2170 2200

visit: www.gap-year.com

Maldives, The Republic of
- Population: 400,000 (2004 estimate)
- Location: South Asia
- Capital: Malé
- Currency: Rufiyaa (MVR); resort islands accept US Dollar (USD)
- Religion: Sunni Muslim (other religions illegal)
- Language: Dhivehi, but English widely spoken in Malé and resort islands
- refer to British High Commission, Colombo, Sri Lanka: +94 (11) 539 0639

Mali, The Republic of
- Population: 12.5 million (2008)
- Location: West Africa
- Capital: Bamako
- Currency: CFA Franc BCEAO (XOF)
- Religion: Muslim, Christian, indigenous beliefs
- Language: French (official), Bambara, and numerous other African languages
- British Embassy Liaison Office, Bamako: +223 2021 3412

Malta, The Republic of
- Population: 402,700
- Location: South Europe
- Capital: Valletta
- Currency: Euro (EUR)
- Religion: Roman Catholic
- Language: Maltese, English
- British High Commission, Valletta: +356 2323 0000

Marshall Islands, Republic of the
- Population: 63,174 (2008)
- Location: Pacific Ocean
- Capital: Majuro
- Currency: US Dollar (USD)
- Religion: Christian (mostly Protestant)
- Language: English, two major Marshallese dialects, Japanese
- refer to British Embassy, Manilia: +63 (2) 858 2200

the gap-year guidebook 2011

Mauritania, The Islamic Repubic of
- Population: 3.1 million (2005 estimate)
- Location: North Africa
- Capital: Nouakchott
- Currency: Ouguiya (MRO)
- Religion: Muslim
- Language: Hassaniya Arabic (official), Pulaar, Soninke, Wolof, French widely used in business
- British Honorary Consul, Nouakchott: +222 525 83 31

Mauritius, The Republic of
- Population: 1.27 million (2008 estimate)
- Location: Southern Africa
- Capital: Port Louis
- Currency: Mauritian Rupee (MUR)
- Religion: Hindu, Christian, Muslim
- Language: English, French, Creole
- British Honorary Consulate, Rodrigues: +230 832 0120

Mexico (The United Mexican State)
- Population: 110 million (2008 estimate)
- Location: Central America
- Capital: Mexico City
- Currency: Mexican Peso (MXN)
- Religion: Roman Catholic, Protestant
- Language: Spanish, at least 62 other regional languages
- British Embassy, Mexico City: +52 (55) 5242 8500

Micronesia, The Federated States of
- Population: 107,665 (2008 estimate)
- Location: Pacific Ocean
- Capital: Palikir
- Currency: US Dollar (USD)
- Religion: Roman Catholic, Protestant
- Language: English, Trukese, Pohnpeian, Yapese, Kosrean, Ulithian, Woleaian, Nukuoro, Kapingamarangi
- refer to British Embassy, Manila: +63 (2) 858 2200

visit: www.gap-year.com

Moldova, The Republic of
- Population: 4.32 million
- Location: East Europe
- Capital: Chisinau
- Currency: Moldovan Leu (MDL)
- Religion: Eastern Orthodox, Jewish, Baptist
- Language: Moldovan, Russian (official)
- British Embassy, Chisinau: +373 22 22 59 02; out of hours +373 69 10 44 42

Monaco, The Principality of
- Population: 32,543 (2006)
- Location: West Europe
- Capital: Monaco
- Currency: Euro (EUR)
- Religion: Roman Catholic
- Language: French (official), Italian, Monegasque, English
- British Honorary Consulate, Monaco: +377 93 50 99 54

Mongolia
- Population: 2.64 million (2007)
- Location: North Asia
- Capital: Ulaanbaatar
- Currency: Togrog (Tughrik) (MNT)
- Religion: Tibetan Buddhist, Shamanist, Muslim (south-west)
- Language: Khalkh Mongol, Kazakh
- British Embassy, Ulaanbaatar: +976 (11) 458 133

Montenegro, Republic of
- Population: 650,575
- Location: South-east Europe
- Capital: Podgorica
- Currency: Euro (EUR)
- Religion: Christian, Muslim
- Language: Montenegrin, Serbian, Bosnian, Albanian, Croatian
- British Embassy, Podgorica: +382 (20) 618 010

Montserrat (British Overseas Territory)
- Population: 4655 (2006)
- Location: Caribbean
- Capital: Plymouth (destroyed by the last volcanic eruption)
- Currency: East Caribbean Dollar (XCD)
- Religion: Christian
- Language: English
- Governor's Office, Brades: +1 (664) 491 2688/9

Morocco, The Kingdom of
- Population: 30.5 million (2006 estimate)
- Location: North Africa
- Capital: Rabat
- Currency: Moroccan Dirham (MAD)
- Religion: Muslim, Christian, Jewish
- Language: Arabic (official), Berber dialects, French (commerce, diplomacy and government)
- British Embassy, Rabat: +212 (537) 63 33 33

Mozambique, The Republic of
- Population: 21.2 million (2008 estimate)
- Location: Southern Africa
- Capital: Maputo
- Currency: Metical (MZN)
- Religion: Roman Catholic, Christian, Muslim, indigenous beliefs
- Language: Portuguese (official), over 16 African languages and dialects
- British High Commission, Maputo: +258 21 356 000

Myanmar (see Burma)

Namibia, The Republic of
- Population: 2.08 million (2008 estimate)
- Location: Southern Africa
- Capital: Windhoek
- Currency: Namibian Dollar (NAD)
- Religion: Christian
- Language: English (official), Afrikaans, German, and several indigenous languages
- British High Commission, Windhoek: +264 (61) 274800

visit: www.gap-year.com

Nauru, The Republic of
- Population: 13,770 (2008 estimate)
- Location: Pacific Ocean
- Capital: Yaren District (unofficial)
- Currency: Australian Dollar (AUD)
- Religion: Protestant, Roman Catholic
- Language: Nauruan (official), English (commerce and government, widely understood)
- refer to British High Commission, Suva, Fiji: +679 322 9100

Nepal
- Population: 29.5 million (2008 estimate)
- Location: South Asia
- Capital: Kathmandu
- Currency: Nepalese Rupee (NPR)
- Religion: Hindu, Buddhist, Muslim
- Language: Nepali (official), Newari (mainly in Kathmandu), Tibetan languages (mainly hill areas), Indian languages (mainly Terai areas). Nepal has over 30 languages and many dialects.
- British Embassy, Kathmandu: +977 (1) 441 0583/1281/4588/1590

Netherlands, The Kingdom of The
- Population: 16.5 million (2009)
- Location: North Europe
- Capital: Amsterdam
- Currency: Euro (EUR)
- Religion: Roman Catholic, Protestant, Muslim
- Language: Dutch
- British Embassy, The Hague: +31 (0) 70 4270 427

New Zealand
- Population: 4.26 million (2008)
- Location: Pacific Ocean
- Capital: Wellington
- Currency: New Zealand Dollar (NZD)
- Religion: Anglican, Presbyterian, Roman Catholic, Methodist, Baptist
- Language: English, Maori
- British High Commission, Wellington: +64 (4) 924 2888

the gap-year guidebook 2011

Nicaragua, The Republic of
- Population: 5.1 million (2005)
- Location: Central America
- Capital: Managua
- Currency: Cordoba (NIO)
- Religion: Roman Catholic, Evangelical Protestant
- Language: Spanish (official), English, Miskito, Creole, Mayanga, Garifuna, Rama
- British Honorary Consul, Managua: +505 254 5454/3839

Niger, The Republic of
- Population: 12 million (2005 estimate)
- Location: West Africa
- Capital: Niamey
- Currency: CFA Franc BCEAO (XOF)
- Religion: Muslim
- Language: French (official), Arabic, local languages widely spoken
- British Honorary Consul, Niamey: +227 9687 8130

Nigeria, The Federal Republic of
- Population: 144.7 million (2006)
- Location: West Africa
- Capital: Abuja
- Currency: Naira (NGN)
- Religion: Muslim, Christian, traditional beliefs
- Language: English (official), Hausa, Yoruba, Igbo
- British High Commission, Abuja: +234 (9) 413 2010/2011/3885-7

Norway, The Kingdom of
- Population: 4.6 million (2006)
- Location: North Europe
- Capital: Oslo
- Currency: Norwegian Kroner (NOK)
- Religion: Church of Norway (Evangelical Lutheran)
- Language: Norwegian (bokmål and nynorsk), Sami
- British Embassy, Oslo: +47 23 13 27 00

visit: www.gap-year.com

Oman, The Sultanate of
- Population: 3.3 million (2007)
- Location: Middle East
- Capital: Muscat
- Currency: Oman Rial (OMR)
- Religion: Ibadhi Muslim, Sunni Muslim, Shi'a Muslim, Hindu, Christian
- Language: Arabic (official), English, Farsi, Baluchi, Urdu
- British Embassy, Muscat: +968 24 609 000; (out of hours emergencies) +968 9920 0865

Pakistan, The Islamic Republic of
- Population: 162.4 million
- Location: South Asia
- Capital: Islamabad
- Currency: Rupee (PKR)
- Religion: Muslim, Hindu, Christian
- Language: Punjabi, Sindhi, Pashtun, Urdu, Balochi, English and other local languages
- British High Commission, Islamabad: +92 51 201 2000

Palau, The Republic of
- Population: 827,900 (2007)
- Location: Pacific Ocean
- Capital: Suva
- Currency: United States Dollar (USD)
- Religion: Christian, Hindu, Muslim
- Language: English, numerous Fijian dialects, Gujarati, Fijian Hindi
- refer to British Ambassador, Manila, The Philippines: +63 (2) 858 2200

Palestine (The Occupied Palestinian Territories)
- Population: 4 million (2007 estimate)
- Location: Middle East
- Currency: New Israeli Shekel (ILS), Jordanian Dinar (JOD) (West Bank Only)
- Religion: Muslim, Christian
- Language: Arabic, English widely spoken
- British Consulate-General, Gaza: +972 (08) 283 7724

Panama, The Republic of
- Population: 3.23 million (2006)
- Location: Central America
- Capital: Panama City
- Currency: US Dollar (USD) (known locally as the Balboa (PAB))
- Religion: Roman Catholic, Protestant, Jewish, Muslim
- Language: Spanish (official), English
- British Embassy, Panama City: +507 269 0866

Papua New Guinea, The Independent State of
- Population: 6 million
- Location: South-east Asia,
- Capital: Port Moresby
- Currency: Kina (PGK)
- Religion: Christian according to its constitution, Roman Catholic, Evangelical Lutheran, Evangelical Alliance, Pentecostal, Baptist, Anglican, Seventh Day Adventist, United Church, Buddhist, Muslim, Hindu
- Language: English, Pidgin, Hiri Motu, over 820 different languages
- British High Commission, Port Moresby: +675 325 1677

Paraguay, The Republic of
- Population: 6.2 million
- Location: Central South America
- Capital: Asunción
- Currency: Guarani (PYG)
- Religion: Roman Catholic, Mennonite, Protestant, Latter-day Saints, Jewish, Russian Orthodox
- Language: Spanish (official), Guaraní (official)
- British Honorary Consulate, Asunción: +595 (21) 210 405

Peru, The Republic of
- Population: 28.22 million (2007 estimate)
- Location: Western South America
- Capital: Lima
- Currency: Nuevo Sol (PEN)
- Religion: Roman Catholic
- Language: Spanish (official), Quechua (official), Aymara and several minor Amazonian languages
- British Embassy, Lima: +51 (1) 617 3000 (main); 3053/3054 (consular)

visit: www.gap-year.com

Philippines, The Republic of the
- Population: 92.23 million (2009 estimate)
- Location: South-east Asia
- Capital: Metro Manila
- Currency: Peso (PHP)
- Religion: Roman Catholic, Protestant, Muslim
- Language: Filipino (official), English (official)
- British Embassy, Manila: +63 (2) 858 2200

Pitcairn, Henderson, Ducie & Oeno Islands (British Overseas Territory)
- Population: 51
- Location: South Pacific
- Capital: Adamstown
- Currency: New Zealand Dollar (NZD)
- Religion: Seventh Day Adventist
- Language: English, Pitkern (a mix of English and Tahitian)
- British High Commission, Auckland, New Zealand: +64 (9) 366 0186

Poland, The Republic of
- Population: 38.1 million
- Location: Central Europe
- Capital: Warsaw
- Currency: Zloty (PLN)
- Religion: Roman Catholic, Eastern Orthodox, Protestant
- Language: Polish
- British Embassy, Warsaw: +48 (22) 311 00 00

Portugal (The Portuguese Republic)
- Population: 10.6 million
- Location: South-west Europe
- Capital: Lisbon
- Currency: Euro (EUR)
- Religion: Roman Catholic, Protestant
- Language: Portuguese
- British Embassy, Lisbon: +351 (21) 392 4000

the gap-year guidebook 2011

Qatar, The State of
- Population: 1.4 million (2008)
- Location: Middle East
- Capital: Doha
- Currency: Qatari Riyal (QAR)
- Religion: Muslim
- Language: Arabic (official), English, Urdu
- British Embassy, Doha: +974 496 2000

Romania
- Population: 22.6 million
- Location: South-east Europe
- Capital: Bucharest
- Currency: New Leu (RON)
- Religion: Orthodox, Roman Catholic, Protestant, Reformed, Greek Catholic, Unitarian
- Language: Romanian (official), English, French, German
- British Embassy, Bucharest: +40 (21) 201 7200

Russia Federation, The
- Population: 142 million (2008)
- Location: North Asia
- Capital: Moscow
- Currency: Ruble (RUB)
- Religion: Orthodox Christian, Muslim, Jewish, Buddhist
- Language: Russian, Tatar
- British Embassy, Moscow: +7 (495) 956 7200

Rwanda, The Republic of
- Population: 8 million (estimated)
- Location: Central Africa
- Capital: Kigali
- Currency: Rwandan Franc (RWF)
- Religion: Roman Catholic, Protestant, Muslim, indigenous beliefs
- Language: Kinyarwanda (official), French (official), English (official), Kiswahili (used in commercial centres and by army)
- British Embassy, Kigali: +250 584 098/586 072

visit: www.gap-year.com

Saint Helena (British Overseas Territory)
- Population: 4000
- Location: Atlantic Ocean
- Capital: Jamestown
- Currency: St Helena Pound (SHP)
- Religion: Christiantiy, Bahá'í
- Language: English
- Governor's Office, Jamestown: +290 2555

Saint Kitts & Nevis (The Federation of St Christopher & Nevis)
- Population: 50,000
- Location: Caribbean
- Capital: Basseterre
- Currency: East Caribbean Dollar (XCD)
- Religion: Anglican, Roman Catholic, Evangelical Protestant
- Language: English
- British High Commission in Barbados: +1 (246) 430 7800

Saint Lucia
- Population: 171,100 (2007 estimate)
- Location: Caribbean
- Capital: Castries
- Currency: East Caribbean Dollar (XCD)
- Religion: Roman Catholic, Anglican, Methodist, Baptist, Jewish, Hindu, Muslim
- Language: English (official), French patois (Kweyol)
- British High Commission, Castries: +1 (758) 452 2484/5 (resides in Barbados)

Saint Vincent and the Grenadines
- Population: 109,022
- Location: Caribbean
- Capital: Kingstown
- Currency: East Caribbean Dollar (XCD)
- Religion: Anglican, Methodist, Roman Catholic, Seventh-Day Adventist, Hindu, other Protestant
- Language: English
- British High Commission, Kingstown: +784 456 5981 (resides in Barbados)

the gap-year guidebook 2011

Samoa, The Independent State of
- Population: 214,765 (2005 estimate)
- Location: South Pacific
- Capital: Apia
- Currency: Samoan Tala (WST)
- Religion: Roman Catholic, Methodist, Latter-day Saints
- Language: Samoan, English
- British Honorary Consulate, Apia: +685 27123

São Tomé & Príncipe, The Democratic State of
- Population: 158,000 (UN 2007 estimate)
- Location: West Africa
- Capital: São Tomé
- Currency: Dobra (STD)
- Religion: Christian
- Language: Portuguese, Lungwa Santomé, and other creole dialects
- Refer to the British Embassy in Luanda, Angola: +244 222 334582

Saudi Arabia, The Kingdom of
- Population: 27.6 million (2007 estimate)
- Location: Middle East
- Capital: Riyadh
- Currency: Saudi Riyal (SAR)
- Religion: Muslim (Sunni, Shia). The public practice of any other religion is forbidden
- Language: Arabic, English
- British Embassy, Riyadh: +966 (0) 1 488 0077

Senegal, The Republic of
- Population: 11.6 million (2005 UN estimate)
- Location: West Africa
- Capital: Dakar
- Currency: CFA Franc BCEAO (XOF)
- Religion: Muslim, Christian, indigenous beliefs
- Language: French (official), Wolof, Malinke, Serere, Soninke, Pular (all national)
- British Embassy, Dakar: +221 33 823 7392/9971

visit: www.gap-year.com

Serbia, The Republic of
- Population: 7.5 million (2002)
- Location: South-east Europe
- Capital: Belgrade
- Currency: Serbian Dinar (RSD)
- Religion: Serbian Orthodox, Muslim, Roman Catholic, Christian
- Language: Serbian (majority), Romanian, Hungarian, Slovak, Croatian, Albanian (Kosovan), Ukranian, Bosniak, Montenegrin, Bulgarian, Ruthenian, Roma. Vlach, Macedonian
- British Embassy, Belgrade: +381 (11) 2645 055

Seychelles, The Republic of
- Population: 82,247 (2007 estimate)
- Location: Indian Ocean
- Capital: Victoria
- Currency: Seychelles Rupee (SCR)
- Religion: Roman Catholic, Anglican, Muslim, Hindu
- Language: English, French, Creole (Seselwa)
- British High Commission, Mahe: +248 283 666

Sierra Leone, The Republic of
- Population: 6.2 million (2008 UN estimate)
- Location: West Africa
- Capital: Freetown
- Currency: Leone (SLL)
- Religion: Muslim, Christian, indigenous beliefs
- Language: English (official), Krio (English-based Creole), indigenous languages widely spoken
- British High Commission, Freetown: +232 (22) 232 961

Singapore, The Republic of
- Population: 4.84 million (2008)
- Location: South-east Asia
- Capital: Singapore
- Currency: Singapore Dollar (SGD)
- Religion: Taoist, Buddhist, Muslim, Christian, Hindu
- Language: Mandarin, English, Malay, Tamil
- British High Commission, Singapore: +65 6424 4200

the gap-year guidebook 2011

Slovakia (The Slovak Republic)
- Population: 5.39 million (2002)
- Location: Central Europe
- Capital: Bratislava
- Currency: Euro (EUR)
- Religion: Roman Catholic, Atheist, Protestant, Orthodox
- Language: Slovak (official), Hungarian
- British Embassy, Bratislava: +421 (2) 5998 2000

Slovenia, The Republic of
- Population: 2 million
- Location: Central Europe
- Capital: Ljubljana
- Currency: Euro (EUR)
- Religion: Roman Catholic
- Language: Slovene, Italian, Hungarian, English
- British Embassy, Ljubljana: +386 (1) 200 3910

Solomon Islands
- Population: 530,000
- Location: Pacific Ocean
- Capital: Honiara
- Currency: Solomon Islands Dollar (SBD)
- Religion: Christian, traditional beliefs
- Language: English, Pidgin, 92 indigenous languages
- British High Commission, Honiara: +677 21705/6

Somalia (The Somali Democratic Republic)
- Population: 8.86 million (2006 estimate)
- Location: East Africa
- Capital: Mogadishu
- Currency: Somali Shilling (SOS)
- Religion: Sunni Muslim
- Language: Somali (official), Arabic, Italian, English
- British Embassy, Mogadishu: +252 (1) 20288/9

visit: www.gap-year.com

South Africa, Republic of
- Population: 43.8 million (2007 estimate)
- Location: Southern Africa
- Capital: Pretoria/Tshwane
- Currency: Rand (ZAR)
- Religion: Predominately Christian but all principal religions are represented
- Language: 11 official languages: Afrikaans, English, Ndebele, Sepedi, Sesotho, Swati, Tsonga, Tswana, Venda, Xhosa, Zulu
- British High Commission, Pretoria: +27 (12) 421 7500

South Georgia & South Sandwich Islands (British Overseas Territories)
- Population: no indigenous population
- Location: Atlantic Ocean
- Capital: King Edward Point
- Currency: United Kingdom Pound Sterling (GBP)
- Language: English
- Governor's Office, Stanley, Falkland Islands: +500 282 00

Spain, The Kingdom of
- Population: 44 million
- Location: South-western Europe
- Capital: Madrid
- Currency: Euro (EUR)
- Religion: Roman Catholic, Protestant
- Language: Castilian Spanish (official), Catalan, Galician, Basque
- British Embassy, Madrid: +34 (91) 700 8200

Sri Lanka, The Democratic Socialist Republic of
- Population: 19.4 million (2008, UN)
- Location: South Asia
- Capital: Colombo
- Currency: Rupee (LKR)
- Religion: Buddhist, Hindu, Muslim, Christian
- Language: Sinhalese, Tamil, English
- British High Commission, Colombo: +94 (11) 5390639

the gap-year guidebook 2011

Sudan, The Republic of
- Population: 33.61 million (2003)
- Location: North Africa
- Capital: Khartoum City
- Currency: Sudanese pound (SDG)
- Religion: Muslim, Christian, indigenous religions
- Language: Arabic (official), Nubian, Ta Bedawie, dialects of Nilotic, Nilo-Hamitic, Sudanic languages, English
- British Embassy, Khartoum: +249 (183) 777 105

Suriname, The Republic of
- Population: 437,024 (2004)
- Location: Northern South America
- Capital: Paramaribo
- Currency: Suriname Dollar (SRD)
- Religion: Hindu, Muslim, Roman Catholic, Dutch Reformed, Moravian, Jewish, Bahá'í
- Language: Dutch (official), English, Sranan Tongo (Creole), Hindustani, Javanese
- British Honorary Consulate, Paramaribo: +597 402 558

Swaziland, The Kingdom of
- Population: 1.1 million (2006 estimate)
- Location: Southern Africa
- Capital: Mbabane
- Currency: Lilangeni (SZL)
- Religion: Christian, indigenous beliefs
- Language: English, Siswati
- British Honorary Consulate, Mbabane: +268 551 6247

Sweden, The Kingdom of
- Population: 9.1 million (2008)
- Location: North Europe
- Capital: Stockholm
- Currency: Swedish Krona (SEK)
- Religion: Lutheran, Roman Catholic, Orthodox, Baptist, Muslim, Jewish, Buddhist
- Language: Swedish, English widely spoken
- British Embassy, Stockholm: +46 (8) 671 3000

visit: www.gap-year.com

Switzerland (The Swiss Confederation)
- Population: 7.5 million (2007)
- Location: Central Europe
- Capital: Berne
- Currency: Swiss Franc (CHF)
- Religion: Roman Catholic, Protestant, Muslim
- Language: Swiss German (official), French, Italian, Rhaeto-Rumantsch
- British Embassy, Berne: +41 (31) 359 7700

Syria (The Syrian Arab Republic)
- Population: 20 million
- Location: Middle East
- Capital: Damascus
- Currency: Syrian Pound (also called Lira) (SYP)
- Religion: Sunni Muslim, Shi'a Muslim, Alawite, Druze, other Muslim sects, Christian, Jewish
- Language: Arabic (official), Kurdish, Armenian, Aramaic, Circassian, some French, English
- British Embassy, Damascus: +963 (11) 339 1513/1541 (consular)

Taiwan (Province of the People's Republic of China)
- Population: 22.9 million (2007)
- Location: East Asia
- Capital: Taipei
- Currency: New Taiwan Dollar (TWD)
- Religion: Buddhist, Taoist, Christian
- Language: Mandarin Chinese (official), Taiwanese, Hakka
- British Trade & Cultural Office, Taipei: +886 (2) 8758 2088

Tajikistan, Republic of
- Population: 7 million (2004 UN)
- Location: Central Asia
- Capital: Dushanbe
- Currency: Somoni (TJS)
- Religion: Sunni Muslim, Ismaili Shiite, Russian Orthodox Christian, Jewish
- Language: Tajik, Russian
- British Embassy, Dushanbe: +992 372 24 22 21

Tanzania, United Republic of
- Population: 40.4 million (UN, 2007)
- Location: East Africa
- Capital: Dodoma (official)
- Currency: Tanzania Shilling (TZS)
- Religion: Christian, Muslim, indigenous beliefs
- Language: Kiswahili, English
- British High Commission, Dar es Salaam: +255 (022) 211 0101

Thailand, Kingdom of
- Population: 65 million (2007 estimate)
- Location: South-east Asia
- Capital: Bangkok
- Currency: Baht (THB)
- Religion: Buddhist, Muslim, Christian, Hindu
- Language: Thai, Yawi
- British Embassy, Bangkok: +66 (0) 2 305 8333

Tibet – see China

Timor-Leste, Democratic Republic of
- Population: 1.1 million (2008)
- Location: South-east Asia
- Capital: Dili
- Currency: US Dollar (USD)
- Religion: Roman Catholic (majority), Protestant, Muslim, Hindu, Buddhist
- Language: Tetum (official), Portuguese (official), Bahasa Indonesian, English
- refer to British Embassy, Jakarta: +62 (21) 2356 5200

Togo (Togolese Republic)
- Population: 4.7 million
- Location: West Africa
- Capital: Lomé
- Currency: CFA Franc BCEAO (XOF)
- Religion: Christian, Muslim, indigenous beliefs
- Language: French, Kabiye, Ewe
- The British Ambassador to Togo resides in Accra, Ghana: +223 21 221665; in a genuine emergency contact the Honorary Consul in Togo: +228 2222714

visit: www.gap-year.com

Tonga, Kingdom of
- Population: 101,991 (2006)
- Location: Pacific Ocean
- Capital: Nuku'alofa
- Currency: Pa'anga (TOP)
- Religion: Christian
- Language: Tongan, English
- refer to British High Commission, Suva, Fiji: +679 322 9100

Trinidad and Tobago, Republic of
- Population: 1.05 million (2007 estimate)
- Location: Caribbean
- Capital: Port of Spain
- Currency: Trinidad and Tobago Dollar (TTD)
- Religion: Roman Catholic, Hindu, Anglican, Muslim, Presbyterian
- Language: English (official), Spanish
- British High Commission, Port of Spain: +1 (868) 622 2748

Tristan da Cunha (British Overseas Territory)
- Population: 275
- Location: Atlantic Ocean
- Capital: Edinburgh of the Seven Seas
- Currency: Sterling (GBP)
- Religion: Christian
- Language: English
- Administrator's Office: +870 764 341 816

Tunisia (Tunisian Republic)
- Population: 9.92 million (2003)
- Location: North Africa
- Capital: Tunis
- Currency: Tunisian Dinar (TND)
- Religion: Muslim, Christian
- Language: Arabic, French
- British Embassy, Tunis: +216 71 108 700

Turkey, Republic of
- Population: 71.9 million (2008)
- Location: South-east Europe
- Capital: Ankara
- Currency: New Turkish Lira (TRY)
- Religion: Muslim
- Language: Turkish, Kurdish
- British Consulae, Izmir: +90 (232) 463 5151

Turkmenistan
- Population: 5.1-6.9 million
- Location: Central Asia
- Capital: Ashgabat
- Currency: Manat (TMM)
- Religion: Sunni Muslim
- Language: Russian, Turkmen
- British Embassy, Ashgabat: +993 (12) 363 462/63/64

Turks and Caicos Islands (British Overseas Territories)
- Population: 32,000 (2006)
- Location: Atlantic Ocean
- Capital: Grand Turk
- Currency: US Dollar (USD)
- Religion: Christian
- Language: English, some Creole
- Governor's Office, Grand Turk: +1 (649) 946 2309

Tuvalu
- Population: 12,177 (2008 estimate)
- Location: Pacific Ocean
- Capital: Funafuti
- Currency: Australian Dollar (AUD), Tuvaluan Dollar (TVD) (coinage only)
- Religion: Church of Tuvalu, Bahá'í
- Language: Tuvaluan, English, Samoan, Kiribati
- refer to British High Commission, Suva, Fiji: +679 322 9100

visit: www.gap-year.com

Uganda Republic
- Population: 28.9 million (2006 estimate)
- Location: Central Africa
- Capital: Kampala
- Currency: Uganda Shilling (UGX)
- Religion: Christian, Muslim
- Language: English (official national language), Luganda, Swahili
- British High Commission, Kampala: +256 (31) 231 2000

Ukraine
- Population: 46.2 million (estimate)
- Location: East Europe
- Capital: Kyiv (Kiev)
- Currency: Hryvna (UAH)
- Religion: Ukrainian Orthodox, Ukrainian Greek Catholic, Jewish, Muslim
- Language: Ukrainian (official), Russian, Romanian, Polish, Hungarian
- British Embassy, Kyiv: +380 44 490 3660

United Arab Emirates
- Population: 4.6 million (2005 estimate)
- Location: Middle East
- Capital: Abu Dhabi
- Currency: Dirham (AED)
- Religion: Muslim, Hindu
- Language: Arabic (official)
- British Embassy, Abu Dhabi: +971 (2) 610 1100

United Kingdom
- Population: 60.6 million (2006)
- Location: Western Europe
- Capital: London
- Currency: United Kingdom Pound Sterling (GBP)
- Religion: Church of England, although all other faiths are practised
- Language: English, Welsh (in Wales), Gaelic (in Scotland)
- Foreign & Commonwealth Office: +44 (0) 20 7008 1500

United States of America
- Population: 306 million (2009 estimate)
- Location: North America
- Capital: Washington, DC
- Currency: US Dollar (USD)
- Religion: Protestant, Roman Catholic, Latter-day Saints, Jewish, Muslim
- Language: English, Spanish
- British Embassy, Washington DC: +1 (202) 588 6500

Uruguay
- Population: 3.5 million (2008)
- Location: Southern South America
- Capital: Montevideo
- Currency: Peso Uruguayan (UYU)
- Religion: Roman Catholic, Protestant, Jewish, Atheist
- Language: Spanish
- British Embassy, Montevideo: +598 (2) 622 36 30/50

Uzbekistan, Republic of
- Population: 26.5 million (2004 UN)
- Location: Central Asia
- Capital: Tashkent
- Currency: Som (UZS)
- Religion: Sunni Muslim
- Language: Uzbek, Russian, Tajik
- British Embassy, Tashkent: +998 71 120 1500/1516 (consular/visa)

Vanuatu, Republic of
- Population: 215,446 (2008 estimate)
- Location: South Pacific
- Capital: Port Vila
- Currency: Vatu (VUV)
- Religion: Presbyterian, Anglican, Roman Catholic, Seventh Day Adventist
- Language: Bislama (offical), English (official), French (official), plus over 130 vernacular languages
- refer to British High Commission, Suva, Fiji: +679 322 9100

visit: www.gap-year.com

Venezuela, The Bolivarian Republic of
- Population: 28.2 million (2008 estimate)
- Location: Northern South America
- Capital: Caracas
- Currency: Bolivar Fuerte (VEF)
- Religion: Roman Catholic
- Language: Spanish
- British Embassy, Caracas: +58 (212) 263 8411

Vietnam, The Socialist Republic of
- Population: 83 million
- Location: South-east Asia
- Capital: Hanoi
- Currency: Vietnamese Dong (VND) (US dollar widely accepted)
- Religion: Buddhist, Roman Catholic, Protestant, Cao Dai, Hoa Hao
- Language: Vietnamese, minority languages also spoken
- British Embassy, Hanoi: +84 (4) 3936 0500

Yemen, Republic of
- Population: 20 million (estimate)
- Location: Middle East
- Capital: Sana'a
- Currency: Yemeni Rial (YER)
- Religion: Muslim
- Language: Arabic
- British Embassy, Sana'a: +967 (1) 308 100

Zambia, Republic of
- Population: 11.8 million (2006)
- Location: Southern Africa
- Capital: Lusaka
- Currency: Kwacha (ZMK)
- Religion: Christian, Muslim, Hindu, indigenous beliefs
- Language: English (official language of government), plus six further official languages
- British High Commission, Lusaka: +260 (211) 423200

Zimbabwe, Republic of
- Population: 12.1 million (2007)
- Location: Southern Africa
- Capital: Harare
- Currency: Zimbabwean Dollar (ZWD)
- Religion: Christian, indigenous beliefs, small communities of Hindu, Muslim and Jewish
- Language: English (official), Shona, Ndebele
- British Embassy, Harare: +912 125 160/167

3 Business Colleges

Office work is based on information technology, so being trained in this field is a great start to earning quick cash. Office temping is a very common job that pays reasonably well and there is usually plenty of it around.

Office skills are pretty basic to many careers and, in an increasingly global market, could lead to chances to work abroad - so you can even combine travel or living in another culture with work.

Work experience ASAP

The big question is: "How do I get work experience when everywhere I go rejects me because I haven't got work experience?" This could ruin your whole **gap-**year plan. For simple menial work, such as stacking shelves or fruit picking, it shouldn't be too much of a problem, but those types of jobs don't pay particularly well.

If you need money fast then you might have to look elsewhere.

Gap-year recruiters tend to expect their clients to have no work experience at all, so it could be a good idea to get ahead of the game and get some experience under your belt, before you leave school. Even if the work is basic (filing, making the tea), it shows that you can function within a working environment.

If you're reading this while you're in Year 12, then you have quite a lot of time left and we advise you to use it to get as much work experience as possible. This will seriously impress your future employers.

We're not saying that you have to spend every week of your holidays working, although many teenagers do now combine weekend and holiday working - such as retail jobs - with study.

You can always do with a bit more cash. It may seem tedious but think how much more impressive you'll be at job interviews later on, with a fatter CV and references in hand.

Skills for work

What are the skills that you need in order to get that vital job? Don't forget that you only have a limited time, so you don't want to be training for too long as that will cut down on your earning time and therefore enjoyment time. This is why many people choose to go into trades such as bartending or retail, where the company tends to provide the training, though this might not prove to be nearly as lucrative as office work.

If you've done a computer based course during sixth form, then that could well prove to be enough. If you can type at around 40-45 words per minute, or you're comfortable designing websites, then you stand a good chance of landing a fairly well-paid job.

the gap-year guidebook 2011

Qualifications - who needs them?

Qualifications are needed when you can't otherwise prove that you're capable of whatever the job involves. For example, if you're not French and have never lived in France, then you'll have to have a qualification showing that you can *speak* French, if that's what the job involves. In office work the agency that you use will put you through some tests first, before putting your name forward to the employer.

More important than any paper qualification, is that your typing speed and accuracy are strong enough to take you through the tests agencies will ask you to undertake. Practice is vital in building up your speeds but you shouldn't despair if you don't reach that magic 45 words per minute, there are other options available to help you build up your speeds while you are working.

Many offices, especially the smaller ones, will offer a trial, for around three days, just to make sure that you have what it takes. This saves them from sorting through an array of paperwork and qualifications.

What if I'm just no good?

Well, you'll just have to get good then, won't you? Training for information technology has dramatically changed recently. Skills that used to take a full year can now take as little as one month. The prices have dropped too.

Evening courses at a local FE college can be under £100 and public libraries also run courses on the internet. IT is already very firmly in schools' curricula so most of you should already have the skills to cope within the office. If not, then get going and get trained.

Which college?

There are lots of different things to look at when choosing a college. Convenience (location, hours) is very important, along with price. However, you don't want to compromise the quality of the qualification you will receive because of practical concerns.

A good idea might be to check with an agency about the value of a qualification from particular colleges. Or check with the actual college on the employment record of their past students.

Finding the right course

Of course you want to start earning as soon as possible, so is it worth spending a longer time studying for a qualification that you don't really need?

How do you know which course is best for you? Can you compare different word processing courses against each other; surely word processing is just word processing? Also, you don't want to pay to learn something that you already know how to do. To help with this little dilemma the City & Guilds, which awards over a million certificates a year, defines the levels of its qualifications (which continue up to Level 7).

visit: www.gap-year.com

Level 1: Introductory awards for those new to the area covering routine tasks or basic knowledge and understanding.

Level 2: Qualifications for those with some knowledge of, and ability in, the areas that acknowledge individual responsibility.

Level 3: Qualifications that recognise complex work involving supervisory ability.

If you think that you already know level two, for example, then it's worth your while going straight onto level 3.

How much to pay?

The most important thing here is to get value for money. Of course the better the course the more expensive it's likely to be, but what things can you check for to make sure that you're not being conned? Be aware of the VAT and any other hidden costs that there might be. To test the value of the course compare the total hours of tuition to the price, check out each course and just be sure that what you are going to do will be of benefit, before parting with any money.

Over the next pages you'll find a list of colleges, from all over the country, which run intensive business skills courses. It is only an indicator of what's available, not a guarantee of quality.

We're happy to hear from (and report about) any training centres that offer short courses in office skills.

Aberdeen College of Further Education	enquiry@abcol.ac.uk www.abcol.ac.uk Tel: +44 (0) 1224 612 330
Abingdon and Witney College	enquiry@abingdon-witney.ac.uk www.abingdon-witney.ac.uk Tel: +44 (0) 1235 555 585
Accrington & Rossendale College	www.accross.ac.uk Tel: +44 (0) 1254 389 933
Alton College	enquiries@altoncollege.ac.uk www.altoncollege.ac.uk Tel: +44 (0) 1420 592 200
Amersham & Wycombe College	www.amersham.ac.uk Tel: +44 (0) 1494 735 555
Andover College	info@andovercollege.ac.uk www.andovercollege.ac.uk Tel: +44 (0) 1264 360 003
Aylesbury College	customerservice@aylesbury.ac.uk www.aylesbury.ac.uk Tel: +44 (0) 1296 588 588

Ayr College	enquiries@ayrcoll.ac.uk www.ayrcoll.ac.uk Tel: +44 (0) 1292 265 184
Banff & Buchan College	info@banff-buchan.ac.uk www.banff-buchan.ac.uk Tel: +44 (0) 1346 586 100
Barking College	admissions@barkingcollege.ac.uk www.barkingcollege.ac.uk Tel: +44 (0) 1708 770 000
Barnet College	admissions@barkingcollege.ac.uk www.barnet.ac.uk Tel: +44 (0) 20 8266 4000
Barnfield College	enquiries@barnfield.ac.uk www.barnfield.ac.uk Tel: +44 (0) 1582 569 500
Barnsley College	programme.enquiries@barnsley.ac.uk www.barnsley.ac.uk Tel: +44 (0) 1226 216 216
Barry College	enquiries@barry.ac.uk www.barry.ac.uk Tel: +44 (0) 1446 725 000
Barton Peveril College	enquiries@imail.barton.ac.uk www.barton-peveril.ac.uk Tel: +44 (0) 238 036 7200
Basingstoke College of Technology	information@bcot.ac.uk www.bcot.ac.uk Tel: +44 (0) 1256 354 141
Bedford College	info@bedford.ac.uk www.bedford.ac.uk Tel: +44 (0) 800 074 0234
Belfast Metroplitan College	central_admissions@belfastinstitute.ac.uk www.belfastmet.ac.uk Tel: +44 (0) 28 9026 5000
Bexhill College	enquiries@bexhillcollege.ac.uk www.bexhillcollege.ac.uk Tel: +44 (0) 1424 214 545
Bexley College	enquiries@bexley.ac.uk www.bexley.ac.uk Tel: +44 (0) 1322 442 331

visit: www.gap-year.com

Bishop Auckland College	enquiries@bacoll.ac.uk www.bacoll.ac.uk Tel: +44 (0) 1388 443 000
Blackburn College	www.blackburn.ac.uk Tel: +44 (0) 1254 551 44
Blackpool & The Fylde College	visitors@blackpool.ac.uk www.blackpool.ac.uk Tel: +44 (0) 1253 504 343
Bolton Community College	info@bolton-community-college.ac.uk www.bolton-community-college.ac.uk Tel: +44 (0) 1204 907 200
Borders College	enquiries@borderscollege.ac.uk www.borderscollege.ac.uk Tel: +44 (0) 8700 505 152
Boston College	info@boston.ac.uk www.boston.ac.uk Tel: +44 (0) 1205 365 701
Bournemouth & Poole College	enquiries@thecollege.co.uk www.thecollege.co.uk Tel: +44 (0) 1202 205 205
Bournville College	info@bournville.ac.uk www.bournville.ac.uk Tel: +44 (0) 1274 433 333
Bracknell & Wokingham College	study@bracknell.ac.uk www.bracknell.ac.uk Tel: +44 (0) 845 330 3343
Bradford College	admissions@bradfordcollege.ac.uk www.bradfordcollege.ac.uk Tel: +44 (0) 1274 433 333
Braintree College	enquiries@braintree.ac.uk www.braintree.ac.uk Tel: +44 (0) 1376 321 711
Bridgwater College	information@bridgwater.ac.uk www.bridgwater.ac.uk Tel: +44 (0) 1278 455464
Brockenhurst College	enquiries@brock.ac.uk www.brock.ac.uk Tel: +44 (0) 1590 625 555

Appendix | 3 - Business colleges

Bromley College	info@bromley.ac.uk www.bromley.ac.uk Tel: +44 (0) 20 8295 7000
Brooklands College	info@brooklands.ac.uk www.brooklands.ac.uk Tel: +44 (0) 1932 797 797
Budmouth Technology College	peerc@budmouth.dorset.sch.uk www.budmouth.dorset.sch.uk Tel: +44 (0) 1305 830 500
Burnley College	student.services@burnley.ac.uk www.burnley.ac.uk Tel: +44 (0) 1282 711 200
Burton College	enquiries@burton-college.ac.uk www.burton-college.ac.uk Tel: +44 (0) 1283 494 400
Bury College	information@burycollege.ac.uk www.burycollege.ac.uk Tel: +44 (0) 161 280 8280
Cambridge Regional College	enquiry@camre.ac.uk www.camre.ac.uk Tel: +44 (0) 1223 418 20
Cannock Chase Technical College	enquiry@cannock.ac.uk www.cannock.ac.uk Tel: +44 (0) 1543 462 200
Canterbury College	courseenquiries@cant-col.ac.uk www.cant-col.ac.uk Tel: +44 (0) 1227 811 111
Cardonald College	enquiries@cardonald.ac.uk www.cardonald.ac.uk Tel: +44 (0) 141 272 3333
Carlisle College	info@carlisle.ac.uk www.carlisle.ac.uk Tel: + 44 (0) 1228 822 703
Castle College	learn@castlecollege.ac.uk www.castlecollege.ac.uk Tel: +44 (0) 845 845 0500
Causeway Institute	admissions@causeway.ac.uk www.causeway.ac.uk Tel: +44 (0) 28 7035 4717

visit: www.gap-year.com

Central Sussex College	www.centralsussex.ac.uk Tel: +44 (0) 845 155 0043
Chesterfield College	advice@chesterfield.ac.uk www.chesterfield.ac.uk Tel: +44 (0) 1246 500 500
Cirencester College	student.services@cirencestercollege.ac.uk www.cirencestercollege.ac.uk Tel: +44 (0) 1255 640 99
City & Islington College	courseinfo@candi.ac.uk www.candi.ac.uk Tel: +44 (0) 20 7700 9200
City College Brighton & Hove	info@ccb.ac.uk www.ccb.ac.uk Tel: +44 (0) 1273 667 788
City College Coventry	info@staff.covcollege.ac.uk www.covcollege.ac.uk Tel: +44 (0) 2476 791 000
City College Manchester	www.ccm.ac.uk Tel: +44 (0) 800 013 0123
City College Norwich	information@ccn.ac.uk www.ccn.ac.uk Tel: +44 (0) 1603 773 311
City College Plymouth	reception@cityplym.ac.uk www.cityplym.ac.uk Tel: +44 (0) 1752 305 300
City College Southampton	enquiries@southampton-city.ac.uk www.southampton-city.ac.uk Tel: +44 (0) 023 8048 4848
City Lit	www.citylit.ac.uk Tel: +44 (0) 207 492 2600
City of Bath College	www.citybathcoll.ac.uk Tel: +44 (0) 1225 312 191
City of Bristol College	enquiries@cityofbristol.ac.uk www.cityofbristol.ac.uk Tel: +44 (0) 117 312 5000
City of Sunderland College	www.citysun.ac.uk Tel: +44 (0) 191 511 6060
City of Westminster College	www.cwc.ac.uk Tel: +44 (0) 20 7723 8826

the gap-year guidebook 2011

City of Wolverhampton College	www.wolverhamptoncollege.ac.uk Tel: +44 (0) 1902 836 000
Clydebank College	info@clydebank.ac.uk www.clydebank.ac.uk Tel: +44 (0) 141 951 2122
Coatbridge College	mail@coatbridge.ac.uk www.coatbridge.ac.uk Tel: +44 (0) 1236 422 316
Colchester Institute	www.colchester.ac.uk Tel: +44 (0) 1206 518 000
Coleg Abertawe	enquiries@swancoll.ac.uk www.swancoll.ac.uk Tel: +44 (0) 1792 284 000
Coleg Castell Nedd	enquiries@nptc.ac.uk www.nptc.ac.uk Tel: +44 (0) 1639 648 000
Coleg Glan Hafren	enquiries@glan-hafren.ac.uk www.glan-hafren.ac.uk Tel: +44 (0) 29 20 250 250
Coleg Glannau Dyfrdwy	www.deeside.ac.uk Tel: +44 (0) 1244 831 531
Coleg Gorseinon	admin@gorseinon.ac.uk www.gorseinon.ac.uk Tel: +44 (0) 1792 890 700
Coleg Gwent	info@coleggwent.ac.uk www.coleggwent.ac.uk Tel: +44 (0) 1495 333 333
Coleg Llysfasi	admin@llysfasi.ac.uk www.llysfasi.ac.uk Tel: +44 (0) 1978 790 263
Coleg Menai	student.services@menai.ac.uk www.menai.ac.uk Tel: +44 (0) 1248 370 125
Coleg Merthyr Tudful	www.merthyr.ac.uk Tel: +44 (0) 1685 726 006
Coleg Morgannwg	www.morgannwg.ac.uk Tel: +44 (0) 1685 887 500
Coleg Penybont	enquiries@bridgend.ac.uk www.bridgend.ac.uk Tel: +44 (0) 1656 302 302

visit: www.gap-year.com

Coleg Sir Gar	admissions@colegsirgar.ac.uk www.colegsirgar.ac.uk Tel: +44 (0) 1554 748 000
College of North East London	admissions@staff.conel.ac.uk www.conel.ac.uk Tel: +44 (0) 208 802 3111
College of North West London	courenq@cnwl.ac.uk www.cnwl.ac.uk Tel: +44 (0) 208 208 5000
College of West Anglia	enquiries@col-westanglia.ac.uk www.col-westanglia.ac.uk Tel: +44 (0) 1553 761 144
Collyer's, The College of Richard Collyer	admin@collyers.ac.uk www.collyers.ac.uk Tel: +44 (0) 1403 210 822
Cornwall College	enquiries@cornwall.ac.uk www.cornwall.ac.uk Tel: +44 (0) 1209 616 161
Craven College	www.craven-college.ac.uk Tel: +44 (0) 1756 791 41
Croydon College	info@croydon.ac.uk www.croydon.ac.uk Tel: +44 (0) 208 686 5700
CRTS International Study Centre	admission@crts.co.uk www.crts.co.uk Tel: +44 (0) 20 8801 0371
Cumbernauld College	info@cumbernauld.ac.uk www.cumbernauld.ac.uk Tel: +44 (0) 1236 731 811
Darlington College of Technology	enquire@darlington.ac.uk www.darlington.ac.uk Tel: +44 (0) 1325 503 050
Dearne Valley College	www.dearne-coll.ac.uk Tel: +44 (0) 1709 513 333
Derby College	enquiries@derby-college.ac.uk www.derby-college.ac.uk Tel: +44 (0) 1322 520 200
Derwentside College	www.derwentside.ac.uk Tel: +44 (0) 1207 585 900

Appendix | 3 - Business colleges

Dewsbury College	info@dewsbury.ac.uk www.dewsbury.ac.uk Tel: +44 (0) 1924 436 221
Dudley College	www.dudleycol.ac.uk Tel: +44 (0) 1384 363 546
Dumfries & Galloway College	info@dumgal.ac.uk www.dumgal.ac.uk Tel: +44 (0) 1387 261 261
Dundee College	enquiry@dundeecollege.ac.uk www.dundeecoll.ac.uk Tel: +44 (0) 1382 834 800
Dunstable College	enquiries@dunstable.ac.uk www.dunstable.ac.uk Tel: +44 (0) 1582 477 776
Ealing, Hammersmith & West London College	cic@wlc.ac.uk www.wlc.ac.uk Tel: +44 (0) 20 8741 1688
East Berkshire College	info@eastberks.ac.uk www.eastberks.ac.uk Tel: +44 (0) 845 373 250
East Devon College	enquiries@admin.eastdevon.ac.uk www.edc.ac.uk Tel: +44 (0) 1884 235 200
East Riding College	info@eastridingcollege.ac.uk www.eastridingcollege.ac.uk Tel: +44 (0) 845 120 0037
East Surrey College	www.esc.ac.uk Tel: +44 (0) 1737 788 444
East Tyrone College of Further & Higher Education	info@etcfhe.ac.uk www.etcfhe.ac.uk Tel: +44 (0) 28 8772 2323
Eastleigh College	goplaces@eastleigh.ac.uk www.eastleigh.ac.uk Tel: +44 (0) 238 091 1299
Edinburgh's Telford College	mail@ed-coll.ac.uk www.ed-coll.ac.uk Tel: +44 (0) 131 559 4000
Enfield College	courseinformation@enfield.ac.uk www.enfield.ac.uk Tel: +44 (0) 20 8443 3434

visit: www.gap-year.com

Epping Forest College	informationcentre@epping-forest.ac.uk www.epping-forest.ac.uk Tel: +44 (0) 208 508 8311
Esher College	eshercollege@esher.ac.uk www.esher.ac.uk Tel: +44 (0) 20 8398 0291
Evesham & Malvern Hills College	www.evesham.ac.uk Tel: +44 (0) 1386 712 600
Exeter College	info@exe-coll.ac.uk www.exe-coll.ac.uk Tel: +44 (0) 1392 205 223
Fareham College	info@fareham.ac.uk www.fareham.ac.uk Tel: +44 (0) 1329 815 200
Farnborough College of Technology	info@farn-ct.ac.uk www.farn-ct.ac.uk Tel: +44 (0) 1252 407 040
Farnham College	enquiries@farnham.ac.uk www.farnham.ac.uk Tel: +44 (0) 1252 716 988
Fermanagh College	admissions@fermanaghcoll.ac.uk www.fermanaghcoll.ac.uk Tel: +44 (0) 28 6632 2431
Filton College	info@filton.ac.uk www.filton.ac.uk Tel: +44 (0) 117 931 2121
Franklin College	college@franklin.ac.uk www.franklin.ac.uk Tel: +44 (0) 1472 875 000
Furness College	www.furness.ac.uk Tel: +44 (0) 1229 825 017
Gateshead College	www.gateshead.ac.uk Tel: +44 (0) 191 4900 300
Gloscat	info@gloscat.ac.uk www.gloscat.ac.uk Tel: +44 (0) 1242 532 000
Godalming College	college@godalming.ac.uk www.godalming.ac.uk Tel: +44 (0) 1483 423 526

Great Yarmouth College	info@gyc.ac.uk www.gyc.ac.uk Tel: +44 (0) 1493 655 261
Guildford College	info@guildford.ac.uk www.guildford.ac.uk Tel: +44 (0) 1483 448 500
Halesowen College	info@halesowen.ac.uk www.halesowen.ac.uk Tel: +44 (0) 121 602 7777
Harrogate College	www.leedsmet.ac.uk/harrogate Tel: +44 (0) 1423 879 466
Hartlepool College of Further Education	enquiries@hartlepoolfe.ac.uk www.hartlepoolfe.ac.uk Tel: +44 (0) 1429 295 000
Hartpury College	enquire@hartpury.ac.uk www.hartpury.ac.uk Tel: +44 (0) 1452 700 283
Havant College	enquiries@havant.ac.uk www.havant.ac.uk Tel: +44 (0) 23 9248 3856
Havering College	information@havering-college.ac.uk www.havering-college.ac.uk Tel: +44 (0) 1708 455 011
Herefordshire College of Technology	enquiries@hct.ac.uk www.hereford-tech.ac.uk Tel: +44 (0) 800 032 1986
Highbury College	info@highbury.ac.uk www.highbury.ac.uk Tel: +44 (0) 23 9231 3373
Holy Cross Sixth Form College	information@holycross.ac.uk www.holycross.ac.uk Tel: +44 (0) 161 762 4500
Hopwood Hall College	enquiries@hopwood.ac.uk www.hopwood.ac.uk Tel: +44 (0) 161 643 7560
Hove College	courses@hovecollege.co.uk www.hovecollege.co.uk Tel: +44 (0) 1273 772577

visit: www.gap-year.com

Huddersfield Technical College	info@hudcoll.ac.uk www.huddcoll.ac.uk Tel: +44 (0) 1484 536 521
Hull College	info@hull-college.ac.uk www.hull-college.ac.uk Tel: +44 (0) 1482 329 943
Huntingdonshire Regional College	college@huntingdon.ac.uk www.huntingdon.ac.uk Tel: +44 (0) 1480 379 100
Interlink College London	ictbs@interlinktech.co.uk www.interlinktech.co.uk Tel: +44 (0) 208 531 1118
Inverness College	info@inverness.uhi.ac.uk www.inverness.uhi.ac.uk Tel: +44 (0) 1463 273 000
Isle of Man College	www.iomcollege.ac.im Tel: +44 (0) 1624 648 200
Itchen College	info@itchen.ac.uk www.itchen.ac.uk Tel: +44 (0) 23 8043 5636
Jewel & Esk Valley College	info@jevc.ac.uk www.jevc.ac.uk Tel: +44 (0) 131 660 1010
John Wheatley College	advice@jwheatley.ac.uk www.jwheatley.ac.uk Tel: +44 (0) 141 778 2426
Josiah Mason College	enquiries@jmc.ac.uk www.jmc.ac.uk Tel: +44 (0) 121 603 4757
Keighley College	www.keighley.ac.uk Tel: +44 (0) 1535 618 600
Kendal College	admissions@kendal.ac.uk www.kendal.ac.uk Tel: +44 (0) 1539 814 709
Kensington & Chelsea College	www.kcc.ac.uk Tel: +44 (0) 207 573 3600
Kidderminster College	www.kidderminster.ac.uk Tel: +44 (0) 1562 820 811
Kilmarnock College	www.kilmarnock.ac.uk Tel: +44 (0) 1563 523 501

the gap-year guidebook 2011

College	Contact
Kingston College	info@kingston-college.ac.uk www.kingston-college.ac.uk Tel: +44 (0) 208 546 2151
Knowsley Community College	info@knowsleycollege.ac.uk www.knowsleycollege.ac.uk Tel: +44 (0) 845 155 1055
Lakes College	info@lcwc.ac.uk www.lcwc.ac.uk Tel: +44 (0) 1946 839 300
Lambeth College	courses@lambethcollege.ac.uk www.lambethcollege.ac.uk Tel: +44 (0) 207 501 5010
Lancaster & Morecambe College	www.lmc.ac.uk Tel: +44 (0) 800 306 306
Langside College	enquireuk@langside.ac.uk www.langside.ac.uk Tel: +44 (0) 141 272 3600
Lauder College	www.lauder.ac.uk Tel: +44 (0) 1383 845 010
Leeds College of Technology	info@lct.ac.uk www.lct.ac.uk Tel: +44 (0) 113 297 6300
Leeds Thomas Danby	info@leedsthomasdanby.ac.uk www.leedsthomasdanby.ac.uk Tel: +44 (0) 113 249 4912
Leicester College	info@leicestercollege.ac.uk www.leicestercollege.ac.uk Tel: +44 (0) 116 224 2240
Lewisham College	info@lewisham.ac.uk www.lewisham.ac.uk Tel: +44 (0) 208 692 0353
Lews Castle College	www.lews.uhi.ac.uk Tel: +44 (0) 1851 770 000
Lincoln College	enquiries@lincolncollege.ac.uk www.lincolncollege.ac.uk Tel: +44 (0) 1522 876 000
Liverpool Community College	www.liv-coll.ac.uk Tel: +44 (0) 151 252 1515

visit: www.gap-year.com

Loughborough College	info@loucoll.ac.uk www.loucoll.ac.uk Tel: +44 (0) 845 166 2952
Lowestoft College	www.lowestoft.ac.uk Tel: +44 (0) 1502 583 521
Ludlow College	info@ludlow-college.ac.uk www.ludlow-college.ac.uk Tel: +44 (0) 1584 872 846
Macclesfield College	info@macclesfield.ac.uk www.macclesfield.ac.uk Tel: +44 (0) 1625 410 000
Manchester College of Arts & Technology	enquiries@mancat.ac.uk www.mancat.ac.uk Tel: +44 (0) 161 953 5995
Matthew Boulton College of Further & Higher Education	ask@matthew-boulton.ac.uk www.matthew-boulton.ac.uk Tel: +44 (0) 121 446 4554
Merton College	info@merton.ac.uk www.merton.ac.uk Tel: +44 (0) 20 8408 6400
Middlesbrough College	courseinfo@mbro.ac.uk www.mbro.ac.uk Tel: +44 (0) 1642 333 333
Mid-Kent College	www.midkent.ac.uk Tel: +44 (0) 1634 402 020
Milton Keynes College	info@mkcollege.ac.uk www.mkcollege.ac.uk Tel: +44 (0) 1908 684 444
Moray College	www.moray.ac.uk Tel: +44 (0) 1343 576 000
Morley College	enquiries@morleycollege.ac.uk www.morleycollege.ac.uk Tel: +44 (0) 207 928 8501
Motherwell College	information@motherwell.ac.uk www.motherwell.ac.uk Tel: +44 (0) 1698 232 425
Nelson & Colne College	reception@nelson.ac.uk www.nelson.ac.uk Tel: +44 (0) 1282 440 200

Appendix | 3 - Business colleges

College	Contact
Nescot	info@nescot.ac.uk www.nescot.ac.uk Tel: +44 (0) 20 8394 1731
New College Durham	help@newdur.ac.uk www.newdur.ac.uk Tel: +44 (0) 191 375 4000
New College Nottingham	enquiries@ncn.ac.uk www.ncn.ac.uk Tel: +44 (0) 115 9100 100
New College Pontefract	reception@newcollpont.ac.uk www.newcollpont.ac.uk Tel: +44 (0) 1977 702 139
New College Stamford	www.stamford.ac.uk Tel: +44 (0) 1780 484 300
New College Swindon	admissions@newcollege.ac.uk www.newcollege.ac.uk Tel: +44 (0) 808 172 1721
Newbury College	info@newbury-college.ac.uk www.newbury-college.ac.uk Tel: +44 (0) 1635 845 000
Newham College of Further Education	admissions@newham.ac.uk www.newham.ac.uk Tel: +44 (0) 208 257 4000
North Devon College	postbox@ndevon.ac.uk www.ndevon.ac.uk Tel: +44 (0) 1271 345 291
North East Worcestershire College	info@ne-worcs.ac.uk www.ne-worcs.ac.uk Tel: +44 (0) 1527 570 020
North Glasgow College	www.north-gla.ac.uk Tel: +44 (0) 141 558 9001
North Hertfordshire College	www.nhc.ac.uk Tel: +44 (0) 1462 424 239
North Nottinghamshire College	webcontact@nnc.ac.uk www.nnotts-col.ac.uk Tel: +44 (0) 1909 504 504
North Trafford College	www.ntc.ac.uk Tel: +44 (0) 161 886 7070

visit: www.gap-year.com

North Warwickshire & Hinckley College	the.college@nwhc.ac.uk www.nwhc.ac.uk Tel: +44 (0) 24 7624 3000
North West Kent College	course.enquiries@nwkcollege.ac.uk www.nwkcollege.ac.uk Tel: +44 (0) 1322 629 400
North West Regional College	info@nwrc.ac.uk www.nwrc.ac.uk Tel: +44 (0) 28 7127 6000
Northampton College	www.northamptoncollege.ac.uk Tel: +44 (0) 1604 734 567
Northern Regional College	info@nrc.ac.uk www.nrc.ac.uk Tel: +44 (0) 28 9085 5000
Northumberland College	advice.centre@northland.ac.uk www.northland.ac.uk Tel: +44 (0) 1670 841 200
Norton Radstock College	www.nortcoll.ac.uk Tel: +44 (0) 1761 433 161
Oaklands College	advice.centre@oaklands.ac.uk www.oaklands.ac.uk Tel: +44 (0) 1727 737 080
Orkney College	orkney.college@uhi.ac.uk www.orkney.uhi.ac.uk Tel: +44 (0) 1856 569 000
Orpington College	enquiries@orpington.ac.uk www.orpington.ac.uk Tel: +44 (0) 1689 899 700
Oxford & Cherwell Valley College	enquiries@ocvc.ac.uk www.ocvc.ac.uk Tel: +44 (0) 1865 550 550
Oxford Media & Business School	courses@oxfordbusiness.co.uk www.oxfordbusiness.co.uk Tel: +44 (0) 1865 240 963
Palmer's College	enquiries@palmers.ac.uk www.palmers.ac.uk Tel: +44 (0) 1375 370 121
Park Lane College	www.parklanecoll.ac.uk Tel: +44 (0) 845 045 7275

the gap-year guidebook 2011

College	Contact
Paston College	enquiries@paston.ac.uk www.paston.ac.uk Tel: +44 (0) 1692 402 334
Penwith College	enquire@penwith.ac.uk www.penwith.ac.uk Tel: +44 (0) 1736 335 000
Perth College	pc.enquiries@perth.uhi.ac.uk www.perth.ac.uk Tel: +44 (0) 1738 877 000
Peterborough Regional College	info@peterborough.ac.uk www.peterborough.ac.uk Tel: +44 (0) 845 872 8722
Pitmans Training Group	www.pitman-training.com Tel: +44 (0) 1937 548500
Portsmouth College	registry@portsmouth-college.ac.uk www.portsmouth-college.ac.uk Tel: +44 (0) 23 9266 7521
Prior Pursglove College	www.pursglove.ac.uk Tel: +44 (0) 1287 280 800
Queen Mary's College	info@qmc.ac.uk www.qmc.ac.uk Tel: +44 (0) 1256 417 500
Quest Business Training	info@questcollege.co.uk www.questcollege.co.uk Tel: +44 (0) 20 7373 3852

Our ten week **gap**-year course covers the skills essential for temping and making your **gap**-year a truly challenging time. Lessons, seminars and workshops cover important interview techniques, skills and training. Alternatively, take a four or six week class to acquire practical office skills such as touch typing, MS Office and telephone techniques – they will be of lifelong benefit.

College	Contact
Redcar & Cleveland College	webenquiry@cleveland.ac.uk www.cleveland.ac.uk Tel: +44 (0) 1642 473 132
Reid Kerr College	sservices@reidkerr.ac.uk www.reidkerr.ac.uk Tel: +44 (0) 141 581 2222
Riverside College	www.riversidecollege.ac.uk Tel: +44 (0) 151 257 2800

visit: www.gap-year.com

Royal Forest of Dean	enquiries@rfdc.ac.uk www.rfdc.ac.uk Tel: +44 (0) 1594 833 416
Salisbury College	enquiries@salisbury.ac.uk www.salisbury.ac.uk Tel: +44 (0) 1722 344 344
Sandwell College	enquiries@sandwell.ac.uk www.sandwell.ac.uk Tel: +44 (0) 121 556 6000
Selby College	www.selby.ac.uk Tel: +44 (0) 1757 211 000
Shipley College	enquiries@shipley.ac.uk www.shipley.ac.uk Tel: +44 (0) 1274 327 222
Skelmersdale & Ormskirk Colleges	info@skelmersdale.ac.uk www.skelmersdale.ac.uk Tel: +44 (0) 1695 728 744
Solihull College	enquiries@solihull.ac.uk www.solihull.ac.uk Tel: +44 (0) 121 678 7000
South Cheshire College	info@s-cheshire.ac.uk www.s-cheshire.ac.uk Tel: +44 (0) 1270 654 654
South Devon College	enquiries@southdevon.ac.uk www.southdevon.ac.uk Tel: +44 (0) 1803 540 540
South Downs College	www.southdowns.ac.uk Tel: +44 (0) 23 9279 7979
South East Essex College	admissions@southend.ac.uk www.southend.ac.uk Tel: +44 (0) 1702 220 400
South East Regional College	www.serc.ac.uk Tel: +44 (0) 28 4461 5815
South Kent College	www.southkent.ac.uk Tel: +44 (0) 845 207 8220
South Lanarkshire College	admissions@slc.ac.uk www.south-lanarkshire-college.ac.uk Tel: +44 (0) 141 641 6600
South Leicestershire College	www.slcollege.ac.uk Tel: +44 (0) 116 288 5051

South Nottingham College	enquiries@snc.ac.uk www.snc.ac.uk Tel: +44 (0) 115 914 6400
South Thames College	studentservices@south-thames.ac.uk www.south-thames.ac.uk Tel: +44 (0) 208 918 7777
South Trafford College	enquiries@stcoll.ac.uk www.stcoll.ac.uk Tel: +44 (0) 161 952 4600
South Tyneside College	www.stc.ac.uk Tel: +44 (0) 191 427 3500
South West College	www.swc.ac.uk Tel: +44 (0) 28 8224 5433
Southern Regional College	www.src.ac.uk Tel: +44 (0) 28 3752 2205
Southgate College	admiss@southgate.ac.uk www.southgate.ac.uk Tel: +44 (0) 208 982 5050
Southport College	www.southport-college.ac.uk Tel: +44 (0) 1704 500 606
Southwark College	info@southwark.ac.uk www.southwark.ac.uk Tel: +44 (0) 207 815 1500
St David's Catholic College	enquiries@st-davids-coll.ac.uk www.st-davids-coll.ac.uk Tel: +44 (0) 29 2049 8555
St Helens College	www.sthelens.ac.uk Tel: +44 (0) 1744 733 766
St Mary's College	reception@stmarysblackburn.ac.uk www.stmarysblackburn.ac.uk Tel: +44 (0) 1254 580 464
St Vincent College	info@stvincent.ac.uk www.stvincent.ac.uk Tel: +44 (0) 239 258 8311
Stafford College	www.staffordcoll.ac.uk Tel: +44 (0) 1785 223 800
Stanmore College	enquiry@stanmore.ac.uk www.stanmore.ac.uk Tel: +44 (0) 20 8420 7700

visit: www.gap-year.com

Stockport College	admissions@stockport.ac.uk www.stockport.ac.uk Tel: +44 (0) 161 958 3100
Stockton Riverside College	www.stockton.ac.uk Tel: +44 (0) 1642 865 400
Stoke on Trent College	info@stokecoll.ac.uk www.stokecoll.ac.uk Tel: +44 (0) 1782 208 208
Stourbridge College	info@stourbridge.ac.uk www.stourbridge.ac.uk Tel: +44 (0) 1384 344 344
Stow College	enquiries@stow.ac.uk www.stow.ac.uk Tel: +44 (0) 141 332 1786
Stratford-upon-Avon College	college@stratford.ac.uk www.strat-avon.ac.uk Tel: +44 (0) 1789 266 245
Strode College	courseinfo@strode-college.ac.uk www.strode-college.ac.uk Tel: +44 (0) 1458 844 400
Stroud College	enquire@stroudcol.ac.uk www.stroud.ac.uk Tel: +44 (0) 1453 763 424
Suffolk New College	info@suffolk.ac.uk www.suffolk.ac.uk Tel: +44 (0) 1473 255 885
Sussex Downs College	info@sussexdowns.ac.uk www.sussexdowns.ac.uk Tel: +44 (0) 1273 483 188
Swindon College	studentservices@swindon-college.ac.uk www.swindon-college.ac.uk Tel: +44 (0) 1793 491 591
Tameside College	www.tameside.ac.uk Tel: +44 (0) 161 908 6789
Tamworth & Lichfield College	enquiries@tamworth.ac.uk www.tamworth.ac.uk Tel: +44 (0) 1827 310 202
Taunton's College	email@tauntons.ac.uk www.tauntons.ac.uk Tel: +44 (0) 23 8051 1811

Thames Valley University	www.tvu.ac.uk Tel: +44 (0) 118 967 5000
Thanet College	www.thanet.ac.uk Tel: +44 (0) 1843 605 040
The Adam Smith College	enquiries@adamsmith.ac.uk www.adamsmithcollege.ac.uk Tel: +44 (0) 800 413 280
The Blackpool Sixth Form College	enquiries@blackpoolsixth.ac.uk www.blackpoolsixth.ac.uk Tel: +44 (0) 1253 394 911
The City College	admissions@citycollege.ac.uk www.citycollege.ac.uk Tel: +44 (0) 20 7253 1133
The College Ystrad Mynach	enquiries@ystrad-mynach.ac.uk www.ystrad-mynach.ac.uk Tel: +44 (0) 1443 816 888
The Community College Hackney	enquiries@tcch.ac.uk www.tcch.ac.uk Tel: +44 (0) 207 613 9123
The Henley College	info@henleycol.ac.uk www.henleycol.ac.uk Tel: +44 (0) 1491 579 988
The Isle of Wight College	info@iwcollege.ac.uk www.iwightc.ac.uk Tel: +44 (0) 1983 526 631
The North Highland College	info@northhighland.ac.uk www.nhcscotland.com Tel: +44 (0) 1847 889 000
The Oldham College	info@oldham.ac.uk www.oldham.ac.uk Tel: +44 (0) 161 624 5214
The Sheffield College	www.sheffcol.ac.uk Tel: +44 (0) 114 260 2600
Thomas Rotherham College	enquiries@thomroth.ac.uk www.thomroth.ac.uk Tel: +44 (0) 1709 300 600
Thurrock & Basildon College	enquire@tab.ac.uk www.thurrock.ac.uk Tel: +44 (0) 845 601 5746

visit: www.gap-year.com

Totton College	info@totton.ac.uk www.totton.ac.uk Tel: +44 (0) 2380 874 874
Tower Hamlets College	advice@tower.ac.uk www.tower.ac.uk Tel: +44 (0) 207 510 7510
Tresham Institute of Further & Higher Education	info@tresham.ac.uk www.tresham.ac.uk Tel: +44 (0) 845 658 8990
Truro College	enquiry@trurocollege.ac.uk www.trurocollege.ac.uk Tel: +44 (0) 1872 267 000
Tyne Metropolitan College	www.ntyneside.ac.uk Tel: +44 (0) 191 229 5000
University of Derby – Buxton	www.derby.ac.uk Tel: +44 (0) 1298 71100
Uxbridge College	enquiries@uxbridgecollege.ac.uk www.uxbridgecollege.ac.uk Tel: +44 (0) 1895 853 333
Varndean College	www.varndean.ac.uk Tel: +44 (0) 1273 508 011
Wakefield College	info@wakefield.ac.uk www.wakcoll.ac.uk Tel: +44 (0) 1924 789 789
Walsall College	www.walsallcollege.ac.uk Tel: +44 (0) 1922 657 000
Waltham Forest College	info@waltham.ac.uk www.waltham.ac.uk Tel: +44 (0) 208 501 8000
Warrington Collegiate	learner.services@warrington.ac.uk www.warr.ac.uk Tel: +44 (0) 1925 494 494
Warwickshire College	enquiries@warkscol.ac.uk www.warkscol.ac.uk Tel: +44 (0) 1926 318 000
West Cheshire College	info@west-cheshire.ac.uk www.west-cheshire.ac.uk Tel: +44 (0) 1244 677 677

West Kent College	enquiries@wkc.ac.uk www.wkc.ac.uk Tel: +44 (0) 1732 358 101
West Lothian College	enquiries@west-lothian.ac.uk www.west-lothian.ac.uk Tel: +44 (0) 1506 418181
West Nottinghamshire College	www.wnc.ac.uk Tel: +44 (0) 1623 627 191
West Thames College	info@west-thames.ac.uk www.west-thames.ac.uk Tel: +44 (0) 20 8326 2000
Westminster Kingsway College	courseinfo@westking.ac.uk www.westking.ac.uk Tel: +44 (0) 870 060 9800
Weston College	enquiries@weston.ac.uk www.weston.ac.uk Tel: +44 (0) 1934 411 411
Weymouth College	lgs@weymouth.ac.uk www.weymouth.ac.uk Tel: +44 (0) 1305 761 100
Wigan & Leigh College	www.wigan-leigh.ac.uk Tel: +44 (0) 1942 761 600
Wiltshire College	info@wiltscoll.ac.uk www.wiltscoll.ac.uk Tel: +44 (0) 1249 464 644
Wirral Metropolitan College	www.wmc.ac.uk Tel: +44 (0) 151 551 7777
Woking College	www.woking.ac.uk Tel: +44 (0) 1483 761 036
Worcestershire College of Technology	college@wortech.ac.uk www.wortech.ac.uk Tel: +44 (0) 1905 725 555
Yale College	www.yale-wrexham.co.uk Tel: +44 (0) 1978 311 794
Yeovil College	info@yeovil.ac.uk www.yeovil.ac.uk Tel: +44 (0) 1935 423 921
Yorkshire Coast College	enquiries@ycoastco.ac.uk www.yorkshirecoastcollege.ac.uk Tel: +44 (0) 1723 372 105

visit: www.gap-year.com

index

0044 Ltd 64
2Way Development 243
3M United Kingdom Plc 362

A

A Broader View Volunteers Corp 267
AA (Automobile Association) 406
Acacia Adventure Holidays 155
Academia Hispánica Córdoba...303
Accademia del Giglio 299
Accademia Italiana 299
Accent Français 295
Accenture 362
ACE European Group Ltd 85
Acorn Venture Ltd 205
Action Aid 245
Action Centres UK 245
Action Professionals Ltd 325
Actors College of Theatre and Television............................292
Adventure Alternative 211
Adventure Bound 325
Adventure Centre 65
Adventure First Aid 61
Adventure Ireland 334
Adventure Tours Australia 155
Adventure Tours NZ 155
Adventure Travellers Club P Ltd 156
Aegean Center for the Fine Arts 285
Aether Mobile Ltd 64
Afreco Tours 156
Africa & Asia Venture...245
Africa Travel Co 156
African Conservation Experience..200
African Conservation Trust 227
African Gap Year 227
African Horizons 156
African Impact..245
African Leadership Academy..283

AgriVenture 200
AIDE (The Association of International Development & Exchange) 245
AIL Madrid Spanish Language School 303
Alaska Heritage Tours 156
Aldeburgh Music 359
Alderleaf Wilderness College 287
All Out Africa 227
All Outdoors California Whitewater Rafting 337
Allaboard Sailing Academy 337
Alliance & Leicester plc 362
Alliance Française de Londres 295
Alltracks Limited 329
Alpin Raft 337
Alpine Exploratory 156
Altitude Futures - Gap Course Verbier 329
Amanzi Travel 227
American Institute for Foreign Study (AIFS) 289
Amigos Spanish School 303
Amnesty International 378
An Óige - Irish Youth Hostel Association 149
Andean Trails 157
AO Nang Divers 339
Appalachian Wildwaters 339
Aquatic Explorers 339
Arcadia Group plc 362
Archaeology Abroad 399
Argentina Travel Plan 157
Ariège Arts 292
Art History Abroad (AHA) 289
ARTIS - Art Research Tours 286
Ashbourne Arts Ltd 378
Ashburton Cookery School 401
Asociacion Nuevos Horizontes 246
ATD Fourth World 246
Atelier Montmiral 286
Attwoolls Camping & Leisure 65
Au Pair Ecosse 199
Au Pair in America (APIA) 199
Australia Travel Plan 157
Avon Ski & Action Centre 334
Azafady 227

B

Backbeat Tours 307
Backpacker Travel Auctions 157
Barque Picton Castle 339

Base Camp Group	334
BASI (British Association of Snowsport Instructors)	329
BASP UK Ltd	417
BBC Recruitment	362
Be More - Volunteering in South Africa	269
Beamish, The North of England Open Air Museum	378
Bear Creek Outdoor Centre	335
Beaumont Château Ltd (UK Office)	205
Belle Isle School of Cookery	401
Bellis Training Australia	205
Berkshire College of Agriculture	409
Berlitz - London	411
Bermuda Sub Aqua Club	339
BERUDEP	246
Best Backpackers Insurance	85
Bicycling Empowerment Network	157
Big Squid Scuba Diving Training and Travel	417
BIMM - Brighton Institute of Modern Music	413
Bishop Burton College	409
Black Feather - The Wilderness Adventure Company	157
Blanche Macdonald Centre	291
BLS French Courses	295
Blue Insurances Ltd	85
Blue Ventures	227
BMS World Mission	246
Boots UK Limited	85
Born Free Foundation	378
Borneo Anchor Travel & Tours/Sabah Divers	158
Brathay Exploration Group	246
Brazil Travel Plan	158
Bridge Year, Spanish Programs	305
BridgeClimb Sydney	158
Brighton Festival	359
Brightsparks Recruitment	366
Britannia Sailing East Coast	332
British Hang Gliding & Paragliding Association Ltd	417
British Midland Airways Ltd	153
British Mountaineering Council	418
British Offshore Sailing School - BOSS	418
British Red Cross	378
British Sub Aqua Club	418
Brook School of Photography	415
Brooks Institute	309
BSES Expeditions	229
BTCV	379
Bucks and Spurs	325

BUNAC (British Universities North America Club) 205
BUPA Travel Services 85
Burton Manor 400
BWS Germanlingua 298

C

c4 Images & Safaris 309
Cactus TEFL 310
Cadbury Schweppes plc 362
Cairns Dive Centre 175
Caledonia Languages Abroad 301
Camberwell College of Arts 400
Cambodia Travel Plan 158
Cameroon Association for the Protection
and Education of the Child (CAPEC) 246
Camp America 205
Camp Challenge Pte Ltd 335
Camp Leaders In America 205
Camphill Communities in the UK 379
Camphill Community Ballybay 247
Camphill Community Ballytobin 247
Camphill Community Dingle 247
Camphill Community Duffcarrig 247
Camphill Community Dunshane 247
Camphill Community Greenacres 247
Camphill Community Jerpoint 249
Camphill Community Kyle 249
Camps International Limited 229
Cancer Research UK 363
Canning House 411
Canvas Holidays 207
Canyon Voyages Adventure Co 335
Cape Trib Horse Rides 325
Cape York Motorcycle Adventures 158
Capel Manor College 409
Cardrona Alpine Resort 329
Careforce 379
Carrick-on-Suir Camphill Community 249
Castaway Resorts 207
Catalina Ocean Rafting 339
Cats Protection League 379
Cave Diving Florida 339
CCUSA 207
Center for Purposeful Living 289
Central Scotland Forest Trust 379
Centre for Alternative Technology 379

Centro Linguistico Italiano Dante Alighieri	200
Centro Machiavelli	299
CERAN Lingua International	301
CESA Languages Abroad	305
Challenge Rafting	341
Challenges Worldwide	249
Changing Worlds	269
Cheap Flights	153
Cheltenham Festivals	359
Chichester College	409
Childcare International	199
Children with Leukaemia	380
Children's Country Holidays Fund	380
China Travel Plan	158
Christian Aid Gap Year	380
Churchtown - A Vitalise Centre	380
CIAL Centro de Linguas	303
Cicerones de Buenos Aires Asociación Civil	249
CILC - Cheltenham International Language Centre	423
City Year	251
Civil Service Recruitment	363
Class Afloat	283
Class VI River Runners	335
Club Direct Ltd.	86
CMEF, Centre Méditerranéen d'Etudes Françaises	295
CMS (Church Mission Society)	251
Coleman The Outdoor Company	66
Colgate-Palmolive (UK) Ltd	363
College Northside	295
Columbus Direct	86
CommsFactory	64
Comunicacion Language School	305
Concordia International Volunteers	229
Conservation Volunteers Australia	229
Conservation Volunteers New Zealand	229
Conservation Volunteers Northern Ireland	380
CookAbility	401
Cookery at The Grange	403
Cookery School at Little Portland Street	403
Coral Cay Conservation	231
Cordillera Blanca Trek	159
Cosmic Volunteers	251
Cotswold Outdoor Ltd	66
Council for British Archaeology	399
Council on International Educational Exchange (CIEE)	283
Country Music Travel	307

Craigdon Mountain Sports	66
CRCC Asia Ltd	211
CREES The Rainforest Education and Resource Centre	231
Crewseekers Limited	332
CricketCoachMaster Academy	418
Cross-Border Development	231
Cross-Cultural Solutions	251
CSV (Community Service Volunteers)	380
Cuba Travel Plan	159
Cultural Canvas Thailand	251
Cultural Experiences Abroad (CEA)	289
Curling in Kent	418
Cutting Edge Food & Wine School	403

D

Dart River Safaris	341
Dartington International Summer School	413
Deep Sea Divers Den	341
Delaney International	199
Deloitte	363
Deutsch-Institut Tirol	329
Digitalmasterclass	415
DIKEMES - International Center for Hellenic and Mediterranean Studies	299
Direct Travel Insurance	86
Discover Adventure Ltd.	252
Discover Nepal	231
Dive Kaikoura	341
Diversity	341
Do Something Different	159
Dogs Trust	381
Dogtag Ltd	87
Dolphin Encounter	159
Domus Academy	291
Don Quijote	305
Dorset Expeditionary Society/Leading Edge Expeditions	159
Downunder Worldwide Travel Insurance	87
Dragoman	159
Dragon Charm	200
DramaScene	408
Driving Standards Agency	406
DVLA (Driver and Vehicle Licencing Agency)	406
Dvorak Expeditions	326
Dyer Island Cruises	231

E

Earth Events	418

Earthwatch Institute ... 231
Earthwise Valley ... 233
Eastern Institute of Technology ... 289
EasyJet Plc ... 153
Ebookers (Flightbookers Ltd) ... 153
Eco Trails Kerala ... 160
Ecobrands ... 61
Ecoteer ... 233
Ecuador Volunteer ... 252
Edinburgh Festival Fringe ... 359
Edinburgh School of Food and Wine ... 403
EF International Language Schools ... 301
Egypt Horse Tours ... 160
Egypt Travel Plan ... 160
EICAR - The International Film School of Paris ... 292
EIL (Experiment for International Living) ... 252
El Casal ... 289
Elite Sailing ... 341
Elizabeth Finn Care ... 381
EMI Group plc ... 363
Emmaus UK ... 381
En Famille Overseas ... 297
Endsleigh Insurance Services Ltd ... 87
Enforex ... 305
English Heritage ... 381
Entabeni Nature Guide Training School ... 233
Equine Adventures ... 160
Equitours - Worldwide Horseback Riding Adventures ... 160
Escuela Internacional ... 305
Essential Croatia ... 233
Essential Travel Ltd ... 87
ETC - The English Training Centre ... 423
Eurolanguages ... 301
Eurolingua Institute ... 301
Europass ... 300
European Film College ... 292
Expanish ... 306
Experience Seminars ... 415
Explore Worldwide Ltd ... 160
Explorers Tours ... 419

F

Facilities Management Catering ... 366
Fair Dinkum Bike Tours ... 161
Fauna Forever Tambopata ... 233
Federation EIL International Office ... 252

the gap-year guidebook 2011

Flashpoint Academy 293
Flexicover Direct 87
Florence by Bike 153
Florence Institute of Design International 291
Fly Gap 323
Flybubble Paragliding 419
Flying Fish UK Ltd 333
Flying Kiwi 161
Food of Course 403
Foreign & Commonwealth Office 363
Fräulein Maria's Bicycle Tours 161
Friends of Conservation 233
Friends of The Earth 381
Frontier 235
Full Sail University 293
Future Publishing Plc 364

G

Galapagos Conservation Trust 235
Gap Aid 61
Gap Guru 269
Gap Medics 269
Gap Year Diver Ltd 343
Gap Year for Grown Ups 115
Gap Year South Africa 252
Gapforce 235
Gapyear Trackers 61
German Academic Exchange Service (DAAD) 298
Gibbs Denley 87
Glasgow Ski & Snowboard Centre 419
GlaxoSmithKline UK 364
Glencree Centre for Peace and Reconciliation 253
Global Action Nepal 235
Global Adventure Challenges Ltd 382
Global Choices 200
Global Vision International 235
Global Volunteer Network 235
Global Volunteers 253
Globelink International Ltd. 89
Go Differently Ltd 161
Go Gap Year 62
Go Outdoors 66
Go Travel Insurance 89
Go Workabout 207
Goa Way 175
Goal-Line Soccer Clinics 333

Goethe Institut 298
Golders Green Teacher Training Centre 423
Gordon Ramsay's Tante Marie School of Cookery 403
Grangemockler Camphill Community 253
Gravity Assisted Mountain Biking 326
Grayline Tours of Hong Kong 161
Great Lake Skydive Centre 323
Greek Embassy Education Office 299
Green Dragons 419
Greenforce 237
Greenpeace 382
Greyhound Lines Inc 175
Groundwork Oldham & Rochdale 382

H

Habitat for Humanity Great Britain 253
Haka Tours 161
Harris Mountains Heli-Ski 331
Harrogate International Festival 359
Hawaii Ocean Rafting 343
Hay Festival 360
Hearing Dogs for Deaf People 382
Heatherley School of Art 400
Hellenic International Studies in the Arts (HISA) 286
High & Wild 162
High Places Ltd 162
Highland Experience Tours 162
Hike Japan 326
Holloway Arts Festival 360
Hollywood Film & Acting Academy 293
Hong Kong Institute of Languages 294
Hong Kong Language Learning Centre 294
Hope For The Nations Children's Charity 253
Hostelbookers.com 149
Hostelling International 149
Hostelling International - Canada 149
Hostelling International - Iceland 149
Hostelling International - USA 149
Hot Recruit 367
HSBC Holdings plc 364

I

i volunteer 253
i-to-i 255
IBM 364
ICE Snowsports Ltd 331

ICYE (Inter Cultural Youth Exchange) UK 255
Il Sillabo 300
ILA (Independent Living Alternatives)..382
Ilkley Literature Festival 360
IMI plc 364
Immigration New Zealand 207
In the Saddle Ltd..162
IndaPidal 306
India Travel Plan 162
Indonesia Travel Plan 162
Inlingua International 302
Inside Japan Tours 177
Inspire 115
Institut ELFCA 297
Institut Français 297
Institut Savoisien d'Etudes Françaises pour Etrangers 297
Institute of International Education 283
Instituto Donatello 300
Insure and Go 89
InterExchange 201
InterHealth Worldwide 62
International Academy..333
International House London 411
International House Madrid 306
International Rail 153
Internet Outpost 65
Intrepid Expeditions 62
Intrepid Travel 163
Island Divers 343
IST Plus...201
Istituto di Lingua e Cultura Italiana Michelangelo..290
Istituto di Moda Burgo...291
Istituto Europeo 300
Italian Cultural Institute in London 411
ITC - Intensive TEFL Courses 424
Itchy Feet Ltd 66
IVCS 255
IVS (International Voluntary Service) 255

J

Jagged Globe 326
Jazz Summer School 307
JET - Japan Exchange and Teaching Programme UK 115
Jobs In The Alps 209
John Hall Venice 286
Joint Ventures 163

Joseph Van Os Photo Safaris 309
Josephite Community Aid 255
Journey Latin America 177
JS Travel Insurance 89
Jubilee Sailing Trust 419
Jungle Surfing Canopy Tours 163

K

Kande Horse Trails 163
Karen Hilltribes Trust 255
Kem Investments - Gap4Africa 257
Kenya Travel Plan 163
Kichijoji Language School 300
Kings World Trust for Children 257
Kingswood Learning & Leisure Group 367
Kiwi Experience 154
Kiwi River Safaris 343
Knowledge Exchange Institute (KEI) 290
KT Adventure 163
Kudu Expeditions Ltd 163
Kumuka Worldwide 177
Kuoni Challenge for Charity 164
Kwa Madwala Private Game Reserve 237

L

L'Arche 257
L'Oréal (UK) Ltd 364
Lake District Summer Music 413
Language Courses Abroad 302
Languages @ Lunchtime 411
Laos Travel Plan 164
Latin Link 382
Lattitude Global Volunteering 257
Launchpad Australia 209
Le Cordon Bleu 405
Learn Languages Abroad 302
Leicester College - St Margaret's 407
Leiths School of Food & Wine 405
Lexia Study Abroad 290
Lichfield Festival 360
Lifesaver Systems 62
Lifesavers (The Royal Life Saving Society) 62
Link Ethiopia 211
Live Travel 164
London 2012 383
London Fencing Club 419

the gap-year guidebook 2011

London Music School 414
London Photo Tours & Workshops 309
London School of Photography 416
London School of Sound 414
London Scuba Diving School 420
Lorenzo de' Medici 300
LTTC - London Teacher Training College 424
Lucasfilm 201
Lyon Bleu International 297

M

Maasai International Challenge Africa 201
Macmillan Cancer Support (UK Office - Volunteering) 383
Madventurer 257
Magic Travellers Network 154
Majestic Wine Warehouse 365
Malaysia Travel Plan 164
Mananan International Festival of Music and the Arts 360
Manchester International Festival 361
Marie Curie Cancer Care (Head Office) 377
Marine Divers Ltd 343
Mark Warner Ltd 209
Marks & Spencer Plc 365
Megalong Australian Heritage Centre 326
Melbourne Street Art Tour 164
Mendip Outdoor Pursuits 420
Mente Argentina 306
Metallo Nobile 291
Metropolitan Film School 408
Mexico Travel Plan 164
Mind 383
Mind The Gap Year 89
Modern Language Studies Abroad (MLSA) 302
Mokai Gravity Canyon 323
Morocco Travel Plan 165
Mountain Beach Mountain Bike Holidays 177
Mountain Kingdoms Ltd 165
Mountaineering Council of Ireland 326
Mountbatten Institute 201
MRL Insurance Direct 89
Murray School of Cookery 405
Museum of London 383
Music Worldwide Drum Camp 414
My Mate Back Home 65

visit: www.gap-year.com

N

NABA - Nuova Accademia de Belle Arti	291
NashCamp	307
National Mountaineering Centre	420
Natives.co.uk	209
Navigator Travel Insurance Services Ltd	90
Neilson Active Holidays Ltd	177
Nepal Travel Plan	165
Neptune's Dive College	343
New Zealand Skydiving School	323
Newcastle College	407
Nigel Turner Photographic Workshop	310
Nikwax Ltd	66
Nimbus Paragliding	323
NLMS Music Summer School	414
Nomad Travel & Outdoor	67
Non-Stop Ski	331
NONSTOP Adventure Ltd	115
Norfolk and Norwich Festival Ltd	361
North London Parachute Centre Ltd	420
North London Piano School	414
NSPCC	383
NYFA (New York Film Academy)	293
Nzone	324

O

Oasis Overland	117
Oasis UK	257
Objective Travel Safety Ltd	63
Obninsk Humanities Centre	303
Ocean Rafting	344
Office of International Education, Iceland	283
OISE Oxford	302
Olympic Bike Travel	165
On The Go Tours	165
OnTheMountain Pro Snowsports Instructor Training in Switzerland	331
Orangutan Foundation	237
Orchards Cookery	405
Outbike	165
Outdoor Interlaken AG	331
Outreach International	237
Oxford International Study Centre	413
OxfordTEFL	424
Oyster Worldwide Limited	259
OzBus UK Ltd	154
OzSail	344

P

Palmar Voyages	167
Páramo Directional Clothing Systems	67
Park Lane College	67
Pathfinders Africa	167
Paul's Xtreme Skydiving	324
PCFE Film School	293
PDSA	383
Peace River Refuge & Ranch	237
Peak Leaders	335
Pebbles	199
Penguin Group UK	365
Penrith Whitewater Stadium	344
Pepper	259
Peregrine Adventures Ltd	167
Peru Travel Plan	167
Peru's Challenge	259
Petersburg Studies	290
PGL Recruitment Team	367
Photo Holidays France	310
Photo Opportunity Ltd	416
Photofusion	416
Photographers on Safari	310
Pichilemu Institute of Language Studies	306
Picture Weddings - Digital wedding photography workshops	416
PJ Scuba	333
Plan UK	384
Planet Au Pair	199
Plas Menai	335
Play Soccer	333
Plumpton College	410
PocketComms Ltd	65
Pocono Whitewater Rafting	344
Pod Zorbing	420
Polimoda Institute of Fashion Design and Marketing	291
PoloSkool Ltd	327
Poole Harbour Watersports	420
Portsmouth Festivities	361
ProAdventure Limited	421
Project O	201
Project Trust	239
Projects Abroad	269
Province of London Curling Club	421
ProWorld (Real Projects...Real Experience)	239
Pura Aventura	167

Q

Queenstown Resort College	285
Quest Overseas	259
Qufu Shaolin Kung Fu School China	327

R

RAC Motoring Services	407
RADA (Royal Academy of Dramatic Art)	408
RAF	365
Raging Thunder	335
Rail Europe Ltd.	154
Rainforest Concern	384
Rainforest Nature	239
Raleigh International	259
Rapid Sensations Rafting	336
Real Gap Experience	239
Red Cedar Songwriter Camp	308
ReefDoctor Org Ltd	239
Remote Trauma Limited	63
Rempart	240
Rickshaw Travel	167
Ride With Us	168
Right Cover Travel Insurance	90
River Deep Mountain High	336
River Expeditions	344
River Rats Rafting	336
RMIT Training	292
RNLI	384
Road2Argentina	290
Rock UK	384
Rock'n Ropes	327
Rodbaston College	410
Rogue Wilderness Adventures	336
Round the World Insurance	90
Royal Agricultural College	410
Royal Botanic Gardens	384
RSPB (Royal Society for the Protection of Birds)	384
RSPCA	385
Rua Reidh Lighthouse	327
Ryanair	154

S

S & N Genealogy	365
SA Volunteers	240
Sabah Divers	344
SACI Florence	286

Saddle Skedaddle	168
Safari Par Excellence	168
Sahara Travel	168
SAI - Study Abroad Italy	286
Sainsbury's Travel Insurance	90
Salisbury International Arts Festival	361
Samaritans	385
Saracen Sailing Mallorca	344
Saxoncourt Training & Recruitment	211
Scenic Air AG	168
School of Archaeology & Ancient History	399
Scoil Acla - Irish Music Summer School	308
Scope	377
Scottish Youth Hostel Association	151
Scuba Junkie	345
Scuola Leonardo da Vinci	285
Selective Asia	168
Sense	385
Serenje Orphans School Home	261
SHAD	385
Shelter	385
Shoestring Polo Ltd.	327
Shoot Experience Ltd	416
Shumba Experience	240
Sim4travel Ltd	65
Simón Bolivar Spanish School	306
Simon Watkinson Photo Training	416
SIT Study Abroad	290
Ski Academy Switzerland	333
Ski le Gap	331
Ski-Exp-Air	332
Skillshare International UK	261
Skydive Arizona	324
Skydive Brid	421
Skydive Cairns	324
Skydive Las Vegas	324
Skydive Switzerland GmbH	324
Skydive Taupo	325
Smile Society	261
Snatch Recruitment	365
Snowcard Insurance Services Limited	90
SnowSkool	332
Snowsport Consultancy	332
Songwriter Girl Camps	308
SOS Rhino	377
South Africa Travel Plan	169

visit: www.gap-year.com

South Cambridgeshire Equestrian Centre 421
Southern African Wildlife College 240
Southern Cross Tours & Expeditions 169
Southern Regional College 169
Spaceships 151
Spanish Study Holidays 306
Sparsholt College 410
Specialtours Ltd. 169
Spirit of Adventure Trust 261
Sport Lived Ltd 336
Sporting Opportunities 327
Sportscotland National Centre Cumbrae 421
SPW (Students Partnership Worldwide) 261
St John Ambulance 63
STA Travel 177
Starfish Ventures Ltd 240
Steve Outram Crete Photo Tours & Workshops 310
Straits Sailing 345
Stray Ltd 154
Studio Escalier 287
Suffolk Sailing 63
Suffolk Ski Centre 421
Sumatran Orangutan Society 240
SummerKeys 308
SummerSongs Inc. 308
Sunrise Volunteer Programmes 241
Sunsail 345
Suntrek 169
Sunvil 169
SuperBon Painting Retreat 287
Surfaris 336
Surfing Queensland 345
Sussex Hang Gliding & Paragliding 422
Sussex Polo Club 422
Swiss Youth Hostels 151
Syndicat Mixte Montaigu-Rocheservière 212

T

Talking Mandarin Language Centre 294
Taller Flamenco 308
Tanzed 261
TASIS, The American School in Switzerland 297
Task Brasil Trust 263
Taupo Bungy 325
TEFL Training LLP 424
Thailand Travel Plan 171

the gap-year guidebook 2011

The Acting Center	293
The adventure company	171
The Avenue Cookery School	405
The Bertinet Kitchen	405
The Blue Cross	385
The Book Bus Foundation	263
The Bridge Camphill Community	263
The British Institute of Florence	287
The British Kodály Academy	414
The Bundu Safari Company	171
The Career Break Guru	117
The Central School of Speech and Drama	408
The Children's Trust	386
The Cordon Vert	406
The DJ Academy Organisation	415
The Ethical Project Company	263
The Fashion Retail Academy	407
The Foundation for Center for Research of Whales	203
The Gables School of Cookery	406
The Gorilla Organisation	241
The Great Marine Project	241
The Imaginative Traveller	171
The Instant Mosquito Net Company Ltd	63
The Institute for Public Policy Research (IPPR)	203
The Instructor Training Co	334
The Japan Foundation - London Language Centre	413
The Language House	311
The Lawn Tennis Association	422
The Leap Overseas Ltd	241
The Los Angeles Film School	293
The Marchutz School	287
The Monkey Sanctuary Trust	386
The National Magazine Company Ltd	366
The National Trust	386
The National Trust for Scotland	386
The New England Wild Flower Society & Garden in the Woods	203
The Open College of Equine Studies	410
The Oriental Caravan	171
The Oxford School of Drama	408
The Photography School	417
The Prince's Drawing School	400
The Prince's Trust	386
The Random House Group Ltd	366
The Recording Workshop	415
The Royal Photographic Society	417
The Russia Experience	171

The Russian Language Centre	303
The Simon Community	386
The Talland School of Equitation	422
The Trained Eye	417
The US-UK Fulbright Commission	285
The Wildlife Trusts	387
The Worldwrite Volunteer Centre	263
The Yamasa Institute	301
The Year Out Group	409
Think Pacific	265
Thomas Cook	155
Ticket To Ride	345
Timberline Adventures	173
Tollymore Mountain Centre	422
Top Deck	173
Torquay Wind & Surf Centre	337
Total Nannies	200
Travel Nation	179
Travel Talk	179
Travelbag Ltd	179
Travellers Auto Barn	151
Travellers Connected.com	173
Travellers Contact Point	155
Travellers Worldwide	285
TravelPharm	64
TrekAmerica Travel Limited	179
Trekforce Worldwide	241
Tribes Travel	173
Tropical Adventures	242
Tucan Travel	173
Turtle Conservation Project	242
TVI Actors Studio - Los Angeles	294
Twin Work & Volunteer	203

U

UK Parachuting	422
UK Skydiving Ltd	422
UK Songwriting Festival	415
UKSA (United Kingdom Sailing Academy)	423
Ultimate Gap Year	64
UNA Exchange	242
UNHCR	366
UNICEF (United Nations Childrens Fund)	387
United DJ Mixing School	308
Universidad de Navarra - ILCE	307
University College London - Institute of Archaeology	399

the gap-year guidebook 2011

University College London - Slade School of Fine Art 400
University of Bristol - Department of Archaeology & Anthropology 399
University of London - School of Oriental and African Studies 413
University of the Arts - Central Saint Martins College of Art and Design 400
University of the Arts - London College of Fashion 407
University of the Arts - London Milan Courses 407
University of the Arts - Wimbledon College of Art 401
University of the Arts London - Chelsea College of Art and Design..............................401
University of Wales Institute - Cardiff School of Art and Design....................................401
University of Westminster - School of Media, Arts & Design 408
Up To Date Fashion Academy 292
USIT 179

V

Vancouver Film School 294
Vango 67
VAP (Volunteer Action for Peace)...265
Venice School of Photography Workshops Ltd 310
VentureCo Worldwide 117
Vietnam Travel Plan 174
Vinspired 387
Virgin Radio 366
Vis-à-Vis 298
Visas Australia Ltd 211
Visitoz 211
Vitalise..387
Vivisto Ltd 242
Vodkatrain 174
Volunteer Latin America 265
Volunteer Reading Help..387
Volunteers Making a Difference - vMaD..242
Voluntour South Africa 267
Voluntours 243

W

Wake up Sydney ....
Walks Worldwide..174
War on Want 377
Warwickshire College - Moreton Morrell 410
WaterAid 267
Wavehunters UK 345
Wayward Bus Touring Company Pty Ltd 174
Webbe's Cookery School 406
Wellington Riding 423
Welsh Jazz Society 309
Wesser and Partner..377

visit: www.gap-year.com

Where There Be Dragons	285
Whipalong Volunteer Program	267
Whistler Summer Snowboard Camps	332
White Peak Expeditions	329
Whizz-Kidz	387
Wild at Heart Youth Adventures	174
Wilderness Aware Rafting	337
Wilderness Awareness School	243
Wilderness Escapes	337
Willing Workers in South Africa (WWISA)	267
Winchester Hat Fair	361
Wind, Sand & Stars	174
Windsor TEFL	424
Work the World Ltd	203
World Expeditions	175
World Nomads Ltd	90
World Rhythms Arts Program (WRAP)	309
WorldLink Education US Office	294
Worldtrekker Travel Insurance	90
Worldwide Experience	243
Worldwide Travel Insurance Services Ltd	91
WorldWide Volunteering for Young People	267
WWOOF (World Wide Opportunities on Organic Farms)	243

X

X-isle Sports	423
Xtreme-gap.com	334

Y

Year Out Drama	409
Yeomans Outdoors	67
Yomps	175
Youth Hostel Association	388
Youth Hostel Association New Zealand	151
Youth Hostels Association of India	151
Youth Music Theatre	361
YSP - Your Safe Planet Ltd	64

Z

Ze-Bus	155

Notes | Your ideas and plans

visit: www.gap-year.com

Notes | Your ideas and plans

the gap-year guidebook 2011

Notes | Your ideas and plans

visit: www.gap-year.com

Notes | Your ideas and plans

the gap-year guidebook 2011

Notes | Your ideas and plans

visit: www.gap-year.com

Notes | Your ideas and plans

Notes | Your ideas and plans

visit: www.gap-year.com

Notes | Your ideas and plans

the gap-year guidebook 2011

Notes | Your ideas and plans

visit: www.gap-year.com